MATERIALS

IN

THE LAW OF BUSINESS CONTRACTS

by

Leonard Lakin
Professor of Law

and

Leona Beane
Associate Professor of Law

The Bernard M. Baruch College

of

The City University of New York

**KENDALL/HUNT
PUBLISHING COMPANY**
Dubuque, Iowa

This edition has been printed directly
from the authors' manuscript copy.

Copyright © 1982 by Kendall/Hunt Publishing Company

Revised Printing, 1984

Library of Congress Catalog Card Number: 82-82926

ISBN 0-8403-3387-0

Printed in the United States of America
10 9 8 7 6 5 4

PREFACE

We have prepared and organized these materials consisting of (1) New York statutes, (2) court decisions and (3) essay and multiple-choice questions for use in a course dealing with the law of business contracts. These materials are intended to accompany a textbook on the law of business contracts and will round out the student's study of the subject matter.

The study of statutes is essential in the study of the law of business contracts because many rules governing the law of contracts today are set forth in statutes. The statutes have either codified the common law rules developed by courts of law or have expressly changed the earlier common law rule. The study of statutes affords the student the opportunity to develop the skills of analytical, critical and logical thinking. Finally, the application of statutory rules of law is frequently required to resolve legal issues posed in business problems.

Reading and briefing court decisions will help the student to understand and appreciate how and why a court applies a rule of contract law to the facts of a particular case to determine the rights of parties to a contract. Moreover, reading and briefing court decisions also will help the student to develop the intellectual ability to critically analyze and evaluate facts and opposing legal arguments advanced by parties involved in actual litigation.

Answering essay and multiple-choice questions is also a very valuable aid in the student's study of the law of contracts. First, the student will be able to use and apply rules of contract law that he has studied to resolve legal issues involved in common business problems. The business major will encounter many similar business problems in his or her professional career. Thus, the knowledge of contract law has practical value and vividly demonstrates that law is not a set of abstract legal principles studied in a vacuum. Second, problem-solving reinforces the learning process and makes the study of law more rewarding and meaningful as the student finds that his knowledge has practical application to the business world. Third, when the student writes carefully reasoned answers to essay questions for classroom discussion, he has the opportunity to practice and develop his writing and reasoning skills that are so important in the business and professional world. Fourth, public accounting majors will become familiar with the substance and form of CPA contract law questions which appear regularly on the CPA Law Examination since some of our essay and multiple-choice questions are taken from prior CPA Law Examinations.

We have also included a glossary of legal terms and phrases at the end of the book which will be helpful to students.

We wish to record our appreciation to Professors James V. Sullivan and Edward G. Tarangioli, retired members of our law department, for giving us permission to use and revise essay questions originally developed by them for an earlier version of this book. We also record our appreciation to the American Institute of Certified Public Accountants for permission to reprint materials from the Uniform CPA Law Examinations between 1973–1982.

Leonard Lakin
Leona Beane

The Uniform Commercial Code:

From Genesis to Adoption

(The following material is reprinted from the textbook: A
Guide to Secured Transactions by Professors Leonard Lakin
and Howard J. Berger.)

...The history of the adoption of the Uniform Commercial Code is best
understood in the light of the various uniform statutes adopted, one at a time
and without reference to each other, over the years by different states...The
movement towards individual and separate uniform commercial laws began in the
late nineteenth century with the principal impetus coming from the increased
volume of interstate commerce as a product of the industrial revolution. The
early expression of the need for uniformity of law in all of the states led to
the creation in 1890 of the National Conference of Commissioners on Uniform
State Laws which continues to be an active organization to this day. Its primary purpose was and is to draft legislation which would uniformly be adopted
by all the state legislatures and which would regulate in all states a particular form of commercial transaction. Almost all of its members are appointed
by the governors of the fifty states. The average number of commissioners
from each state is between three and four, who serve without compensation. The
Conference, over the years, has been considered one of the most distinguished
legal organizations in the United States.

The first major project of the Conference was the promulgation of a Uniform Negotiable Instruments Law in 1896. Other uniform laws separately promulgated by the Conference over the years were as follows:

UNIFORM ACT	PROMULGATED	LAST ENACTED	NO. OF STATES ENACTED
Uniform Negotiable Instruments Law	1896	1928	48
Uniform Sales Act	1906	1941	34
Uniform Warehouse Receipt Act	1906	1945	48
Uniform Stock Transfer Act	1909	1947	48
Uniform Bill of Lading Act	1909	1947	31
Uniform Conditional Sales Act	1918	1945	10
Uniform Trust Receipt Act	1933	1955	32

However, by the 1930's, there was a growing chorus of criticism that the
various uniform acts were not being uniformly interpreted by the states that
had adopted them, that only three of the seven uniform acts had been adopted
by all the states, and that drastic revision was necessary to keep pace with
the modern day needs of the American businessman. Indeed, in 1938 the Merchants Association of New York City sponsored a congressional bill for a

federal sales act to govern all interstate sales transactions. In view of the sentiment that the Uniform Sales Act was not doing the job it was intended to do, the Conference was then considering a revision of the Uniform Negotiable Instruments Law, which it had prepared in 1896.

Then in 1940, at the fiftieth annual meeting of the Conference, the president of the Conference, William A. Schnader, one of the most influential commissioners, called for a comprehensive uniform commercial code to replace the independent and fragmented laws that had proliferated over the years. "Could not a great uniform commercial code be prepared," he asked, "which would bring the commercial law up to date, and which would become the uniform law of our fifty-three jurisdictions (forty-eight states, District of Columbia, territories of Alaska and Hawaii, Puerto Rico and the Virgin Islands) by the passage of only fifty-three acts, instead of many times that number?" Therefore, it was successfully proposed that the Conference abandon the practice of sponsoring piecemeal legislation and scrap all of the earlier uniform acts in favor of a single comprehensive uniform commercial code.

Work began promptly on what was called a Uniform Revised Sales Act which was to be a major subdivision of the proposed Uniform Commercial Code. In 1942 the American Law Institute, a prestigious group of some 1,200 lawyers organized in 1923, agreed to participate in the drafting of the proposed Code. The joint project was financed by a two hundred and fifty thousand dollar grant from the Maurice and Laura Falk Foundation in Pittsburgh, Pennsylvania; by a one hundred thousand dollar contribution form the Beaumont Foundation of Cleveland, Ohio, and by donations from ninety-eight business and financial concerns and law firms.

The Institute and the Conference appointed an editorial board consisting of five men—two representing each of the permanent organizations, and the chief reporter, Professor Karl Llewellyn of Columbia University School of Law, and numerous drafting committees of many nationally prominent judges, lawyers, and law teachers. The basic concept on which the Uniform Commercial Code is based is that commercial transactions involve a single subject of law although they have many parts. Therefore, they should be regulated by one uniform law. The desired uniformity was to be achieved by replacing the above-listed seven acts, which were for the most part no longer in accord with modern business practices, by a Uniform Commercial Code which would modernize and coordinate all uniform acts in the field of commercial law as well as adopt new provisions where no uniform acts existed on important and closely related commercial problems such as secured transactions.

Drafts and revised drafts of the proposed Uniform Commercial Code were continuously considered and reconsidered over a decade by more than one thousand lawyers and related financial and trade groups, such as the American Bankers Association, and warehouse and farming groups. Thus it has been said that probably no enactment since the adoption of the Federal Constitution has received so much study from so many and so distinguished a group of legal scholars as has the Uniform Commercial Code between the time it was first conceived in 1940 and the time its sponsors offered the Code to the state legislatures for adoption a decade or so later. Indeed, the Code has been widely recognized as bearing "the stamp of approval of a large body of American scholarship."

The Uniform Revised Sales Act, as a major subdivision of the proposed Code, was approved by the Conference in 1943 and by the American Law Institute in 1944. On January 1, 1945, the comprehensive joint project of the Conference and the American Law Institute officially began. The American Bar Association also participated in the project, offering its own criticisms and suggestions. Four years later in 1949 the first complete draft of the proposed Uniform Commercial Code, consisting of the following nine integrated articles with notes and comments, was released:

Article 1   General Provisions
Article 2   Sales
Article 3   Commercial Paper
Article 4   Bank Deposits and Collections
Article 5   Letters of Credit
Article 6   Bulk Transfers
Article 7   Documents of Title
Article 8   Investment Securities
Article 9   Secured Transactions

The Code's range, as can be seen, is extensive, covering and encompassing the entire field of commercial law and unifying the law formerly encompassed by a multitude of uniform laws. Five of the seven uniform laws were promulgated between 1896 and 1909 and antedated the problems of mass production and interstate distribution.

In September 1951, the final text of the proposed Code was completed and approved by the Conference and the American Law Institute and by the American Bar Association. During the next year, a limited number of further amendments were made and in October 1952, an official edition of the Code with explanatory comments was published as the "1952 Official Text and Comments Edition." And in that same year, the Code was introduced "for educational purposes only" in the legislatures of New York, California, and Mississippi and in seven additional state legislatures during the following year. Pennsylvania was the first state to enact the Code (1953), which became effective in 1954 by a unanimous vote in that state legislature. As the proposed Code was thereafter studied by different legislatures and other interested groups, further objections and suggestions were made. Furthermore, as a result of extensive study of the proposed Code by the New York Law Revision Commission between 1953 and 1956, substantial amendments were made by the sponsoring organizations and the "1958 Official Text and Comments Edition" was thereafter published.

This 1958 version of the Code was next adopted in Massachusetts, effective in 1960. Further amendments were enacted by the sponsoring organizations based on experiences with the Code in Pennsylvania, Massachusetts, and Kentucky leading to the 1962 version of the Code which was subsequently enacted in every state (as well as in the District of Columbia, the Virgin Islands, and Puerto Rico) except Louisiana. In each adopting state the Code was not only endorsed but actively supported by chambers of commerce, industrial associations, labor unions, insurance associations, and individual insurance companies, teachers associations, retail trade boards, farm credit banks, and other groups. In summary, the Code, unlike the codes of continental Europe, was not professors' law: in a relatively short time, compared to the time prior uniform acts took to be adopted by most of the states, the Uniform Commercial Code was the law of the land in every state except Louisiana. A summary of the number of states adopting the Code effective in the year shown reveals the growing acceptance of the Code:

| | EFFECTIVE IN |
YEAR	ADDITIONAL STATES
1954	1
1958	1
1960	1
1961	2
1962	6
1963	4
1964	8
1965	5
1966	8
1967	8
1968	5
Total	49

Unquestionably, the Uniform Commercial Code was the most ambitious codification ever undertaken in the Anglo-American legal system. The Code, as we have seen, replaces seven uniform acts, the model collection code of the American Bankers' Association and myriad statutes dealing with banking, selling, and securities and a mass of common law concerned with personal property. The Code deals with today's problems, modernizes concepts and terminology, and eliminates a variety of problems which existed because of antiquated concepts.

The purpose of the entire Uniform Commercial Code is stated as follows:

"Section 1-102. Purposes; Rules of Construction.

* * *

"(2) Underlying purposes and policies of this Act
are
  (a) to simplify, clarify and modernize the law
     governing commercial transaction;
  (b) to permit the continued expansion of commercial practices through custom, usage and
     agreement of the parties;
  (c) to make uniform the law among the various
     jurisdictions."

* * *

Implicit in the foregoing purposes is the proposition that to the extent necessary, the Code will grow and adapt to commercial practices as those change in the course of time. Moreover, to avoid narrow construction of the Uniform Commercial Code by the courts, Section 1-102 (1) sets forth the basic principle that "This Act shall be liberally construed and applied to promote its underlying purposes and policies."

Furthermore, the national sponsors of the Uniform Commercial Code have wisely set up a Permanent Editorial Board which meets regularly each year to consider problems which are bound to arise and to approve and promulgate amendments on a continuing basis, because the Code is not a static body of law. This Board will insure that the Code will remain current and will always serve the growing and changing needs of the business community. As a result of their efforts, amendments were subsequently enacted and a revised Uniform Commercial Code was enacted in 1972 and further revised in 1978. This represents a completely radical and innovative departure from the attitude of the Conference to prior uniform laws, which were promulgated and then left to the mercy of every legislature to amend from time to time because the Conference unfortunately did not establish a permanent editorial board to perform that function on a uniform and national basis.

TABLE OF CONTENTS

	Page #
PREFACE	iii
HISTORY OF THE U.C.C.	v
TABLE OF CASES	xiii
TABLE OF STATUTES	xiv
1. FORMATION OF CONTRACTS: OFFER AND ACCEPTANCE	1
Statutes	1
Case 1	16
Case 2	19
Case 3	21
Case 4	22
Case 5	25
Case 6	28
Case 7	31
Case 8	34
Case 9	38
Case 10	41
Case 11	43
Essay Questions	50
Multiple Choice Questions	57
2. STATUTE OF FRAUDS	66
Statutes	66
Case 12	71
Case 13	76
Case 14	79
Case 15	84
Essay Questions	87
Multiple Choice Questions	92
3. CONSIDERATION	95
Statutes	95
Case 16	100
Case 17	102
Case 18	105
Case 19	109
Case 20	111
Case 21	115
Case 22	118
Essay Questions	121
Multiple Choice Questions	127
4. CAPACITY OF PARTIES	129
Statutes	129
Case 23	135
Case 24	139
Essay Questions	142

5. REALITY OF ASSENT - FRAUD, MISREPRESENTATION, DURESS, MISTAKE, UNDUE INFLUENCE 144
        Statutes 144
        Case 25 147
        Case 26 150
        Case 27 154
        Essay Questions 157
        Multiple Choice Questions 160

6. ILLEGALITY 162
        Statutes 162
        Case 28 207
        Case 29 209
        Case 30 213
        Case 31 215
        Case 32 218
        Case 33 221
        Case 34 225
        Case 35 229
        Case 36 234
        Case 37 238
        Case 38 241
        Essay Questions 244
        Multiple Choice Questions 245

7. PERFORMANCE; DEFECTIVE PERFORMANCE; SUBSTANTIAL PERFORMANCE; IMPOSSIBILITY OF PERFORMANCE; CONDITIONS; BREACH OF CONTRACT; DAMAGES; REMEDIES 246
        Statutes 246
        Case 39 258
        Case 40 261
        Case 41 263
        Case 42 265
        Case 43 267
        Case 44 269
        Essay Questions 272
        Multiple Choice Questions 279

8. THIRD PARTY BENEFICIARIES AND ASSIGNMENTS 281
        Statutes 281
        Case 45 289
        Case 46 292
        Essay Questions 295
        Multiple Choice Questions 298

9. INTERPRETATION: RULES OF CONSTRUCTION: PAROL EVIDENCE RULE ... 300
        Statutes 300
        Case 47 303
        Essay Questions 304
        Multiple Choice Questions 305

                                                                    Page #
10. STATUTE OF LIMITATIONS 307
            Statutes 307
            Multiple Choice Questions 311

GLOSSARY OF COMMON LEGAL TERMS AND PHRASES 312

TABLE OF CASES

	Case #	Page #
AM Broadcasting Companies v. Wolf	35	229
Amend v. Hurley	26	150
Ansorge v. Kane	1	16
Appelgate v. MacFadden Corp.	44	269
Austin Instrument, Inc. v. Loral Corporation	27	154
Bellizzi v. Huntley	40	261
Braun v. C.E.P.C. Distributors, Inc.	19	109
Ciofalo v. Vic Tanney Gyms, Inc.	28	207
Crabtree v. Elizabeth Arden Sales Corp.	12	71
Dombrowski v. Somers	3	21
Duplex Safety Boiler Co. v. C. Henry Garden et al	43	267
Farash v. Sykes Datatronics, Inc.	15	84
Feld v. Henry S. Levy & Sons, Inc.	20	111
Gelder Medical Group v. Webber	34	225
Gross v. Sweet	29	209
Hamer v. Sidway	16	100
I & I Holding Corp. v. Gainsburg	21	115
Jacob & Youngs v. Kent	39	258
Jaffray v. Davis	17	102
Joseph Martin, Jr., Delicatessen v. Schumacher	6	28
Jungmann v. Atterbury	41	263
Kane v. Kane et al.	24	139
Karpinski v. Ingrasci	33	221
Kleinschmidt Div. of SCM Corp. v. Futuronics	2	19
Matter of Marlene Indus. Corp. v. Carnac Textiles, Inc.	8	34
McConnell v. Commonwealth Pictures Corporation	31	215
Minneapolis & c, R'y v. Columbus R'g Mill	4	22
Municipal Consultants v. Town of Ramapo	9	38
Murray v. Cunard Steamship Co.	10	41
Nassau Hotel Co. v. Barnett	46	292
Petterson v. Pattberg	5	25
Post v. Merrill Lynch Etc.	37	238
Purchasing Associates, Inc. v. Weitz	36	234
Reno v. Bull	25	147
Reynolds v. Robinson	47	303
Richardson Press v. Albright	13	76
Schlegel v. Cooper's Glue Factory	22	118
Schnell v. Perlmon	18	105
Seaver v. Ransom	45	289
Seidlitz v. Auerbach	32	218
State of New York v. Avco Financial Service of New York, Inc.	38	241
Sternlieb v. Normandie Nat. Sec. Corp.	23	135
Thomaier v. Hoffman Chevrolet, Inc.	14	79
Tomkins v. Dudley	42	265
Trevor v. Wood	7	31
Union Exchange Nat. Bank v. Joseph	30	213
Weinberg v. D.M. Restaurant Corp.	11	43

TABLE OF STATUTES

The statutory materials in this book consist of various New York Statutes dealing with the law of contracts. These statutes have been included either entirely or partially, or have been abstracted, summarized, or listed by title. These statutes have been taken from the following.

1. Uniform Commercial Code (U.C.C.)
2. New York General Obligations Law (G.O.L.)
3. New York General Business Law
4. New York Personal Property Law
5. New York Civil Practice Law and Rules (C.P.L.R.)
6. New York Education Law
7. New York Penal Law
8. New York Judiciary Law
9. New York Real Property Law
10. New York Banking Law
11. New York Business Corporation Law (B.C.L.)
12. New York Estates, Powers and Trust Law (E.P.T.L.)
13. New York General Construction Law
14. Racing, Pari-Mutuel Wagering and Breeding Law

The following table of statutes should be consulted to locate applicable statutes which are included in this book.

UNIFORM COMMERCIAL CODE (U.C.C.)

Section		Page
1-103	Supplementary General Principles of Law Applicable	300
1-106	Remedies To Be Liberally Construed	300
1-107	Waiver Or Renunciation Of Claim Or Right After Breach	98
1-201	General Definitions	4
1-203	Obligation Of Good Faith	5,300
1-204	Time; Reasonable Time; "Seasonable"	300
1-205	Course of Dealing And Usage of Trade	300
1-206	Statute Of Frauds For Kinds Of Personal Property Not Otherwise Covered	70
1-207	Performance Or Acceptance Under Reservation Of Rights	98
2-103	Definitions	2
2-104	Definitions: "Merchant"; "Between Merchants"	2
2-105	Definitions: ..."Goods"; "Future Goods"	2
2-106	Definitions: "Contract"; "Agreement"; "Contract For Sale"; "Sale";	3
2-107	Goods To Be Severed From Realty	3
2-201	Formal Requirements; Statute Of Frauds	69
2-202	Final Written Expression; Parol or Extrinsic Evidence	302
2-203	Seals Inoperative	98

Page

2-204 Formation In General.. 5

2-205 Firm Offers... 5

2-206 Offer And Acceptance In Formation Of Contract................... 5

2-207 Additional Terms In Acceptance Or Confirmation................ 5

2-208 Course Of Performance Or Practical Construction.............. 301

2-209 Modification, Rescission And Waiver.......................... 99,247

2-210 Delegation Of Performance; Assignment of Rights.............. 282

2-301 General Obligations Of Parties............................... 301

2-302 Unconscionable Contract Or Clause............................ 178

2-304 Price Payable In Money, Goods, Realty, Or Otherwise.......... 7

2-305 Open Price Term.. 7

2-306 Output, Requirements And Exclusive Dealings.................. 7

2-308 Absence Of Specified Place For Delivery...................... 302

2-309 Absence Of Specific Time Provisions.......................... 8,302

2-310 Open Time For Payment.. 8

2-311 Options And Cooperation Respecting Performance............... 8,247

2-328 Sale By Auction.. 8

2-403 Power To Transfer; Good Faith Purchaser Of Goods............. 145

2-601 Buyer's Rights On Improper Delivery.......................... 248

2-602 Manner And Effect Of Rightful Rejection...................... 248

2-606 What Constitutes Acceptance Of Goods......................... 248

2-607 Effect Of Acceptance; Notice Of Breach; Burden Of Establish-
       ing Breach After Acceptance;................................. 248

2-608 Revocation Of Acceptance In Whole Or In Part................. 249

2-609 Right To Adequate Assurance Of Performance................... 249,282

2-610 Anticipatory Repudiation..................................... 249

2-611 Retraction Of Anticipatory Repudiation....................... 249

2-612 "Installment Contract"; Breach............................... 250

2-613 Casualty To Identified Goods................................. 250

2-614 Substituted Performance...................................... 250

2-615 Excuse By Failure Of Presupposed Conditions.................. 251

2-616 Procedure On Notice Claiming Excuse.......................... 251

2-701 Remedies For Breach Of Collateral Contracts Not Impaired..... 251

2-703 Seller's Remedies In General................................. 251

2-708 Seller's Damages For Non-Acceptance Or Repudiation........... 252

2-709 Action For The Price... 252

2-710 Seller's Incidental Damages.................................. 252

2-711 Buyer's Remedies In General.................................. 252

2-712 "Cover"; Buyer's Procurement Of Substitute Goods............. 253

2-713 Buyer's Damages For Non-Delivery Or Repudiation.............. 253

2-714 Buyer's Damages For Breach In Regard To Accepted Goods....... 253

2-715 Buyer's Incidental And Consequential Damages................. 253

2-716 Buyer's Right To Specific Performance Or Replevin............ 254

2-717 Deduction Of Damages From The Price.......................... 254

2-718 Liquidation Or Limitation Of Damages;........................ 254

2-719 Contractual Modification Or Limitation Of Remedy............. 255

2-720 Effect Of "Cancellation" Or "Rescission" On Claims For
       Antecedent Breach.. 255

2-721 Remedies For Fraud... 145,255

2-725 Statute Of Limitations In Contracts For Sale................. 310

		Page
3-408	Consideration	99
8-319	Statute Of Frauds - Investment Securities	69
9-203	Attachment And Enforceability Of Security Interest; Proceeds; Formal Requisites	70
9-206	Agreement Not To Assert Defenses Against Assignee;	283
9-318	Defenses Against Assignee; Modification Of Contract After Notification Of Assignment; Term Prohibiting Assignment Ineffective; Identification And Proof Of Assignment	283

NEW YORK GENERAL OBLIGATIONS LAW (G.O.L.)

1-202	Definitions	129
3-101	When Contracts May Not Be Disaffirmed On Grounds Of Infancy	129
3-102	Obligations Of Certain Minors For Hospital, Medical And Surgical Treatment And Care	129
3-105	Judicial Approval of Certain Contracts For Services Of Infants;	130
3-107	Certain Contracts Of Parents Or Guardians Respecting Employment Of Infants Not Enforceable Unless Approved	131
3-109	Payment of Wages To Minor; When Valid	131
3-112	Limited Liability Of Parents Or Certain Legal Guardians Having Custody Of An Infant For Malicious And Destructive Acts Of Such Infant	132
3-301	Powers Of Married Woman	134
3-305	Contract Of Married Woman Not to Bind Husband	134
5-321	Agreements Exempting Lessors From Liability For Negligence Void And Unenforceable	178
5-322	Agreements Exempting Caterers And Catering Establishments from Liability for Negligence Void and Unenforceable	179
5-323	Agreements Exempting Building Service or Maintenance Contractors From Liability For Negligence Void And Unenforceable	179
5-324	Agreements By Owners, Contractors, Subcontractors or Suppliers To Indemnify Architects, Engineers And Surveyors From Liability Caused By Or Arising Out Of Defects In Maps, Plans, Designs And Specifications Void And Unenforceable	179
5-325	Garages And Parking Places; Agreements Exempting From Liability For Negligence Void	179
5-326	Agreements Exempting Pools, Gymnasiums, Places Of Public Amusement or Recreation And Similar Establishments From Liability For Negligence Void And Unenforceable	180
5-327	Consumers Right to Recover Attorneys Fees	205
5-331	Certain Covenants And Restrictions In Conveyance And Other Agreements Affecting Real Property	180
5-332	Unsolicited And Voluntarily Sent Merchandise Deemed Unconditional Gift	9
5-401	Illegal Wagers, Bets And Stakes	162
5-411	Contracts On Account Of Money Or Property Wagered, Bet Or Staked Are Void	162
5-501	Rate of Interest; Usury Forbidden	167
5-511	Usurious Contracts Void	168
5-513	Recovery Of Excess	168

5-515   Borrower Bringing An Action Need Not Offer To Repay..............168
5-519   Return Of Excess A Bar To Further Penalties.....................169
5-521   Corporations Prohibited From Interposing Defense Of Usury.......169
5-524   Taking Security Upon Certain Property For Usurious Loans........169

5-701   Agreements Required To Be In Writing........................... 66
5-702   Requirements For Use Of Plain Language In Consumer Trans-
        actions ("Plain English Law")................................. 11
5-703   Conveyances and Contracts Concerning Real Property Required
        To Be In Writing.. 67
5-901   Certain Provisions Of Leases Of Personal Property Inoperative
        Unless Notice Thereof Given To Lessee......................... 9
5-903   Automatic Renewal Provision Of Contract For Service, Mainten-
        ance Or Repair Unenforceable By Contractor Unless Notice
        Thereof Given To Recipient Of Services........................ 10
5-905   Certain Provisions Of Leases To Be Inoperative Unless Express
        Notice Thereof Is Given To Tenant............................. 10
5-1101 Agreements Relating To Securities............................. 95
5-1103 Written Agreement For Modification Or Discharge............... 95
5-1105 Written Promise Expressing Past Consideration................. 95
5-1107 Written Assignment... 95
5-1109 Written Irrevocable Offer.................................... 1
5-1111 Execution By Agent In Real Property Transactions; Written
        Authorization Required....................................... 68
5-1113 Written Or Published Promise Or Reward....................... 95
5-1115 Promises And Warranties In Conveyance Made Without Consider-
        ation.. 96

5-1301 How Interest Calculated......................................170
5-1311 Uniform Vendor And Purchaser Risk Act.......................246
13-101 Transfer Of Claims..281
13-105 Effect Of Transfer Of Claim Or Demand.......................281
13-109 Definition Of "Transfer"....................................281
15-301 When Written Agreement Or Other Instrument Cannot Be Changed
        By Oral Executory Agreement, Or Discharged Or Terminated By
        Oral Executory Agreement Or Oral Consent Or By Oral Notice.... 96
15-303 Release In Writing Without Consideration Or Seal............. 96
15-501 Executory Accord... 97
15-503 Offer Of Accord Followed By Tender..........................1;98
17-101 Acknowledgement or New Promise Must Be In Writing...........307
17-103 Agreements Waiving the Statute of Limitations...............307

NEW YORK GENERAL BUSINESS LAW

    5   Labor Prohibited On Sunday...................................206
    6   Persons Observing Another Day As A Sabbath...................206
    8   Trades, Manufactures, And Mechanical Employments Prohibited
        On Sunday..206
   11   Serving Civil Process On Sunday..............................206
198-a   Warranties 256
  200   Safes; Limited Liability 14
  201   Liability For Loss Of Clothing & Other Personal Property Limited. 14
  340   Contracts Or Agreements For Monopoly Or In Restraint Of Trade
        Illegal And Void 180

		Page
349	Deceptive Acts And Practices Unlawful	182
350	False Advertising Unlawful	181
350-a	False Advertising	181
350-d	False Advertising - Construction	181
380-		
380-s	Fair Credit Reporting Act (Article 25)	191
380-b	Permissible Dissemination Of Reports	191
380-c	Preparation And/ Or Procurement Of Investigative Consumer Reports	192
380-d	Disclosure To Consumers	193
380-e	Methods And Conditions Of Disclosure To Consumers	193
380-f	Procedure for Resolving Disputes	194
380-i	Requirements On Users Of Consumer Reports	195
380-j	Prohibited Information	196
380-m	Civil Liability For Negligent Noncompliance	197
380-o	Obtaining Information Under False Pretense: Penalty	197
380-p	Unauthorized Disclosures By Officers Or Employees; Penalty	198
512	Limitations Of Liability For Unauthorized Use Of A Credit Card	198
515	Issuance of Credit Cards	198
517	Statements Of Account	198
600-		
603	Debt Collection Procedures Act (Article 29H)	188
600	Definitions - Debt Collection Procedures Act	188
601	Prohibited Practices	188
602	Violations and Penalties	189
620-		
631	Health Club Services Act (Article 30)	184
620	Legislative Intent - Health Club Services	185
622	Escrow Required	185
623	Contract Restrictions	185
624	Rights of Cancellation of Contracts for Services	186
625	Assignment of Contracts For Services	187,285
626	Deceptive Acts Prohibited	187
627	Contracts Void and Unenforceable	187
628	Private Right of Action	187
629	Violations	187
701-		
707	Creditor Billing Errors (Article 34)	189
703	Notice of Error and Response	190
707	Penalties	190

NEW YORK PERSONAL PROPERTY LAW

46-		
49-b	Assignment of Earnings (Article 3-A)	286
46	Definitions	286
49-b	Income Deduction by Court Order In Support Cases	287
46-c	Formal Requisites of Assignment of Less Than One Thousand Dollars And of Assignments Securing Certain Guarantees Amounting to Fifteen Hundred Dollars or Less	287

		Page
46-e	Personal Execution of Assignment By Assignor; Delivery of Copies of Papers.	287
46-f	Limit On Interest and Other Charges	171
301-315	<u>Motor Vehicle Retail Instalment Sales Act</u> (Article 9)	202
401-422	<u>Retail Instalment Sales Act</u> (Article 10)	198
402	Provisions of Retail Instalment Contracts and Obligations	199
403	Restrictions on Retail Instalment Contracts and Obligations	284
404	Credit Service Charge Limitation	171
406	Notice Of Assignment; Payments	285
413	Retail Instalment Credit Agreements	201
414	Penalties	202
416	Waiver	202
425-431	<u>Door-To-Door Sales Protection Act</u> (Article 10-A)	11
425	Short Title; Purpose	12
426	Definitions	12
427	Buyer's or Other Obligor's Right To Cancel	12
428	Form of Notice; Statement Of Buyer's Rights	13
429	Restoration Of Down Payment	13
430	Duty Of Buyer	13
431	Restriction On Assignment Of Obligation	13,284

NEW YORK CIVIL PRACTICE LAW AND RULES (C.P.L.R.)

203	Methods Of Computing Periods Of Limitation Generally	308
211	Actions To Be Commenced Within Twenty Years	308
213	Actions To Be Commenced Within Six Years	144,308
213-a	Actions To Be Commenced Within 4 Years Residential Overcharge	309
214	Actions To Be Commenced Within Three Years	309
214-a	Action For Medical Malpractice	309
215	Actions To Be Commenced Within One Year	309
1201	Representation Of Infant, Incompetent Person, or Conservater	133
1206	Disposition Of Proceeds Of Claim Of Infant, Judicially Declared Incompetent Or Conservatee	133
1207	Settlement Of Action Or Claim By Infant, Judicially Declared Incompetent Or Conservatee, By Whom Motion Made; Special Proceeding; Notice; Order Of Settlement.	133
3002	Actions and Relief Not Barred For Inconsistency	144
3004	Where Restoration of Benefits Before Judgment Unnecessary	144
3005	Relief Against Mistake Of The Law	144
5004	Rate Of Interest	167
5205	Personal Property Exempt from Application to the Satisfaction of Money Judgments	203
5206	Real Property Exempt from Application to the Satisfaction of Money Judgments	204
5231	Income Execution	205
5252	Dismissal Or Lay Off Of Employee To Avoid Compliance With Wage Assignment or Income Execution	288
7501	Effect of Arbitration Agreement	68

NEW YORK EDUCATION LAW

		Page
281	Loans And Extensions Of Credit To Infants	132
6501	Admission To A Profession (Licensing)	172
6503	Practice Of A Profession	172
6509	Definitions Of Professional Misconduct	173
6512	Unauthorized Practice A Crime	173
6513	Unauthorized Use Of A Professional Title A Crime	174
6515	Restraint Of Unlawful Acts	174
6522	Practice Of Medicine And Use Of Title "Physician"	174
6524	Requirements For A Professional License (as Medical Doctor)	174
6602	Practice Of Dentistry And Use Of Title "Dentist"	175
7401	Definition Of Practice Of Public Accountancy	175
7402	Practice Of Public Accountancy And Use Of Title "Certified Public Accountant" Or "Public Accountant"	175
7404	Requirements For A License As A Certified Public Accountant	175
7408	Special Provisions	176

NEW YORK PENAL LAW

135.60	Coercion In The Second Degree	165
155.05	Larceny; Defined	164
180.00	Commercial Bribing In The Second Degree	166
180.03	Commercial Bribing In The First Degree	166
180.05	Commercial Bribe Receiving In The Second Degree	167
190.20	False Advertising	182
190.40	Criminal Usury In The Second Degree	170
190.60	Scheme To Defraud In The Second Degree	146
190.65	Scheme To Defraud In The First Degree	146

NEW YORK JUDICIARY LAW

460	Examination And Admission Of Attorneys	176
478	Practicing Or Appearing As Attorney-At-Law Without Being Admitted And Registered	176
484	None But Attorneys To Practice In The State	177
486	Practice Of Law By Attorney Who Has Been Disbarred, Suspended, Or Convicted Of A Felony	177

NEW YORK RACING, PARI-MUTUEL WAGERING AND BREEDING LAW

101	New York State Racing And Wagering Board	163
104	Prohibition Of Wagering By Certain Officials, Employees And Minors	163
213	Licenses For Participants And Employees At Race Meetings	163
216	Penalty For Unlawful Racing And Betting	163
601	Declaration Of Policy And Statement Of Purpose--New York City Off-Track Betting Corporation Law	164
603	New York City Off-Track Betting Corporation	164
604	Powers Of The Corporation	164
605	Policing Of Off-Track Betting	164

NEW YORK REAL PROPERTY LAW

235-b   Warranty of Habitability.. 184
235-c   Unconscionable Lease or Clause.................................. 178
442-d   Actions for Commission; License Prerequisite.................... 172

NEW YORK BANKING LAW

6-f   Alternative Mortgage Instruments Made By Banks, Trust Companies,
        Savings Banks, Savings And Loan Associations And Credit Unions... 170

14-a   Rate Of Interest; Banking Board To Adopt Regulations............ 167

NEW YORK BUSINESS CORPORATION LAW (B.C.L.)

625   Infant Shareholders and Bondholders............................ 132

NEW YORK ESTATES, POWERS AND TRUST LAW (E.P.T.L.)

13-2.1 Agreements Involving A Contract To Establish A Trust, To Make
        A Testamentary Provision Of Any Kind, And By A Personal
        Representative To Answer For The Debt Or Default Of A Decedent,
        Required To Be In Writing...................................... 68

NEW YORK GENERAL CONSTRUCTION LAW

44-a   Seal On Written Instrument 98

ADDITIONAL U.C.C. SECTIONS ON WARRANTY

2-312   Warranty Of Title 256
2-313   Express Warranties By Affirmation, Promise, Description, Sample.. 256
2-314   Implied Warranty: Merchantability 256
2-315   Implied Warranty: Fitness For Particular Purpose 256
2-316   Exclusion Or Modification Of Warranties 256

FORMATION OF CONTRACTS: OFFER AND ACCEPTANCE

There are several New York statutes which govern the formation of contracts. Some of these statutes relate to all contracts while others relate only to specific types of contracts such as contracts for the sale of goods, real property, services, and insurance.

Statutes included herewith encompass various sections of the Uniform Commercial Code which is effective in New York, the New York General Obligations Law, as well as several other New York statutes and also statutes that specifically relate to the formation of contracts involved in "consumer" transactions.

Where there are no New York statutes governing the formation of contracts, the common law rules of contract law will apply.

FORMATION OF CONTRACTS: OFFER AND ACCEPTANCE

NEW YORK GENERAL OBLIGATIONS LAW:

Section 5-1109. Written Irrevocable Offer

Except as otherwise provided in section 2-205 of the uniform commercial code with respect to an offer by a merchant to buy or sell goods, when an offer to enter into a contract is made in writing signed by the offeror, or by his agent, which states that the offer is irrevocable during a period set forth or until a time fixed, the offer shall not be revocable during such period or until such time because of the absence of consideration for the assurance of irrevocability. When such a writing states that the offer is irrevocable but does not state any period of time of irrevocability, it shall be construed to state that the offer is irrevocable for a reasonable time. (eff. Sept. 27, 1964 - originally enacted in 1941, and was previously contained in Personal Property Law 33(5)).

Section 15-503. Offer of Accord Followed By Tender

1. An offer in writing, signed by the offeror or by his agent, to accept a performance therein designated in satisfaction or discharge in whole or in part of any claim, cause of action, contract, obligation, or lease, or any mortgage or other security interest in personal or real property, followed by tender of such performance by the offeree or by his agent before revocation of the offer, shall not be denied effect as a defense or as the basis of an action or counterclaim by reason of the fact that such tender was not accepted by the offeror or by his agent.

2. If executed by an agent, any offer required by this section to be in writing which affects or relates to real property or an interest therein as defined in section 5-101 in any manner stated in subdivisions one or two of section 5-703 of this chapter shall be void unless such agent was thereunto authorized in writing. (1963 - originally enacted in 1937, and was previously contained in Personal Property Law 33-b(1)).

1

FORMATION OF CONTRACTS - OFFER AND ACCEPTANCE

UNIFORM COMMERCIAL CODE: ARTICLE 2: SALE OF GOODS

The Uniform Commercial Code (UCC) became effective in New York State on September 27, 1964 and is in effect in 49 states (except Louisiana). Article 2 of the UCC governs sales transactions involving the sale of goods.

The following material includes several sections of Articles 1 and 2 which contain definitions of terms used in Article 2, in addition to several statutes in Article 2 specifically governing the formation of contracts for the sale of goods.

It should be noted that common law rules of contract law will govern all contracts relating to real property, employment, services, and insurance, and intangibles such as patents and copyrights, as well as contracts for the sale of goods if there is no specific UCC provision in Article 2.

DEFINITIONS

Section 2-103. Definitions

(1) In this Article, unless the context otherwise requires

    (a) "Buyer" means a person who buys or contracts to buy goods.
    (b) "Good faith" in the case of a merchant means honesty in fact and the observance of reasonable commercial standards of fair dealing in the trade.
    (c) "Receipt" of goods means taking physical possession of them.
    (d) "Seller" means a person who sells or contracts to sell goods.
    ....

Section 2-104. Definitions: "Merchant"; "Between Merchants"...

(1) "Merchant" means a person who deals in goods of the kind or otherwise by his occupation holds himself out as having knowledge or skill peculiar to the practices or goods involved in the transaction or to whom such knowledge or skill may be attributed by his employment of an agent or broker or other intermediary who by his occupation holds himself out as having such knowledge or skill.

    ....

(3) "Between merchants" means in any transaction with respect to which both parties are chargeable with the knowledge or skill of merchants.

Section 2-105. Definitions: ..."Goods"; "Future Goods"...

(1) "Goods" means all things (including specially manufactured goods) which are movable at the time of identification to the contract for sale other than the money in which the price is to be paid, investment securities(Article 8) and things in action. "Goods" also includes the unborn young of animals and growing crops and other identified things attached to

realty as described in the section on goods to be severed from realty (Section 2-107).

(2) Goods must be both existing and identified before any interest in them can pass. Goods which are not both existing and identified are "future" goods. A purported present sale of future goods or of any interest therein operates as a contract to sell.

(3) There may be a sale of a part interest in existing identified goods.

. . .

(5) "Lot" means a parcel or a single article which is the subject matter of a separate sale or delivery, whether or not it is sufficient to perform the contract.

(6) "Commercial unit" means such a unit of goods as by commercial usage is a single whole for purposes of sale and division of which materially impairs its character or value on the market or in use. A commercial unit may be a single article (as a machine) or a set of articles (as a suite of furniture or an assortment of sizes) or a quantity (as a bale, gross, or carload) or any other unit treated in use or in the relevant market as a single whole.

Section 2-106.   Definitions: "Contract"; "Agreement"; "Contract for Sale"; "Sale";....

(1) In this Article unless the context otherwise requires "contract" and "agreement" are limited to those relating to the present or future sale of goods. "Contract for sale" includes both a present sale of goods and a contract to sell goods at a future time. A "sale" consists in the passing of title from the seller to the buyer for a price (Section 2-401). A "present sale" means a sale which is accomplished by the making of the contract.

(2) Goods or conduct including any part of a performance are "conforming" or conform to the contract when they are in accordance with the obligations under the contract.

(3) "Termination" occurs when either party pursuant to a power created by agreement or law puts an end to the contract otherwise than for its breach. On "termination" all obligations which are still executory on both sides are discharged but any right based on prior breach or performance survives.

(4) "Cancellation" occurs when either party puts an end to the contract for breach by the other and its effect is the same as that of "termination" except that the cancelling party also retains any remedy for breach of the whole contract or any unperformed balance.

Section 2-107.   Goods To Be Severed From Realty...

(1) A contract for the sale of minerals or the like (including oil and gas) or a structure or its materials to be removed from realty is a contract

for the sale of goods within this Article if they are to be severed by the seller but until severance...is effective only as a contract to sell.

(2) A contract for the sale apart from the land of growing crops or other things attached to realty and capable of severance without material harm thereto but not described in subsection (1) or of timber to be cut is a contract for the sale of goods within this Article whether the subject matter is to be severed by the buyer or by the seller even though it forms part of the realty at the time of contracting, and the parties can by identification effect a present sale before severance.

.... (eff. July 2, 1978)

Section 1-201. General Definitions

Subject to additional definitions contained in the subsequent Articles of this Act which are applicable to specific Articles or Parts thereof, and unless the context otherwise requires, in this Act:

(1) "Action" in the sense of a judicial proceeding includes recoupment, counterclaim, set-off, suit in equity and any other proceedings in which rights are determined.

(2) "Aggrieved party" means a party entitled to resort to a remedy.

(3) "Agreement" means the bargain of the parties in fact as found in their language or by implication from other circumstances including course of dealing or usage of trade or course of performance as provided in this Act....Whether an agreement has legal consequences is determined by the provisions of this Act, if applicable; otherwise by the law of contracts....

....

(9) "Buyer in ordinary course of business" means a person who in good faith and without knowledge that the sale to him is in violation of the ownership rights or security interests of a third party in the goods buys in ordinary course from a person in the business of selling goods of that kind but does not include a pawnbroker..."Buying" may be for cash or by exchange of other property or on secured or unsecured credit and includes receiving goods or documents of title under a pre-existing contract for sale ...

....

(11) "Contract" means the total legal obligation which results from the parties' agreement as affected by this Act and any other applicable rules of law...

....

(19) "Good faith" means honesty in fact in the conduct or transaction concerned.

....

(29) "Party", as distinct from "third party", means a person who has engaged in a transaction or made an agreement within this Act.

(30) "Person" includes an individual or an organization...

....

4

(32) "Purchase" includes taking by sale, discount, negotiation, mortgage, pledge, lien, issue or re-issue, gift or any other voluntary transaction creating an interest in property.

(33) "Purchaser" means a person who takes by purchase.

(34) "Remedy" means any remedial right to which an aggrieved party is entitled with or without resort to a tribunal.

....

(36) "Rights" includes remedies.

....

(38) "Send" in connection with any writing or notice means to deposit in the mail or deliver for transmission by any other usual means of communication with postage or cost of transmission provided for and properly addressed... to an address specified thereon or otherwise agreed, or if there be none to any address reasonable under the circumstances. The receipt of any writing or notice within the time at which it would have arrived if properly sent has the effect of a proper sending.

(39) "Signed" includes any symbol executed or adopted by a party with present intention to authenticate a writing....

....

(41) "Telegram" includes a message transmitted by radio, teletype, cable, any mechanical method of transmission, or the like.

(42) "Term" means that portion of an agreement which relates to a particular matter.

....

(46) "Written" or "writing" includes printing, typewriting or any other intentional reduction to tangible form.

(some definitions have been amended, effective date 1981).

Section 1-203. Obligation Of Good Faith

Every contract or duty within this Act imposes an obligation of good faith in its performance or enforcement.

FORMATION OF CONTRACTS - OFFER AND ACCEPTANCE

UNIFORM COMMERCIAL CODE: ARTICLE 2 - SALE OF GOODS

Section 2-204. Formation In General

(1) A contract for sale of goods may be made in any manner sufficient to show agreement, including conduct by both parties which recognizes the existence of such a contract.

(2) An agreement sufficient to constitute a contract for sale may be found even though the moment of its making is undetermined.

(3) Even though one or more terms are left open a contract for sale

does not fail for indefiniteness if the parties have intended to make a contract and there is a reasonably certain basis for giving an appropriate remedy.

Section 2-205. Firm Offers

An offer by a merchant to buy or sell goods in a signed writing which by its terms gives assurance that it will be held open is not revocable, for lack of consideration, during the time stated or if no time is stated for a reasonable time, but in no event may such period of irrevocability exceed three months; but any such term of assurance on a form supplied by the offeree must be separately signed by the offeror.

Section 2-206. Offer and Acceptance In Formation Of Contract

(1) Unless otherwise unambiguously indicated by the language or circumstances

    (a) an offer to make a contract shall be construed as inviting acceptance in any manner and by any medium reasonable in the circumstances;

    (b) an order or other offer to buy goods for prompt or current shipment shall be construed as inviting acceptance either by a prompt promise to ship or by the prompt or current shipment of conforming or non-conforming goods, but such a shipment of non-conforming goods does not constitute an acceptance if the seller seasonably notifies the buyer that the shipment is offered only as an accommodation to the buyer.

(2) Where the beginning of a requested performance is a reasonable mode of acceptance an offeror who is not notified of acceptance within a reasonable time may treat the offer as having lapsed before acceptance.

Section 2-207. Additional Terms In Acceptance Or Confirmation

(1) A definite and seasonable expression of acceptance or a written confirmation which is sent within a reasonable time operates as an acceptance even though it states terms additional to or different from those offered or agreed upon, unless acceptance is expressly made conditional on assent to the additional or different terms.

(2) The additional terms are to be construed as proposals for addition to the contract. Between merchants such terms become part of the contract unless:

    (a) the offer expressly limits acceptance to the terms of the offer;

    (b) they materially alter it; or

    (c) notification of objection to them has already been given or is given within a reasonable time after notice of them is received.

(3) Conduct by both parties which recognizes the existence of a contract is sufficient to establish a contract for sale although the writings of
the parties do not otherwise establish a contract. In such case the terms of
the particular contract consist of those terms on which the writings of
the parties agree, together with any supplementary terms incorporated under
any other provisions of this Act.

Section 2-304. Price Payable In Money, Goods, Realty, Or Otherwise

(1) The price can be made payable in money or otherwise. If it is
payable in whole or in part in goods each party is a seller of the goods
which he is to transfer....

.....

Section 2-305. Open Price Term

(1) The parties if they so intend can conclude a contract for sale even
though the price is not settled. In such a case the price is a reasonable
price at the time for delivery if

(a) nothing is said as to price; or
(b) the price is left to be agreed by the parties and they fail
       to agree; or
(c) the price is to be fixed in terms of some agreed market or
       other standard as set or recorded by a third person or agency
       and it is not so set or recorded.

(2) A price to be fixed by the seller or by the buyer means a price for
him to fix in good faith.

(3) When a price left to be fixed otherwise than by agreement of the
parties fails to be fixed through fault of one party the other may at his
option treat the contract as cancelled or himself fix a reasonable price.

(4) Where, however, the parties intend not to be bound unless the
price be fixed or agreed and it is not fixed or agreed there is no contract.
In such a case the buyer must return any goods already received or if unable
so to do must pay their reasonable value at the time of delivery and the
seller must return any portion of the price paid on account.

Section 2-306. Output, Requirements and Exclusive Dealings

(1) A term which measures the quantity by the output of the seller or
the requirements of the buyer means such actual output or requirements as may
occur in good faith, except that no quantity unreasonably disproportionate to
any stated estimate or in the absence of a stated estimate to any normal or
otherwise comparable prior output or requirements may be tendered or
demanded.

(2) A lawful agreement by either the seller or the buyer for exclusive
dealing in the kind of goods concerned imposes unless otherwise agreed an
obligation by the seller to use best efforts to supply the goods and by the
buyer to use best efforts to promote their sale.

<u>Section 2-309</u>. <u>Absence of Specific Time Provisions</u>

(1) The time for shipment or delivery or any other action under a contract if not provided in this Article or agreed upon shall be a reasonable time....

....

<u>Section 2-310</u>. <u>Open Time for Payment</u>

Unless otherwise agreed

(a) payment is due at the time and place at which the buyer is to receive the goods even though the place of shipment is the place of delivery;...

....

<u>Section 2-311</u>. <u>Options and Cooperation Respecting Performance</u>

(1) An agreement for sale which is otherwise sufficiently definite (subsection (3) of Section 2-204) to be a contract is not made invalid by the fact that it leaves particulars of performance to be specified by one of the parties. Any such specification must be made in good faith and within limits set by commercial reasonableness.

....

<u>Section 2-328</u>. <u>Sale By Auction</u>

(1) In a sale by auction if goods are put up in lots each lot is the subject of a separate sale.

(2) A sale by auction is complete when the auctioneer so announces by the fall of the hammer or in other customary manner. Where a bid is made while the hammer is falling in acceptance of a prior bid the auctioneer may in his discretion reopen the bidding or declare the goods sold under the bid on which the hammer was falling.

(3) Such a sale is with reserve unless the goods are in explicit terms put up without reserve. In an auction with reserve the auctioneer may withdraw the goods at any time until he announces completion of the sale. In an auction without reserve, after the auctioneer calls for bids on an article or lot, that article or lot cannot be withdrawn unless no bid is made within a reasonable time. In either case a bidder may retract his bid until the auctioneer's announcement of completion of the sale, but a bidder's retraction does not revive any previous bid.

....

STATUTORY PROVISIONS RELATING TO SPECIFIC TYPES OF CONTRACTS

NEW YORK GENERAL OBLIGATIONS LAW:

Section 5-332. Unsolicited And Voluntarily Sent Merchandise Deemed Unconditional Gift

(1) No person, firm, partnership, association or corporation, or agent or employee thereof, shall, in any manner, or by any means, offer for sale goods, wares, or merchandise, where the offer includes the voluntary and unsolicited sending of such goods, wares, or merchandise not actually ordered or requested by the recipient, either orally or in writing. The receipt of any such goods, wares, or merchandise shall for all purposes be deemed an unconditional gift to the recipient who may use or dispose of such goods, wares, or merchandise in any manner he sees fit without any obligation on his part to the sender.

If after any such receipt deemed to be an unconditional gift under this section, the sender continues to send bill statements or requests for payment with respect thereto, an action may be brought by the recipient to enjoin such conduct, in which action there may also be awarded reasonable attorney's fees and costs to the prevailing party.

.... (eff. July 1, 1970).

FORMATION OF CONTRACTS - AUTOMATIC RENEWAL PROVISIONS

Some agreements provide for the automatic renewal of the agreement unless notice of intent to terminate is given. Statutes have been enacted whereby such provision in certain types of contracts would be ineffective unless written notice calling attention to such provision is given within specific time periods. A list of the relevant statutes is provided, and the full text of two of the sections is included herewith.

REQUIREMENTS OF NOTICE FOR EFFECTIVENESS OR ENFORCEABILITY

NEW YORK GENERAL OBLIGATIONS LAW:

Section 5-901. Certain provisions of leases of personal property inoperative unless notice thereof given to lessee.
Section 5-903. Automatic renewal provision of contract of service, maintenance or repair unenforceable by contractor unless notice thereof given to recipient of services.
Section 5-905. Certain provisions of leases to be inoperative unless express notice thereof is given to tenant.

Section 5-903. Automatic Renewal Provision Of Contract For Service, Maintenance Or Repair Unenforceable By Contractor Unless
Notice Thereof Given To Recipient Of Services

(1) As used in this section, "person" means an individual, firm, company,
partnership or corporation.

(2) No provision of a contract for service, maintenance or repair to or
for any real or personal property which states that the term of the contract
shall be deemed renewed for a specified additional period unless the person
receiving the service, maintenance or repair gives notice to the person
furnishing such contract service, maintenance or repair of his intention to
terminate the contract at the expiration of such term, shall be enforceable
against the person receiving the service, maintenance or repair, unless the
person furnishing the service, maintenance or repair, at least fifteen days
and not more than thirty days previous to the time specified for serving such
notice upon him, shall give to the person receiving the service, maintenance
or repair written notice, served personally or by certified mail, calling
the attention of that person to the existence of such provision in the
contract.

(3) Nothing herein contained shall be construed to apply to a contract
in which the automatic renewal period specified is one month or less. (eff.
1963)

Section 5-905. Certain Provisions Of Leases To Be Inoperative Unless
Express Notice Thereof Is Given To Tenant

No provision of a lease of any real property or premises which states
that the term thereof shall be deemed renewed for a specified additional
period of time unless the tenant gives notice to the lessor of his intention
to quit the premises at the expiration of such term shall be operative unless
the lessor, at least fifteen days and not more than thirty days previous to
the time specified for the furnishing of such notice to him, shall give to
the tenant written notice, served personally or by registered or certified
mail, calling the attention of the tenant to the existence of such provision
in the lease. (eff. 1963)

FORMATION OF CONTRACTS - "CONSUMER" TRANSACTIONS

Some statutes have been designed specifically to protect consumers
involved in consumer transactions in the formation of contracts. In protecting the consumer, the statutes at times depart from general rules of
contract law. Most of these statutes relating to consumer transactions are
contained in the New York General Obligations Law, the New York Personal
Property Law, and the New York General Business Law. A representative
selection of some of these statutory provisions follows:

NEW YORK GENERAL OBLIGATIONS LAW

Section 5-702. Requirements For Use Of Plain Language In Consumer Transactions

(a) Every written agreement entered into after November first, nineteen hundred seventy-eight, for the lease of space to be occupied for residential purposes, or to which a consumer is a party and the money, property or service which is the subject of the transaction is primarily for personal, family or household purposes must be:

1. Written in a clear and coherent manner using words with common and every day meanings;

2. Appropriately divided and captioned by its various sections. Any creditor, seller or lessor who fails to comply with this subdivision shall be liable to a consumer who is a party to a written agreement governed by this subdivision in an amount equal to any actual damages sustained plus a penalty of fifty dollars. The total class action penalty against any such creditor, seller or lessor shall not exceed ten thousand dollars in any class action or series of class actions arising out of the use by a creditor, seller or lessor of an agreement which fails to comply with this subdivision. No action under this subdivision may be brought after both parties to the agreement have fully performed their obligation under such agreement, nor shall any creditor, seller or lessor who attempts in good faith to comply with this subdivision be liable for such penalties. This subdivision shall not apply to agreements involving amounts in excess of fifty thousand dollars nor prohibit the use of words or phrases or forms of agreement required by state or federal law, rule or regulation or by a governmental instrumentality ... (eff. 1978)

Note: The above statute is known as the "Plain English Law." Similar statutes have been enacted which require that certain specific types of contracts be written in plain language. See, for example, New York Insurance Law Section 142-a. "Requirements for the use of readable and understandable insurance policies."

NEW YORK PERSONAL PROPERTY LAW: DOOR-TO-DOOR SALES PROTECTION ACT

Section 425. Short title; purpose.
Section 426. Definitions
Section 427. Buyer's or other obligor's right to cancel.
Section 428. Form of notice; statement of buyer's rights.
Section 429. Restoration of down payment.
Section 430. Duty of Buyer.
Section 431. Restriction on assignment of obligation.

Section 425. Short title; purpose

This act may be cited as the door-to-door sales protection act. The purpose of this act is to afford consumers a "cooling-off" period to cancel contracts which are entered into as a result of high pressure door-to-door sales tactics.

Section 426. Definitions
In this article:
(1) "Door-to-door sale" shall mean a sale, lease or rental of consumer goods or services in which the seller or his representative personally solicits the sale, including those in response to or following an invitation by the buyer, and the buyer's agreement or offer to purchase is made at a place other than the place of business of the seller. The term "door-to-door sale" does not include a transaction:...
....
(c) conducted and consummated entirely by man or telephone;...,or
(d) in which the buyer has initiated the contact and specifically requested the seller to visit his home for the purpose of repairing or performing mantenance upon the buyer's personal property...., or
(e) pertaining to the sale or rental of real property,..., or
(f) where the purchase price whether under single or multiple contracts, does not exceed twenty-five dollars and the products, goods or merchandise purchased is capable of delivery at one time.

(2) "Consumer goods or services" shall mean goods or services purchased, leased, or rented primarily for personal, family or household purposes, including courses of instruction or training regardless of the purpose for which they are taken.

(3) "Seller" shall mean any person, partnership, corporation or association engaged in the door-to-door sale of consumer goods or services.

(4) "Place of business" shall mean the main or permanent branch office or local address of the seller.

(5) "Purchase price" shall mean the total price paid or to be paid for the consumer goods or services, including all interest and service charges.

(6) "Business day" shall mean any calendar day except Sunday, or the following business holidays:....
....
Section 427. Buyer's Or Other Obligor's Right to Cancel

(1) In addition to any right otherwise to revoke an offer, the buyer or other person obligated for any part of the purchase price may cancel [the] door-to-door sale until midnight of the third business day after the day on which the buyer has signed an agreement or offer to purchase relating to such sale.

....

12

Section 428. Form of Notice; Statement of Buyer's Rights

(1) In a door-to-door sale, the seller shall furnish to the buyer

(a) a fully completed receipt or copy of any contract pertaining to such sale at the time of its execution, which is in the same language, e.g. Spanish, as that principally used in the oral sales presentation and which shows the date of the transaction and contains the name and address of the seller, and in immediate proximity to the space reserved in the contract for the signature of the buyer or on the front page of the receipt if a contract is not used and in not less than ten-point bold face type, a statement... [informing the consumer of his rights]...

Section 429. Restoration Of Down Payment

(1) Within ten days after a door-to-door sale has been cancelled or an offer to purchase revoked, the seller shall tender to the buyer all payments made by the buyer and any note or other evidence of indebtedness.
                              ....
[Note - penalties may be imposed for failure of seller to comply].

Section 430. Duty of Buyer

(1) ...the buyer upon demand shall tender to the seller any goods delivered by the seller pursuant to the sale but need not tender at any place other than his residence. If the seller fails to demand possession of such goods within a reasonable time after cancellation or revocation, the goods shall become the property of the buyer without obligation to pay for them. For the purpose of this section, twenty days shall be presumed to be a reasonable time.

(2) The buyer shall take reasonable care of the goods in his possession both before cancellation or revocation and for a reasonable time thereafter, during which time the goods are otherwise at the seller's risk.

(3) If the seller has performed any services pursuant to a door-to-door sale prior to its cancellation, the seller shall not be entitled to compensation therefor.

Section 431. Restriction On Assignment of Obligation

See Assignments

See Also, topics of Illegality and Assignments, for other statutes that place limitations and restrictions in transactions involving consumers.

FORMATION OF CONTRACTS - LIMITATION OF LIABILITY BY STATUTE

There are some statutes that place limitations on recovery and limitations of liability of innkeeper and hotel and restaurant check rooms in certain circumstances.

NEW YORK GENERAL BUSINESS LAW

Section 200. Safes; Limited Liability

Whenever the proprietor or manager of any hotel, motel, inn or steamboat shall provide a safe in the office of such hotel, motel or steamboat, or other convenient place for the safe keeping of any money, jewels, ornaments, bank notes, negotiable securities or precious stones, belonging to the guests of or travelers in such hotel, motel, inn or steamboat, and shall notify the guests or travelers thereof by posting a notice stating the fact that such safe is provided, in which such property may be deposited, in a public and conspicuous place and manner in the office and public rooms, and in the public parlors of such hotel, motel, or inn, or saloon of such steamboat; and if such guest or traveler shall neglect to deliver such property, to the person in charge of such office for deposit in such safe, the proprietor or manager of such hotel, motel, or steamboat shall not be liable for any loss of such property, sustained by such guest or traveler by theft or otherwise; but no hotel, motel or steamboat proprietor, manager or lessee shall be obliged to receive property on deposit for safe keeping, exceeding five hundred dollars in value; and if such guest or traveler shall deliver such property, to the person in charge of such office for deposit in such safe, said proprietor, manager or lessee shall not be liable for any loss thereof, sustained by such guest or traveler by theft or otherwise, in any sum exceeding the sum of five hundred dollars unless by special agreement in writing with such proprietor, manager or lessee.... (eff. June 1, 1960, as amended)

Section 201. Liability For Loss Of Clothing And Other Personal Property Limited

1. No hotel or motel keeper except as provided in the foregoing section shall be liable for damage to or loss of wearing apparel or other personal property in the lobby, hallways or in the room or rooms assigned to a guest for any sum exceeding the sum of five hundred dollars, unless it shall appear that such loss occurred through the fault or negligence of such keeper, nor shall he be liable in any sum exceeding the sum of one hundred dollars for the loss of or damage to any such property when delivered to such keeper for storage or safe keeping in the store room, baggage room or other place elsewhere than in the room or rooms assigned to such guest, unless at the time of delivering the same for storage or safe keeping such value in excess of one hundred dollars shall be stated and a written receipt, stating such value, shall be issued by such keeper, but in no event shall such keeper be liable beyond five hundred dollars, unless it shall appear that such loss occurred through his fault or negligence,...; as to property deposited by guests or patrons in the parcel or check room of any hotel, motel or restaurant, the delivery of which is evidenced by a check or receipt therefor and for which

no fee or charge is exacted, the proprietor shall not be liable beyond two hundred dollars, unless such value in excess of two hundred dollars shall be stated upon delivery and a written receipt, stating such value, shall be issued, but he shall in no event be liable beyond three hundred dollars, unless such loss occurs through his fault or negligence. Notwithstanding anything hereinabove contained, no hotel or motel keeper shall be liable for damage to or loss of such property by fire, when it shall appear that such fire was occasioned without his fault or negligence.

2. A printed copy of this section shall be posted in a conspicuous place and manner in the office or public room and in the public parlors of such hotel or motel. No hotel, motel or restaurant proprietor shall post a notice disclaiming or misrepresenting his liability under this section. (originally eff. June 1, 1960, as amended, and subsequently amended eff. 90 days after May 31, 1983).

FORMATION OF CONTRACTS

MUTUAL ASSENT

CASE NO. 1

ANSORGE v. KANE

244 N.Y. 395   Feb. 23, 1927

INTRODUCTION

It is a fundamental common law rule that there is no enforceable contract unless the parties have agreed on all the material terms. By contrast, the failure of parties to agree on trivial or immaterial terms does not prevent a contract from being enforceable. Thus, the major question a court must frequently decide is whether the particular term not agreed to is material or immaterial. A court will decide the question based on a careful analysis of the other terms agreed to. This leading case illustrates the analysis used and shows that sometimes a higher court reaches a different conclusion than a lower court.

POUND, J. The main point is simply stated. Defendant owned real property in Flushing, N.Y.. Plaintiff desired to purchase it. Through her agent the parties came together March 25, 1925, and made a memorandum of purchase and sale which describes the property and acknowledges the receipt of $500 as binder thereon and then provides:

"The price is $32,625; payable $12,625 cash; balance of $20,000 to remain on 1st mortgage for five years. The sum to be paid on signing of contract on March 26, 1925, to be agreed on. The balance of cash payment on passing of title on May 26, 1925."

The parties never agreed on the sum to be paid on signing the contract. When the owner refused to sign a contract or execute a deed, the court below ordered specific performance at the suit of the purchaser. That the parties had not agreed was held immaterial. It was said that the agreement in substance was that the balance of the cash payment would be payable when title passed unless the parties in the interim agreed otherwise....

Appellant contends that the scheme or plan of the parties was left incomplete by the failure to name the sum to be paid when the contract was signed; and that until the sum was named the contract was unenforceable....The memorandum states the price to be paid, but it does not state all the terms of payment....The fundamental question here presented is whether there was any contract; any actual meeting of minds on all the material elements of the agreement.

If a material element of a contemplated contract is left for future negotiations, there is no enforceable contract....The price is a material element of any contract of sale, and an agreement to agree thereon in the future is too indefinite to be enforceable....

16

The terms of payment may be no less material. Is this memorandum in effect an agreement to convey the property described if the parties can agree upon the amount to be paid on the signing of the contract but for no sale if they do not agree? Or is the agreement on the sum to be paid on signing the contract a minor and nonessential detail of the transaction? That is the question before us....The memorandum was on its face a mere binder. The formal contract was to be prepared and executed on the next day. As a part of the agreement was left to future negotiations, the contract was embryonic. It never reached full time. It was not for nothing that the parties provided that a sum should be agreed on to be paid on the signing of the contract; nor was it a minor matter for the owner whether nothing should be paid when the contract was signed and she should wait two months for her money, or whether she should receive a substantial sum, the stronger to bind the agreement, on which she also might receive interest, or even a greater increment, if she had her hands on it. In this connection we observe that the broker demanded that his full commission of ten percent, be paid on the signing of the contract which further suggests that the down payment had more than theoretical importance to the vendor.

The parties had decided to purchase and sell. They had agreed on the purchase price. They had not agreed on the terms of payment. The law implies nothing as to such terms as it does in cases where the rate of interest and date of maturity of a mortgage are not stated...or where it appears that an agreement is to take effect and be acted upon before the details reserved for future agreement, such as time of delivery, are settled, when an implication may arise that, in the event of a failure to agree, the terms shall be such as are reasonable or customary....The amount to be paid on the signing of the contract was an important element of the complete contract. It was left open. The contract was never completed. The transaction was destitute of legal effect. Specific performance is therefore impossible. If the contract had been partly performed by the act of the purchaser in taking possession and making improvements, as in Morris v. Ballard and Roberge v. Winne, equity might grant relief, but that question is not presented. The parties have nothing to stand on but their legal rights.

The judgement of the Appellate Division and that of the Special Term should be reversed and the complaint dismissed, with costs in all courts.

(Judgment for defendant seller.)

DISCUSSION QUESTIONS

1.   The rule of law in this case is the law applied today for all types of contracts except contracts for the sale of goods which are governed by a statute called the Uniform Commercial Code (UCC). The policy of Article 2 ("Sales") of the UCC is to favor the formation of a sales contract even where the parties do not agree upon all of the material terms. This policy is given effect by provisions of the UCC which state that, for example, if the price is not settled, then the price is a reasonable price at the time for delivery. Similarly, the UCC expressly provides that if the parties have not otherwise agreed (1) the place for delivery of goods is the seller's place of business or if he has none his residence, (2) payment is due at the time and place at which

17

the buyer is to receive the goods, and (3) the time for shipment or delivery or any other action under a contract shall be a reasonable time. Thus, as to certain material terms the UCC "fills the gaps". Why did the UCC adopt its rule to create enforceable contracts when the parties did not agree on certain material terms, by "filling the gaps", thereby departing from the fundamental common law rule applicable to all other contracts--that there is no enforceable contract unless the parties agree to all the material terms?

2.   Do you think a statute similar to the UCC should be enacted to "fill the gaps" to create an enforceable contract in every type of contract even though the parties have not agreed on all the material terms?

FORMATION OF CONTRACTS: WHEN NOT FORMED

CASE NO. 2

KLEINSCHMIDT DIV. OF SCM CORP. v. FUTURONICS

395 N.Y.S. 2d 151   April, 1977

INTRODUCTION

Under the Uniform Commercial Code, if parties intend to contract for the
sale of goods, a contract will result even if one or more terms are left open.
This rule is opposite the rule applicable in all other contracts such as real
estate and employment contracts where the parties must agree on all material
terms. However, before the U.C.C. rule applies there must be evidence that the
parties intend to contract. The following case illustrates this basic requirement.

MEMORANDUM.

In this case, there is evidence from which the trial court could have inferred agreement with respect to Lots II and III. There were, of course, the
various serious communications, arguably reading as if the parties had reached
firm agreement on many things. Futuronics urged, especially on oral argument,
that Kleinschmidt's shipment, for "first unit testing", of several units comprised in Lots II and III was "Conduct * * * which recognizes the existence of
a contract" (Uniform Commercial Code, Sect. 2-207, subd. (3)). The trial court
however, found that no agreement had been reached. It could have found otherwise. But that is not the point. The point is that the trial court, with all
of the evidence before it, determined that no agreement had been reached, and
in making that determination, the court made no error of law.

Under the Uniform Commercial Code, if the parties have intended to contract, and if an appropriate remedy may be fashioned, a contract for sale does
not fail for indefiniteness if terms, even important terms, are left open
(Sect. 2-204, subd. (3)). It is no longer true that dispute over material
terms inevitably prevents formation of a binding contract. What is true, and
decisive in this case, is that when a dispute over material terms manifests a
lack of intention to contract, no contract results.

The basic philosophy of the sales article of the Uniform Commercial Code
is simple. Practical business people cannot be expected to govern their actions with reference to nice legal formalisms. Thus, when there is basic
agreement, however manifested and whether or not the precise moment of agreement may be determined, failure to articulate that agreement in the precise
language of a lawyer, with every difficulty and contingency considered and
resolved, will not prevent formation of a contract (see Uniform Commercial Code
Sect. 2-204). But, of equal importance, if there be no basic agreement, the
Code will not imply one. In this case, it was found as a fact by the trial
court, a finding supportable by the evidence and affirmed by the Appellate
Division, that there was no basic agreement.

Without agreement there can be no contract, and, of course, without a contract there can be no breach. This principle, basic as it is to contract law, finds explicit recognition in the Uniform Commercial Code (Sect. 1-201, subds. (3), (11); Sect. 2-204, subds. (1), (2)). The principle should be dispositive of this case.

Accordingly, the order of the Appellate Division should be affirmed, with costs.

DISCUSSION QUESTION

1.   How could the seller have avoided the result in this case?

CASE NO. 3

DOMBROWSKI v. SOMERS

393 N.Y.S. 2d 706   February 1977

INTRODUCTION

It is a fundamental rule of contract law that parties to a contract must agree on all the material terms before there is an enforceable contract. The material terms agreed to must be definite and certain, not vague or ambiguous. The following case illustrates the legal result that flows from the use of "loose language".

MEMORANDUM.

By this action plaintiff seeks compensation for housekeeping chores rendered pursuant to an alleged oral agreement between herself and the decedent Edward Vogel, whose household she was sharing.

Three witnesses testified that they heard Vogel say he would "take care of" plaintiff. None recalled any reference to a specific date. The claim itself was not filed until 18 months after the decedent's death.

The words to "take care of", in the context of this record, are too vague to spell out a meaningful promise. Even if they were not, standing alone, they would be legally insufficient to support a finding that there was a contract to compensate plaintiff during her lifetime rather than one to do so by bequest. In the latter case, an enforceable agreement would be required to be in writing ....In short, plaintiff has not met her burden of proof as a matter of law....

Accordingly, the order of the Appellate Division is reversed and the complaint dismissed.

DISCUSSION QUESTIONS

1. How could the plaintiff have avoided this result?

2. Could the plaintiff recover the fair and reasonable valuable of the of the household services she rendered under the doctrine of quasi-contract or quantum meruit?

FORMATION OF CONTRACTS: MUTUAL ASSENT

CASE NO. 4

MINNEAPOLIS, & c., R'Y v. COLUMBUS R'G MILL

119 U.S. 49   Nov. 1866

INTRODUCTION

An offeree who receives an offer from an offeror will frequently attempt to "accept" the offer in <u>different</u> terms than those stated in the offer (e.g. by "accepting" the <u>seller's</u> offer but for a <u>lesser</u> quantity than what the seller offers to sell). Under the common law rules of contract law the offeree's acceptance must "mirror" the offeror's offer. Thus, the acceptance must be an <u>unconditional</u> acceptance of each and every term contained in the offer or there is no acceptance which would create a contract. The legal question arises whether the offeree's "qualified acceptance" is a rejection, and, if so, whether the offeree can later accept the offer. This leading United States Supreme Court decision illustrates the common law rule of law applicable to such cases.

This was an action by a railroad corporation established at Minneapolis in the State of Minnesota against a manufacturing corporation established at Columbus in the State of Ohio. The petition alleged that on December 19, 1879, the parties made a contract by which the plaintiff agreed to buy of the defendant, and the defendant sold to the plaintiff, two thousand tone of iron rails of the weight of fifty poundsper yard, at the price of fifty four dollars per ton gross, to be delivered free on board cars at the defendant's rolling mill in the month of March, 1880, and to be paid for by the plaintiff in cash when so delivered. The answer denied the making of the contract. It was admitted at the trial that the following letters and telegrams were sent at their dates, and were received in due course, by the parties, through their agents:

December 5, 1879. Letter from plaintiff to defendant:

"Please quote me prices for 500 to 3000 tons 50lb. steel rails, and for 2000 to 5000 tone 50lb. iron rails, March 1880 delivery."

December 8, 1879. Letter from defendant to plaintiff:

"Your favor of the 5th inst. at hand. We do not make steel rails. For iron rails, we will sell 2000 to 5000 tons of 50 lb. rails for fifty-four ($54.00) dollars per gross ton for spot cash, F.O.B. cars at our mill, March delivery, subject as follows: In case of strike among our workmen, destruction of or serious damage to our works by fire or the elements, or any causes of delay beyond our control, we shall not be held accountable in damages. If our offer is accepted, shall expect to be notified of same prior to Dec. 20th, 1879."

December 16, 1879. Telegram from plaintiff to defendant:

"Yours of the 8th came duly to hand. I telegraphed you today to enter our order for twelve hundred (1200) tons 50 lb. iron rails for next March delivery, at fifty-four dollars (54.00) F.O.B. cars at your mill. Please send contract. Also please send me templet of your 50lb. rail. Do you make splices? If so, give me prices for splices for this lot of iron."

December 18, 1879. Telegram from defendant to plaintiff received same day: "We cannot book your order at present at that price."

December 19, 1879. Telegram from plaintiff to defendant:

"Please enter an order for two thousand tons rails, as per your letter of the eighth. Please forward written contract. Reply."

December 22, 1879. Telegram from plaintiff to defendant:

"Did you enter my order for two thousand tons rails, as per my telegram of December nineteenth? Answer."

After repeated similar inquiries by the plaintiff, the defendant, on January 19, 1880, denied the existence of any contract between the parties.

The jury returned a verdict for the defendant, under instructions which need not be particularly stated; and the plaintiff alleged exceptions, and sued out this writ of error.

Mr. Justice Gray, after making the foregoing statement of the case, delivered the opinion of the court.

The rules of law which govern this case are well settled. As no contract is complete without the mutual assent of the parties, an offer to sell imposes no obligation until it is accepted according to its terms. So long as the offer has been neither accepted nor rejected, the negotiation remains open, and imposes no obligation upon either party; the one may decline to accept, or the other may withdraw his offer; and either rejection or withdrawal leaves the matter as if no offer had ever been made. A proposal to accept, or an acceptance, upon terms varying from those offered, is a rejection of the offer, and puts an end to the negotiation, unless the party who makes the original offer renews it, or assents to the modification suggested. The other party, having once rejected the offer, cannot afterwards revive it by tendering an acceptance of it. If the offer does not limit the time for its acceptance, it must be accepted within a reasonable time. If it does, it may, at any time within a reasonable time. If it does, it may, at any time within the limit and so long as it remains open, be accepted or re- jected by the party to whom, or be withdrawn by the party by whom, it was made.

The defendant, by the letter of December 8, offered to sell to the plain- tiff two thousand to five thousand tons of iron rails on certain terms specified, and added that if the offer was accepted the defendant would expect to be notified prior to December 20. This offer, while it remained open, without having been rejected by the plaintiff or revoked by the defend- ants would authorize the plaintiff to take at his election any number of tons

23

not less than two thousand nor more than five thousand, on the terms specified.
The offer, while unrevoked, might be accepted or rejected by the plaintiff
at any time before December 20. Instead of accepting the offer made, the plaintiff, on December 16, by telegram and letter, referring to the defendant's
letter of December 8, directed the defendant to enter an order for twelve
hundred tons on the same terms. The mention, in both telegram and letter,
of the date and terms of the defendant's original offer, shows that the
plaintiff s order was not an independant proposal, but an answer to the
defendant's offer, a qualified acceptance of that offer, varying the number
of tons and therefore,in law a rejection of the offer. On December 18, the
defendant by telegram declined to fulfill the plaintiff's order. The negotiation between the parties was thus closed, and the plaintiff could not afterwards fall back on the defendant's original offer. The plaintiff's attempt
to do so, by telegram of December 19, was therefore ineffectual and created
no rights against the defendant.

(Judgment for Defendant seller)

DISCUSSION QUESTIONS

1.   How could the buyer in this case "bargain " over the quantity without
rejecting the offer and without losing his right to accept the offer?

2.   Article 2 of the Uniform Commercial Code (UCC) governs the law of sales
contracts involving the sales of goods. Article 2 does not follow many
common law rules of contract law. Rather Article 2 provides different rules
of law concerning the formation of contracts for the sale of goods in order
to give effect to the practices and expectations of merchants in the market-
place. Thus, for example, Section 2-207 of the UCC provides that an offeree
who gives a definite and seasonable expression of acceptance (e.g."I accept")
will thereby create a contract for the sale of goods even though his acceptance "states terms additional to or different from those offered or agreed
upon, unless acceptance is expressly made conditional on assent to the
additional or different terms."
Under Section 2-207 of the UCC, do the additional or different terms become
a part of the contract?

3.   How could an offeror (seller) avoid the legal effect of having the
offeree's additional or different terms which accompany his acceptance
become part of the contract under the UCC?

CASE NO. 5

PETTERSON v. PATTBERG

248 N.Y. 86   May 1928

INTRODUCTION

Sometimes an offeror makes an offer (orally or in writing) which requires that the offeree perform an act in order to accept the offer, and thereby create a contract. This kind of contract is called a unilateral contract - a promise in exchange for an act. The legal question arises whether such an offeror who requests the offeree to perform an act can withdraw his offer at any time before the act is _fully_ performed. This leading case illustrates the common law rule applicable to such cases.

Kellogg, J. The evidence given upon the trial sanctions the following statement of facts: John Petterson was the owner of a parcel of real estate in Brooklyn, known as 5301 Sixth Avenue. The defendant was the owner of a bond executed by Petterson, which was secured by a third mortgage upon the parcel. On April 4th, 1924, there remained unpaid upon the principal the sum of $5,450. This amount was payable in installments of $250 on April 25th, 1924, and upon a like monthly date every three months thereafter. Thus the bond and mortgage had more than five years to run before the entire sum became due. Under date of the 4th of April, 1924, the defendant wrote Petterson as follows: "I hereby agree to accept cash for the mortgage which I hold against premises 5301 6th Ave., Brooklyn, N.Y. It is understood and agreed as a consideration I will allow you $780 providing said mortgage is paid on or before May 31, 1924 and the regular quarterly payment due April 25, 1924, is paid when due." On April 25, 1924, Petterson paid the defendant the installment of principal due on that date. Subsequently, on a day in the latter part of May, 1924, Petterson presented himself at the defendant's home, and knocked at the door. The defendant demanded the name of his caller. Petterson replied: "It is Mr. Petterson. I have come to pay off the mortgage." The defendant answered that he had sold the mortgage. Petterson stated that he would like to talk with the defendant, so the defendant partly opened the door. Thereupon Petterson exhibited the cash and said he was ready to pay off the mortgage according to the agreement. The defendant refused to take the money. Prior to this conversation Petterson had made a contract to sell the land to a third person free and clear of the mortgage to the defendant. Meanwhile, also, the defendant had sold the bond and mortgage to third party. It, therefore, became necessary for Petterson to pay to such person the full amount of the bond and mortgage. It is claimed that he thereby sustained a loss of $780, the sum which the defendant agreed to allow upon the bond and mortgage if payment in full of principal, less that sum, was made on or before May 31st, 1924. The plaintiff has had a recovery for the sum thus claimed, with interest.

Clearly the defendant's letter proposed to Petterson the making of a unilateral contract, the gift of a promise in exchange for the performance of an act. The thing conditionally promised by the defendant was the reduction of the mortgage debt. The act requested to be done, in consideration of the offered promise, was payment in full of the reduced principal of the debt prior to the due date thereof. "If an act is requested, that very act and no other must be given." (Williston on Contracts, sec. 73) It is elementary that any offer to enter into a unilateral contract may be withdrawn before the act requested to be done has been performed....A bidder at a sheriff's sale may revoke his bid at any time before the property is struck down to him.... The offer of a reward in consideration of an act to be performed is revocable before the very act requested has been done.... So, also, an offer to pay a broker commissions, upon a sale of land for the offeror, is revocable at any time before the land is sold, although prior to revocation the broker performs services in an effort to effectuate a sale.... An interesting question arises when, as here, the offeree approaches the offeror with the intention of proffering performance and, before actual tender is made, the offer is withdrawn. Of such a case Williston says: "The offeror may see the approach of the offeree and know that an acceptance is contemplated. If the offeror can say 'I revoke' before the offeree accepts, however brief the interval of time between the two acts, there is no escape from the conclusion that the offer is terminated.".... In this instance Petterson, standing at the door of the defendant's house, stated to the defendant that he that come to pay off the mortgage. Before a tender of the necessary monies had been made the defendant informed Petterson that he had sold the mortgage. That was a definite notice to Petterson that the defendant could not perform his offered promise and that a tender to the defendant, who was no longer the creditor, would be ineffective to satisfy the debt. "An offer to sell property may be withdrawn before acceptance without any formal notice to the person to whom the offer is make. It is sufficient if that person had actual knowledge that the person who made the offer had done some act inconsistent with the continuance of the offer, such as selling the property to a third person.".... Thus, it clearly appears that the defendant's offer was withdrawn before its acceptance had been tendered. It is unnecessary to determine, therefore, what the legal situation might have been had tender been made before withdrawal. It is the individual view of the writer that the same result would follow. This would be so, for the act requested to be performed was the completed act of payment, a thing incapable of performance unless assented to by the person to be paid.... Clearly an offering party has the right to name the precise act performance of which would convert his offer into a binding promise. Whatever the act may be until it is performed the offer must be revocable. However, the supposed case is not before us for decision. We think that in this particular instance the offer of the defendant was withdrawn before it became a binding promise, and, therefore, that no contact was ever made for the breach of which the plaintiff may claim damages.

(JUDGMENT FOR DEFENDANT)

DISCUSSION QUESTIONS

1.   How could the debtor have avoided the legal result reached in this case while he was trying to perform the requested act after he received the creditor's offer? Should the debtor have entered into an agreement with the creditor that provided that the creditor would not withdraw his offer for a stipulated time <u>before</u> the debtor undertook to perform the requested act?

2.   Is there a New York statute in effect today which changes the rule of law in this case? What does the statute provide?

3.   Under some circumstances a court will rule that the offeror cannot lawfully withdraw his offer where the offeror knows that the offeree has partially - but not fully - performed the requested act. Give one example and the rationale for the rule.

FORMATION OF CONTRACT: DEFINITENESS

CASE NO. 6

Joseph Martin, Jr., Delicatessen v. Schumacher

436 NYS 2d 247   Jan. 1981

INTRODUCTION

It is a fundamental common law rule of law that the parties <u>must agree on material terms</u> if there is to be a contract. The legal question thus arises whether a real estate lease agreement between landlord and tenant which provides that the tenant "may renew this lease for an additional period of five years at annual rentals to be agreed upon" is sufficiently definite to be an enforceable contract where the parties subsequently do not agree on the annual rentals.

Fuchsberg, Judge, This case raises an issue fundamental to the law of contracts. It calls upon us to review a decision of the Appellate Division, which held that a realty lease's provision that the rent for a renewal period was "to be agreed upon" may be enforceable.

The pertinent factual and procedural contexts in which the case reaches this court are uncomplicated. In 1973, the appellant, as landlord, leased a retail store to the respondent for a five-year term at a rent graduated upwards from $500 per month for the first year to $650 for the fifth. The renewal clause stated that "the Tenant may renew this lease for an additional period of five years at annual rentals to be agreed upon; Tenant shall give Landlord thirty (30) days written notice, to be mailed certified mail, return receipt requested, of the intention to exercise such right". It is not disputed that the tenant gave timely notice of its desire to renew or that, once the landlord made it clear that he would do so only at a rental starting at $900 a month, the tenant engaged an appraiser who opined that a fair market rental value would be $545.41.

The tenant thereupon commenced an action for specific performance in Supreme Court, Suffolk County, to compel the landlord to extend the lease for the additional term at the appraiser's figure or such other sum as the court would decide was reasonable. For his part, the landlord in due course brought a holdover proceeding in the local District Court to evict the tenant. On the landlord's motion for summary judgment, the Supreme Court, holding that a bold agreement to agree on a future rental was unenforceable for uncertainty as a matter of law, dismissed the tenant's complaint....

It was on appeal by the tenant from these orders that the Apellate Division, expressly overruling an established line of cases in the process, reinstated the tenant's complaint and granted consolidation. In so doing, it reasoned that a "a renewal clause in a lease providing for future agreement on the rent to be paid during the renewal term is enforceable if it is established that the parties' intent was not to terminate in the event of a failure to agree". It went on to provide that, if the tenant met that burden, the trial court could proceed to set a "reasonable rent". One of the Justices, concurring, would have eliminated the first step and required the trial court to proceed directly to the fixation of the rent. Each party now appeals....

We begin our analysis with the basic observation that, unless otherwise mandated by law (e.g. residential emergency rent control statutes), a contract is a private "ordering" in which a party binds himself to do, or not to do, a particular thing.... This liberty is no right at all if it is not accompanied by freedom not to contract. The corollary is that, before one may secure redress in our courts because another has failed to honor a promise, it must appear that the promisee assented to the obligation in question.

It also follows that, before the power of law can be invoked to enforce a promise, it must be sufficiently certain and specific so that what was promised can be ascertained. Otherwise, a court, in intervening, would be imposing its own conception of what the parties should or might have undertaken rather than confining itself to the implementation of a bargain to which they have mutually committed themselves. Thus, definiteness as to material matters is of the very essence in contract law. Impenetrable vagueness and uncertainty will not do....

Dictated by these principles, it is rightfully well settled in the common law of contracts in this State that a mere agreement to agree, in which a material term is left for future negotiations, is unenforceable.... This is especially true of the amount to be paid for the sale or lease of real property.... The rule applies all the more, and not the less, when, as here, the extraordinary remedy of specific performance is sought....

This is not to say that the requirement for definiteness in the case before us now could only have been met by explicit expression of the rent to be paid. The concern is with substance, not form. It certainly would have sufficed for instance, if a methodology for determining the rent was to be found within the four corners of the lease, for a rent so arrived at would have been the end product of agreement between the parties themselves. Nor would the agreement have failed for indefiniteness because it invited recourse to an objective extrinsic event, condition or standard on which the amount was made to depend. All of these, inter alia, would have come within the embrace of the maxim that what can be made certain is certain.... (escalation of rent keyed to building employees' future wage increases); (rental increase to be adjusted for upward movement in US Consumer Price Index)....

But the renewal clause here in fact contains no such ingredients. Its unrevealing, unamplified language speaks to no more than "annual rentals to be agreed upon". Its simple works leave no room for legal construction or resolution of ambiguity. Neither tenant nor landlord is bound to any formula. There is not so much as a hint at a commitment to be bound by the "fair market rental value" which the tenant's expert reported or the "reasonable rent" the Appellate Division would impose, much less any definition of either. Nowhere is there an inkling that either of the parties directly or indirectly assented upon accepting the clause, to subordinate the figure on which it ultimately would insist, to one fixed judicially, as the Appellate Division decreed be done, or, for that matter, by an arbitrator or other third party.

(Judgment for Appellant - Landlord)

DISCUSSION QUESTIONS

1.   How could the tenant have avoided the decision in this case?

2.   What does Article 2 of the Uniform Commercial Code (UCC) provide when a seller and buyer agree upon <u>quantity</u> being sold but do <u>not</u> agree on <u>price</u>, <u>delivery terms</u> and <u>payment terms?</u> Does the omission of such material terms prevent a contract being formed if the parties intend to contract for the sale of goods according to the UCC?

3.   Why does the UCC provide a different rule to contracts for the sale of goods than the common law rule applicable to real estate contracts?

FORMATION OF CONTRACTS: WHEN ACCEPTANCE EFFECTIVE
CASE NO. 7
TREVOR   v.   WOOD
36 N.Y. 307   (1868)

INTRODUCTION

Under the common law rule of contracts, parties may agree on the method of communication. The question then arises when does an acceptance become effective to form or create a contract-upon dispatch or upon receipt? The following leading case illustrates the application of the common law rule and its rationale.

Appeal from a judgment of the Supreme Court rendered at General Term, in the first district, reversing a judgment entered upon the report of Hon. Wm. MITCHELL, referee, and ordering a new trial before the same referee.

The appellants have stipulated that if the judgment be affirmed, judgment absolute may be entered against them.

The appellants are dealers in bullion in New York, and the respondents are dealers in bullion in New Orleans. In 1859 they agreed to deal with each other in the purchase and sale of dollars, and that all communications between them in reference to such transactions should be by telegraph.

On 30th January, 1860, the appellants telegraphed from New York to the respondents, at New Orleans, asking at what price they would sell one hundred thousand Mexican dollars. On the 31st of the same month, the respondents answered that they would deliver fifty thousand at seven and one-quarter; and on the same day the appellants telegraphed from New York to the defendants, at New Orleans, as follows:
"To John Wood & Co.--Your offer fifty thousand Mexicans at seven and one-quarter accepted; send more if you can.
                    TREVOR & COLGATE."

At the same time the appellants sent by mail to the respondents a letter acknowledging the receipt of the respondents' telegram, and copying the appellants' telegraphic answer. On the same day the respondents had also sent by mail a letter to the appellants, copying respondents' telegram of that date. On the next day (1st February, 1860), the appellants again telegraphed to the respondents as follows:
"To John Wood & Co.--Accepted by telegraph yesterday your offer for fifty thousand Mexicans; send as many more, same price.
Reply.   TREVOR & COLGATE."

This telegram, as well as that of 31st of January, from the appellants, did not reach the respondents until 10 a.m. on 4th February, 1860, in consequence of some derangement in a part of the line used by the appellants, but which was not known to the appellants until 4th February, when the telegraph company reported the line down. On 3rd February the respondents telegraphed to the appellants as follows: "No answer to our dispatch--dollars are sold;" and on the same day they wrote by mail to the same effect. The appellants received this dispatch on the same day, and answered it on the same day as follows: "To John Wood & Co-- Your offer was accepted on receipt; and again the next day: "The dollars must come, or we will hold you responsible. Reply. Trevor & Colgate." And again on 4th February insisting on the dollars being sent "by this or next steamer," and saying "don't fail to send the dollars at any price."

On the same 4th of February the respondents telegraphed to appellants, "No dollars to be had. We may ship by steamer twelfth, as you propose, if we have them". No dollars were sent, and this action was brought to recover damages from an alleged breach of contract in not delivering them. The referee found for the plaintiff $219.33.

SCRUGHAM, J. The offer of the respondents was made on the 31st of January, and they did not attempt to revoke it until the 3rd of February. The offer was accepted by the appellants before, but the respondents did not obtain knowledge of the acceptance until after this attempted revocation. The principal question, therefore, which arises in the case, is whether a contract was created by this acceptance before knowledge of it reached the respondents.

The case of Mactier v. Frith, in the late Court of Errors (6 Wend., 103), settles this precise question, and was so regarded by this court in Vassar v. Camp (1 Kern., 432), where it is said that the principle established in the case of Mactier v. Frith was that it was only necessary "that there should be a concurrence of the minds of the parties upon a distinct proposition manifested by an overt act; and that the sending of a letter announcing a consent to the proposal was a sufficient manifestation and consummated the contract from the time it was sent."

There is nothing in either the case of Mactier v. Frith nor in that of Vassar v. Camp, indicating that this effect is given to the sending of a letter, because it is sent by mail through the public post-office, and in fact the letter referred to in the first case could not have been so sent, for it was to go from the city of New York to Jacmel, in the island of St. Domingo, between which places there was at that time no communication by mail.

The sending of a letter accepting the proposition is regarded as an acceptance, because it is an overt act clearly manifesting the intention of the party sending it to close with the offer of him to whom it is sent, and thus marking that "aggregatio mentium" which is necessary to constitute a contract.

Mr. Justice Marcy in delivering the leading opinion in Mactier v. Frith, says: "What shall constitute an acceptance will depend in a great measure upon circumstances. The mere determination of the mind unacted on can never be an acceptance. Where the offer is by letter the usual mode of acceptance is by sending of a letter announcing a consent to accept; where it is made by a messenger a determination to accept returned through him or sent by another would seem to be all the law requires if the contract may be consummated without writing. There are other modes which are equally conclusive upon the parties; keeping silent under certain circumstances is an assent to a proposition; anything that shall amount to a manifestation of a formed determination to accept, communicated or put in the proper way to be communicated to the party making the offer, would doubtless complete the contract.

It was agreed between these parties that their business should be transacted through the medium of the telegraph. The object of this agreement was to substitute the telegraph for other methods of communication, and to give to their transactions by it the same force and validity they would derive if they had been performed through other agencies. It cannot, therefore, be said that the appellants did not put their acceptance in a proper way to be communicated to the respondents, for they adopted the method of communication which had been used in the transaction by the respondents, and which had been selected by prior agreement between them as that by means of which their business should be transacted.

Under these circumstances the sending of the dispatch must be regarded as an acceptance of the respondents' offer and thereupon the contract became complete.

I cannot conceive upon what principle an agreement to communicate by telegraph can be held to be in effect a warranty by each party that his communication to the other shall be received. On the contrary, by agreeing beforehand to adopt that means of communication, the parties mutually assume its hazards, which are principally as to the prompt receipt of the dispatches.

The referee finds as a fact that the respondents answered the telegram of the appellants asking at what price they would sell 100,000 Mexican dollars by another telegram as follows, viz.:
"TREVOR & COLGATE, New York.
    "Will deliver fifty thousand at seven and one-quarter per Moses Taylor. Answer.   JOHN WOOD & CO."
    It was proved on the trial that this telegram was sent by the respondents, and a letter of the same date, signed by them, repeating the telegram and stating that they had sent it, was read in evidence.
    This affords sufficient evidence of subscription by the respondents to take the cases out of the statute of frauds.
    The judgment should be reversed.   Judgment reversed.

DISCUSSION QUESTIONS
1. Would your answer be that no contract was formed in this case if the buyer used a different means of communication than was used by the seller? Why?
2. How could the seller avoid the result of this decision when the seller and buyer agree on the method of communication?

FORMATION OF CONTRACTS
THE BATTLE OF THE FORMS

CASE NO. 8

MATTER OF MARLENE INDUS. CORP. v. CARNAC TEXTILES, INC.

408 NY 2d 410   July, 1978

INTRODUCTION

Article 2 of the Uniform Commercial Code (UCC) governs the law of contracts for the sale of goods. The UCC has been adapted by all states except
Louisiana. The UCC rules for the formation of a contract for the sale of
goods are very different than the common law rules in effect today which
govern the formation of other types of contracts, such as real estate contracts and employment contracts. These differences are largely explained by
the desire of the draftsmen of the UCC to recognize and give effect in
statutory language in Article 2 - to the usual business practices and business
expectations of merchants who deal with each other in the United States.
Thus, Article 2 provides that contracts are formed for the sale of goods and
are enforceable - even where not signed by the party to be charged - where,
under the same circumstances, these would be no contract formed or the contract would not be enforceable under the Statute of Frauds - when the subject
matter of the contract involves real property or services.

This leading case illustrates the common practice in the business world
where a merchant buyer submits his contract to the merchant seller when he
orders merchandise and the merchant seller then sends his written acknowle-
ment to the merchant buyer. Each form or contract contains terms most favorable to the party who prepared it and neither party signs the other party's
form or contract. When a dispute arises and the parties seek to enforce their
respective forms or contract against the other we have what is generally described as "the battle of the forms". The legal question then arises which
form or contract will govern where there are contradictory provisions. This
leading case provides the answer and the background why the UCC adapted its
rule.

GABRIELLI, Judge. This appeal involves yet another of the many conflicts
which arise as a result of the all too common business practice of blithely
drafting, sending, receiving, and filing unread numerous purchase orders,
acknowledgments, and other divers forms containing a myriad of discrepant terms
Both parties agree that they have entered into a contract for the sale of
goods; indeed, it would appear that there is no disagreement as to most of
the essential terms of their contract. They do disagree, however, as to
whether their agreement includes a provision for the arbitration of disputes
arising from the contract.

Petitioner Marlene Industries Corp. (Marlene) appeals from a an order of
the Appellate Division which, one Justice dissenting, affirmed a judgment
of Supreme Court denying an application to stay arbitration. here should be
a reversal and arbitration should be stayed, for we conclude that the parties
did not contract to arbitrate.

The dispute between the parties, insofar as it is relevant on this appeal is founded upon an alleged breach by Marlene of a contract to purchase certain fabrics from respondent Carnac Textiles, Inc. (Carnac). The transaction was instituted when Marlene orally placed an order for the fabrics with Carnac. Neither party contends that any method of dispute resolution was discussed at that time. Almost immediately thereafter, Marlene sent Carnac a "purchase order" and Carnac sent Marlene an "acknowledgement of order". Marlene's form did not provide for arbitration; it did declare that it would not become effective as a contract unless signed by the seller, and that its terms could not be "superceded by an unsigned contract notwithstanding retention". Carnac's form, on the other hand, contained an arbitration clause placed in the midst of some 13 lines of small type "boilerplate". It also instructed the buyer to "sign and return one copy of this confirmation". However, neither party signed the other's form. When a dispute subsequently arose, Carnac sought arbitration, and Marlene moved for a stay.

The courts below have denied the application to stay arbitration, the Appellate Division reasoning that "as between merchants where 'a writing in confirmation of the contract and sufficient against the sender is received and the party receiving it has reason to know its contents' written notice of objection should be given within 10 days after it is received".... Since Marlene had retained without objection the form containing the arbitration clause, the court concluded that Marlene was bound by that clause. We disagree.

This case presents a classic example of the "battle of the forms", and its solution is to be derived by reference to section 2-207 of the Uniform Commercial Code, which is specifically designed to resolve such disputes. The courts below erred in applying subdivision (2) of section 2-201, for that statute deals solely with the question whether a contract exists which is enforceable in the face of a Statute of Frauds defense; it has no application to a situation such as this, in which it is conceded that a contract does exist and the dispute goes only to the terms of that contract. In light of the disparate purposes of the two sections, application of the wrong provision will often result in an erroneous conclusion. As has been noted by a recognized authority on the code, "the easiest way to avoid the miscarriages this confusion perpetrates is simply to fix in mind that the two sections have nothing to do with each other. Though each has a special rule for merchants sounding very much like the other, their respective functions are unrelated. Section 2-201(2) has its role in the context of a challenge to the use of the statute of frauds to prevent proof of an alleged agreement, whereas the merchant rule of section 2-207(2) is for use in determining what are the terms of an admitted agreement"....

Subdivision (2) of section 2-207 is applicable to cases such as this, in which there is a consensus that a contract exists, but disagreement as to what terms have been included in that contract. Subdivision (1) of section 2-207 was intended to abrogate the harsh "mirror-image" rule of common law, pursuant to which any deviation in the language of a purported acceptance from the exact term of the offer transformed that "acceptance" into a counter-offer and thus precluded contract formation on the basis of those two documents alone.... Under subdivision (1) of section 2-207, however, an acceptance containing additional terms will operate as an acceptance unless it is "expressly made conditional on assent to the additional or different terms". Having thus departed from the common-law doctrine, it became necessary for the code to make some provision as to the effect upon the contract of such additional terms in an acceptance. Subdivision (2) was designed to deal with that problem.

Before continuing, we would note that the section speaks of both acceptances and written confirmations. It is thus intended to include at least two distinct situations: one in which the parties have reached a prior oral contract and any writings serve only as confirmation of that contract; and one in which the prior dealings of the parties did not comprise actual formation of a contract, and the writings themselves serve as offer and/or acceptance. In either case, the writing or writings may contain additional terms, and in either case the effect of such additional terms under the code is the same. Thus, on this appeal, since the prior discussions of the parties did not reach the question of dispute resolution, it is unnecessary to determine whether those discussions rose to the level of contact formation, or whether no contract was created until the exchange of forms. Therefore, whether Marlene's form is an offer and Carnac's an acceptance, or whether both are mere confirmations of an existing oral contract, the result in this case is the same, and that result is dependent upon the operation of subdivision (2) of section 2-207

Subdivision (2) of section 2-207 provides that any additional terms in an acceptance or a written confirmation are to be considered merely proposals for additions to the contract, and that such terms normally will not become a part of the contract unless expressly agreed to by the other party. As with many sections of the code, however, there is a special provision for merchants:

"(2) The additional terms are to be construed as proposals for additions to the contract. Between merchants such terms become part of the contract unless:

"(a) the offer expressly limits acceptance to the terms of the offer;
"(b) they materially alter it; or
"(c) notification of objection to them has already been given or is given or is given within a reasonable time after notice of them is received" (Uniform Commercial Code, 2-207, subd. (2)).

The parties to this dispute are certainly merchants, and the arbitration clause is clearly a proposed additional term, whether Carnac's form be considered an acceptance of an oral or written offer or a written confirmation of an oral agreement. As such, it became a part of the contract unless one of the three listed exceptions is applicable. We hold that the inclusion of an arbitration agreement materially alters a contract for the sale of goods, and thus, pursuant to section 2-207 (subd. (2), par. (b)), it will not become a part of such a contract unless both parties explictly agree to it.

It has long been the rule in this State that the parties to a commercial transaction "will not be held to have chosen arbitration as the forum for the resolution of their disputes in the absence of an express, unequivocal agreement to that effect; absent such an explicit commitment neither party may be compelled to arbitrate".... The reason for this requirement, quite simply, is that by agreeing to arbitrate a party waives in large part many of his

36

normal rights under the procedural and substantive law of the State, and it would be unfair to infer such a signifcant waiver on the basis of anything less than a clear indication of intent....

Since an arbiration agreement in the context of a commercial transaction "must be clear and direct, and must not depend upon implication, inveiglement or subtlety***(its) existnece * * * should not depend solely upon the conflicting fine print of commercial forms which cross one another but never meet".... Thus, at least under this so-called "New York Rule"...it is clear that an arbitration clause is a material addition which can become part of a contract only if it is expressly assented to by both parties. Applying these principles to this case, we conclude that the contract between Marlene and Carnac does not contain an arbitration clause; hence, the motion to permanently stay arbitration should have been granted.

Accordingly, the order appealed from should be reversed, with costs.

(Judgment for Buyer.)

DISCUSSION QUESTION

1.   How could the seller have avoided the decision in this case?

MUNICIPAL CONSULTANTS,   v. TOWN OF RAMAPO

417 N.Y. 2d 148   May 1979

INTRODUCTION

Parties often negotiate the terms of their contract by oral communication, in person or by telephone. The legal question arises whether the oral contract must then be reduced to writing and signed before the contract becomes effective, if there is no statute of frauds which legally requires specific contract to be in writing and signed. The following case illustrates the rule of law applicable when the statute of frauds does not apply.

GABRIELLI, Judge.

The issue in this case is whether the Town of Ramapo is contractually obligated to receive and pay for the services offered by the petitioner Municipal Consultants & Publishers, Inc. (Municipal). For the reasons which follow we conclude that there existed an enforceable contract between the parties, and we therefore affirm the order of the Appellate Division.

On June 10, 1976 Municipal, at the request of the town, submitted a written proposal in the form of a contract to the Town of Ramapo offering to codify its ordinances and local laws for a sum specified in the proposal. On July 21 Municipal agreed to certain changes suggested by the town attorney, but no formal action was taken at that time on behalf of the town on the proposal. Finally, on February 9, 1977 the town board formally acted on it, and agreed to engage petitioner's services.

By resolution No. 77-54 the town (1) authorized the town attorney to accept the proposal; (2) authorized the supervisor to sign the agreement, and (3) provided payment for the work. The resolution adopted by the town board on February 9, 1977, in pertinent part, provided that:

"RESOLVED by the Town Board of the Town of Ramapo that authorization be hereby granted for the Town Attorney to accept the proposal submitted by Municipal Consultants & Publishers, Inc., of 64 Seneca Street, Geneva, New York to codify Ordinances and Local Laws of the Town of Ramapo, and

"BE IT FURTHER RESOLVED that the Supervisor be hereby authorized to execute the Agreement between the Town of Ramapo and Municipal Consultants & Publishers, Inc., and

"BE IT FURTHER RESOLVED that the sum of $10,000.00 for the first 450 pages or less and $20.00 per page for each additional page in excess of 450 pages, be hereby paid to Municipal Consultants & Publishers, Inc. for services rendered."

On February 15, 1977, the town attorney notified Municipal that the agreement had been approved, forwarded copies of the agreement for Municipal to execute, and stated he looked forward to a long and pleasant relationship.

Ramapo's supervisor, however, never signed the contract. It appears that one of Municipal's competitors, long after the passage of the resolution authorizing the agreement, offered to do the work for a lesser sum. The parties met in an attempt to work out their differences but to no avail. This article 78 proceeding ensued requesting that the court declare the contract valid and enforceable and also to direct the supervisor and town attorney to deliver an executed copy of the agreement.

The primary issue presented is whether the contract is enforceable against the town without the signature of the supervisor.

(1-3) Generally, where the parties contemplate that a signed writing is required there is no contract until one is delivered....This rule yields, however, when the parties have agreed on all contractual terms and have only to commit them to writing. When this occurs, the contract is effective at the time the oral agreement is made, although the contract is never reduced to writing and signed. Where all the substantial terms of a contract have been agreed on, and there is nothing left for future settlement, the fact, alone, that it was the understanding that the contract should be formally drawn up and put in writing, did not leave the transaction incomplete and without binding force, in the absence of a positive agreement that it should not be binding until so reduced to writing and formally executed....Here, of course, there was no understanding that the agreement would not be binding, short of formal execution by the supervisor; and the facts of the case before us fall within the legal framework of the last above-cited cases. All the terms of the contract had been negotiated and agreed upon. They were, in fact, expressed in Municipal's written standard contract which had been modified in several slight respects through negotiations. There was no understanding or agreement that the contract would not be binding until both parties had signed it, and therefore it is enforceable although it was never memorialized with a mutually signed writing.

We now further address the question of whether the authorizing resolution No. 77-54 constituted an acceptance of the proposal. The resolution of the town board authorized the town attorney to accept the contract on behalf of the board and authorized, but did not specifically direct, in so many words, the supervisor to sign the agreement on behalf of the town (cf. Village of Lake George v. Town of Caldwell, 3 A.D.2d 550, 552, 162 N.Y.S.2d 762, 764, affd. 5 N.Y.2d 727, 177 N.Y.S.2d 711, 152 N.E.2d 668). Because the supervisor never signed the agreement the town maintains that it never fully assented to it. This concept we reject.

Subdivision 6 of section 64 of the Town Law reposes exclusive authority in the town board to award contracts; and it further provides that "the same shall be executed by the supervisor in the name of the town after approval by the town board" (emphasis added). The section does not recognize any discretion on the part of the supervisor to pass on the award of contracts; in fact it is quite the opposite, in effect, by instructing him or directing that he act. The ministerial nature of the supervisor's function is further emphasized by section 29 of the Town Law which delineates the powers and duties of the supervisor. Despite the breadth of the responsibilities outlined therein, nowhere does there appear any authority or responsibility to agree to or to have any discretionary authority in anywise relating to the execution of contracts authorized or adopted by the board.

Hence, the town board's resolution which authorized the supervisor to sign the agreement on its behalf was an acceptance of the offer made by Municipal. Nothing further was necessary to create an enforceable contract. The supervisor's refusal to perform the ministerial act of signing the contract was therefore unlawful, and an article 78 proceeding in the nature of mandamus lay to compel his action....

Accordingly, the order of the Appellate Division should be affirmed, with costs.

(Judgment for plaintiff.)

DISCUSSION QUESTION

1. How could the Town of Ramapo have avoided the result of this decision?

FORMATION OF CONTRACTS

MUTUAL ASSENT
CASE NO. 10
MURRAY v. CUNARD STEAMSHIP CO.
235 N.Y. 162   March 1923

INTRODUCTION

Tickets are frequently issued or sold to the public which are then used to obtain admission to an event or are given in exchange for property which is left with the issuer of the ticket to identify the property (e.g. car in parking lot). These tickets frequently contain language that states the ticket holder's rights are limited to those rights stated on the ticket. Usually, liability is partially or totally eliminated in the event the ticket holder suffers personal injury or property loss. Parties rarely read such tickets or consider such tickets to be contracts especially where liability is partially or totally eliminated. Instead, parties consider such tickets as only a means of identification (that the ticket holder has paid the purchase price or to identify property deposited with the issuer).

The legal questions arise (1) what requirements must be met before a ticket will be judicially raised from mere evidence of identification only (not a contract) to the level of an enforceable contract, (2) where a court determines that a particular ticket is a contract, will a ticket holder be bound by the contract (a) if he did not read it and (b) after he surrenders it, and (3) to what extent will courts enforce conditions and limitations contained in tickets which are contracts. Sometimes a higher court will reach a different conclusion concerning these questions than a lower court, as is illustrated by this leading case.

CARDOZO, J. The plaintiff left New York on April 24, 1920, as a second cabin passenger on the defendant's steamship Mauretania. On April 28 he broke his knee cap by a fall upon the deck. Plaintiff spent several months in the hospital in Ireland, after leaving the ship when it arrived in London. His final discharge from the hospital was about the middle of November. After remaining some weeks in Ireland, he sailed for New York on January 8, 1921. On February 24, 1921, without preliminary notice, this action was begun.

The plaintiff's ticket, issued to him some days before the departure of the vessel, is described in large type as a "cabin passage contract ticket". It provides, again in large type, that "this contract ticket is issued by the company and accepted by the passenger on the following terms and conditions." One of the terms and conditions is that no action shall be maintained either for injury to property or for personal injury to the passenger unless commenced within one year after the termination of the voyage. That requirement was obeyed. Another term or condition is that no action shall be maintained for injury to the passenger unless written notice of the claim be delivered to the company within 40 days after debarcation. That requirement was not obeyed. At the top of the ticket is printed a notice: "The attention of passengers is specially directed to the terms and conditions of this contract."

We assume, without intending to decide, that the plaintiff's narrative, if accepted, would sustain a finding by the jury that the defendant had been

41

negligent. We assume also that a contract exonerating the defendant altogether from liability for negligent injury to a passenger would be ineffective and void because opposed to public policy....Exoneration, however, is not to be confused with regulation. "A stipulation for written notice within a reasonable time stands on a different footing, and of this there is no doubt.".... The court enforced the contract. "Very probably," it was said, "an exception might be implied if the accident made notice within the time impracticable"... There is no evidence that this plaintiff was physically or mentally unable to give notice of the injury....Even if we were to assume in his favor that there was incapacity for a time, with a resulting extension of the period for notice, he did not make a move within forty days thereafter. Limitations of this kind have their justification in the need of some safeguard to protect the carrier against fraud. Passengers on steamships scatter in all directions when the voyage is at an end. If claims may be presented at any time within the term of years permitted by the Statute of Limitations, the opportunity for investigation will often be lost beyond recall. "The practice of fraud is too common to be ignored"....

The plaintiff argues that he is not bound by the conditions of the ticket because he did not read them. The omission does not help his case. The law is settled in this state that a ticket in this form issued by a steamship company for a voyage across the ocean, is more than a mere token or voucher. It is a contract, creating the obligation and defining the terms of carriage... This is not a case of a mere notice on the back of a ticket, separate either in substance or in form from the body of the contract....Here the condition is wrought into the tissue, the two inseparably integrated. This ticket, to the most casual observer, is as plainly a contract, burdened with all kinds of conditions, as if it were a bill of lading or a policy of insurance. "No one who could read could glance at it without seeing that it undertook to prescribe the particulars which should govern the conduct of the parties until the passenger reached the port of destination"....In such circumstances, the act of acceptance gives rise to an implication of assent....The passenger who omits to read takes the risk of omission.

The plaintiff is not helped by his surrender of the ticket when he went aboard the ship, after he had then held it several days with ample time to read it. A contract valid and reasonable in its inception does not become invalid and unreasonable thereafter, because the passenger who has assented, is unable, when the voyage is over, to recall the terms of the assent. If some aid to memory is required, his business is to make for himself a note of the conditions, or to procure from the carrier a copy, which doubtless would be given for the asking. He had abundant opportunity both on the ship and later to inquire about the terms of carriage, if he supposed them to be important. We should indulge in the merest speculation if we were to say that the surrender of the ticket was the cause of the omission of the notice. Whether it was or not, his contract remained the same. He is charged as if he had signed. The obligation of one who signs is not defeated by proof that the document had been lost or that its contents have been forgotten.

The judgment of the Appellate Division and that of the Trial Term should be reversed, and complaint dismissed, with costs in all courts.

(Judgment for defendant.)

DISCUSSION QUESTIONS

1. Read CIOFALO v. VIC TANNEY GYMS, INC. in this book which involved the legal question of whether contracting parties may lawfully include a valid exculpatory clause in their contract.

442 N.Y.S. 2d 965   June, 1981

INTRODUCTION

Many public businesses such as hotels, motels and restaurants have successfully lobbied for legislation in the various states since the early part
of this century to limit their liability to guests or customers when they lose
personal property that they checked with the hotel, motel or restaurant. These
statutes vary from state to state but usually provide that hotels and motels
must post conspicuous signs in the room setting forth the terms of limited
liability and how the guest may arrange for increased liability on the part of
the hotel or motel. No similar posting of notice is usually required by a
restaurant. The legal effect of these limited liability statutes is that a
guest or customer can recover the value of property lost by the hotel, motel
or restaurant only if he can prove (1) negligence or (2) noncompliance with the
state statute. If he cannot, then his maximum recovery is usually limited to
a range of between fifty and one hundred dollars. The following case involved
the liability of a restaurant under the New York statute when a $7,500 Russian
sable fur was lost by a restaurant in Rockefeller Center.

MEYER, Judge. Section 201 of the General Business Law has no bearing
upon an action against a restaurant owner sued for the conversion of a coat
checked by a patron. It does limit recovery by a patron who sues for negligence: to the value of the coat if negligence be shown, a fee or charge is
exacted for checking the coat, and a value in excess of $75 is declared and a
written receipt stating such value is issued when the coat is delivered to the
checkroom attendant; to $100 if a value in excess of $75 is declared and the
other conditions are met but negligence cannot be shown; to $75 in any event
if no fee or charge is exacted or a value in excess of $75 is not declared and
a written receipt obtained when the coat is delivered. For the reasons hereafter stated, the order of the Appellate Division,...affirming judgment of
$9,578.75 entered February 7, 1979 for plaintiff after trial by jury must be
modified by reducing the amount awarded to $75.

I

Plaintiff's complaint contained but one cause of action predicated upon
the negligence of defendant restaurant owner. Defendant moved for summary
judgment limiting plaintiff's recovery to $75. The affidavits presented by
defendant established that neither defendant's president nor anyone else in
his employ could explain the disappearance of the Russian sable fur coat which
plaintiff checked with defendant's checkroom attendant, that no value had been
declared by plaintiff nor had any written receipt stating a value been given,
acknowledged that no sign had been posted but stated that section 201 of the
General Business Law did not require posting by a restaurant, and quoted a
portion of plaintiff's deposition in which she acknowledged that no charge had
been made for the checking of the coat. Plaintiff cross-moved for summary
judgment. Her affidavit noted the admission of defendant's president that
tipping was discretionary and characterized it as contrary to common knowledge.

Attached to it also was the deposition of the coatroom attendant in which she conceded that on the night in question she received $20 to $30 in tips.

Special Term denied both the motion and cross motion. On appeal the Appellate Division modified and remanded for trial as to damages, holding that plaintiff was entitled to judgment on liability but that on the issue of damages there existed questions of fact concerning whether defendant restaurant had "exacted" a fee or charge and whether the loss was the result of theft by defendant, its agent, servants or employees....On remand the Trial Judge, after testimony by defendant's president that the checkroom attendant received an hourly rate of pay plus a percentage of the tips given her, the owner receiving the balance of the tips, ruled that notwithstanding that there was no sign concerning tips nor other open solicitation of them and that some people received their coats without leaving any tip, the gratuities paid the checkroom attendant constituted, as a matter of law, the exaction of a fee within the meaning of the section. He noted further that the issue of theft by defendant or its employees had become academic, that were that not so he would have directed a verdict for plaintiff on that ground also because defendant had presented no evidence on the question of theft. He submitted to the jury, therefore, only the question of the value of plaintiff's coat. The jury fixed that value at $7,500 and judgment was entered for that sum plus interest and costs.

On appeal from the judgment entered on the jury's verdict, the Appellate Division affirmed, without opinion, but granted defendant leave to appeal to our court from the final judgment....For the reasons stated below we hold that (1) the tip or gratuity customarily given a checkroom attendant is not a "fee or charge * * * exacted" for the checking service within the meaning of section 201 of the General Business Law; (2) restaurants are not required to post the provisions of section 201 in order to be entitled to its limitation of liability; and (3) in granting summary judgment to plaintiff rather than defendant and in affirming the judgment entered February 7, 1979 the Appellate Division erred; its order of affirmance must, therefore, be modified and judgment directed to be entered for plaintiff in the amount of $75 with interest from March 3, 1975.

II

Subdivision 1 of section 201 of the General Business Law provides in relevant part: "(A)s to property deposited by guests or patrons in the parcel or check room of any hotel, motel or restaurant, the delivery of which is evidenced by a check or receipt therefor and for which no fee or charge is exacted, the proprietor shall not be liable beyond seventy-five dollars, unless such value in excess of seventy-five dollars shall be stated upon delivery and a written receipt, stating such value, shall be issued, but he shall in no event be liable beyond one hundred dollars, unless such loss occurs through his fault or negligence." In a case strikingly similar to the instant case, Honig v. Riley,...that language was construed by this court. Plaintiff Honig sought to recover the value of the fur coat she left at the checkroom of defendant's restaurant on New Year's Eve 1925. She received a check but was not questioned as to value and made no statement to the attendant concerning value. The Trial Judge charged that plaintiff was entitled to full value of the coat if they found defendant to have been negligent. On appeal by defendant from a judgment of $850 entered on the jury's verdict and affirmed by the Appellate Term and

and the Appellate Division, this court reversed and directed reduction of the judgment to $75. In an opinion by Jedge CARDOZO, we said..."The defendant maintains that where property is deposited in a parcel or check room without statement of value or delivery of the prescribed receipt, there is a limit of liability to $75 for loss from any cause. Disclosure of the value, if followed by a receipt, will extend liability for fault or negligence up to the limit of the value stated, though even then the liability, if any, as insurer will be $100 and no more. The plaintiff on her side maintains, and the courts below have held, that the exemption from liability in excess of $75 where the value is not disclosed, is not to be read as a limitation of liability for loss from any cause, but is confined to losses not due to the fault or negligence of the proprietor.

"We think the defendant's construction is the true one, however clumsy and inartificial may be the phrasing of the statute. A limitation of liability affecting merely the measure of recovery is applicable, if not otherwise restrained, to loss for any cause. * * * From the beginning of the section to the end, the exemption from liability in excess of the prescribed maximum is absolute where value is concealed. Only where value is stated and a receipt delivered is the exemption made dependent upon freedom from negligence or other fault."

Under that reading of the statute plaintiff's recovery is limited to $75, no value having been declared or receipt obtained, unless it can be found that a "fee or charge (was) exacted." The ruling of the lower courts that the acceptance by the checkroom attendant of a gratuity in which the restaurant owner shares constitutes an "exaction", made not as a finding of fact but as a matter of law was, however, erroneous....

When the service cannot be obtained without the payment of a fixed sum a fee has been exacted, but when, as the papers on the summary judgment motions showed, plaintiff acknowledges that no charge was made and presents no evidence that there was a sign indicating a fixed charge, or of solicitation of any kind or that the giving and the amount were other than discretionary with the customer, there has, as a matter of law, been no exaction of a fee or charge.

III

Plaintiff argued on the original motions, and the dissenter in this court agrees, that section 201 is not applicable because defendant failed to comply with subdivision 2 of the section. That subdivision requires that "A printed copy of this section shall be posted in a conspicuous place and manner in the office or public room and in the public parlors of such hotel or motel." While that provision was not added to the section until 1960 (L.1960, ch.840), section 206 has since 1909 required posting of a printed copy of section 201. Section 206 is by its terms limited, however, to a "hotel or inn" just as subdivision 2 of section 201 is limited to a "hotel or motel." To read subdivision 2 to require posting by a restaurant because subdivision 1 groups "hotel, motel or restaurant" together is to fly in the face of usual rules of statutory construction that a statute (in this instance, subdivision 2's posting requirement) is to be read and given effect as it was written, and that the courts under guise of interpretation may not enlarge or change the scope of a legislative enactment....If posting by restaurants is to be required as a condition

45

of the limitation of liability granted them by subdivision 1 of section 201, it is the Legislature rather than this court that must impose the requirement.

(Judgment for plaintiff for $75.00 only.)

FUCHSBERG, Judge (dissenting).

Invited, of course, to do so by its management, plaintiff, a restaurant patron, deposited her fur coat, now found to have been worth $7,500, at the defendant's cloakroom at the plush Rainbow Grill in Rockefeller Center. Without explanation, it was never to be returned. Yet, the majority would relegate her to a recovery of $75. Neither the history or public policy of the statutory scheme which governs such a case, nor the common sense or the elementary fairness that go with a living law will abide such a result. I therefore vote to uphold the Trial Term award to the plaintiff for the full amount of her loss as thereafter unanimously affirmed by the Appellate Division. Here follow my reasons, grounded, I would like to believe, on principle, practicality and, withal, sound law.

I start with section 201 of the General Business Law, which as we have seen, so drastically and arbitrarily limits the amount which even the grievously damaged patron-bailor may recover for the loss of property entrusted without separate fee to restaurants, hotels or, since they arrived on the scene, motels. Indeed, its provisions, enacted, as the legislative history makes clear, at the instance of restaurant and hotel industry functionaries, are so harsh that, even when a restaurateur, hotelkeeper or motel owner to whom an article is committed is proved to have knowingly engaged a dishonest checkroom attendant, collectable damages may not exceed the more munificient sum of $100. This cap, I might add, has remained unaltered since it was fixed in the antedeluvian monetary times of 57 years ago.

But, as one might have suspected, there had to be and, indeed, are compensating provisions designed to ameliorate the confiscatory nature of this scheme or at least to warn those who otherwise could be caught within its web. So, when a patron requests a receipt containing the declared value of the item he or she decides to check, the limitations are inoperative, and the restaurant hotel or motel resumes its traditional liability for full value (General Business Law, Sect. 201).

Now, it goes without saying that, unless a restaurant proffers receipts and invites declarations, or unless patrons in some other manner are advised of the existence of this option (or, for that matter, of the limitations that prevail in the absence of its exercise), it would be but a secret, and, therefore, ineffective privilege. It was to avoid this paradoxical consequence that the Legislature, apparently recognizing that almost no one is likely to consult the Consolidated Laws before deciding to dine out, enacted section 206 as an auxiliary to the statutory scheme. In my view, this provision, a precondition to the enforcement of the limitation preferences granted restaurants by section 201, requires them to informatively post a printed copy of the statute in a conspicuous place and manner. This, concededly, the defendant here did not do. Yet, because the posting appendage, though part of what Judge CARDOZO called a "connected plan" embracing both restaurants and hotels (Honig v. Riley, 244 N.Y. 105, 109, 155 N.E. 65), does not refer to restaurants by name, the majority, by choosing to deal with section 206 as though it stood in isolation rather than as a dependent part of a whole, would stultify the salurary purpose it was intended to achieve.

It takes no missionary zeal to observe that, while canons of construction are helpful, they can never take the place of reasoned analysis (Beary v. City of Rye, 44 N.Y.2d 398, 410-411, 406 N.Y.2d 9, 377 N.E.2d 453; Becker v. Huss Co., 43 N.Y.2d 527, 533, 402 N.Y.S.2d 980, 373 N.E.2d 1205). Signposts at best they are not to be followed blindly when they appear to point in the wrong direction. All the more is this so when we treat with a statute which Judge CARDOZO also deservedly characterized as "clumsy and inartificial" (Honig v. Riley, supra, 244 N.Y. at p. 109, 155 N.E. 65). For, the notion that, because words are plain, their meaning is also plain is "merely pernicious oversimplification" (United States v. Monia, 317 U.S. 424, 431, 63 S.Ct. 409, 87 L.Ed. 376 (FRANKFURTER, J., dissenting), quoted in People v. Brooks, 34 N.Y.2d 475, 478, 358 N.Y.S.2d 395, 315 N.E.2d 460). So, when words, read literally, lead to an unreasonable result plainly at variance with the policy of legislation as a whole, a court must look "to the purposes of the act" (New York State Bankers Assn. v. Albright, 38 N.Y.2d 430, 437, 381 N.Y.S.2d 17, 343 N.E.2d 735). Or, as we suggested, in Brooks, the goal of judicial inquiry is not always to be satisfied by a "mechanical" reading of a statute, but rather by understanding that its phrases have "'some purpose or object to accomplish, whose sympathetic and imaginative discovery is the surest guide to their meaning'" (People v. Brooks, supra, 34 N.Y.2d at p. 478, 358 N.Y.S.2d 395, 315 N.E.2d 460, quoting Cabell b. Markham, 2nd Cir. 148 F.2d 737, 739 (LEARNED HAND J.)).

Turning then to the purpose of the statute before us now, its genesis goes back to the days when, if food and drink were to be provided outside the home, it was primarily the business of the innkeeper to provide it. In this unitary concept, the same responsibility was borne toward the wayfarer who applied for lodging and the one who applied for a meal. One of these in the beginning was that of absolute liability, as an insurer, for the loss of a guest's property and, later, a combination of statutorily fixed limited liability matched by compulsory safeguards against loss....However, with time, as a growing urban population developed an everincreasing habit of taking meals at restaurants, the obligation of its proprietors was reduced to that imposed by the general law of negligence....

Then, the year 1924 saw the birth of the legislation which Judge CARDOZO so critically was to describe that same year and which we, as his successors, today confront. Its intended goal and format, as described in hotel terms by the counsel to the New York State Hotel Association and the Hotel Association of New York City, who did the drafting, is revealing: "Heretofore the hotel-keeper has been practically at the mercy of the unscrupulous guest and has often been compelled to pay heavy claims for the loss of property from store-rooms and checking-rooms in cases where, when the property was originally deposited with the hotel-keeper, he had no knowledge of the real value thereof nor was such value called to his attention by the guest. The * * * bill relieves the situation and at the same time works no hardship on the guest, for all he is required to do is to notify the hotel-keeper of the value of the property at the time of depositing the same. Furthermore, when so notified, the hotelkeeper at all times continues to be liable for the full value of such property in case of negligence, and copies of the law are required to be posted pursuant to Section 206 of the General Business Law" (emphasis added; legislative bill jacket, Document No. 3, L. 1924, ch. 506).

As formally enacted, however, the bill,,to be known as section 201, without further definition, put restaurants within the ambit of its general protection. Then, significantly, when it was construed by this court, Judge CARDOZO made clear that, however ineptly presented, its inclusion of restaurants made them part of an integrated whole. Specifically, he not only referred to them "in conjunction with the provisions immediately preceding it as part of a connected plan," but also declared that "the statute is not aimed at the protection of proprietors of restaurants exclusively". Crucially, he went on to say that, "(f)or the prupose of the new exemption, proprietors of inns and proprietors of restaurants are grouped as a single class" (Honig v. Riley, 244 N.Y. 105, 110, 155 N.E. 65 supra (emphasis added)).

That sensible crossover among the different sections of the General Business Law was intended is well illustrated by these observations. For "the new exemption" for "proprietors of restaurants" to which Honig refers is also contained in article 12 of the General Business Law under what ordinarily might be regarded as the misleading heading "Hotels and Boarding Houses". It follows from this most confusing arrangement that the posting requirement applicable to hotels, if they are to make any sense, must be deemed equally applicable to restaurants.

It was in the same wein that, in 1960, section 201 was amended to include, as had been the case with restaurants, the newly emerging motel industry as well. On that occasion, in language again reflecting the recognized trade-off between the benefits and obligations of the statutory framework, the Department of Commerce and the Association of the Bar of the City of New York advised the Governor that those desiring the protection should be "subjected to the posting provisions of the law" (legislative bill jacket, Document Nos. 14, 31, L. 1960, ch. 840).

Sound policy too supports this conclusion. In the past, this court, dehors the present context, has repeatedly emphasized that it would be misleading and unfair to allow a hotel to assert a limited liability when it had not posted a copy of a statute so that a guest would be notified of the true situation and acts with knowledge"....It would be equally misleading and unfair for one who patronizes a restaurant to be confronted with a defense of limited liability without such notice. (claim check limiting damages recoverable for loss at parcel room in railroad terminal, though otherwise comporting with public policy, held inadequate in absence of "conspicuous signs * * * calling attention to the limitation * * * or that there was any opportunity afforded to plaintiffs to assent to or dissent from the alleged contract")).

In fine, history and policy lead to inexorable conclusions: The Legislature did not intend to extend the salutary benefits of section 201 of the General Business Law to the proprietors of either restaurants, hotels or motels without appropriate notice of the condition--exaction of a receipt containing a statement of value--without which the most extensive loss would bring but a pittance. When the bill was originally enacted, it would have served nothing but an impermissibly overprecious and overliteral reading to assume it intended to charge only hotels with its posting requirement, when, though its hotel sponsors had ignored restaurants, the Legislature affirmatively and expressly took the trouble to include them within the "connected" statutory scheme....

Therefore, while, no doubt, the statutory language could be clearer, it surely is remiss not to give effect to the clearcut underlying intent that, at least for checkroom posting purposes, restaurants are in the "same class" with the other kinds of establishments to be found in the related subdivisions of the statute.

It is for all these reasons that the order of the Appellate Division should be affirmed.

DISCUSSION QUESTIONS

1. Do you agree with the majority or dissenting opinion?
2. How could the plaintiff have avoided the result of this decision?
3. Since valuable personal property is usually insured and the insured would recover the value of the lost property, the effect of this decision is that the insurance company after it pays the insured, could only recover $75.00 from a restaurant in New York State in cases similar to this. Do insurance companies therefore pass along to all their insured the ultimate loss they incur in cases like this?
4. If restaurants had greater liability, would they decline to check valuable property or pass along the cost of their losses in the form of higher prices to the public?
5. Read CIOFALO v. VIC TANNEY GYMS, INC. in this book which involved the legal question of whether contracting parties may lawfully include a valid exculpatory clause in their contract.
6. In 1983, Section 201 of the New York General Business Law (p.15 in this book) was amended to provide that "No hotel, motel or restaurant proprietor shall post a notice disclaiming or misrepresenting his liability under this section." Assuming a restaurant posted a notice in a conspicious place and manner which stated "We are not liable for the loss of any personal property checked with us", what legal effect would such notice have on the restaurant's liability to a patron?

1. O Corporation hired E as sales manager under a written five year employment contract which provided that E would receive an annual salary of $50,000
and "a fair share of the profits" each year. Shortly after the end of the
first year a dispute arose as to what constituted a "fair share of the
profits". E resigned and sued O Corporation for breach of contract seeking
recovery of ten percent of the profits earned by O Corporation during the
first year which E claimed was a "fair share". O Corporation contends there
is no contract.

(a) In an action for breach of contract, judgment for whom? Explain.

(b) Does E have any other legal theory under which he may recover from O
     Corporation? Explain.

2. D Corporation entered into a written employment agreement with E on
September 1, which provided in part that employment will commence on the
following January 1 and "will continue for a period of time to be mutually
agreed upon". One month before January 1 D Corporation notified E that it
had changed its mind and would not employ him. In an action brought by E
against D Corporation for breach of contract, D Corporation contends there
is no contract. Judgment for whom? Explain.

3. On October 1, B received a letter from S as follows:

> "I understand that you are interested in buying a pick-up
> truck. I will sell you mine for $4,000 all cash, and will
> have it ready for delivery on November 15.
>
>   (Signed) S"

B then telephoned S and inquired: "Can I have 20 days to think over your
offer?" S replied: "O.K. You have an irrevocable option for 20 days.
Write me when you decide."

On October 6, B wrote S: "I am still very much interested in your offer.
I'm a little short of cash at the moment and would like to know if you
would consider taking $2,000 cash and my 90-day note for the other $2,000?

>   (Signed) B"

S did not reply. On October 10, without B's knowledge, S sold and delivered
the truck to T for $4,250 cash.

On October 15, B wrote S: "I have decided to accept your offer and will pay
you $4,000 in cash when I pick up the truck on Nov. 15.

>   (Signed) B"

S wrote back: "The truck is sold."

B sues S for damages for breach of contract. Judgment for whom? Explain.

4. (a) S, a merchant, wrote B, a merchant:

                    "August 1,

     I offer to sell you 1 Labelette, Model A, price $9,000.
     This is a firm offer for 30 days.

                         (Signed) S."

On August 10, B received a letter from S:

     "I hereby revoke my offer of August 1."

On August 17, B wrote S:

     "I hereby accept your offer of August 1."

     (1) Is there a contract under common law? Explain.

     (2) Is there a contract under the Uniform Commercial Code? Explain.

     (b) Assume that S's offer stated that it was a firm offer for four
          months, and that on November 15 B mailed an acceptance. Is there
          a contract? Explain.

     (c) Assume that S's offer stated that it was a firm offer for four
          months and that on November 5, B received a letter from S, dated
          November 2:

     "I hereby revoke my offer of August 1".

and that on November 15 B mailed an acceptance. Is there a contract?
Explain.

5. On May 1, S, a textile manufacturer, mailed to B, a merchant, a written
and signed offer to sell 1,000 bolts of blue denim (with a sample enclosed)
at $40 per bolt. Each bolt would contain 25 square yards. The offer stated
that "it would remain open for 10 days from the above date (May 1) and that
it could not be withdrawn prior to that date."

Two days later, S, noting a sudden increase in the price of blue denim,
changed his mind. After making great personal efforts to contact B, S sent
B a letter revoking the offer of May 1. The letter was mailed on May 4 and
received by B on May 5.

B chose to disregard the letter of May 4; instead, he happily continued to watch the price of blue denim rise. On May 9, B mailed a letter accepting the original offer. The letter was sent by registered mail and was properly addressed and contained the correct postage. However, it was not received by S until May 12 due to a delay in the mails.

B demanded delivery of the goods according to the terms of the offer of May 1, but S has refused, claiming there is no contract.

(a) Is there a contract under common law? Explain.

(b) Is there a contract under the Uniform Commercial Code? Explain.

(c) If S and B were not merchants, would there be a contract under New York General Obligations Law Section 5-1109? Explain.

6. S, a wholesale appliance dealer, had thirty-five dishwashers which he wishes to sell. He telephoned B, a retailer, and offered him the entire lot at a most advantageous price. B recognized that it was a real bargain, but felt he could not handle that number alone. Consequently, he asked S to give him a ten-day option on the thirty-five dishwashers. B explained that in the meantime he would be arranging financing and storage and attempting to get another retailer to agree to take some of the dishwashers. S said he would consider this request and that he would contact B again.

Having no other prospective buyer at the moment, S decided to grant B's request. He typed out and signed the following option:

> "I, S, do hereby promise B that my offer to sell thirty-five (35) dishwashers (described below at the prices indicated) will be held open for ten days from this date (April 15), and will not be withdrawn prior to the expiration of such time."

S then sent this writing to B by mail and B received it the next day.

On April 16, another retailer, came to S's store and inquired about the dishwashers. He offered to buy them immediately for cash.

S send B a letter on April 17 revoking his offer, telling him that he was going to sell the dishwashers to another party. This letter was received by B on April 20. B disregarded the revocation and on April 22 sent S a letter accepting the offer. This letter was delayed in the mail and did not reach S until April 30.

(a) Is the option binding upon S according to:

    (1) Common law? Explain.

    (2) the Uniform Commercial Code? Explain.

    (3) New York General Obligations Law Section 5-1109, if the parties

were <u>not</u> merchants? Explain.

(b) Assume that the option was binding. Was there a timely acceptance according to:

    (1) common law? Explain.

    (2) the Uniform Commercial Code? Explain.

7. B, a merchant, wrote S, a merchant:

    "Ship within 2 weeks 1 Labelette, model A, price $9,000, F.O.B. Chicago.

                      (Signed) B."

S replied by letter:

    "Your order received. Shipment will be made within 2 weeks.

                      (Signed) S."

Two days later, and before S had done anything to fill the order, S received a telegram from B:

    "Cancel my order. Do not need Labelette. Sorry."

(a) Is there a contract under common law? Explain.

(b) Is there a contract under the Uniform Commercial Code? Explain.

8. S, a manufacturer, send B, an owner of a chain of retail stores, an offer to sell 100 television sets for $30,000, terms C.O.D.

B wrote to S:

    "I accept your offer: payment 2/10, net 30 days."

S tendered delivery of the TV sets to B and demanded cash on delivery. B refused to pay on delivery, and S withheld delivery.

S then brought an action against B to recover damages for breach of contract.

(a) Judgment for whom at common law? Explain.

(b) Judgment for whom under the Uniform Commercial Code? Explain.

(c) Assume that B's letter read as follows:

53

"I accept your offer provided that you agree to a credit sale, 2/10 net 30."

Is there a contract under the Uniform Commercial Code if S made no reply? Explain.

9. S, a wholesale fruit dealer, sent the following letter to B, a fruit merchant:

"Feb. 1

Offer 1000 boxes of Los Angeles, San Gabriel oranges, at $10.60 per box, F.O.B. Los Angeles: March delivery.

Unless I receive your acceptance by 2 P.M. on Feb. 4, I will dispose of them elsewhere.

(Signed)   ."

S's letter was received by B on Feb. 2, at 3 P.M.

At 1 P.M. on Feb. 2, S mailed B the following letter:

"I regret to inform you I am compelled to withdraw my offer dated Feb. 1.

(Signed) S."

S's second letter was not received by B until Feb. 3.

Meanwhile, at 5 P.M. on Feb. 2, B mailed the following letter to S:

"I accept your offer dated Feb. 1.

(Signed) B."

Because of a severe snowstorm which disrupted all means of communication, B's letter was not delivered to S until 4 P.M. on Feb. 4.

Is there a binding contract between S and B? Explain.

10. S offered to sell B a ten acre tract of commercial property for $250,000. S's letter indicated the offer would expire on March 1 at 3:00 P.M. and that any acceptance must be received in her office by that time. On February 28, B decided to accept the offer and mailed an acceptance at 4:00 P.M. B indicated that in the event the acceptance did not arrive on time, he would assume there was a contract if he did not hear anything from S in five days. The letter arrived on March 2. S never responded to B's letter. B claims a contract was entered into and is suing S for breach of contract. Judgment for whom? Explain.

54

11. In auditing the accounts of B the following problem was revealed as a result of an examination of the "purchase orders outstanding" file. The correspondence between B and S was as follows:

(Letter of April 20 from B to S)

April 20.

S:

Please advise on lowest price you can make us on our order of ten car loads of Mason green jars, complete with caps, packed one dozen in a case, either delivered here, or f.o.b. cars your place as you prefer. State terms and cash discount.

Very truly yours,
(Signed) B

(To this S replied)

April 23.

B:

Replying to your favor of April 20, we quote you Mason green jars, complete, in one dozen boxes, delivered railroad depot your city: pints, $4.50, quarts, $5.00, half gallons, $6.50 per gross, for immediate acceptance, and shipment not later than May 15, sixty days acceptance, or 2 off, cash in ten days.

Yours truly,
(Signed) S

(In response to the above letter B replied by telegram)

April 24.

S:

Your letter April 23 received. Enter our order ten car loads as per your quotation. Specifications will be mailed promptly.

(Signed) B

(The final communication was S's telegram sent in response to the above telegram)

April 24.

B:

Impossible to book your order. Output all sold.

(Signed)   S

B insists that a contract was created by its April 24 telegram.
However, S insists there was no contract and it had the right
to decline to fill the order at the time it sent its April 24th
telegram.

These additional facts were noted. The price of Mason green
jars has increased rapidly since April 24. The term "car
load" is an expression invariably used in the trade as being
equivalent to 100 gross.

(a) Is there a contract under common law? Explain.

(b) Is there a contract under the Uniform Commercial Code?
Explain.

12. On March 10 S sent a written offer to B to sell 3,000
tons of steel rails on certain specified terms. B received
this letter on March 11 and on March 25 telegraphed to S an
acceptance which reached him at 3 P.M. on that day. On the
same day, March 25, at 2 P.M. S mailed to B a revocation of
his March 10 offer which was received the following day.

(a) Is there a contract? Explain.

(b) Assume there is a contract. When was the contract formed
according to:

(1) common law? Explain.

(2) the Uniform Commercial Code? Explain.

QUESTIONS   FORMATION OF CONTRACTS: OFFER AND ACCEPTANCE

1. Jackson paid Brady $100 for a 90-day option to purchase Brady's 160-acre farm for $32,000. The option agreement was in writing and signed by both parties. The agreement referred only to the option, its period, a legal description of the farm, and the purchase price. Thirty days later, Jackson wrote Brady.

    "I hereby exercise my option to purchase your farm for $32,000 subject to your replacing the well pump and related plumbing fixtures." Jackson's letter

    a. Rejects Brady's offer and terminates the option agreement.
    b. Accepts Brady's offer leaving customary details to be worked out during formalization of the contract.
    c. Accepts Brady's offer leaving a matter to be negotiated during formalization of the contract.
    d. Has no effect on the option agreement.

    Questions 2 and 3. Each of the following items begins by a statement of facts or an opening statement followed by two independent statements numbered I and II. You are to evaluate each statement and determine whether it is true. Your answer for each item should be selected from the following responses.

    a. I only is true.
    b. II only is true.
    c. Both I and II are true.
    d. Neither I nor II is true.

    Questions 2 and 3 are based on the following information:

    On September 4, Farr offered to sell his farm to Jackson for $10,000. The offer was received by Jackson on September 7. Jackson wrote back on September 10 asking whether or not this was a "firm price." Farr replied, I will not accept a penny less."

2. Jackson wired Farr his acceptance of the original offer on September 17. The telegram was received by Farr on September 18. Farr refuses to perform.

    I.   Since Farr used the mails as his means of communication, the purported acceptance by telegram is invalid.
    II. Had Farr mailed a revocation to Jackson prior to his receipt of Jackson's telegram purporting to accept the offer, no contract would have resulted, even though Farr received Jackson's telegram ten minutes after mailing his revocation.

3. Jackson lost interest in the purchase of the farm as a result of Farr's refusal to budge from the offering price. Therefore, on September 20, Jackson assigned the offer to Martin Stark who had expressed an interest

in the farm. Stark promptly mailed his acceptance at the asking price of $10,000 to Farr. Farr refuses to perform.

   I. Jackson has validly assigned his rights to Stark.
  II. A contract was formed upon Stark's posting his acceptance.

Questions 4 and 5 are based on the following information:

Ambrose undertook to stage a production of a well-known play. He wired Belle, a famous actress, offering her the lead at $1,000 per week (for six evening performances per week) for six weeks from the specified opening night, plus $1,000 for a week of rehearsal prior to the opening. The telegram also said, "Offer ends in three days."

4. Assuming Belle's reply was received by Ambrose within the time limit, it would

   a. Be an effective acceptance if she telephoned Ambrose and accepted within the three-day period and prior to receiving any indication of revocation of the offer even though Ambrose had previously dispatched a letter to Belle revoking the offer.
   b. Be an effective acceptance only if she replied by telegram.
   c. Be an effective acceptance if she replied immediately, "Fine if Howard is my leading man."
   d. Not be an effective acceptance if she replied, "Fine, but I hope you will try to line up Howard as my leading man."

5. Ambrose's death

   a. Would not terminate the offer if it occurred after Belle sent a telegraphed acceptance but before receipt of the telegram at Ambrose's office.
   b. Would terminate any contract previously made with Belle.
   c. On the day of the offer would not prevent Belle from subsequently accepting within the three-day period.
   d. Transforms the offer into an offer to enter into a unilateral contract.

6. An outstanding offer to sell a tract of real property is terminated at the time the

   a. Buyer learns of the seller's death.
   b. Seller posts his revocation if the original offer was made by mail.
   c. Buyer posts a rejection of the offer if the original offer was received by mail.
   d. Buyer learns of the sale of the property to a third party.

7. Donaldson Retailers engaged in lengthy negotiations for the purchase of an office building from Universal Real Estate, Inc. The parties reached an impasse on the price. Universal's written offer to sell was $150,000. Donaldson replied by telegram offering $140,000 - "Take

58

it or leave it." Universal filed the telegram away for future reference but did not respond. Donaldson then sent a letter stating that Universal was to disregard its prior communication and that it accepted the offer at $150,000. Universal wrote back stating, "The price is now $160,000 take it or leave it." Donaldson promptly telegraphed Universal that it held Universal to its original offer of $150,000. Under these circumstances

a. The purported contract in unenforceable in any event under the Statute of Frauds.
b. No contract was formed.
c. Since the same means of communication was not used throughout the transaction, there can be no contract.
d. Donaldson's reply offering $140,000 constituted a mere counter-proposal which did not terminate the original offer.

8. An offer is generally effective when it is

a. Dispatched.
b. Signed.
c. Mailed.
d. Received.

9. Unless the offer specifies otherwise, an acceptance is generally effective when it is

a. Signed.
b. Received by the offeror.
c. Delivered by the communicating agency.
d. Dispatched by the offeree.

10. Baker Corporation sent a letter to Sampson Company in which Baker offered to purchase 10 acres of certain real estate from Sampson for $4,000. Sampson responded that it would sell 8 of these acres at that price. Baker and Sampson have created

a. A contract for sale of 8 acres for $4,000.
b. A contract for sale of 10 acres for $4,000.
c. A contract to sell 8 acres for $3,200.
d. No contract in this action.

11. Vantage telephoned Breyer on December 18 and offered to sell a plot of land to Breyer for $5,000. Vantage promised to keep the offer open until December 27. Breyer said he was interested in the land but wanted to inspect it before making any commitment. Which of the following best describes the legal significance of these events?

a. Vantage may revoke the offer at will.
b. Vantage may not revoke the offer prior to December 27.
c. A contract was formed on December 18.
d. Breyer's response constituted a rejection and counteroffer.

12. A written option to buy land generally cannot be revoked before acceptance if the offer

    a. Is supported by consideration from the offeree.
    b. Allows a specific time for acceptance.
    c. Is made exclusively to one person.
    d. By its terms is not revocable before acceptance.

13. Waldo Carpets, Inc., decided to sell a portion of its two-acre property and the president of Waldo wrote several prospective buyers the following letter:

Dear Sir:

We are sending this solicitation to several prospective buyers because we are interested in selling one acre of our property located in downtown Metropolis. If you are interested, please communicate with me at the above address. Under no circumstances, will we consider a price of less than $90,000.

                                    Cordially,

                                    James Waldo,
                                    President
                                    Waldo Carpets, Inc.

In this situation

    a. The Statute of Frauds does not apply because the real property being sold is the division of an existing tract which had been properly recorded.
    b. Markus, a prospective buyer who telegraphed Waldo that he would buy at $90,000 and forwarded a $90,000 surety bond to guarantee his performance, has validly accepted the offer.
    c. Waldo must sell to the highest bidder.
    d. Waldo's communication did not constitute an offer to sell.

14. Milbank undertook to stage a production of a well-known play. He wired Lucia, a famous actress, offering her the lead in the play at $2,000 per week for six weeks from the specified opening night plus $1,000 for a week of rehearsal prior to the opening. The telegram also said, "Offer ends in three days." Lucia wired an acceptance the same day she received it. The telegram acceptance was temporarily misplaced by the telegraph company and did not arrive until five days after its dispatch. Milbank, not hearing from Lucia, assumed she had declined and abandoned the production. Which of the following is correct if Lucia sues Milbank?

    a. The contract was automatically terminated when Milbank decided not to proceed.
    b. Lucia has entered into a valid contract and is entitled to recover

damages if Milbank fails to honor it.

    c. Lucia may not take any other engagement for the period involved if she wishes to recover.

    d. Milbank is excused from any liability since his action was reasonable under the circumstances.

15. Normally, the offer initiates the process by which a contract is created. Therefore, the offer is critical insofar as satisfying basic contract law requirements. Which of the following statements is incorrect?

    a. The offer may only be expressed in words.

    b. The offer must be communicated to the other party.

    c. The offer must be certain enough to determine the liability of the parties.

    d. The offer must be accepted by the other party.

16. Fashion Swimming Pools, Inc., mailed a letter to Direct Distributors offering a three-year franchise dealership. The offer stated the terms in detail and at the bottom stated that "the offer would not be withdrawn prior to October 1." Under the circumstances, which of the following is correct?

    a. The offer is an irrevocable option which cannot be withdrawn prior to October 1.

    b. A letter of acceptance from Direct to Fashion sent on October 1, but not received until October 2, would not create a valid contract.

    c. The Statute of Frauds would not apply to the proposed contract.

    d. The offer cannot be assigned to another party if Direct chooses not to accept.

17. Mayer wrote Jackson and offered to sell Jackson a building for $50,000. The offer stated it would expire 30 days from July 1. Mayer changed his mind and does not wish to be bound by his offer. If a legal dispute arises between the parties regarding whether there has been a valid acceptance of the offer, which of the following is correct?

    a. The offer cannot be legally withdrawn for the stated period of time.

    b. The offer will not expire prior to the 30 days even if Mayer sells the property to a third person and notifies Jackson.

    c. If Jackson phoned Mayer on August 1 and unequivocally accepted the offer, it would create a contract, provided he had no notice of withdrawal of the offer.

    d. If Jackson categorically rejects the offer on July 10th, Jackson cannot validly accept within the remaining stated period of time.

18. Gregor paid $100 to Henry for a thirty-day written option to purchase Henry's commercial real property for $75,000. Twenty days later Henry received an offer from Watson to purchase the property for $85,000. Henry promptly notified Gregor that the option price was now $85,000, or the option was revoked. Gregor said he would not pay a penny more than $75,000 and that he still had 10 days remaining on the option. On

the 28th day of the option, Gregor telephoned Henry that he had decided to exercise the option; he tendered his $75,000 check the next day which was to be held in escrow until delivery of the deed. Henry refused to accept the tender stating that he had decided not to sell and that he was going to retain the property for the present. Which of the following best describes the legal rights of the parties involved?

    a. Henry effectively revoked his offer to sell because he did this prior to Gregor's acceptance.

    b. Consideration given for the option is irrelevant because the option was in writing and signed by Henry.

    c. Because Gregor's acceptance was not in writing and signed, it is invalid according to the Statute of Frauds.

    d. Gregor's acceptance was valid, and in the event of default he may obtain the equitable remedy of specific performance.

19. Abacus Corporation sent Frame Company an offer by a telegram to buy its patent on a calculator. The Abacus telegram indicated that the offer would expire in ten days. The telegram was sent on February 1, and received on February 2, by Frame. On February 8, Abacus telephoned Frame and indicated they were withdrawing the offer. Frame telegraphed an acceptance on the 11th of February. Which of the following is correct?

    a. The offer was an irrevocable offer, but Frame's acceptance was too late.

    b. Abacus' withdrawal of the offer was ineffective because it was not in writing.

    c. Since Frame used the same means of communication, acceptance was both timely and effective.

    d. No contract arose since Abacus effectively revoked the offer on February 8.

20. Dustin received a telephone call on Monday from his oil supplier. The supplier offered him 1,000 barrels of heating oil at $48 a barrel, the current price in a rapidly changing market. Dustin said he would take the offer under advisement. The next day, the market price rose to $50 a barrel and Dustin sent the supplier a letter late that afternoon accepting the offer at $48 a barrel. The letter arrived in the usual course on Thursday morning, by which time the market price had moved to $56 a barrel. The supplier called Dustin and said it would not accept his order. Dustin insisted that he had a contract. Which of the following is correct?

    a. Acceptance took place on dispatch of Dustin's letter

    b. Acceptance did not take place upon dispatch as the offer had already expired.

    c. Acceptance did not take place because the only means of acceptance Dustin could use was the phone.

    d. Acceptance could only be made by a signed writing.

21. Which of the following offers for the sale of the Lazy L Ranch is enforceable?

a. Owner tells buyer she will sell the ranch for $35,000 and that the offer will be irrevocable for ten days.

b. Owner writes buyer offering to sell the ranch for $35,000 and stating that the offer will remain open for ten days.

c. Owner telegraphs buyer offering to sell the ranch for $35,000 and promises to hold the offer open for ten days.

d. Owner writes buyer offering to sell the ranch for $35,000 and stating that the offer will be irrevocable for ten days if buyer will pay $1.00. Buyer pays.

22. Water Works had a long-standing policy of offering employees $100 for suggestions actually used. Due to inflation and a decline in the level and quality of suggestions received, Water Works decided to increase the award to $500. Several suggestions were under consideration at that time. Two days prior to the public announcement of the increase to $500, a suggestion by Farber was accepted and put into use. Farber is seeking to collect $500. Farber is entitled to

a. $500 because Water Works had decided to pay that amount.

b. $500 because the suggestion submitted will be used during the period that Water Works indicated it would pay $500.

c. $100 in accordance with the original offer.

d. Nothing if Water Works chooses not to pay since the offer was gratuitous.

23. Nichols wrote Dilk and offered to sell Dilk a building for $50,000. The offer stated it would expire 30 days from July 1. Nichols changed his mind and does not wish to be bound by his offer. If a legal dispute arises between the parties regarding whether there has been a valid acceptance of the offer, which of the following is correct?

a. The offer will not expire prior to the 30 days even if Nichols sells the property to a third person and notifies Dilk.

b. If Dilk categorically rejects the offer on July 10th, Dilk can not validly accept within the remaining stated period of time.

c. If Dilk phoned Nichols on August 1 and unequivocally accepted the offer, it would create a contract, provided he had no notice of withdrawal of the offer.

d. The offer can not be legally withdrawn for the stated period of time.

24. Marglow Supplies Inc., mailed a letter to Wilson Distributors on September 15, offering a three-year franchise dealership. The offer stated the terms in detail and at the bottom stated that the offer would not be withdrawn prior to October 1. Which of the following is correct?

a. The statute of frauds would not apply to the proposed contract.

b. The offer is an irrevocable option which can not be withdrawn prior to October 1.

c. The offer can not be assigned to another party by Wilson if Wilson chooses not to accept.

d. A letter of acceptance from Wilson to Marglow sent on October 1, but not received until October 2, would not create a valid contract.

25. Park owed Collins $1,000 and $2,000, respectively, on two separate unsecured obligations. Smythe had become a surety on the $2,000 debt at the request of Park when Park became indebted to Collins. Both debts matured on June 1. Park was able to pay only $600 at that time, and he forwarded that amount to Collins without instructions. Under these circumstances

    a. Collins must apply the funds pro rata in proportion to the two debts.
    b. Collins must apply the $600 to the $2,000 debt if there is no surety on the $1,000 debt.
    c. Smythe will be discharged to the extent of $400 if Collins on request of Smythe fails to apply $400 to the $2,000 debt.
    d. Collins is free to apply the $600 to the debts as he sees fit.

26. A contract is said to be executory when

    a. Any of the obligations thereunder remain to be performed.
    b. All of the obligations thereunder have been performed.
    c. It is in writing.
    d. It is informal.

27. Which of the following contracts falls within common law rules and is not covered by the Uniform Commercial Code?

    a. A requirement contract for the purchase of fuel oil.
    b. A contract for the sale of 200 chess sets.
    c. Contract for the sale of goods which are manufactured according to the buyer's specifications.
    d. An employment contract which by its terms has a set period of eighteen months.

28. One of a CPA's major concerns regarding contractual questions arising in the examination of a client's financial statement is

    a. The proper court to initiate a lawsuit.
    b. The question of who has the burden of proof.
    c. Whether consideration has been provided by both parties to a contract.
    d. The admissibility of evidence in court.

29. The distinction between contracts covered by the Uniform Commercial Code and contracts which are not covered by the code is

    a. Basically dependent upon whether the subject matter of the contract involves the purchase or sale of goods.
    b. Based upon the dollar amount of the contract.
    c. Dependent upon whether the Statute of Frauds is involved.
    d. Of relatively little or no importance to the CPA since the laws are invariably the same.

30. The basic distinction between a bilateral contract and a unilateral contract according to common law rules is

    a. That one must be signed, sealed and delivered, whereas the other need not.
    b. There is only one promise involved when the contract is unilateral.
    c. The Statute of Frauds applies to one and not the other.
    d. One is assignable whereas the other is not.

31. Which of the following represents the basic distinction between a bilateral contract and a unilateral contract?

    a. Specific performance is available if the contract is unilateral whereas it is not if the contract is bilateral.
    b. There is only one promise involved if the contract is unilateral whereas there are two promises is the contract is bilateral.
    c. The Statute of Frauds applies to a bilateral contract but not a unilateral contract.
    d. The rights under a bilateral contract are assignable whereas rights under a unilateral contract are not assignable.

32. Where a client accepts the services of an accountant without an agreement concerning payment there is

    a. An implied in fact contract.
    b. An implied in law contract.
    c. An express contract.
    d. No contract.

33. In determining whether a bilateral contract has been created, the courts look primarily at

    a. The fairness to the parties.
    b. The objective intent of the parties.
    c. The subjective intent of the parties.
    d. The subjective intent of the offeror.

34. Justin made an offer to pay Benson $1,000 if Benson would perform a certain act. Acceptance of Justin's offer occurs when Benson

    a. Promises to complete the act.
    b. Prepares to perform the act.
    c. Promises to perform and begins preliminary performance.
    d. Completes the act.

STATUTE OF FRAUDS

The Statute of Frauds is a collection of statutes which provides that certain contracts be in writing (or be signed by the party against whom enforcement is being sought) in order for the contract to be enforceable. The original Statute of Frauds was enacted in England in 1677.

Most of the provisions of the Statute of Frauds in New York State are contained in Section 5-701 of the N.Y. General Obligations Law. That statute uses the terminology "every agreement, promise or undertaking is void, unless... in writing..." Although the legislature has used the word "void", this has been interpreted by legal scholars and the courts to mean "unenforceable". Therefore, the statute would render the oral contract provision unenforceable, and not void, if it were required to be in writing pursuant to the Statute of Frauds.

Various **statutes** in New York State containing Statute of Frauds provisions are included herein.

NEW YORK GENERAL OBLIGATIONS LAW:

Section 5-701. Agreements Required To Be In Writing

Every agreement, promise or undertaking is void, unless it or some note or memorandum thereof be in writing, and subscribed by the party to be charged therewith, or by his lawful agent, if such agreement, promise or undertaking:

1. By its terms is not to be performed within one year from the making thereof or the performance of which is not to be completed before the end of a lifetime;

2. Is a special promise to answer for the debt, default or miscarriage of another person;

3. Is made in consideration of marriage, except mutual promises to marry;

....

5. Is a subsequent or new promise to pay a debt discharged in bankruptcy;

6. Notwithstanding section 2-201 of the uniform commercial code, if the goods be sold at public auction, and the auctioneer at the time of the sale, enters in a sale book, a memorandum specifying the nature and price of the property sold, the terms of the sale, the name of the purchaser, and the name of the person on whose account the sale was made, such memorandum is equivalent in effect to a note of the contract or sale, subscribed by the party to be charged therewith;

...

9. Is a contract to assign or an assignment, with or without consideration to the promisor, of a life or health or accident insurance policy, or a
promise, with or without consideration to the promisor, to name a beneficiary
of any such policy. This provision shall not apply to a policy of industrial
life or health or accident insurance.

10. Is a contract to pay compensation for services rendered in negotiating
a loan, or in negotiating the purchase, sale, exchange, renting or leasing of
any real estate or interest therein, or of a business opportunity, business,
its good will, inventory, fixtures or an interest therein, including a
majority of the voting stock interest in a corporation and including the
creating of a partnership interest. "Negotiating" includes procuring an
introduction to a party to the transaction or assisting in the negotiation
or consummation of the transaction. This provision shall apply to a contract
implied in fact or in law to pay reasonable compensation but shall not apply
to a contract to pay compensation to an auctioneer, an attorney at law, or a
duly licensed real estate broker or real estate salesman. (eff. Sept. 27,
1964 - originally enacted in 1897, and was previously contained in the
Personal Property Law).

Section 5-703. Conveyances and Contracts Concerning Real Property
Required To Be In Writing

1. An estate or interest in real property, other than a lease for a term
not exceeding one year, or any trust or power, over or concerning real
property, or in any manner relating thereto, cannot be created, granted,
assigned, surrendered or declared, unless by act or operation of law, or by a
deed or conveyance in writing, subscribed by the person creating, granting,
assigning, surrendering or declaring the same, or by his lawful agent,
thereunto authorized by writing. But this subdivision does not affect the
power of a testator in the disposition of his real property by will; nor
prevent any trust from arising or being extinguished by implication or
operation of law, nor any declaration of trust from being proved by a writing
subscribed by the person declaring the same.

2. A contract for the leasing for a longer period than one year, or for
the sale, of any real property, or an interest therein, is void unless the
contract or some note or memorandum thereof, expressing the consideration, is
in writing, subscribed by the party to be charged, or by his lawful agent
thereunto authorized in writing.

3. A contract to devise real property or establish a trust of real
property, or any interest therein or right with reference thereto, is void
unless the contract or some note or memorandum thereof is in writing and
subscribed by the party to be charged therewith, or by his lawfully authorized
agent.

4. Nothing contained in this section abridges the powers of courts of
equity to compel the specific performance of agreements in cases of part

performance. (eff. 1963 - originally enacted in 1897, and was previously contained in the Personal Property Law).

Section 5-1111. Execution By Agent In Real Property Transactions; Written Authorization Required

If executed by an agent, any agreement, promise, undertaking, assignment or offer required by section 5-1103, 5-1105, 5-1107 or 5-1109 to be in writing, which affects or relates to real property or an interest therein in any manner stated in sub-divisions one or two of section 5-703 of this chapter, shall be void unless such agent was thereunto authorized in writing. (eff. 1963 - originally enacted in 1897).

NEW YORK CIVIL PRACTICE LAW AND RULES: (C.P.L.R.)

Section 7501. Effect Of Arbitration Agreement

A written agreement to submit any controversy thereafter arising or any existing controversy to arbitration is enforceable without regard to the justiciable character of the controversy and confers jurisdiction on the courts of the state to enforce it and to enter judgment on an award. In determining any matter arising under this article, the court shall not consider whether the claim with respect to which arbitration is sought is tenable, or otherwise pass upon the merits of the dispute. (eff. 1963 - originally enacted in 1876).

NEW YORK ESTATES, POWERS AND TRUST LAW: (E.P.T.L.)

Section 13-2.1 Agreements Involving A Contract To Establish a Trust, to Make a Testamentary Provision Of Any Kind, And By A Personal Representative To Answer For The Debt or Default Of A Decedent, Required To Be In Writing

(a) Every agreement, promise or undertaking is **unenforceable unless** it or some note or memorandum thereof is in writing and subscribed by the party to be charged therewith, or by his lawful agent, if such agreement, promise or undertaking:

(1) Is a contract to establish a trust

(2) Is a contract to make a testamentary provision of any kind.

(3) Is a promise by a personal representative to answer for the debt or default of his decedent. (eff. Sept. 1, 1967 - portions were originally enacted in 1897).

UNIFORM COMMERCIAL CODE: ARTICLE 2: SALE OF GOODS

Section 2-201. Formal Requirements; Statute of Frauds

(1) Except as otherwise provided in this section a contract for sale of goods for the price of $500 or more is not enforceable by way of action or defense unless there is some writing sufficient to indicate that a contract for sale has been made between the parties and signed by the party against whom enforcement is sought or by his authorized agent or broker. A writing is not insufficient because it omits or incorrectly states a term agreed upon but the contract is not enforceable under this paragraph beyond the quantity of goods shown in such writing.

(2) Between merchants if within a reasonable time a writing in confirmation of the contract and sufficient against the sender is received and the party receiving it has reason to know its contents, it satisfies the requirements of subsection (1) against such party unless written notice of objection to its contents is given within ten days after it is received.

(3) A contract which does not satisfy the requirements of subsection (1) but which is valid in other respects is enforceable

(a) if the goods are to be specially manufactured for the buyer and are not suitable for sale to others in the ordinary course of the seller's business and the seller, before notice of repudiation is received and under circumstances which reasonably indicate that the goods are for the buyer, has made either a substantial beginning of their manufacture or commitments for their procurement; or

(b) if the party against whom enforcement is sought admits in his pleading, testimony or otherwise in court that a contract for sale was made, but the contract is not enforceable under this provision beyond the quantity of goods admitted; or

(c) with respect to goods for which payment has been made and accepted or which have been received and accepted (Section 2-606).

UNIFORM COMMERCIAL CODE:

Section 8-319. Statute of Frauds - Investment Securities.

A contract for the sale of securities is not enforceable by way of action or defense unless

(a) there is some writing signed by the party against whom enforcement is sought or by his authorized agent or broker sufficient to indicate that a contract has been made for sale of a stated quantity of described securities at a defined or stated price; or

(b) delivery of a certificated security or transfer instruction has been accepted, or transfer of an uncertificated security has been registered and the transferee has failed to send written objection to the issuer within ten days after receipt of the initial transaction statement confirming such registration or payment has been made but the contract is enforceable under this provision only to the extent of such delivery, registration or payment; or

(c) within a reasonable time a writing in confirmation of the sale or purchase and sufficient against the sender under paragraph (a) has been received by the party against whom enforcement is sought and he has failed to send written objection to its contents within ten days after its receipt; or

(d) the party against whom enforcement is sought admits in his pleading, testimony or otherwise in court that a contract was made for sale of a stated quantity of described securities at a defined or stated price. (as amended eff. 12/21/82, retroactive to 9/1/82).

Section 1-206. Statute of Frauds For Kinds of Personal Property Not Otherwise Covered.

(1) Except in the cases described in subsection (2) of this section contract for the sale of personal property is not enforceable by way of action or defense beyond five thousand dollars in amount or value of remedy unless there is some writing which indicates that a contract for sale has been made between the parties at a defined or stated price, reasonably identifies the subject matter, and is signed by the party against whom enforcement is sought or by his authorized agent.

(2) Subsection (1) of this section does not apply to contracts for the sale of goods (Section 2-201) nor of securities (Section 8-319) nor to security agreements (Section 9-203).

Section 9-203. Attachment And Enforceability of Security Interest; Proceeds; Formal Requisites

(1) ...a security interest is not enforceable against the debtor or third parties with respect to the collateral and does not attach unless:

(a) ...the debtor has signed a security agreement which contains a description of the collateral ....

STATUTE OF FRAUDS: SUFFICIENCY OF MEMORANDUM
CASE NO. 12
CRABTREE v. ELIZABETH ARDEN SALES CORP.

305 N.Y. 48. Jan. 1953

INTRODUCTION

The New York state Statute of Frauds states that certain specified agreements are "void, unless...some note or memorandum thereof be in writing, and subscribed by the party to be charged". This leading case answers the following important legal questions: 1. whether the memorandum of the agreement may be "pieced together" from more than one document, 2. whether only one or every one of the documents "pieced together" must be subscribed, 3. what is required to connect or "piece together" all the documents to produce a written memorandum of the agreement to satisfy the Statute of Frauds, 4. how soon after the oral agreement is made must the written memorandum thereof be subscribed, and 5. whether the written memorandum must be prepared and subscribed with the intention of evidencing the oral agreement.

Fuld, J.

In September of 1947, Nate Crabtree entered into preliminary negotiations with Elizabeth Arden Sales Corporation, manufacturers and sellers of cosmetics, looking toward his employment as sales manager. Interviewed on September 26th, by Robert P. Johns, executive vice-president and general manager of the corporation, who had apprised him of the possible opening, Crabtree requested a three-year contract at $25,000 a year. Explaining that he would be giving up a secure well-paying job to take a position in an entirely new field of endeavor--which he believed would take him some years to master--he insisted upon an agreement for a definite term. And he repeated his desire for a contract for three years to Miss Elizabeth Arden, the corporation's president. When Miss Arden finally indicated that she was prepared to offer a two-year contract, based on an annual salary of $20,000 for the first six months, $25,000 for the second six months and $30,000 for the second year, plus expenses of $5000 a year for each of those years, Crabtree replied that that offer was "interesting". Miss Arden thereupon had her personal secretary make this memorandum on a telephone order blank that happened to be at hand:

"EMPLOYMENT AGREEMENT WITH

NATE CRABTREE   Date Sept. 26, 1947

At 681-5th Ave.   6: PM

****

Begin   20000.
6 Months   25000.
6 "   30000.
      5000.--per year
      Expense money

(2 years to make good)

```
                    Arrangement with
                     Mr. Crabtree
                    By Miss Arden
                    Present Miss Arden
                           Mr. John
                           Mr. Crabtree
                           Miss OLeary"
```

A few days later, Crabtree 'phoned Mr. Johns and telegraphed Miss Arden; he accepted the "invitation to join the Arden organization", and Miss Arden wired back her "welcome". When he reported for work, a "payroll change" card was made up and initialed by Mr. Johns, and then forwarded to the payroll department, reciting that it was prepared on September 30, 1947, and was to be effective as of October 22d, it specified the names of the parties, Crabtree's "Job Classification" and, in addition, contained the notation that "This employee is to be paid as follows:

"First six months of employment	$20,000. per annum
Next six months of employment	25,000. " "
After one year of employment	30,000. " "

Approved by RPJ (initialed)"

After six months of employmnet, Crabtree received the scheduled increase from $20,000 to $25,000, but the further specified increase at the end of the year was not paid. Both Mr. Johns and the comptroller of the corporation, Mr. Carstens, told Crabtree that they would attempt to straighten out the matter with Miss Arden, and with that in mind, the comptroller prepared another "payroll change" card, to which his signature is appended, noting that there was to be a "Salary increase" from $25,000 to $30,000 a year, "per contractual arrangements with Miss Arden". The latter, however, refused to approve the increase and, after further fruitless discussion, plaintiff left defendant's employ and commenced this action for breach of contract.

At the ensuing trial, defendant denied the existence of any agreement to employ plaintiff for two years, and further contended that, even if one had been made, the statute of frauds barred its enforcement. The trial court found against defendant on both issues and awarded plaintiff damages of about $14,000 and the Appellate Division, two justices dissenting, affirmed. Since the contract relied upon was not to be performed within a year, the primary question for decision is whether there was a memorandum of its terms subscribed by defendant, to satisfy the statute of frauds....

Each of the two payroll cards-the one initialed by defendant's general manager, the other signed by its comptroller-unquestionably constitutes a memorandum under the statute. That they were not prepared or signed with the intention of evidencing the contract, or that they came into existence subsequent to its execution, is of no consequence...; it is enough, to meet the statute's demands, that they were signed with intent to authenticate the information contained therein and that such information does evidence the terms of the contract. Those two writings contain all of the essential terms of the contract-the parties to it, the position that plaintiff was to assume, the salary that he was to receive-except that relating to the duration of plaintiff's employment. Accordingly, we must consider whether that item, the length of the contract, may be supplied by reference to the earlier unsigned office memorandum, and, if so, whether its notation, "2 years to make good", sufficiently designates a period of employment.

The statute of frauds does not require the "memorandum to be in one document. It may be pieced together out of separate writings, connected with one another either expressly or by the internal evidence of subject-matter and occasion." Where each of the separate writings has been subscribed by the party to be charged, little if any difficulty is encountered. Where, however, some writings have been signed, and others have not-as in the case before us-there is basic disagreement as to what constitutes a sufficient connection permitting the unsigned papers to be considered as part of the statutory memorandum. The courts of some jurisdictions insist that there be a reference, of varying degrees of specificity, in the signed writing to that unsigned, and, if there is no such reference, they refuse to permit consideration of the latter in determining whether the memorandum satisfies the statute. That conclusion is based upon a construction of the statute which requires that the connection between the writings and defendant's acknowledgment of the one not subscribed, appear from examination of the papers alone, without the aid of parol evidence. The other position-which has gained increasing support over the years-is that a sufficent connection between the papers is established simply by a reference in them to the same subject matter or transaction. The statute is not pressed "to the extreme of a literal and rigid logic"... and oral testimony is admitted to show the connection between the documents and to establish the acquiescence, of the party to be charged, to the contents of the one unsigned.

The view last expressed impresses us as the more sound, and we now definitively adopt it, permitting the signed and unsigned writing to be read together, provided that they clearly refer to the same subject matter of transaction.

The language of the statute - "Every agreement***is void, unless***some note or memorandum thereof be in writing, and subscribed by the party to be charged",...does not impose the requirement that the signed acknowledgment of the contract must appear from the writings alone, unaided by oral testimony. The danger of fraud and perjury, generally attendant upon the admission of parol evidence is at a minimum in a case such as this. None of the terms of the contract are supplied by parol. All of them must be set out in the various writings presented to the court, and at least one writing, the one establishing a contractual relationship between the parties, must bear the signature of the party to be charged, while the unsigned document must on its face refer to the same transaction as that set forth in the one that was signed. Parol evidence to portray the circumstances surrounding the making of the memorandum - serves only to connect the separate documents and to show that there was assent, by the party to be charged, to the contents of the one unsigned. If that testimony does not convincingly connect the papers, or does not show assent to the unsigned paper, it is within the province of the judge to conclude as a matter of law, that the statute has not been satisfied. True, the possibility still remains that, by fraud or perjury, an agreement never in fact made may occasionally be enforced under the subject matter or transaction test. It is better to run that risk, though, than to deny enforcement to all agreements, merely because the signed document made no specific mention of the unsigned writing. As the United States Supreme Court declared, in sanctioning the admission of parol evidence to establish the connection between the signed and unsigned writings. "There may be cases in which it would be a violation of reason and common sense to ignore a reference which derives its significance from such (parol) proof. If there is ground for any doubt in the matter, the general rule should be enforced. But where there is no ground for doubt, its enforcement would aid, instead of discouraging, fraud."....

Turning to the writings in the case before us - the unsigned office memo, the payroll change form initialed by the general manager Johns, and the paper signed by the comptroller Carstens - it is apparent, and most patently, that all three refer on their face to the same transaction. The parties, the position to be filled by plaintiff, the salary to be paid him, are all identically set forth; it is hardly possible that such detailed information could refer to another or a different agreement. Even more, the card signed by Carstens notes that it was prepared for the purpose of a "Salary increase per contractual arrangem nts with Miss Arden". That certainly constitutes a reference of sorts to a more comprehensive "arrangement," and parol is permissible to furnish the explanation.

The corroborative evidence of defendant's assent to the contents of the unsigned office memorandum is also convincing. Prepared by defendant's agent, Miss Arden's personal secretary, there is little likelihood that that paper was fraudulently manufactured or that defendant had not assented to its contents. Furthermore, the evidence as to the conduct of the parties at the time it was prepared persuasively demonstrates defendant's assent to its terms. Under such circumstances, the courts below were fully justified in finding that the three papers constituted the "memorandum" of their agreement within the meaning of the statute.

Nor can there by any doubt that the memorandum contains all of the essential terms of the contract. Only one term, the length of the employment, is in dispute. The September 26th office memorandum contains the notation, "2 years to make good". What purpose, other than to denote the length of the contract term, such a notation could have, is hard to imagine. Without it, the employment would be at will...and its inclusion may not be treated as meaningless or purposeless. Quite obviously, as the courts below decided, the phrase signifies that the parties agreed to a term, a certain and definite term, of two years, after which, if plaintiff did not "make good", he would be subject to discharge. And examination of other parts of the memorandum supports that construction. Throughout the writings, a scale of wages, increasing plaintiff's salary periodically, is set out; that type of arrangement is hardly consistent with the hypothesis that the employment was meant to be at will. The most that may be argued from defendant's standpoint is that "2 years to make good", is a cryptic and ambiguous statement. But, in such a case, parol evidence is admissible to explain its meaning.... Having in mind the relations of the parties, the course of the negotiations and

74

plaintiff's insistence upon security of employment, the purpose of the phrase
- or so the trier of the facts was warranted in finding - was to grant plaintiff the tenure he desired.

(Judgment Affirmed For Plaintiff)

DISCUSSION QUESTION

1.   Assume the statute of frauds applied to a particular type of contract
(e.g. a contract which could not be performed within one year from the date
it was made). Would one party be able to enforce the oral contract against
the other if there were no note or memorandum thereof subscribed by the party
to be charged if the two parties shook hands upon making their oral contract
in the presence of three witnesses?

STATUTE OF FRAUDS: GUARANTEES

CASE NO. 13

RICHARDSON PRESS v. ALBRIGHT

234 N.Y. 497   Nov. 1918

INTRODUCTION

The New York Statute of Frauds provides that "every agreement, promise, or undertaking is void, unless it or some note or memorandum thereof be in writing, and subscribed by the party to be charged therewith, or by his lawful agent, if such agreement, promise or undertaking...is a special promise to answer for the debt, default or miscarriage of another person." Under this statute, a party who guarantees payment of another party's debt is liable under his guaranty <u>only if his guaranty is in writing and sub-scribed (i.e. signed at the bottom) by him or his lawful agent</u>. Thus, with one exception, an <u>oral</u> guaranty is <u>unenforceable</u> no matter how many witnesses are present and regardless of the amount guaranteed. The exception is that a party who gives an oral guaranty and receives direct benefit as a result of giving his oral guaranty is liable to the creditor. The legal question arises whether a stockholder who orally guarantees the debt of the corporation in which he is a stockholder receives direct benefit so that he is liable under the exception to the general rule. This case illustrates the judicial analysis by a court to determine whether or not a stockholder receives "direct benefit" when a creditor extends credit to the corporation in which he is a stockholder.

POUND, J. Plaintiff [sues] on a balance of about four thousand dollars alleged to be due on account for materials furnished to Oceanic Publishing Company, a corporation, for which it is alleged that defendant agreed to pay. The complaint was dismissed at the close of plaintiff's evidence and the question is whether sufficient evidence was adduced to establish prima facie defendant's liability as a primary principal debtor.

Defendant was a large stockholder in Oceanic Publishing Company, which was publishing a semi-monthly periodical entitled "Dogs in America" which plaintiff was printing for it. On February 29, 1912, plaintiff brought to the attention of defendant by letter the fact that it had been carrying a large account with his company which was past due and asked him to make some arrangement for the systematic payment of it. On March 1 defendant answered, explaining that he had nothing to do with the direct management of the company; that the president, Vandergrift, conducted the business; that he expected that Vandergrift would soon resign and allow him to assume the management of the paper and that he would be glad to meet the representative of plaintiff to make arrangements for the payment of the back account due it and for future issues. This letter contains no promise to pay plaintiff the debt of Oceanic Publishing Company, but it contains a personal assurance that defendant will furnish Oceanic Publishing Company money to pay for each future issue.

The parties met on March 4, and Aberle, plaintiff's representative, testifies as follows:

"I met Mr. Albright on that morning and Mr. Albright stated to me in substance -- at least he said directly, 'I am now in charge of the Oceanic Publishing Company. I will run it hereafter, Mr. Vandergrift has withdrawn.' He inquired about the size of the account and I had a statement with me, which I showed him. The exact figure I haven't here now. It was something like $3,000. We discussed the thing generally, and he said, 'Well, you can't expect me to pay all of this.' He says, 'I will agree to pay you $1,500, in three payments, $500 weekly. I will further agree to pay each issue hereafter in cash, before you send it out.' This I want to say because we had notified the publishing company that we would not publish hereafter unless the cash was in evidence. That was really in answer to our request. Mr. Davidson, the treasurer of the company, was then present in the office. I asked Mr. Albright to give me this in writing, and he said, 'No, I am an honorable man, my word is my bond. Besides, you have Davidson here as a witness.'" It later appeared that the money was to be forwarded by defendant to Mr. Davidson, the treasurer of the Oceanic Company.

No other promise, original or collateral, was ever made by defendant to plaintiff to pay the debt of Oceanic Publishing Company, and if the promise is to answer for its debt, it is unenforceable, because no note or memorandum in writing was made, sufficient to satisfy the requirements of the Statute of Frauds.

Assuming that defendant in the interview above quoted was speaking for himself and not merely as the representative of his company, it may be said that some of the elements of an original, enforceable, absolute promise on his part to pay $1,500 of the back indebtedness and to pay for future issues unquestionably appear. Technically, at least, defendant had a substantial interest to subserve in making the promise. He had -- or at least he said that he had -- taken control of Oceanic Publishing Company, and was about to reorganize it. It was his desire to have the plaintiff continue to issue "Dogs in America" and perhaps it was a benefit to him to have the periodical appear regularly without a change of publishers. Thus the element of a new consideration moving to him was present. But his beneficial interest was at best remote. Unquestionably the prinicipal debt was not extinguished and credit was still given and to be given to Oceanic Publishing Company.

On this evidence it is urged that defendant became a primary debtor with Oceanic Publishing Company...and that plaintiff was entitled to recover.

But a promise may still be collateral, even though the new consideration moves to the promisor and is beneficial to him. The elements of beneficial interest and new consideration must be present to take the case out of the statute, but the inquiry remains whether the consideration is such that the promisor thereby comes under an independent duty of payment, irrespective of the liability of the principal debtor.... The implied consideration, as indicated by the subsequent dealings of the parties, is that plaintiff will continue to give credit primarily to Oceanic Publishing Company. Plaintiff was notified on March 14, 1912, that defendant admitted no responsibility as to its claim, and it is indisputable that plaintiff thereafter considered that the primary duty of payment remained with the original debtor. It continued to furnish materials and render services to Oceanic Publishing Company, publishing its periodical down to the issue of September 19; it kept no account with defendant on its books; made but one demand on him to furnish money in advance of an issue of the periodical, and that was for the issue of March 7, which brought forth the denial of responsibility; took assignments of accounts from Oceanic Publishing Company; took assignments of stock under an agreement which gave it control of Oceanic Publishing Company; took possession of all its personal property, books and papers, and turned to defendant only when the resources of the original debtor had been completely exhausted. The tenor of the entire transaction was that defendant proposed to help out the Oceanic Company and verbally promised to pay its debts.

When the primary debt continues to exist, the promise of another to pay the debt may be original or it may not be, but it is regarded as original only when the party sought to be charged clearly becomes, within the intention of the parties, a principal debtor primarily liable. If we pick a few phrases from the context, we may draw the conclusion that defendant intended to assume such a relation to plaintiff, but on all the evidence we find but one principal primary debtor and that is Oceanic Publishing Company. The ancient purpose of the Statute of Frauds was to require satisfactory evidence of a promise to answer for the debt of another person and its efficacy should not be wasted by unsubstantial verbal distinctions.

The judgment should be affirmed for the defendant.

DISCUSSION QUESTIONS

1. What could plaintiff printer have done so that defendant would have become a principal debtor who would be primarily liable instead of defendant becoming a guarantor?

2. If a guarantor is liable to the creditor and pays the creditor, does he have any rights against the debtor whose debt he guaranteed?

3. Will a guarantor be liable under his written guaranty if he can prove that the debtor was an infant or insolvent at time he became guarantor or that the debtor subsequently died?

78

STATUTE OF FRAUDS: CONTRACTS FOR THE SALE OF GOODS

CASE NO. 14

THOMAIER v. HOFFMAN CHEVROLET, INC.

410 N.Y.S. 2d 645   Nov. 1978

INTRODUCTION

Article 2 of the Uniform Commercial Code governs the law of contracts for the sale of goods. It contains a statute of frauds section which provides that "a contract for the sale of goods for the price of $500 or more is not enforceable unless there is some writing sufficient to indicate that a contract for sale has been made between the parties and signed by the party against whom enforcement is sought or by his authorized agent or broker." However, there are four instances when an exception is expressly made under the Statute of Frauds section which permits an oral contract to be enforceable even though the oral contract does not satisfy the Statute of Frauds. This case illustrates the general rule and one exception.

GULOTTA, J. On January 4, 1978 plaintiff, Ray Thomaier, placed an order with the defendant dealer, Hoffman Chevrolet, Inc., for a specifically-optioned, 1978 Limited Edition Corvette Coupe. The order form which was utilized in the transaction described the automobile and options desired by the plaintiff, stated its purchase price and provided for delivery to the purchaser "A.S.A.P." (as soon as possible). Plaintiff signed the order form in the place designated for his signature and gave the dealer a substantial deposit in the form of a check for $1,000 to be applied toward the purchase price. This check was subsequently deposited into the account of Hoffman Chevrolet and apparently cleared without incident.

On the same date, Hoffman placed a written order with defendant General Motors Corporation, Chevrolet Motor Division, for the 1978 Limited Edition Corvette Coupe which the plaintiff had just ordered. The order was placed on a form supplied by General Motors, was signed by the dealer, listed the plaintiff's name as "customer" and designated the type of order as "sold" rather than "stock" (i.e., for inventory). Thereafter, by letter dated April 19, 1978 plaintiff was notified by Hoffman that "market conditions" had made his "offer" unacceptable and that his deposit of $1,000 was being refunded. The vehicle was ultimately manufactured by Chevrolet and delivered to Hoffman. Upon the argument of this appeal, Hoffman asserted that the specific vehicle has since been sold to a third party.

The instant controversy revolves about the effect of certain language employed by Hoffman on its purchase order form. In block letters directly above the place where the buyer (e.g., the plaintiff) enters his signature, the form states "THIS ORDER SHALL NOT BECOME BINDING UNTIL ACCEPTED BY DEALER OR HIS AUTHORIZED REPRESENTATIVE." Then, directly below the line where the buyer signs, appear the words "ACCEPTED BY", followed by a blank line, beneath which appear the words "DEALER OR HIS AUTHORIZED REPRESENTATIVE". Neither the dealer nor his authorized representative signed this order form. Accordingly, Hoffman argues, there was no acceptance and therefore no binding contract. In addition, the dealer argues that even if there was a contract, it is unenforceable by virtue of the Statutue of Frauds (see Uniform Commercial Code, sec. 2-201).

Passing only upon the first issue, the Justice at Special Term granted Hoffman's motion for summary judgment dismissing the complaint and denied plaintiff's cross motion for summary judgment. Plaintiff has appealed. The order should be reversed insofar as it has been appealed from.

On the basis of the undisputed facts, a contract was formed as a matter of law no later than the time when the dealer, after having taken and retained plaintiff's substantial ($1,000) down payment, placed an order signed by it for the identical vehicle with the Chevrolet Motor Division of General Motors, designating the vehicle as "sold" and listing the plaintiff's name under the heading "Customer". Section 2-204 of the Uniform Commercial Code provides:

"(1) A contract for sale of goods may be made in any manner sufficient to show agreement, including conduct by both parties which recognizes the existence of such a contract." (Cf. Uniform Commercial Code, sec. 2-207, subd. (3).)

The conduct of Hoffman herein was clearly sufficient to signify an acceptance, notwithstanding its conceded failure to sign the agreement (see Price v. Spielman Motor Sales Co., 261 App. Div. 626, 630, 26 N.Y.S.2d 836, 840 (absence of a written acceptance held unavailing where the defendant-dealer had taken plaintiff's $50 check as a down payment, endorsed it and collected that amount through its bank; the court (per CLOSE, J.) stated: "That act creates an acceptance."); compare and distinguish Scutti Pontiac v. Rund, 92 Misc.2d 881, 402 N.Y.S.2d 144 and Antonucci v. Stevens Dodge, 73 Misc2d 173, 340 N.Y.S.2d 979 (dealers' form contracts similar to the one at bar construed strictly against them)). Section 2-204 of the Uniform Commercial Code further provides:

"(2) An agreement sufficient to constitute a contract for sale may be found even though the moment of its making is undetermined."

Turning to the issue of the Statute of Frauds as a possible bar to recovery, the order form sent by Hoffman to General Motors, either taken alone or when read in conjunction with plaintiff's "purchase order", is a sufficient note or memorandum to satisfy the applicable statute, section 2-201 of the Uniform Commercial Code, which provides, inter alia:

"(1) Except as otherwise provided in this section a contract for the sale of goods for the price of $500 or more is not enforceable by way of action or defense unless there is some writing sufficient to indicate that a contract for sale has been made between the parties and signed by the party against whom enforcement is sought or by his authorized agent or broker. A writing is not insufficient because it omits or incorrectly states a term agreed upon but the contract is not enforceable under this paragraph beyond the quantity of goods shown in such writing."

The Official Comment explains its intended effect (McKinney's Cons. Laws of N.Y., Book 62½, Part 1, Uniform Commercial Code, sec. 2-201, pp. 117-118):

"1. The required writing need not contain all the material terms of the contract and such material terms as are stated need not be precisely stated. All that is required is that the writing afford a basis for believing that the offered oral evidence rests on a real transaction. It may be written in lead pencil on a scratch pad. It need not indicate which party is the buyer and which the seller. The only term which must appear is the quantity term which need not be accurately stated but recovery is limited to the amount stated. The price, time and place of payment or delivery, the general quality of the goods, or any particular warranties may all be omitted. * * *

"Only three definite and invariable requirements as to the memorandum are made by this subsection. First, it must evidence a contract for the sale of goods; second, it must be 'signed', a word which includes any authentication which identifies the party to be charged; and third it must specify a quantity."

Here, the order form sent by Hoffman to General Motors (1) evidences the existence of a contract, (2) is signed by the party to be charged (Hoffman) and (3) implicitly specifies the quantity involved (one). It is therefore sufficient under the applicable Statute of Frauds (cf. General Obligations Law, sec. 5-701). An otherwise sufficient writing directed to a third party is nowhere excluded (see 1 Anderson, Uniform Commercial Code (2d ed.), sec. 2-201:31). However, assuming, arguendo, the absence of a sufficient writing, it is nevertheless my opinion that plaintiff's $1,000 part payment on the indivisible contract operated to take the agreement out of the Statute of Frauds pursuant to section 2-201 (subd. (3), par (c)) of the Uniform Commercial Code, which states:

> "A contract which does not satisfy the requirements of subsection (1) but which is valid in other respects is enforceable.
> *   *   *   *   *   *   *   *   *   *
> "(c) with respect to goods for which payment has been made and accepted or which have been received and accepted (Section 2-606)."

The effect of part payment on a contract for the sale of an indivisible item is not specifically treated by the Uniform Commercial Code, but the weight of authority is clearly to the effect that such payment will render an indivisible oral contract enforceable, notwithstanding the Statute of Frauds. As Dean William D. Hawkland observes (A Transactional Guide To The Uniform Commercial Code, vol. 1 sec. 1.1202, pp. 28-29):

> "By failing to distinguish part payment from partial acceptance and receipt, the section does create one problem, neatly illustrated by Williamson v. Martz (11 PaD. & C.2d 33). Here S orally agreed to sell to B two vats for a total price of $1600, B paying $100 on account. Subsequently B refused to take the vats, and S sued for breach of contract. B set up section 2-201 of the Code as his defense and S countered that the partial payment took the matter out of the Statute of Frauds. The court held for B. Subsection 2-201(3)(c) removes the Statute of Frauds only to the extent of payment. Since the payment of $100 cannot be translated into one vat(worth $800), S cannot enforce the contract to the extent of one vat. There being no way to divide up a vat, S is barred completely by the Statute.
> "Though this case seems to follow the plain meaning of subsection 2-201 (3)(c), the result appears to be excessively restrictive. The payment of $100 indicates a contract whose quantity term must be at least one unit. The court, therefore could safely enforce the agreement to the extent of one vat, and, thus give the S a recovery of $800. The payment of $100 of course, does not necessarily prove a contract for two vats, and the court would not be justified in enforcing the contract for such an amount. But is is difficult to see how the contract

could have contemplated less than one vat, assuming as the court did, that vats are indivisible." (Accord 1 Anderson, Uniform Commercial Code (2d ed.), sec. 2-201:43)

I find the foregoing logic persuasive and determinative on the facts of the instant case * * *

As Judge TOMSON correctly observed in the Starr case (supra, 54 Misc. 2d p. 274, 282 N.Y.S. 2d p. 61):

> "Any other conclusion would work an unconscionable result and would encourage rather than discourage fraud * * * The statute of frauds would be used to cut down the trusting buyer rather than to protect the one who, having made his bargain, parted with a portion of the purchase price as an earnest of his good faith."

The facts of the case at bar serve to reinforce Judge TOMSON's observation.

Based on the foregoing, I believe that the order should be reversed insofar as it has been appealed from, Hoffman's motion for summary judgment denied, plaintiff's cross motion for summary judgment granted and the action remanded to Special Term for further proceedings not inconsistent herewith. In the event that it becomes apparent upon the remand of this action that specific performance (and any appropriate consequential damages) will no longer provide a viable remedy, the court shall proceed to order a full assessment of damages in lieu thereof.

DISCUSSION QUESTIONS

1. Why does the statute of frauds rule applicable to contracts for the sales of goods contain an exception where one party can enforce an oral contract against the other to the extent he has made a part payment which the other party has received and accepted?

2. List three other exceptions to the general statute of frauds rule applicable to contracts for the sale of goods where an oral contract for the sale of goods for a price of $500 or more will be enforceable.

3. The signed order sent by Hoffman to General Motors which ordered the automobile which Hoffman orally sold to the plaintiff was held to be "some writing sufficient to indicate that a contract for sale had been made . . . ." which satisfied the Statute of Frauds. Would the court have so held if such signed order were sent a week later after the oral contract was made?

4. If the contract were for the sale of goods which were divisible, what would the court have held?

STATUTE OF FRAUDS

CASE NO. 15
FARASH v. SYKES DATATRONICS, INC.
465 N.Y.S. 2d 917   July 1983

INTRODUCTION

The New York Statute of Frauds provides that a "contract" for the leasing for a longer period than one year, or for the sale, of any real property, or any interest therein, is void unless the contract or some note or memorandum thereof, expressing the consideration, is in writing, subscribed by the party to be charged, or by his lawful agent thereunto authorized in writing." Thus, the Statute of Frauds bars enforcement of an oral lease of real property for a term longer than one year if the party sue raises the defense of the Statute of Frauds. The interesting question then arises whether a party can recover the expenses he incurs in preparing to perform the contract when he cannot enforce the oral contract itself. The following case answers this question and reveals the legal analysis applied by the court to reach its conclusion.

COOKE, Chief Judge. Plaintiff claims that he and defendant entered an agreement whereby defendant would lease a building owned by plaintiff, who was to complete its renovation and make certain modifications on an expedited basis. Defendant, however, never signed any contract and never occupied the building. Plaintiff commenced this litigation, and defendant unsuccessfully moved to dismiss for failure to state a cause of action. On appeal, the Appellate Division, 90 A.D. 2d 965, 456 N.Y.S.2d 556, reversed with two Justices dissenting in part. For the reasons that follow, we now modify.

Plaintiff pleaded three causes of action in his complaint. The first was to enforce an oral lease for a term longer than one year. This is clearly barred by the Statute of Frauds (General Obligations Law, Sec. 5-703, subd. 2). The third cause of action is premised on the theory that the parties contracted by exchanging promises that plaintiff would perform certain work in his building and defendant would enter into a lease for a term longer than one year. This is nothing more than a contract to enter into a lease; it is also subject to the Statute of Frauds * * * . Hence, the third cause of action was properly dismissed.

Plaintiff's second cause of action, however, is not barred by the Statute of Frauds. It merely seeks to recover for the value of the work performed by plaintiff in reliance on statements by and at the request of defendant. This is not an attempt to enforce an oral lease, but is in disaffirmance of the void contract and so may be maintained (see Baldwin v. Palmer, 10 N.Y. 232, 235). That defendant did not benefit from plaintiff's effort does not require dismissal; plaintiff may recover for those efforts that were to his detriment and that thereby placed him in a worse position * * * . "The contract being void and incapable of enforcement in a court of law, the party * * * rendering the services in pursuance thereof, may treat it as a nullity, and recover * * * the value of the services" (Erben v. Lorillard, 19 N.Y. 299, 302; accord Day v. New York Cent. R.R. Co., 51 N.Y. 583, 590).

The dissent's primary argument is that the second cause of action is equivalent to the third, and is also barred by the Statute of Frauds. It is true that plaintiff attempts to take the contract outside the statute's scope and render it enforceable by arguing that the work done was unequivocally referable to the oral argreement. This should not operate to prevent recovery under a theory of quasi contract as a contract implied by law, which "is not a contract at all but an obligation imposed by law to do justice even though it is clear that no promise was ever made or intended" (Calamari and Perillo, Contracts (2d ed), Sec. 1-12, p. 19). Obviously, the party who seeks both to enforce the contract that is unenforceable by virtue of the Statute of Frauds and to recover under a contract implied in law will present contradictory characterizations. This, however, is proper in our courts where pleading alternative theories of relief is accepted. Moreover, the existence of any real promise is unnecessary; plaintiff's attempt to make his acts directly referable to the unenforceable contract simply is irrelevant.

The authorities all recognize that a promisee should be able to recover in the present situation. "(I)f the improvements made by the plaintiff are on land that is not owned by the defendant and in no respect add to his wealth the plaintiff will not be given judgment for reliance upon the contract that the defendant has broken. For such expenditutes as these in reliance on a contract, the plaintiff can get judgment only in the form of damages for consequential injury" (5 Corbin, Contracts, p. 578 (n. omitted)). Thus, plaintiff may recover for those expenditures he made in reliance on defendant's representations * * * and that he otherwise would not have made. The Restatement provides that an injured party who has not conferred a benefit may obtain restitution, but he or she may "have an action for damages, including one for recovery based on * * * reliance" (Restatement, Contracts 2d, Sec. 370, Comment a). "(T)he injured party has a right to damages based on his reliance interest, including expenditures made in preparation for performance or in performance, less any loss that the party in breach can prove with reasonable certainty the injured party would have suffered had the contract been performed" (Restatement, Contracts 2d, Sec. 349). The Restatement recognizes an action such as is involved here (see Restatement, Contracts 2d, Secs. 139, 439, Comment b).

The dissent relies on Bradkin v. Leverton, 26 N.Y. 2d 192, 257 N.E.2d 643 and Miller v. Schloss, 218 N.Y. 400, 113 N.E. 337 for the proposition that plaintiff can recover only if there is an actual benefit to the defendant. Those cases do not state that there can be no recovery for work performed in the absence of any real benefit to defendant. As stated by Professor Williston (12, Williston, Contracts (3d ed.), pp. 282-284, 286-287 (nn. omitted)): "Again, even though the defendant's liability is imposed by law irrespective of the agreement of the parties, and may, therefore, be called quasi contractual, where the defendant is a wrongdoer, the plaintiff may well preferred, and if a complete restoration of the status quo or its equivalent is impossible the plaintiff should at least be replaced in as good a position as he originally was in, although the defendant is thereby compelled to pay more than the amount which the plaintiff's performance has benefited him.

* * * * * * *

"That is, the law should impose on the wrongdoing defendant a duty to restore the plaintiff's former status, not merely to surrender any enrichment or benefit that he may unjustly hold or have received; although if the market value, the benefit to the defendant of what has been furnished exceeds the cost or value to the plaintiff, there is no reason why recovery or this excess should not be allowed . . . .

A lesson in this area can be taken from Professors Calamari and Perillo: "The basic aim of restitution is to place the plaintiff in the same economic position as he enjoyed prior to contracting. Thus, unless specific restitution is obtained in Equity, the plaintiff's recovery is for the reasonable value of services rendered, goods delivered, or property conveyed less the reasonable value of any counter-performance received by him. The plaintiff recovers the reasonable value of his performance whether or not the defendant in any economic sense benefitted from the performance. The quasi-contractual concept of benefit continues to be recognized by the rule that the defendant must have received the plaintiff's performance; acts merely preparatory to performance will not justify an action for restitution. 'Receipts,' however, is a legal concept rather than a description of physical fact. If what the plaintiff has done is part of the agreed exchange, it is deemed to be 'received' by the defendant." (Calamari and Perillo, Contracts (2d ed.), Sec. 15-4, p. 574 (nn. omitted); see, also, id., Sec. 19-44; Perillo, Restitution in a Contractual Context, 73 Col. L. Rev. 1208, 1219-1225).

We should not be distracted by the manner in which a theory of recovery is titled. On careful consideration, it becomes clear that the commentators do not disagree in result, but only in nomenclature. Whether denominated "acting in reliance" or "restitution," all concur that a promisee who partially performs (e.g., by doing work in a building or at an accelerated pace) at a promisor's request should be allowed to recover the fair and reasonable value of the performance rendered, regardless of the enforceability of the original agreement.

Accordingly, the order of the Appellate Division should be modified, with costs to appellant, by reinstating plaintiff's second cause of action and, as so modified, affirmed. (Dissenting opinion by J. JASON, omitted.)

DISCUSSION QUESTIONS

1. How could the tenant have avoided the result reached by the court? Explain.
2. Does the court's decision result in a weakening of the requirement of the Statute of Frauds? Explain.
3. Was the oral lease held to be void or valid but unenforceable?
4. What legal theory did the court rely on to award damages? Explain.
5. Did the court's decision have the same legal and practical effect as enforcing the oral lease?
6. Does this decision stand for the legal proposition that a party who cannot enforce an oral contract because of the Statute of Frauds, may nevertheless always recover all of the expenses he incurs in preparing to perform?

STATUTE OF FRAUDS—ESSAY QUESTIONS

1. B was the owner of Lot No. 1 on which he had built his home. S owned the adjoining Lots No. 2 and 3 which were undeveloped, along with Lot No. 4 on which S's home was located. B wished to acquire Lot No. 2 in order to protect his home site from crowding if Lot No. 2 should be sold to a stranger. Meeting S on the street on January 2, he explained his wish to acquire Lot No. 2 and offered to buy it from S for $7,500 cash. S agreed and promised to deliver a deed to Lot No. 2 in 4 weeks. B paid to S $500 as a deposit or down payment towards the purchase price of $7,500. On February 1, S told B that he had changed his mind. B demands that S perform the contract. S contends that if there is any contract, it is unenforceable.

(a) Was there an offer and acceptance sufficient to constitute a contract? Explain.

(b) In an action by B against S to recover damages for breach of contract, judgment for whom? Explain.

(c) Assuming the contract is enforceable, will a court grant B a decree of specific performance against S upon B paying the balance of $7,000.

Assume that on January 10, B sent S his check for $500 bearing the notation "On account of purchase price of Lot No. 2" and that S cashed the check, but later refused to convey Lot No. 2.

(d) Would B's payment constitute sufficient part performance to enable B to enforce the contract against S? Explain.

(e) If the contract is not enforceable, may B recover his $500? Explain.

Assume that in addition to the payment, B, with S's knowledge and consent, entered on Lot No. 2 and had it cleared of brush on January 20 at a cost of $150, but S still refused to convey.

(f) Would B be entitled to obtain a decree of specific performance to compel S to deliver a deed to Lot No. 2 to B upon B paying the balance of $7,000? Explain.

(g) Would B be entitled to recover his payment plus the cost of clearing the land? Explain.

Assume that on March 1, B instituted a suit for specific performance and that S denied he had agreed to sell. On the trial the Court decided that B was telling the truth, and ordered S to execute and deliver to B a deed to Lot No. 2 upon paying the balance of $7,000.

(h) Is S entitled to have the decision reversed on appeal, if on the appeal S raises for the first time the defense that his agreement was not in writing? Explain.

2. Assume that in the preceding problem S had sent B a receipt for the $500 reading as follows:

"January 11

Received from B $500 on account of $7,500 purchase price of Lot No. 2 at 27 Y Street, Albans, N.Y. Closing in 4 weeks.

(Signed)   S."

(a)   Would B be entitled to a decree of specific performance against S? Explain.

Assume that S is willing to perform but that B refuses.

(b)   Would S be entitled to a decree of specific performance against b? Explain.

(c)   If S decides not to try to enforce the contract against B, is B entitled to the return of his $500 payment? Explain.

3.   On December 15, L agreed orally with T to lease a store to T in Manhattan at $2,500 per month for one year starting January 1.

(a)   Is the oral agreement enforceable? Explain.

Assume that the lease was for three years, that T moved in and paid the rent monthly for six months and that than L notified T to vacate.

(b)   Is the oral agreement enforceable by T for the balance of the three year term? Explain.

(c)   Is the oral agreement enforceable by T for an additional six months? Explain.

Assume that T, with L's consent, had spent $8,000 in installing a new decorative store front.

(d)   Is the oral agreement enforceable by T for the balance of the three year term? Explain.

4.   L and T signed a five year lease for a store in Manhattan at $2,500 per month. Before the lease expired L and T orally agreed that L would repaint the store and that T would thereafter pay $2,600 for the balance of the lease term.

(a)   Is the oral agreement enforceable if, at the time it was made, the lease had 2 years to run? Explain.

(b)   If it had nine months to run? Explain.

5.   On January 15 S and B concluded an oral agreement concerning the sale of
S's apple orchard to B. Payment of the $50,000 purchase price and delivery
of the deed was to take place on March 15.

(a)   Assume that on February 1, B made a $5,000 down payment which S accepted.
      On March 15, B tendered the $45,000 balance to S who refused to accept
      it and offered to return the $5,000 previously paid to him. Will B
      succeed in a suit for breach of contract against S? Explain.

(b)   Assume that on February 10, S wrote B a signed letter which set forth
      all material facts and confirmed their oral agreement. On March 15,
      when B tendered to S the $50,000 purchase price, S refused to accept it
      and refused to deliver the deed.

      (1)   Will B succeed in a suit for breach of contract against S? Explain.

      (2)   Assuming that B has a cause of action against S, is the remedy of
            specific performance available? Explain.

6.   L, a landlord, on December 15, entered into an oral agreement with T to
lease apartment 5W to T for one year starting on January 1 at a rental of
$400 per month. On the same day he hired J as superintendent of the building
for a period of one year starting January 1 at a salary of $800 per month.
On December 20 L changes his mind and notifies T and J that he will not rent
to T or employ J.

(a)   In an action by T against L, judgment for whom if L pleads the Statute
      of Frauds as a defense? Explain.

(b)   In an action by J against L, judgment for whom if L pleads the Statute
      of Frauds as a defense? Explain.

7.   M orally promised W that if W would take care of M during the remainder
of his life, W would have a claim against M's estate for $5,000 and M would
leave W his library collection in his will. W performed fully but on M's
death it was discovered that M had left no will, and that his entire estate
of $50,000 will go to his son. A disinterested witness will testify to the
agreement. What are W's rights?

8.   B, wishing to start his own business, borrowed $15,000 from L. He orally
agreed to repay the loan in two years. B refused to pay when the loan became due. L sued B for breach of contract. B asserts the oral contract is
unenforceable according to the statute of frauds. Judgment for whom?
Explain.

9.   A, 21 years old, and a college student, went to Brentwood Department
Store to buy a new spring outfit. He selected two new suits and a topcoat
for $450 and asked to open up a charge account. The credit manager was
willing to open the account but was concerned about payment. A referred him

to F, his father. On the telephone F told the credit manager, "Go ahead, open the account for him. It will teach him to stand on his own feet if he has to pay his own bills. But don't worry, if A doesn't pay I will." The clothes are given to A and billed to him. He fails to pay. The store sues F who pleads the Statute of Frauds as a defense. Judgment for whom? Explain.

10. Assume in the previous question that the credit manager refused to open the account for A, that he called F on the telephone and F said, "I have an account with your store. Give A the clothes and charge them to my account." The clothes are given to A. Is F liable if he pleads the Statute of Frauds as a defense? Explain.

11. C, a general contractor, had a contract with a local school board for the construction of a $15,000,000 school. He subcontracted the electrical work to W. W had completed a substantial part of the subcontract when he met with financial reverses which made it impossible for him to pay his supplier for materials already delivered. He was refused further deliveries of materials by his supplier until the amount owing was paid. C orally promised the supplier that he would pay W's debt if W did not provided the supplier would complete delivery so that the school could be completed on schedule. The supplier agreed to C's offer and supplied the necessary materials. Upon completion of the electrical work the supplier billed C when W defaulted in making payment to the supplier. C refused to pay contending that the application of the statute of frauds rendered his oral guaranty unenforceable. Is C correct? Explain.

12. S and B entered into an oral agreement under which S agreed to sell to B 8 renovated air-conditioners at $200 each; delivery at B's place of business ten days later; payment C.O.D. B refused to complete the purchase.
(a) In a suit by S against B, would S be entitled to a decree of specific performance if B did not plead the Statute of Frauds?

Assume that in a suit by S against B for damages, (B) pleaded the Statute of Frauds as a defense.
(b) Will S be entitled to judgment, if he can prove:
    (1) that B made a down payment of $200? Explain
    (2) that B took 4 air-conditioners at the time the agreement was made? Explain.

13. C a processor of women's clothes, telephoned D, a dealer in sewing machines on March 1 and ordered a Model M machine for $2,500 as described in D's catalog. On March 2 D telephoned M, the manufacturer, and ordered the machine for $2,000.

On March 3 M sent D a confirmatory letter in which M outlined in detail the arrangement between D and M. D received this letter on March 4. On March 5 D sent a similar letter to C which C received on March 7. On March 15 C wrote D cancelling his order.

D received this letter on March 17. D in turn wrote M on March 18 requesting M to cancel his order. M refused, whereupon D informed C that he was compelled to hold him to his order in view of M's attitude.

(a)   May M hold D to his contract: *No*

    (1)   under common law? Explain. *STATUTE OF FRAUDS*

    (2)   under the Uniform Commercial Code? Explain. *YES ORAL BETWEEN MERCHANTS IF CONFIM IS REC*

(b)   May D hold C to his contract:

    (1)   under common law? Explain. *No*

    (2)   under the Uniform Commercial Code? Explain. *No OBJECTED WITHIN 10 DAYS*

14.   During the examination of the financial statements of the W Watch Company the following problem was discovered. On January 16, C, one of W's salesmen, called upon P, the vice president of purchasing for X Department Stores. He showed P the new line of mod watches with large, bright-colored faces. P ordered 150 watches from $5 to $20 each at a total cost of $1,475. Delivery was to be made not later than March 15. C wrote the orders in his order book as P orally indicated the quantity of each watch he desired. Neither party signed anything.

C promptly submitted the X Department Stores' order to the sales department. The next day the order was recorded and a memorandum was sent to X Department Stores in care of P. The memorandum described the transaction indicating the number and prices of the watches purchased and was signed by S. A. Williams, vice president of marketing; however, the total price and delivery terms were excluded erroneously.

P received the memo on January 20. He read it and placed it in his goods-on-order file. On February 20, the market for mod watches collapsed and fair market value of the watches dropped to approximately $700. P promptly notified W Watch Company by phone that X Department Stores was not interested in the mod watches and would refuse delivery. W Watch Company filed suit against X Department Stores to recover damages for breach of contract. X Department Stores contends (1) there is no contract and (2) if there is a contract it is unenforceable under the Statute of Frauds.

Will W Watch Company prevail in its suit against X Department Stores? Explain.

2 —

A
C
B
A
D
A
D
D

Question 1. The following question begins by a statement of facts
followed by two independent statements numbered I and II. You are to
evaluate each statement and determine whether it is true. Your answer
for the question should be selected from the following responses:

    a. I only is true.
    b. II only is true.
    c. Both I and II are true.
    d. Neither I nor II is true.

On September 4, Farr offered to sell his farm to Jackson for $10,000.
The offer was received by Jackson on September 7. Jackson wrote back on
September 10, asking whether or not this was a "firm price." Farr replied,
"I will not accept a penny less."

Jackson accepted Farr's offer by letter mailed September 17. The letter
was received by Farr on September 21. Farr refuses to perform.

    I. The Statute of Frauds is applicable to the above transaction.
    II. If a contract was formed, specific performance would be an appropri-
        ate remedy under the circumstances.

2. The Statute of Frauds

    a. Does not require that all the terms and provisions of the agreement
       of the parties be contained in a single document.
    b. Requires that both parties sign the written contract.
    c. Defines what constitutes fraudulent conduct by a party in inducing
       another to make a contract.
    d. Applies to all contracts which by their terms require the payment of
       $500 or more.

3. The purpose of the Statute of Frauds is to render agreements unenforceable
   unless they are

    a. Legal.
    b. Not fraudulent.
    c. Written.
    d. Supported by consideration.

4. On May 1, James Arthur orally agreed to a contract as a sales representative of Wonder Insurance Company. The contract terminates April 30, of
   the following year and provides for $10,000 salary plus 1% of the
   insurance premiums charged by the company on the policies which he writes.
   Under these circumstances

    a. Arthur is an undisclosed principal.
    b. The contract in question is not subject to the Statute of Frauds.
    c. Arthur would be permitted to delegate his performance to another
       equally competent person.

d. Arthur's contract is too indefinite and uncertain to be enforceable.

5. Potter orally engaged Arthur as a salesman on April 5, 1980, for exactly one year commencing on May 1, 1980. Which of the following is correct insofar as the parties are concerned?

a) If Arthur refuses to perform and takes another job on April 14, 1980, he will not be liable if he pleads the Statute of Frauds.
b. The contract need not be in writing since its duration is exactly one year.
c. Potter may obtain the remedy of specific performance if Arthur refuses to perform.
d. The parol evidence rule applies.

6. Franklin engaged in extensive negotiations with Harlow in connection with the proposed purchase of Harlow's factory building. Which of the following must Franklin satisfy to establish a binding contract for the purchase of the property in question?

a. Franklin must obtain an agreement signed by both parties.
b. Franklin must obtain a formal, detailed, all-inclusive document.
c. Franklin must pay some earnest money at the time of final agreement.
d. Franklin must have a writing signed by Harlow which states the essential terms of the understanding.

7. Exeter Industries, Inc., orally engaged Werglow as one of its district sales managers for an 8-month period commencing April 1. Werglow commenced work on that date and performed his duties in a highly competent manner for several months. On October 1, the company gave Werglow a notice of termination as of November 1, citing a downturn in the market for its product. Werglow sues seeking either specific performance or damages for breach of contract. Exeter pleads the Statute of Frauds and/or a justified dismissal due to the economic situation. What is the   outcome of the lawsuit.

a. Werglow will prevail because the Statute of Frauds does not apply to contracts such as his.
b. Werglow will prevail because he has partially performed under the terms of the contract.
c. Werglow will lose because the reason for his termination was caused by economic factors beyond Exeter's control.
d. Werglow will lose because such a contract must be in writing and signed by a proper agent of Exeter.

8. Ambrose agreed to pay a specified rental to Lord under a lease agreement calling for rental of one of two identical side-by-side theaters owned by Lord (Theater "A" and Theater "B"). It was later agreed that Theater "A" would be used for the run of the play but not to exceed nine months in return for a fixed weekly fee plus a percentage of gross receipts. Under these circumstances

a. The lease if oral would be void.
b. The lease, even if written, would be illusory since no set lease term is provided.
c. If the interior of Theater "A" was burned out by fire, Lord would probably be excused from performance even though Theater "B" was available and Ambrose was willing to accept the substitution.
d. The lease if oral would be valid and not voidable.

9. Matson loaned Donalds $1,000 at 8% interest for one year. Two weeks before the due date, Matson called upon Donalds and obtained his agreement in writing to modify the terms of the loan. It was agreed that on the due date Donalds would pay $850 to Cranston to whom Matson owed that amount, and pay the balance plus interest to his son Arthur, to whom he wished to make a gift.

Which of the following statements is legally valid with respect to the events described above?

a. Because Matson never received the interest on the Donalds loan, he will not have to include it in his gross income for federal income tax purposes.
b. Matson has irrevocably assigned the debt to Cranston and Arthur.
c. In the event of default by Donalds, Cranston must first proceed against him before seeking recourse against Matson.
d. Neither of the agreements between Matson and Donalds needs to be in writing.

10. Stone engaged Parker to perform personal services for $1,000 a month for a period of three months. The contract was entered into orally on August 1, 1983, and performance was to commence January 1, 1984. On September 15, Parker anticipatorily repudiated the contract. As a result, Stone can

a. Obtain specific performance.
b. Not assign her rights to damages under the contract to a third party.
c. Immediately sue for breach of contract.
d. Not enforce the contract against Parker since the contract is oral.

CONSIDERATION

NEW YORK GENERAL OBLIGATIONS LAW:

Section 5-1101. Agreements Relating to Securities

An agreement, promise or undertaking for the purchase, sale, transfer, assignment or delivery of a certificate or other evidence of debt, issued by the United States or by any state, or a municipal or other corporation, or of any share or interest in the stock of any bank corporation or joint stock association, incorporated or organized under the laws of the United States or of any state, is not void or voidable, for want of consideration, or because of the nonpayment of consideration, or because the vendor, at the time of making such contract, is not the owner or possessor of the certificate or certificates or other evidence of debt, share or interest.

Section 5-1103. Written Agreement For Modification Or Discharge

An agreement, promise or undertaking to change or modify, or to discharge in whole or in part, any contract, obligation, or lease, or any mortgage or other security interest in personal or real property, shall not be invalid because of the absence of consideration, provided that the agreement, promise or undertaking changing, modifying, or discharging such contract, obligation, lease, mortgage or security interest, shall be in writing and signed by the party against whom it is sought to enforce the change, modification or discharge, or by his agent. (1963 - originally enacted in 1897).

Section 5-1105. Written Promise Expressing Past Consideration

A promise in writing and signed by the promisor or by his agent shall not be denied effect as a valid contractual obligation on the ground that consideration for the promise is past or executed, if the consideration is expressed in the writing and is proved to have been given or performed and would be a valid consideration but for the time when it was given or performed. (1963 - originally enacted in 1941).

Section 5-1107. Written Assignment

An assignment shall not be denied the effect of irrevocably transferring the assignor's rights because of the absence of consideration, if such assignment is in writing and signed by the assignor, or by his agent. (1963 - originally enacted in 1941).

Section 5-1113. Written Or Published Promise of Reward

A promise to pay a reward for return of lost or mislaid property is not unenforceable because of absence of consideration if the promise was made in

95

writing or the promisor caused it to be published. (1963)

Section 5-1115. Promises And Warranties In Conveyance Made Without
Consideration

A promise or warranty by the grantor in a deed or conveyance of an estate
or interest in real property and acknowledged or proved in the manner prescribed by law to entitle it to be recorded shall not be denied effect
because of the absence of consideration, if no consideration was intended.
(1963 - originally enacted in 1944, and was previously contained in Real
Property Law 283).

Section 15-303. Release In Writing Without Consideration Or Seal

A written instrument which purports to be a total or partial release of
all claims, debts, demands or obligations, or a total or partial release of
any particular claim, debt, demand or obligation, or a release or discharge in
whole or in part of a mortgage, lien, security interest or charge upon personal or real property shall not be invalid because of the absence of consideration or of a seal. (1963 - originally enacted in 1936, and was derived
from Debtor and Creditor Law 243).

Section 15-301. When Written Agreement Or Other Instrument Cannot Be
Changed By Oral Executory Agreement, Or Discharged Or
Terminated By Oral Executory Agreement Or Oral Consent
Or By Oral Notice

1. A written agreement or other written instrument which contains a
provision to the effect that it cannot be changed orally, cannot be changed
by an executory agreement unless such executory agreement is in writing and
signed by the party against whom enforcement of the change is sought or by
his agent.

2. A written agreement or other written instrument which contains a
provision to the effect that it cannot be terminated orally, cannot be discharged by an executory agreement unless such executory agreement is in
writing and signed by the party against whom enforcement of the discharge
is sought, or by his agent, and cannot be terminated by mutual consent unless
such termination is effected by an executed accord and satisfaction other than
the substitution of one executory contract for another, or is evidenced by a
writing signed by the party against whom it is sought to enforce the termination, or by his agent.

3. a. A discharge or partial discharge of obligations under a written
agreement or other written instrument is a change of the agreement or instrument for the purpose of subdivision one of this section and is not a discharge
or termination for the purpose of subdivision two, unless all executory

obligations under the agreement or instrument are discharged or terminated.

b. A discharge or termination of all executory obligations under a written agreement or other written instrument is a discharge or termination for the purpose of subdivision two even though accrued obligations remaining unperformed at the date of the discharge or termination are not affected by it.

c. If a written agreement or other written instrument containing provision that it cannot be terminated orally also provides for termination or discharge on notice by one or either party, both subdivision two and subdivision four of this section apply whether or not the agreement or other instrument states specifically that the notice must be in writing.

4. If a written agreement or other written instrument contains a provision for termination or discharge on written notice by one or either party, the requirement that such notice be in writing cannot be waived except by a writing signed by the party against whom enforcement of the waiver is sought or by his agent.

5. If executed by an agent, any agreement, evidence of termination, notice of termination or waiver, required by this section to be in writing, which affects or relates to real property or an interest therein as defined in section 5-101 in any manner stated in subdivisions one or two of section 5-703 of this chapter shall be void unless such agent was thereunto authorized in writing.

6. As used in this section the term "agreement" includes promise and undertaking. (1963 - originally enacted in 1941 and was derived from Personal Property Law 33-c(1) and Real Property Law 282(1)).

See, also 5-1109 "Written Irrevocable Offer" included in Formation of Contracts - Offer and Acceptance

CONSIDERATION - ACCORD AND SATISFACTION

NEW YORK GENERAL OBLIGATIONS LAW

Section 15-501. Executory Accord

1. Executory accord as used in this section means an agreement embodying a promise express or implied to accept at some future time a stipulated performance in satisfaction or discharge in whole or in part of any present claim, cause of action, contract, obligation, or lease, or any mortgage or other security interest in personal or real property, and a promise express or implied to render such performance in satisfaction or in discharge of such

claim, cause of action, contract, obligation, lease, mortgage or security interest.

2. An executory accord shall not be denied effect as a defense or as the basis of an action or counterclaim by reason of the fact that the satisfaction or discharge of the claim, cause of action, contract, obligation, lease, mortgage or other security interest which is the subject of the accord was to occur at a time after the making of the accord, provided the promise of the party against whom it is sought to enforce the accord is in writing and signed by such party or by his agent. If executed by an agent, any promise required by this section to be in writing which affects or relates to real property or an interest therein as defined in section 5-101 in any manner stated in subdivision one or two of section 5-703 of this chapter shall be void unless such agent was thereunto authorized in writing.

3. If an executory accord is not performed according to its terms by one party, the other party shall be entitled either to assert his rights under the claim, cause of action, contract, obligation, lease, mortgage or other security interest which is the subject of the accord, or to assert his right under the accord. (1963)

Section 15-503. Offer of Accord Followed By Tender-See Formation Of Contracts - Offer and Acceptance

CONSIDERATION - SEALS INOPERATIVE

NEW YORK GENERAL CONSTRUCTION LAW:

Section 44-a. Seal On Written Instrument

Except as otherwise expressly provided by statute, the presence or absence of a seal upon a written instrument executed after August thirty-first-nineteen hundred forty-one shall be without legal effect. (eff. Sept. 1, 1963)

NEW YORK U.C.C. Section 2-203. Seals Inoperative

The affixing of a seal to a writing evidencing a contract for sale or an offer to buy or sell goods does not constitute the writing a sealed instrument and the law with respect to sealed instruments does not apply to such a contract or offer.

CONSIDERATION - UNIFORM COMMERCIAL CODE SECTIONS

Section 1-107. Waiver Or Renunciation Of Claim Or Right After Breach

Any claim or right arising out of an alleged breach can be discharged in whole or in part without consideration by a written waiver or renunciation signed and delivered by the aggrieved party.

Section 1-207. Performance Or Acceptance Under Reservation Of Rights

A party who with explicit reservation of rights performs or promises performance or assents to performance in a manner demanded or offered by the other party does not thereby prejudice the rights reserved. Such words as "without prejudice", "under protest" or the like are sufficient.

Section 2-209.   Modification Rescission And Waiver

(1)   An agreement modifying a contract within this Article needs no consideration to be binding.

(2)   A signed agreement which excludes modification or rescission except by a signed writing cannot be otherwise modified or rescinded, but except as between merchants such a requirement on a form supplied by the merchant must be separately signed by the other party.

(3)   The requirements of the statute of frauds section of this Article (Section 2-201) must be satisfied if the contract as modified is within its provisions.

(4)   Although an attempt at modification or rescission does not satisfy the requirements of subsection (2) or (3) it can operate as a waiver.

(5)   A party who has made a waiver affecting an executory portion of the contract may retract the waiver by reasonable notification received by the other party that strict performance will be required of any term waived, unless the retraction would be unjust in view of a material change of position in reliance on the waiver.

See, also

    UCC 2-205 "Firm Offers"
    UCC 2-306 "Output, Requirements and Exclusive Dealings"

Said statutes are included in Formation of Contracts - Offer and Acceptance.

CONSIDERATION - UNIFORM COMMERCIAL CODE - COMMERCIAL PAPER

Section 3-408.   Consideration

Want or failure of consideration is a defense as against any person not having the rights of a holder in due course (Section 3-305), except that no consideration is necessary for an instrument or obligation given in payment of or as security for an antecedent obligation of any kind. Nothing in this section shall be taken to displace any statute outside this Act under which a promise is enforceable notwithstanding lack or failure of consideration. Partial failure of consideration is a defense pro tanto whether or not the failure is in an ascertained or liquidated amount.

CONSIDERATION

LEGAL DETRIMENT

CASE NO. 16

HAMER v. SIDWAY

124 N.Y. 538   April 1891

INTRODUCTION

Virtually every contract requires that consideration be given by each party to the other in order for the contract to be enforceable. The legal question arises whether consideration is given when a party incurs a legal detriment by giving up a legal right if the other party receives no benefit. This leading case illustrates the rule of law that legal detriment incurred and not benefit received determines if consideration exists.

PARKER, J. The question which provoked the most discussion by counsel on this appeal, and which lies at the foundation of plaintiff's asserted right of recovery, is whether by virtue of a contract defendant's testator William E. Story became indebted to his nephew William E. Story, 2d, on his twenty-first birthday in the sum of five thousand dollars. The trial court found as a fact that "on the 20th day of March, 1869,...William E. Story agreed to and with William E. Story, 2d, that if he would refrain from drinking liquor, using tobacco, swearing, and playing cards or billiards for money until he should become 21 years of age then he, the said William E. Story, would at that time pay him, the said William E. Story, 2d, the sum of $5,000 for such refraining, to which the said William E. Story, 2d, agreed," and that he "in all things fully performed his part of said agreement."

The defendant contends that the contract was without consideration to support it, and, therefore, invalid. He asserts that the promisee by refraining from the use of liquor and tobacco was not harmed but benefited: that that which he did was best for him to do independently of his uncle's promise, and insists that it follows that unless the promisor was benefited, the contract was without consideration. A contention, which if well founded, would seem to leave open for controversy in many cases whether that which the promisee did or omitted to do was, in fact, of such benefit to him as to leave no consideration to support the enforcement of the promisor's agreement. Such a rule could not be tolerated, and is without foundation in the law. The Exchequer Chamber, in 1875, defined consideration as follows: "A valuable consideration in the sense of the law may consist either in some right, interest, profit or benefit accuring to the one party, or some forbearance, detriment, loss or responsibility given, suffered or undertaken by the other." Courts "will not ask whether the thing which forms the consideration does in fact benefit the promisee or a third party, or is of any substantial value to anyone. It is enough that something is promised, done, forborne or suffered by the party to whom the promise is made as consideration for the promise made to him." (Anson's Prin. of Con. 63.)

"In general a waiver of any legal right at the request of another party

100

is a suffiecient consideration for a promise." (Parsons of Contracts, 444.)

"Any damage, or suspension, or forbearance of a right will be sufficient to sustain a promise." (Kent, vol. 2, 465, 12th ed.)

Pollock, in his work on contracts, page 166, after citing the definition given by the Exchequer Chamber already quoted, says: "The second branch of this judicial description is really the most important one. Consideration means not so much more that one party is profiting as that the other abandons some legal right in the present or limits his legal freedom of action in the future as an inducement for the promise of the first."

Now, applying this rule to the facts before us, the promisee used tobacco, occasionally drank liquor, and he had a legal right to do so. That right he abandoned for a period of years upon the strength of the promise of the testator that for such forbearance he would give him $5,000. We need not speculate on the effort which may have been required to give up the use of those stimulants. It is sufficient that he restricted his lawful freedom of action within certain prescribed limits upon the faith of his uncle's agreement, and now having fully performed the conditions imposed, it is of no moment whether such performance actually proved a benefit to the promisor, and the court will not inquire into it, but were it a proper subject or inquiry, we see nothing in this record that would permit a determination that the uncle was not benefited in a legal sense.

The cases cited by the defendant on this question are not in point.... In Vanderbilt v. Schreyer the plaintiff contracted with defendant to build a house, agreeing to accept in part payment therefor a specific bond and mortgage. Afterwards he refused to finish his contract unless the defendant would guarantee its payment, which was done. It was held that the guarantee could not be enforced for want of consideration. For in building the house the plaintiff only did that which he had contracted to do. And in Robinson v. Jeweet, the court simply held that "The performance of an act which the party is under a legal obligation to perform cannot constitute a consideration for a new contract."

(Judgment for plaintiff.)

CONSIDERATION

SUFFICIENCY OF CONSIDERATION

CASE NO. 17

JAFFRAY v. DAVIS

124 N.Y. 164   Jan. 1891

INTRODUCTION

Creditors and their debtors sometimes enter into agreements pursuant to which a creditor agrees to accept a lesser sum as payment in full of a larger debt. Whether the debtor can then avoid liability for the balance due, after he pays the lesser sum agreed to, depends on whether the debtor has given the creditor any consideration for the creditor's agreement to accept the lesser sum as payment in full. This case illustrates one kind of consideration frequently given by a debtor. When such an agreement is entered into, supported by consideration, and fully performed, there is an accord and satisfaction and the original debt is discharged.

POTTER, J. The facts found by the trial court in this case were agreed upon. They are simple and present a familiar question of law. The facts are that defendants were owing plaintiffs on the 8th day of December, 1886, for goods sold between that date and the May previous at an agreed price, the sum of $7,714.37, and that on the 27th of the same December, the defendants delivered to the plaintiffs their three promissory notes amounting in the aggregate to three thousand four hundred and sixty-two twenty-four-one-hundredths dollars secured by a chattel mortgage on the stock, fixtures and other property of defendants, located in East Saginaw, Michigan, which said notes and chattel mortgage were received by plaintiffs under an agreement to accept same in full satisfaction and discharge of said indebtedness. "That said notes have all been paid and said mortgage discharged or record."

The question of law arising from these facts and presented to this court for its determination is whether such agreement, with full performance, constitutes a bar to this action, which was brought after such performance to recover the balance of such indebtedness over the sum so secured and paid.

One of the elements embraced in the question presents upon this appeal is, viz., whether the payment of a sum less than the amount of a liquidated debt under an agreement to accept the same in satisfaction of such debt forms a bar to the recovery of the balance of the debt. This single question was presented to the English court in 1602, when it was resolved (if not decided) in Pinnel's case "that payment of a lesser sum on the day in satisfaction of a greater, cannot be any satisfaction for the whole," and that this is so, although it was agreed that such payment should satisfy the whole. This simple question has since arisen in the English courts and in the courts of this country in almost numberless instances, and has received the same solution, notwithstanding the courts, while so ruling, have rarely failed, upon any recurrence of the question, to criticize and condemn its reasonableness, justice, fairness or honesty. No respectable authority that I have been able to find has, after such unanimous dispproval by all the courts, held otherwise than was held in Pinnel case....

The steadfast adhesion to this doctrine by the courts in spite of the current of condemnation by the individual judges of the court, and in the face of the demands and conveniences of a much greater business and more extensive mercantile dealings and operations, demonstrate the force of the doctrine of stare decisis. But the doctrine of stare decisis is further illustrated by the course of judicial decisions upon this subject, for while the courts still hold to the doctrine of the Pinnel and Cumber and Wane cases they have seemed to seize with avidity upon any consideration to support the agreement to accept the lesser sum in satisfaction of the larger, or in other words to extract if possible from the circumstances of each case a consideration for the new agreement, and to substitute the new agreement in place of the old and thus to form a defense to the action brought upon the old agreement.

In some states, notably Maine and Georgia, the legislature, in order to avoid the harshness of the rule under consideration, have by statute changed the law upon that subject by providing, "no action can be maintained upon a demand which has been canceled by the receipt of any sum of money less than the amount legally due thereon, or for any good and valuable consideration however small."

In the case at bar the defendants gave their promissory notes upon time for one-half of the debt they owed plaintiff, and also gave plaintiff a chattel mortgage on the stock, fixtures and other personal property of the defendants under an agreement with plaintiff, to accept the same in full satisfaction and discharge of said indebtedness. Defendants paid the notes as they became due, and plaintiff then discharged the mortgage. Under the cases above cited, and upon principle, this new agreement was supported by a sufficient consideration to make it a valid agreement, and this agreement was by the parties substituted in place of the former. The consideration of the new agreement was that the plaintiff, in place of an open book account for goods sold, got the defendants' promissory notes, probably negotiable in form, signed by defendants, thus saving the plaintiff perhaps trouble or expense of proving their account, and got security upon all the defendants' personal property for the payment of the sum specified in the notes, where before they had no security.

It was some trouble at least, and perhaps some expense to the defendants to execute and deliver the security, and they deprived themselves of the legal ownership, or of any exemptions or the power of disposing of this property, and gave the plaintiff such ownership as against the defendants, and the claims thereto of defendants' creditors, if there were any.

It seems to me, upon principle and the decisions of this state and of quite all of the other states, the transactions between the plaintiff and the defendants constitute a bar to this action. All that is necessary to produce satisfaction of the former agreement is a sufficient consideration to support the substituted agreement. The doctrine is fully sustained in the opion of Judge ANDREWS in Allison v. Abendroth, from which I quote: "But it is held

that where there is an independent consideration, or the creditor receives any
benefit or is put in a better position, or one from which there may be legal
possibility of benefit to which he was not entitled except for the agreement,
then the agreement is not nudum pactum, and the doctrine of the common law to
which we have adverted has no application." Upon this distinction the cases
rest which hold that the acceptance by the creditor in discharge of the debt
of a different thing from that contracted to be paid, although of much less
pecuniary value or amount, is a good satisfaction, as for example, a negotiable instrument binding the debtor and a third person for a smaller sum....
Following the same principle it is held that when the debtor enters into a
new contract with the creditor to do something which he was not bound to do
by the original contract, the new contract is a good accord and satisfaction
if so agreed. The case of accepting the sole liability of one of two joint
debtors or copartners in satisfaction of the joint or copartnership debt is an
illustration. This is held to be a good satisfaction, because the sole
liability of one of two debtors "may be more beneficial than the joint liability of both, either in respect of the solvency or of the parties, or the convenience of the remedy." In perfect accord with this principle is the recent
case in this court of Ludington v. Bell, in which it was held that the acceptance by a creditor of the individual note of one of the members of a copartnership after dissolution for a portion of the copartnership debt was a good
consideration for the creditor's agreement to discharge the maker from further liability....

(Judgment for defendants.)

CONSIDERATION

ACCORD AND SATISFACTION

CASE NO. 13

SCHNELL v. PERLMON

238 N.Y. 362   June 1924

INTRODUCTION

In many cases between a creditor and debtor there is a good faith dispute as to whether any money is owed or how much money is owed. In such cases, the debtor frequently tenders a check to the creditor for a lesser sum and writes the legend "paid in full" on the check or indicates that fact in an accompanying letter. The creditor usually crosses out the legend on the check, deposits the check and informs the debtor that he still claims the balance due. The legal question arises whether the creditor is entitled to collect the balance. This case illustrates the rule of law as to the requirements for an unliquidated claim and an accord and satisfaction between a creditor and debtor which discharges the original debt.

CRANE, J. This action is brought to recover an alleged balance due for goods, wares and merchandise sold by the plaintiffs to the defendant. Defendant pleaded an accord and satisfaction.

The trial court directed a verdict for the plaintiffs for the full amount claimed, and the judgment entered theron has been unanimously affirmed by the Appellate Division. That court, however, granted leave to appeal to this court, certifying that in its opinion there is a question of law involved which ought to be reviewed by us.

The question of law referred to arises through the payment by the defendant of an amount less than the agreed price in full payment and satisfaction of the claimed debt. As in all like cases the result depends very much upon the facts of each case, it is therefore, necessary at the outset to state fully the transaction between these parties. The plaintiffs, trading under the firm name of H. Schnell & Co., sold to Sol Perlmon, the defendant, trading under the firm name of Detroit Celery & Produce Co., ten cars of Spanish onions, pursuant to the terms of a written contract dated November 14, 1921. These ten carloads were to consit of 2,500 crates to be shipped by the Michigan Central Railroad from New York to Detroit; all goods sold F.O.B. New York, delivery to the common carrier being delivery to the purchaser. When the onions arrived in Detroit some of them were found to be in a defective condition due to decay consisting of fusarean rot, slimy soft rot, and a bacteria heart rot involving the greater portion of the onions. The defendant had the onions inspected by the Food Products Inspector of the United States Department of Agriculture, who gave five separate certificates certifying to this condition of the onions examined by him and stating that the decay amounted in some of the containers from ten per cent to thirty-five per cent, in others from fifteen to twenty-five percent of the contents. The percentage varied in these certificates, running as high, however, as fifty per cent and as low as three per cent. The defendant notified the plaintiff by letter regarding this condition, and sent them copies of the government official's report. On December 13, 1921, the defendant sent to the plaintiffs five checks in payment of five of the cars shipped and deducted a total of $425 for a percentage of the decay as covered by the government reports. Accompanying these checks was a letter in which an explanation of the deduction was made in the following words: "These deductions are made to cover the percentage of decay on each car. We mailed you, some time ago, the inspection reports covering each of these cars in order that you might satisfy yourself that we are making only reasonable deductions." Each of the checks was marked in full payment of the car number for which payment was remitted.

On December 16th the plaintiffs acknowledged receipt of checks totaling $4,575, which they stated they had placed to the credit of the defendant, but insisted that there was still a balance due of $425 for which they demanded payment. In other words, they accepted the checks but rejected the proposed deduction.

On February 11, 1922, the defendant, who was still indebted to the plaintiffs for five cars, sent to them a check for $2,000 and a promissory note for $2,328.70 with interest paypble in thirty days. On the back of this note there was this notation: "Payment in full of balance owing you on the following cars of Onions:" (giving numbers of cars). A letter also accompanied this note showing the reasons for the deductions mentioned therein, reading as follows:

"We have already advised you the percentage of decay on cars NYC-138745 and NYC-138762 and have deducted off the first car Two Hundred and Eight Dollars ($208.00), representing twenty per cent of the invoice which the Government inspection shows as running from ten to thirty-five per cent decay and an average of fifteen to twenty-five per cent. You know that decay of this particular kind Slimy Soft Rot, hurts the sale of the entire shipment as the onions that are sound lose in value after being sorted over as they are never so bright and clean as when shipment is sound.

"Car NYC-138762 shows the same kind of decay and we have deducted fifteen per cent from the invoice and this in no way represents what we should have deducted as the bad onions affected the sale condition of the others."

The plaintiffs replied to this letter crediting these amounts on the account of the defendant and demanding all the balance due, $801.29, the amount sued for in this action. There is evidence that fusarean rot is a disease which does not develop as a result of transportation but is inherent in the plant itself. "Fusarean rot is a rot that is right inside of the onion." Testimony offered in behalf of the plaintiffs was to the effect that the onions were in good condition when delivered to the railroad. The government reports seem quite conclusive that a large part of the shipment was decayed when it reached Detroit. If the decay was in the heart of the onion it might have been overlooked on inspection in New York, and discovered by more careful examination or because of growth in the meantime, when the onions reached their destination.

The facts, briefly stated, therefore, are: The plaintiffs sold to the defendant onions for an agreed price. The shipment in part was rotten and decayed. The defendant notified the plaintiffs of the fact sending to them the government reports made by the Food Products Inspector. The defendant paid for the goods which were in good condition, deducting $801.29 for those which he claimed to have been decayed. The payment was made by checks and notes and accompanying letters notifying the plaintiffs that if accepted by them they would be in full payment of the amount due, and the balance, $801.29, the amount of the deduction, would thus be paid by agreement or by accord and satisfaction (to use the legal terms). The claim put forth by the defendant for deduction was apparently made in good faith, and in view of the government reports seems to be reasonable and fair. The percentage of the deduction made by the defendant was not as large as the percentage of decay reported by the government reports sent to the plaintiffs and might be less than the amount which the defendant could have recovered if he had sued the plaintiffs for damages or upon their warranty. Under these circumstances, was the trial judge justified in holding as a matter of law that there had been no accord and satisfaction and that the plaintiffs were entitled to the balance claimed?

The general rule is that a liquidated claim, that is, a claim which is not disputed, but admitted to be due, cannot be discharged by any payment of a less amount. In Jackson v. Volkening we find the following language used: "The rule of law is well established, undoubtedly, that where a liquidated sum is due, the payment of part only, although accepted in satisfaction, is not, for want of consideration, a discharge of the entire indebtedness, but this rule is not looked upon with favor and is confined strictly to cases falling within it." In Fuller v. Kemp it was said: "Where the demand is liquidated, and the liability of the debtor is not in good faith disputed, a different rule has been applied. In such cases the acceptance of a less sum than is the creditor's due, will not of itself discharge the debt, even if a receipt in full is given." In Simons v. Supreme Council American Legion of Honor the point was stated in these words: "Now it is the settled law of this state that if a debt or claim be disputed or contingent at the time of payment, when accepted, of a part of the whole debt is a good satisfaction and it matters not that there was no solid foundation for the dispute." And in Eames Vacuum Brake Co. v. Prosser this court said: "It is only in cases where a dispute has arisen between the parties as to the amount due and a check is tendered on one side in full satisfaction of the matter in controversy that the other party will be deemed to have acquiesced in the amount offered by an acceptance and a retention of the check." The term "liquidated," therefore, when used in connection with the subject of accord and satifaction has reference to a claim which the debtor does not dispute; a claim which he admits to be due but, attempts to satisfy by the payment of a smaller amount. Thus in Nassoiy v. Tomlinson this court said: "A demand is not liquidated, even if it appears that something is due, unless it appears how much is due; and when it is admitted that one of two specific sums is due, but there is a genuine dispute as to which is the proper amount, the demand is regarded as unliquidated, within the meaning of that term as applied to the subject of accord and satisfaction."

In this case before us, the full amount claimed by the plaintiffs was not admittedly due. The fact that the contract called for a stated amount or an amount which could be easily figured according to deliveries did not make the claim liquidated within this meaning of the law as applied to accord and satisfaction. The term "liquidated" has an entirely different meaning in this connection that it has when used to determine whether or not interest is payable upon a recovery. The amount claimed by the plaintiffs and specified in the contract was repudiated by the defendant. He denied that he owed the money. He disputed the plaintiffs' demand. The contract had not been fulfilled and completed. Deliveries had not been made as called for. The goods were rotten and decayed, and not as warranted. For the purpose of this subject, to my mind, it makes no difference whether the defendant had a claim for breach of warranty or whether he had a right to reject or claimed a right to reject the imperfect goods. The fact still exists that he insisted with the plaintiffs that he should not be obliged to pay for articles he had not purchased. It is a statement inconsistent with the fact to say that the plaintiffs' claim was liquidated in the sense that it was admitted and acknowledged to be due by the defendant. He disputed it at every step, and sent to the plaintiffs written evidence to justify the honesty and good faith of his statements. Thus there was a difference between these parties over the amount due on this contract. If the plaintiffs had sued the defendant for the full amount, the latter could have defended. There was some evidence at least to indicate that the onions were rotten at the heart when delivered to the railroad. Thus, there never had been a complete delivery and the defendant might have defended, or if there had been acceptance and no rejection within a reasonable time, then the defendant having given notice, could have counterclaimed on his warranty. However we look at it there was relief at law in some form for the defendant. He was not obliged to pay for rotten onions.

Thus within all the cases the claim of the plaintiffs was not liquidated within the meaning of that term as used in the connection. It was a disputed claim. The plaintiffs knew it was disputed. They knew also that the checks and notes which they received and cashed were received in full payment of their disputed claim. They could not under these circumstances keep the money and reject the conditions attached to payment. Having accepted payment the conditions attached and the balance of $801.29 has been satisfied.

Therefore, the judments below must be reversed and judgment directed for the defendant dismissing the complaint, with costs in all courts.

(Judgment for defendant.)

DISCUSSION QUESTIONS

1. What should the creditor have done in this case to avoid the result of accord and satisfaction?

BRAUN v. C.E.P.C. DISTRS.   CASE NO. 19

77 AD 2d 358   Dec. 1980

INTRODUCTION

The common law rule in the United States has been that where a bona fide dispute between creditor and debtor exists and the debtor tenders to the creditor a lesser sum than what the creditor claims is due--as payment in full-- and the creditor cashes the debtor's check, an accord and satisfaction results and the original debt is discharged. The significant legal effect of accord and satisfaction is that the creditor who cashes the debtor's check under such circumstances cannot collect the balance he claims is still due. However, the Uniform Commercial Code has changed this common law rule under certain circumstances as the following case reveals.

BLOOM, J. The facts, as agreed to by the parties, demonstrate that in May, 1978 defendant purchased from plaintiff certain goods required to be specially manufactured. Both parties knew and understood that the goods were to be installed on the fifth floor of 40 Wall Street, New York City, for the use of Manufacturers Hanover Trust Company, then or thereafter to be the occupant of the premises.

By mutual agreement between the parties, the contract was subsequently amended by additions and deletions to the end that the original purchase price of $23,680 was reduced to $18,905.

Plaintiff delivered the goods specifically manufactured. Subsequently, it was notified by defendant that the goods failed to conform to the specifications laid down in the purchase order and that defendant had been required to expend the sum of $4,134.50 in order to conform the goods to the purchase order and to the needs of the Manufacturers Hanover Trust Company and that, by consequence, defendant claimed a set off in the amount of that expenditure against the purchase price.

Thereafter, defendant issued a check payable to plaintiff in the sum of $14,770.50 representing the difference between the agreed purchase price of $18,905 and the claimed set off of $4,134.50. On the reverse side of the check was an endorsement which stated: "Endorsement of this check constitutes payment in full of all claims that Braun Equipment may have against Elaine Products Co. Inc." (Elaine was the name by which defendant was previously known.) Accompanying the check was a letter which indicated that the check was a tender of the amount claimed to be owing and that acceptance thereof constituted a waiver of any further claim against defendant.

Plaintiff endorsed this check and negotiated it. However, prior to such negotiation plaintiff noted immediately following the endorsement placed on the check by defendant, the following: "Notwithstanding the foregoing Braun

Equipment Co. accepts this payment without prejudice and with full reservation of its rights to assert a claim for $4,134.50 due under P.O. 19820, dated May 3, 1978 and Braun Invoice #6349, dated August 12, 1978, for which this payment is accepted in part".

Thus, the issue tendered is whether the plaintiff's negotiation of the check containing defendant's endorsement constituted an accord and satisfaction.

"An agreement whereby one party undertakes to give or perform, and the other to accept in settlement of an existing or matured claim, something other than that which he believes himself entitled to, is an accord, and the execution of such an agreement is a satisfaction. An accord, when followed by a satisfaction, is a bar to the assertion of the original claim, but unless and until followed by a satisfaction it has no effect"....In order for the compromise to be binding, it is necessary that the amount in dispute be unliquidated or, if liquidated, that there be genuine disagreement as to the amount due.

Prior to the enactment of the Uniform Commercial Code, it is highly probable that the negotiation of the check here in question would have constituted an accord and satisfaction and would have discharged defendant from further liability. The amount due from plaintiff to defendant, although liquidated was in dispute and the dispute was a genuine one;....the check issued by defendant was in settlement of that dispute and the plaintiff so understood it; and plaintiff, despite its addendum to plaintiff's endorsement, by its negotiation of the check, accepted it in accordance with the terms of defendant's offer....

Thus, the question resolves itself to whether section 1-207 of the Uniform Commercial Code has changed or altered the pre-existing rule. That section reads as follows: "A party who with explicit reservation of rights performs or promises performance or assents to performance in a manner demanded or offered by the other party does not thereby prejudice the rights reserved. Such words as 'without prejudice', 'under protest' or the like are sufficient".

Defendant would seek to limit applicability the section to installment or continuing contracts. In support of its position it points to language in the official comment referring to "the continuation of performance along the lines contemplated by the contract despite a pending dispute, by adopting the mercantile device of going ahead with delivery, acceptance, or payment 'without prejudice,' 'under protest,' 'under reserve,' 'with reservation of all our rights,' and the like". (Uniform Commercial Code, Sect. 1-207, Official Comment No. 1) There is authority, both academic...and judicial...to support this position. We, however, have held to the contrary, in Ayer v. Sky Club (70 AD' 2d 863). There we noted (p 864) that section 1-207 of the Uniform Commercial Code "permits a party ***to accept whatever he can get by way of payment, so long as he explicitly reserves his rights". Other decisions by New York courts have followed the same rule...as have some of the courts of sister States (citing only Florida cases)....

In the circumstances here presented, we find that plaintiff, by its addendum, to defendant's endorsement, expressly preserved its rights in accordance with section 1-207 of the Uniform Commercial Code thus precluding an accord and satisfaction.

Accordingly, judgment is unanimously rendered in favor of plaintiff and against defendant in the sum of $4,134.50, with interest thereon, but without costs.

DISCUSSION QUESTION
1. How could the debtor have avoided the result in this case?

CONSIDERATION: OUTPUT CONTRACT

CASE NO. 20

FELD v. HENRY S. LEVY & SONS, INC

373 N.Y. 2d 102   July 1975

INTRODUCTIONS

Output contracts require a seller to sell all of his output to a particular buyer and the buyer to buy the seller's output as it is delivered. The Uniform Commercial Code recognizes that such a contract is enforceable even though the quantity is not specified in the contract. The general rule is that a seller may in good faith cease production and terminate his obligations under an output contract without liability to the buyer. The legal question arises whether a seller acts in "good faith" when he ceases production. This leading case demonstrates the judicial analysis employed by the court to determine if the UCC requirement of "good faith" is met.

COOKE, Judge.

Plaintiff operates a business known as the Crushed Toast Company and defendant is engaged in the wholesale bread baking business. They entered into a written contract, as of June 19, 1968, in which defendant agreed to sell and plaintiff to purchase "all bread crumbs produced by the Seller in its factory at 115 Thames Street, Brooklyn, New York, during the period commencing June 19, 1968, and terminating June 18, 1969", the agreement to "be deemed automatically renewed thereafter for successive renewal periods of one year" with the right to either party to cancel by giving not less than six months notice to the other by certified mail. No notice of cancellation was served....

Interestingly, the term "bread crumbs" does not refer to crumbs that may flake off bread; rather, they are a manufactured item, starting with stale or imperfectly appearing loaves and followed by removal of labels, processing through two grinders, the second of which effects a finer granulation, insertion into a drum in an oven for toasting and, finally, bagging of the finished product.

Subsequent to the making of the agreement, a substantial quantity of bread crumbs, said to be over 250 tons, were sold by defendant to plaintiff but defendant stopped crumb production on about May 15, 1969. There was proof by defendant's comptroller that the oven was too large to accommodate the drum, that it was stated that the operation was "very uneconomical", but after said date of cessation no steps were taken to obtain more economical equipment. The toasting oven was intentionally broken down, then partially rebuilt, then completely dismantled in the summer of 1969 and, thereafter, defendant used the space for a computer room. It appears, without dispute, that defendant indicated to plaintiff at different times that the former would resume bread crumb production if the contract price of 6 cents per pound be changed to 7 cents, and also that, after the crumb making machinery was dismantled, defendant sold

111

the raw materials used in making crumbs to animal food manufacturers....

Defendant contends that the contract did not require defendant to manufacture bread crumbs, but merely to sell those it did, and, since none were
produced after the demise of the oven, there was no duty to then deliver and,
consequently from then on, no liability on its part. Agreements to sell all the
goods or services a party may produce or perform to another party are commonly
referred to as "output" contracts and they usually serve a useful commercial
purpose in minimizing the burdens of product marketing (see 1 Williston, Contracts (3d ed.), & 104A). The Uniform Commercial Code rejects the ideas that
an output contract is lacking in mutuality or that it is unenforceable because
of indefiniteness in that a quantity for the term is not specified. Official
Comment 2 to section 2-306...states in part: "Under this Article, a contract
for output...is not too indefinite since it is held to mean the actual good
faith output...of the particular party. Nor does such a contract lack mutuality
of obligation since, under this section, the party who will determine quantity
is required to operate his plant or conduct his business in good faith and
according to commercial standards of fair dealing in the trade so that his output...will proximate a reasonably foreseeable figure."....

The real issue in this case is whether the agreement carries with it an
implication that defendant was obligated to continue to manufacture bread crumbs
for the full term. Section 2-306 of the Uniform Commercial Code, entitled
"Output, Requirements and Exclusive Dealings" provides:

"(1)A term which measure the quantity by the output of the seller
or the requirements of the buyer means such actual output or requirements as may occur in good faith, except that no quantity unreasonably disproportionate to any stated estimate or in the absence
of a stated estimate to any normal or otherwise comparable prior
output or requirements may be tendered or demanded."

"(2) A lawful agreement by either the seller or the buyer for
exclusive dealing in the kind of goods concerned imposes unless
otherwise agreed an obligation by the <u>seller to use best efforts</u>
<u>supply the goods</u> and by the buyer to use best efforts to promote
their sale." (Emphasis supplied.)

The Official Comment thereunder reads in part: "Subsection (2), on exclusive dealing, makes explicit the commercial rule embodied in this Act under
which the parties to such contracts are held to have impliedly, even when not
expressly, bound themselves to use reasonable diligence as well as good faith
in their performance of the contract.... An exclusive dealing agreement brings
into play all of the good faith aspects of the output and requirement problems
of subsection (1). It also raises questions of insecurity and right to adequate assurance under this Article."

Section 2-306 is consistent with prior New York case law.... Every contract of this type imposes an obligation of good faith in its performance....
(Uniform Commercial Code, & 1-203;) Under the Uniform Commercial Code, the
commercial background and intent must be read into the language of any agreement and good faith is demanded in the performance of that agreement...and,

under the decisions relating to output contracts, it is clearly the general rule that good faith cessation of production terminates any further obligations thereunder and excuses further performance by the party discontinuing production....

This is not a situation where defendant ceased its main operation of bread baking.... Rather, defendant contends in a conclusory fashion that it was "uneconomical" or "economically not feasible" for it to continue to make bread crumbs. Although plaintiff observed in his motion papers that defendant claimed it was not economically feasible to make the crumbs, plaintiff did not admit that as a fact. In any event, "economic feasibility", an expression subject to many interpretations, would not be a precise or reliable test.

There are present here interwined questions of fact, whether defendant performed in good faith and whether it stopped its manufacture of bread crumbs in good faith, neither of which can be resolved properly on this record. The seller's duty to remain in crumb production is a matter calling for a close scrutiny of its motives...confined here by the papers to financial reasons. It is undisputed that defendant leveled its crumb making machinery only after plaintiff refused to agree to a price higher than that specified in the agreement and that it then sold the raw materials to manufacturers of animal food. There are before us no componential figures indicating the actual cost of the finished bread crumbs to defendant, statements as to the profits derived or the losses sustained, or data specifying the net or gross return realized from the animal food transactions.

The parties by their contract gave the right of cancellation to either by providing for a six months' notice to the other. The apparent purpose of such a stipulation was to provide an opportunity to either the seller or buyer to conclude their dealings in the event that the transactions were not as profitable or advantageous as desired or expected, or for any other reason. Correspondingly, such a notice would also furnish the receiver of it a chance to secure another outlet or source of supply, as the case might be. Short of such a cancellation, defendant was expected to continue to perform in good faith and could cease production of the bread crumbs, a single facet of its operation, only in good faith. Obviously, a bankruptcy or genuine imperilling of the very existence of its entire business caused by the production of the crumbs would warrant cessation of productions of that item; the yield of less profit from its sale than expected would not. Since bread crumbs were but a part of defendant's enterprise and since there was a contractual right of cancellation, good faith required continued production untill cancellation, even if there be no profit. In circumstances such as these and without more, defendant would be justified, in good faith, in ceasing production of the single item prior to cancellation only if its losses from continuance would be more than trivial, which, overall, is a question of fact.

The order of the Appellate Division should be affirmed, without costs.

(Judgment for buyer. A trial is required to determine if seller acted in good faith.)

DISCUSSION QUESTIONS

1.   How could the seller have provided for an "escape clause" in its contract
to allow it to cease production in "good faith"?

2.   Would the seller act in "good faith" in ceasing production if it produced
evidence that it would incur substantial losses if it continued to perform?
Would the seller's accountant be an expert witness in a trial?

CONSIDERATION

CHARITABLE SUBSCRIPTIONS

CASE NO. 21

I.&.I HOLDING CORP. V. GAINSBURG

276 N.Y. 427   Jan. 1938

INTRODUCTION

Each year billions of dollars are pledged in the United States to charities by donors who sign pledge agreements or subscription agreements. The legal question raised is whether the charity has given the donor any consideration so that it may enforce the donor's subscription agreement. This case illustrate the rule of law and the different legal theories regarding consideration that are employed by courts to enforce charitable subscription agreements.

Hubbs, J. Appellant signed and delivered to Beth Israel Hospital Association a pledge or subscription agreement reading as follows: "To aid and assist the Beth Israel Hospital Association in its humanitarian work, and in consideration of the promises of others contributing for the same purposes, the undersigned does hereby promise to pay to the order of the Beth Israel Hospital Association at the Hospital Building, Stuyvesant Park East, New York City the sum of * * * $5,000 payable in 4 year installments, $1,250 cash. The undersigned further requests each and every other contributor to make his contribution in reliance upon the contribution of the undersigned herewith made."

Respondent is now the holder and owner thereof. The allegation of the complaint, as to consideration, is as follows:

"Seventh. That upon the said subscription and agreement, the said Beth Israel Hospital Association proceeded in its humanitarian work, obtained other like subscriptions, expended large sums of money and incurred large liabilities, and has otherwise duly performed all the conditions on its part to be performed."

The Apellate Division, by a divided court, reversed the judgment of Special Term which dismissed the complaint, found the allegation of consideration sufficient, and struck out the fifth affirmative defense, which was:

"14. That upon information and belief the pledge and agreement described in and alleged in the complaint, copy of which is thereto annexed, was by reason of the nature thereof unassignable in law on the part of the said Hospital Association or corporation."

The appeal to this court is on certified questions, namely:

"1. Does the complaint herein state facts sufficient to constitute a cause of action?

"2. Does the fifth defense contained in the answer state facts sufficient to constitute a defense to the action?

It is unquestioned that the request that other subscribers make contributions in reliance on appellant's contribution, stated as a consideration in the subscription agreement, is not consideration which will support appellant's promise....

The respondent's complaint alleges that the hospital association "has * * * duly performed all the conditions on its part to be performed."

The question presented is whether the subscription agreement, which recites that it is made "to aid and assist" a hospital in carrying on "its humanitarian work," when relied upon by the hospital by proceeding in its work, securing other subscribers, expending large sums of money and incurring large liabilities, is binding upon the subscriber and enforceable. We believe that the allegations of the complaint are broad enough to permit proof as to the conditions upon which the subscription was made and the extent of fulfillment. Evidence may be given, under the allegations in question, that the hospital, after the subscription was given, relying thereon, altered its position to the knowledge of the promisor and in the reasonable belief that the promise would be kept.... Consideration in such a case may be shown from facts outside the subscription agreement....

The subscription agreement need not on its face require the hospital to do or refrain from doing any particular thing, as urged by the appellant. The reliance is not upon a request, but upon the subscription agreement made, as recited, "to aid * * * the hospital * * * in its humanitarian work." The agreement can be read as though it said "to aid and assist the hospital in carrying on its humanitarian work, I agree to pay." Relying on the agreement to aid and assist by paying, the hospital acted. The subscription agreement is not a contract, but an offer to contract, which, when acted upon by incurring liability, becomes a binding obligation. (1 Williston on Contracts (Rev. ed.), 116.) It is a unilateral contract unenforceable until acted upon by the promisee. An invitation or request to carry on its work need not be expressed in the subscription agreement - it may be implied. "Nor need a request to the promisee to perform the services be expressed in the instrument; it may be implied." .... True it is that, under our law, there must be consideration in contracts in order to make them valid.

We realize that the principles upon which courts of differing jurisdictions have placed their decisions sustaining subscriptions for charitable purposes are all subject to criticism from a legalistic standpoint. Nevertheless we feel that we should follow the decisions of our own courts, extending, as they do, over a long period. The principle controlling our decisions has "been too firmly established in this State to be disturbed by judicial decision." .... Our courts have definitely ruled that such subscriptions are enforceable on the ground that they constitute an offer of a unilateral contract which, when accepted by the charity by incurring liability in reliance thereon, becomes a binding obligation.(12 Cornell Law Review, 467; Selected Readings on the Law of Contracts, p. 559.) The view that a subscription is an offer to contract which becomes binding as soon as work has been begun in reliance on the promise is strengthened by the adoption of the following statement in the Restatement of Contracts:

"45. If an offer for a unilateral contract is made, and part of the consideration requested in the offer is given or tendered by the offeree in response thereto, the offeror is bound by a contract, the duty of immediate performance of which is conditional on the full consideration being given or tendered within the time stated in the offer, or if no time is stated therein, within a reasonable time." (American Law Institute, Restatement of the Law of Contracts, vol. 1.)

Courts, in passing on subscription agreements for charitable purposes, have sustained them under the rule of promissory estoppel in cases where the promisee has acted on the promise to pay by incurring liability. We need not go so far as to base our decision on the doctrine of promissory estoppel, as stated in (   ). That doctrine need not be applied to save a subscription where a request or invitation that the promisee go on with its work can be implied from the subscription agreement. It is only when a request or an invitation to carry on cannot be implied in fact that it is necessary to invoke that doctrine. In the complaint there is alleged some consideration. It must be remembered that the case involves only a motion on the pleadings. The cases cited by appellant, where there has been a trial and failure of proof, are not in point. The argument of appellant that the parol evidence rule applies and that under it no new or different consideration can be proved, has no application on this motion on the pleadings.

That the agreement or pledge was assignable in law is also clear. It is a promise to pay "to the order of the Beth Israel Hospital Association." There is no statutory restriction against the assignability of such a subscription and we are referred to no decision tending to deny the assignability of an instrument of this character. This court has indicated the rule applicable

Section 41 of the Personal Property Law (Cons. Laws, ch. 41) Provides:

"Any claim or demand can be transferred, except in one of the following cases: * * *

"(3) Where a transfer thereof is expressly forbidden by a statute of the state, or of the United States, or would contravene public policy."

The order should be affirmed, with costs, the first question certified answered in the affirmative, and the second in the negative.

(Judgement for Respondent)

117

ILLUSORY PROMISES
CASE NO. 22

SCHLEGEL v. COOPER'S GLUE FACTORY

231 N.Y. 459   July 1921

INTRODUCTION

Sellers and buyers frequently enter into contracts whereby either (1)the seller agrees to <u>sell all</u> of his <u>output</u> to one buyer or (2)the buyer agrees to <u>buy all</u> of his <u>requirements</u> from one seller. Courts have held that such contracts are enforceable even though the quantity is indefinite and unknown at the time of contract, provided the seller has an "actual" output or the buyer has "actual" requirements. This case illustrates the rule of law that a buyer's promise to buy his requirements--when in fact he has none--is not a promise that is valid or sufficient consideration. Instead, his so-called promise is an <u>illusory</u> <u>promise</u> which is <u>not</u> sufficient or valid consideration to render the seller's promise enforceable.

MCLAUGHLIN, J. Action to recover damages for alleged breach of contract. The complaint alleged that on or about December 9, 1915, the parties entered into a written agreement by which the defendant agreed to sell and deliver to the plaintiff, and the plaintiff agreed to purchase from the defendant, all its "requirements" of special BB glue for the year 1916, at the price of nine cents per pound. It also alleged the terms of payment, the manner in which the glue was to be packed, the place of delivery, the neglect and refusal of defendant to make certain deliveries, and the damages sustained, for which judgment was demanded. The answer put in issue the material allegations of the complaint. At the trial a jury was waived and the trial proceeded before the trial justice. At its conclusion he rendered a decision awarding the plaintiff a substantial amount. Judgment was entered upon the decision from which an appeal was taken to the Appellate Division, first department, where the same was affirmed, two of the justices dissenting. The appeal to this court followed.

I am of the opinion the judgment appealed from should be reversed, upon the ground that the alleged contract, for the breach of which a recovery was had, was invalid since it lacked mutuality. It consisted solely of a letter written by defendant to plaintiff, the material part of which is as follows:

"GENTLEMEN.--We are instructed by our Mr. Von Schuckmann to enter your contract for your requirements of 'Special BB' glue for the year 1916, price to be 9¢ per lb., terms 2% 20th to 30th of month following purchase. Deliveries to be made to you as per your orders during the year and quality same as heretofore. Glue to be packed in 500 lb. or 350 lb. barrels and 100 lb. kegs, and your special Label to be carefully pasted on top, bottom and side of each barrel or keg. * * *

"PETER COOPER'S GLUE FACTORY,

"W.D. DONALDSON,

"Sales Manager."

At the bottom of the letter the president of the plaintiff wrote:
"Accepted, Oscar Schlegel Manufacturing Company," and returned it to the
defendant.

The plaintiff, at the time, was engaged in no manufacturing business in
which glue was used or required, nor was it then under contract to deliver
glue to any third parties at a fixed price or otherwise. It was simply a jobber, selling, among other things, glue to such customers as might be obtained
by sending out salesmen to solicit orders therefor. The contract was invalid
since a consideration was lacking. Mutual promises or obligations of parties
to a contract, either express or necessarily implied, may furnish the requisite consideration. The defect in the alleged contract here under consideration is that it contains no express consideration, nor are there any mutual
promises of the parties to it from which such consideration can be fairly
inferred. The plaintiff, it will be observed, did not agree to do or refrain
from doing anything. It was not obligated to sell a pound of defendant's glue
or to make any effort in that direction. It did not agree not to sell other
glue in competition with defendant's. The only obligation assumed by it was
to pay nine cents a pound for such glue as it might order. Whether it should
order any at all rested entirely with it. If it did not order any glue, then
nothing was to be paid. The agreement was not under seal, and, therefore,
fell within the rule that a promise not under seal made by one party, with
none by the other, is void. Unless both parties to a contract are bound, so
that either can sue the other for a breach, neither is bound....Had the plaintiff neglected or refused to order any glue during the year 1916, defendant
could not have maintained an action to recover damages against it, because
there would have been no breach of the contract. In order to recover damages,
a breach had to be shown, and this could not have been established by a mere
failure on the part of the plaintiff to order glue, since it had not promised
to give such orders.

There are certain contracts in which mutual promises are implied: Thus,
where the purchaser, to the knowledge, of the seller, has entered into a contract for the resale of the article purchased...where the purchaser contracts
for his requirements of an article necessary to be used in the business
carried on by him...in a canning factory...all the lubricating oil for party's
own use...all the coal needed for a foundry during a specified time...all the
iron required during a certain period in a furnace...and all the ice required
in a hotel during a certain season....In cases of this character, while the
quantity of the article contracted to be sold is indefinite, nevertheless
there is a certain standard mentioned in the agreement by which such quantity
can be determined by an approximately accurate forecast. In the contract here
under consideration there is no standard mentioned by which the quantity of
glue to be furnished can be determined with any approximate degree of accuracy.

The view above expressed is not in conflict with the authorities cited by
the respondent. Thus, in N.Y.C. Iron Works Co. v. U.S. Radiator Co., principally relied upon and cited in the prevailing opinion at the Appellate

Division, "the defendant bound the plaintiff to deal exclusively in goods to be ordered from it under the contract, and to enlarge and develop the market for the defendant's wares so far as possible."

In Fuller & Co. v. Schrenk the contract provided: "It is hereby agreed that in consideration of W. P. Fuller & Co. buying all their supply of German Mirror Plates from the United Bavarian Looking Glass Works, for a period of six months from this date, the said United Bavarian Looking Glass Works" agrees to sell certain mirrors at specified prices.

In Wood v. Duff-Gordon the plaintiff was to have, for the term of one year, the exclusive right to place defendant's indorsement on certain designs, in return for which she was to have one-half of all the profits and revenue derived from any contracts he might make. The point was there made, as here, that plaintiff did not promise that he would use reasonable efforts to place defendant's indorsement and market her designs, but this court held that such a promise was fairly to be implied; that when defendant gave to the plaintiff an exclusive privilege for a period of one year, during which time she could not place her own indorsements, or market her own designs, except through the agency of the plaintiff, that the acceptance of such an exclusive agency carried with it an assumption of its duties.

In the instant case, as we have already seen, there was no obligation on the part of the plaintiff to sell any of the defendant's glue, to make any effort towards bringing about such sale, or not to sell other glues in competition with it. There is not in the letter a single obligation from which it can fairly be inferred that the plaintiff was to do or refrain from doing anything whatever.

The price of glue having risen during the year 1916 from nine to twenty-four cents per pound, it is quite obvious why orders for glue increased correspondingly. Had the price dropped below nine cents it may fairly be inferred such orders would not have been given. In that case, if the interpretation put upon the agreement be the correct one, plaintiff would not have been liable to the defendant for damages for a breach, since he had not agreed to sell any glue.

The judgments of the Appellate Division and trial court should be reversed and the complaint dismissed, with costs in all courts.

(Judgment for defendant seller.)

DISCUSSION QUESTIONS

1.   What could the buyer have given the seller as consideration which would have enabled the buyer to enforce the contract against the seller?

2.   Section 2-306 of the Uniform Commercial Code sets forth the law concerning "output" and "requirements" contracts. After reading that section in the back of this book, give an example of "good faith" and "bad faith" in determining whether a seller or buyer has acted properly in determining his "output" or "requirements".

CONSIDERATION - ESSAY QUESTIONS

1. The Chairman of the board of directors of X Corp. writes to P, the president, who is 60 years old and plans to retire, "The corporation will pay you a pension of $20,000 a year for life if you retire as planned, and agree not to take another job in this industry." P replied, "I promise to do as you wish." Two years later, X Corp. stops the pension payments. P sues for the current installment.

(a) May he recover? Explain.

(b) If X Corp.'s promise had been oral, could P enforce it if X Corp. pleads the Statute of Frauds as a defense? Explain.

2. Assume that X Corp.'s letter to P stated: "In view of the fact that you have been faithful to X Corp. for 30 years and have resisted efforts of our competitors to hire you away from us, the corporation promises to pay you a pension of $20,000 a year for life." P replied, "I accept your pension promise with gratitude."

Is X Corp.'s promise enforceable by P:

(a) under common law? Explain.

(b) in New York today? Explain.

3. D owes C $2,000 on a contract for the purchase of 10 air-conditioners on credit, the terms of payment stating "Payment due 60 days after delivery." Delivery was made on January 2. On March 10, D meets C and tells him, "I'm sorry I missed out on paying you what I owe you. Collections have been slow. If you give me till May 1, I'll pay you what I owe plus interest at 6%." C says, "O.K. I'll give you till May 1." On March 15, C sues D for $2,000. D's defense is that the debt is not due till May 1. Is the defense good:

(a) under the majority rule? Explain.

(b) under New York law today? Explain.

4. A owes B $10,000. B orally agrees to reduce the debt to $8,000 and extend the payment date by 3 months, and in return A gives B as collateral for the debt 10 shares of X Corp. stock owned by A and worth $5,000. A pays the $8,000 before the end of the three months and demands the return of the stock. B refuses and has threatened to sell the stock in order to collect the $2,000 balance he claims is still owed by A. Is A entitled to the return of his stock? Explain.

5. A owes B $10,000 on a promissory note which will become due and payable one year from today. Today B writes to A "I will allow you $1,000 on your note and accept $9,000 in full payment if you pay me the $9,000 before the end of next month. (Signed) B."

(a) Did B's letter constitute an accord? Explain.
(b) Assume A comes to B's house within 2 weeks with the money to pay the $9,000, but, before A can tender the money to B, B tells A that he has negotiated the note to C and consequently cannot accept the money. A year later, A is forced to pay C the entire $10,000. May A recover the $1,000 difference from B? Explain.
(c) Assume A hands B $9,000 in cash within 2 weeks which B receives and keeps. A year later, B sues A for $1,000. May B recover:
    (1) under common law? Explain.
    (2) in New York today? Explain.
(d) Assume A hands B $9,000 in cash within 2 weeks which B refuses to take since he has changed his mind. One year later B sues A for $10,000. How much may B recover? Explain.

6. B borrowed $1,000 from L at 5% interest and gave L a promissory note for $1,050 payable in one year. The year having elapsed, B tendered a check for $900 with these words marked on the back above the space where L would endorse it: "I (L) hereby accept the face amount of this check in complete satisfaction of the debt owed by B." L cashed the check and now seeks to recover the balance from B. Is the entire debt discharged? Explain.

7. C, a building contractor, enters into a written agreement with O, the owner of 27 Y Street, to build for O a new wing on his house for $20,000. After the work is one-half done, C complains about the rising cost of materials and stops work. O says to C "If you go ahead and finish the job I'll pay you a bonus of $3,000". C agrees and finishes the job. C demands payment of $23,000 but O refuses to pay more than $20,000.

(a) How much may C collect from O? Explain.

(b) Assume that C wrote on the bottom of the written contract, "The agreed price for the above work is $23,000" and said to O "I'll go ahead if you sign that", which O did. How much may C collect from O under New York law today? Explain.

8. S, a certified public accountant, accepted an offer from G Corporation to become the Corporation's controller at an annual salary of $75,000. The written and signed contract was for three years and expressly provided that it was "irrevocable by either party except for cause" during that period.

After a year, S became dissatisfied with the agreed compensation he was receiving. He had done an excellent job as controller and several larger competing corporations were attempting to lure him away from G Corporation. S, therefore, demanded a substantial raise and G Corporation agreed in writing to pay him an additional $25,000 at the end of the third year. S remained with G Corporation and performed the same duties he had agreed to perform at the time he initially accepted the position as controller.

At the end of the three years S sought to collect the additional $25,000. G Corporation denied liability beyond the amount agreed to in the original contract.

Can S recover the additional compensation from G Corporation:

(a) under common law? Explain.

(b) in New York today? Explain.

9. The basic facts are the same as stated in the previous problem except that one of F's competitors, J Corp., successfully lured S away from G Corporation by topping G Corporation's offer of additional compensation. J Corp. did this with full knowledge of the terms of the original three-year contract between S and G Corporation.

(a) Does G Corporation have any legal remedy against J Corp.? Explain.

(b) G Corporation, relying on the contract's stated irrevocability for three years, seeks the equitable relief of specific performance against S, i.e., a court order compelling S to perform his contract. Will G Corporation prevail? Explain.

10. S shipped 10 refrigerators to B pursuant to a sales contract under which title to the goods and risk of loss would pass to B upon delivery to X Railroad. The agreed price was $2,000. When the refrigerators were delivered to B, he found they were damaged. An estimate for repairing them showed it would cost up to $300, and an expert opinion was to the effect that they were defective when shipped. B put in a claim to S which S rejected. B then wrote to S, "I don't like to get into a dispute of this nature. I am enclosing my check for $1,700 in full payment of the shipment." S did not reply but he cashed the check and then sued B for $300.

(a) May he recover? Explain.

(b) Did the agreement between S and B constitute an "accord and satisfaction"? Explain.

11. In the previous problem assume that there was no damage to the refrigerators and no dispute, but that B did not pay. One month after payment was due, B wrote to S, "I'll pay you $1,600 if you will accept it in full payment." S wrote back, "Since I have despaired of getting any more out of you, I'll take the $1,600." B paid the $1,600 and S sued for the $400 balance. May he recover:

(a) under common law? Explain.

123

(b) in New York today? Explain.

Assume that there was no correspondence between B and S but that after a delay in payment B sent S a check for $1,600. On the back of the check B wrote "The cashing of this check will constitute full payment of all claims on the sale of 10 refrigerators." S endorsed the check, cashed it, and then sued B for $400.

(c) May he recover? Explain.

12.   In your audit examination of the accounts receivable of your client, S Publishing Corp. the following problem was discovered.

During November and December B, Inc. purchased $5,000 of sheet music and music books from S. The amount of B's indebtedness to S has not been disputed.

Investigation revealed that the following March 1, exasperated with the number and frequency of S's written demands for settlement of the account, B returned to S $1,000 of previously purchased books and a check for $4,000. There was no dispute as to this point.

B's letter to S included a list of books being returned and stated that the credit for the return plus the enclosed check for the balance constituted payment of the account in full.

The following was written on the face of the check: "Complete and final settlement of our account payable."

The letter and check reached S in due course. S cashed the check, but declined to accept the books for credit. On March 7 S wrote B as follows: "We are not crediting your account with these books, but are holding them subject to your disposal."

On March 15, B replied reaffirming its position as indicated in its letter of March 1.

B claimed that there was a general custom throughout the United States permitting the return of such books. S denied that such a custom existed. S's counsel submitted a memorandum stating that there was authority supporting both sides of the proposition and that in fact there was a bona fide dispute as to whether such a custom existed. The attorney's memorandum concluded that "this issue can only be determined by litigation."

Will S succeed in an action against B to recover $1,000? Explain.

13. B has owned and operated a fleet of trucks for several years. B was concerned about obtaining sufficient fuel for his truck operations during the coming year. After negotiations with S Oil Co. the following agreement was signed by both parties:

"July 9

S Oil Co. agrees to supply B with all his requirements
of diesel fuel for next year, price to be $1.00 per
gallon, terms 2% 10 days, net 30 days. Delivery to
be made to B's truck terminal in New York City as per
B's order during the year.

S Oil Co.
by S, President

Accepted: B"

(a) Is the contract sufficiently definite to be enforceable:

(1) under common law? Explain.

(2) under the Uniform Commercial Code? Explain.

(b) If B orders no fuel during the next year because he buys it from X Oil
Co. at 95 cents per gallon, has S Oil Co. a cause of action against B
for damages? Explain.

(c) If B orders 5 times what he needs for his truck operations since he
can resell it at a profit, is S Oil Co. obligated to make the
deliveries? Explain.

(d) Would the contract be enforceable if B were a wholesale jobber, who
would order fuel only when he could resell it at a profit? Explain.

14. S promises in writing to deliver to B at a fixed and stated price all
of S's product line that B may desire during the next eight months. In
exchange for S's promise, B promises in writing that he will buy all he
desires of S's product line during the stipulated period and at the stipulated
price.

Has a contract been made? Explain.

15. D owes $1,000 to A, $5,000 to B and $10,000 to C, all past due. In a
meeting with all three creditors D asserts that he will be able to raise
$8,000 in three months to pay all the debts. He offers to pay each of them
one-half of the respective debts in three months if they all agree to take
the payments in full discharge of his obligations to them. A, B, and C agree.
Thirty days later, D's father dies and D inherits $50,000.

D tenders $8,000 to A, B, and C at the agreed date. The creditors contend
their agreement is unenforceable because there was no consideration given by
D. How much may A, B, and C collect? Explain.

16. A, the owner of a tract of undeveloped land in the City of Shady Crest,

entered into a contract with B, a building contractor and developer, under which B agreed to build 100 houses on the property over three years for $10,000,000. However, due to inflation of building costs and other inadequacies in the plans, A decided, with B's consent, not to go through with the contract.

C, the owner of land adjacent to the development, wanted A to go ahead with the project. To induce A to do so, C wrote to A promising to construct a $2,000,000 shopping center on his land if A went ahead with his project. A consulted B, and in reliance on C's promise, they reinstated the building contract and started work. May A enforce C's promise? Explain.

17. (a) What are the requirements or elements that must be shown in order to establish promissory estoppel?

(b) What is the primary importance of the promissory estoppel doctrine in relation to the law of contracts? Explain.

CONSIDERATION

1. The common-law contract doctrine of consideration

    a. Requires that consideration have a monetary value if it is to be valid.
    b. Recognizes that the forebearance from a legal right constitutes consideration.
    c. Has been abolished in most jurisdictions if the contract is made under seal.
    d. Requires a roughly equal exchange of value by the parties to the contract.

2. Consideration to support a contract generally requires

    a. An adequate exchange.
    b. A bargained for exchange.
    c. A reasonable price.
    d. An adequate price.

3. In order to be valid, consideration must

    a. Be stated in the contract.
    b. Be based upon a legal obligation as contrasted with a moral obligation.
    c. Be performed simultaneously by the parties.
    d. Have a monetary value.

4. Martinson Services, Inc., agreed to rent two floors of office space in Jason's building for five years. An escalation clause in the lease provided for a $200 per month increase in rental in the fifth year of occupancy by Martinson. Near the end of the fourth year, during a serious economic recession, Martinson's business was doing very poorly. Martinson called upon Jason to inform him that Martinson could not honor the lease if the rent was increased in the fifth year. Jason agreed in a signed writing to allow Martinson to remain at the prior rental, and Martinson did so. At the end of the fifth year Martinson moved to another office building. Then, Jason demanded payment of $2,400 from Martinson.

    What is the legal standing of the parties involved?

    a. A binding accord and satisfaction has resulted between the parties.
    b. The agreed upon rent reduction is valid due to the increased burden of performance as a result of events beyond Martinson's control.
    c. Martinson's relinquishment of the legal right to breach the contract provides the consideration for the reduction in rent.
    d. The writing signed by Jason does not bind him to the agreed reduction in rent.

5. Williams purchased a heating system from Radiant Heating, Inc., for his factory. Williams insisted that a clause be included in the contract

calling for service on the heating system to begin not later than the next business day after Williams informed Radiant of a problem. This service was to be rendered free of charge during the first year of the contract and for a flat fee of $200 per year for the next two years thereafter. During the second year of the contract, the heating system broke down and Williams promptly notified Radiant of the situation. Due to other commitments, Radiant did not send a man over the next day. Williams phoned Radiant and was told that the $200 per year service charge was uneconomical and they could not get a man over there for several days. Williams in desperation promised to pay an additional $100 if Radiant would send a man over that day. Radiant did so and sent a bill for $100 to Williams. Is Williams legally required to pay this bill and why?

    a. No, because the pre-existing legal duty rule applies to this situation.

    b. No, because the Statute of Frauds will defeat Radiant's claim.

    c. Yes, because Williams made the offer to pay the additional amount.

    d. Yes, because the fact that it was uneconomical for Radiant to perform constitutes economic duress which freed Radiant from its obligation to provide the agreed-upon service.

6. Montbank's son, Charles, was seeking an account executive position with Dobbs, Smith, and Fogarty, Inc., the largest brokerage firm in the United States. Charles was very independent and wishes no interference by his father. The firm, after several weeks deliberation, decided to hire Charles. They made him an offer on April 12 and Charles readily accepted. Montbanks feared that his son would not be hired. Being unaware of the fact that his son had been hired, Montbanks mailed a letter to Dobbs on April 13 in which he promised to give the brokerage firm $50,000 in commission business if the firm would hire his son. The letter was duly received by Dobbs and they wish to enforce it against Montbanks. Which of the following statements is correct?

    a. Past consideration is no consideration, hence there is no contract.

    b. The pre-existing legal duty rule applies and makes the promise unenforceable.

    c. Dobbs will prevail since the promise is contained in a signed writing.

    d. Dobbs will prevail based upon promissory estoppel.

7. In general, which of the following requirements must be satisfied in order to have a valid contract?

    a. A writing.

    b. Consideration.

    c. Mutual promises.

    d. Signatures of all parties.

CAPACITY OF PARTIES: INFANCY

NEW YORK GENERAL OBLIGATIONS LAW:

<u>Section 1-202</u>. <u>Definition</u>

As used in this chapter, the term "infant" or "minor" means a person who has not attained the age of eighteen years. (eff. Sept. 1, 1974)

<u>Section 3-101</u>. <u>When Contracts May Not Be Disaffirmed On Ground Of Infancy</u>

1. A contract made on or after September first, nineteen hundred seventy-four by a person after he has attained the age of eighteen years may not be disaffirmed by him on the ground of infancy.

. . . .

3. A husband and wife, with respect only to real property they occupy or which they affirm they are about to occupy as a home, regardless of the minority of either or both and without limitation of the powers of any such person who is of full age, shall each have power (a) to enter into and contract for a loan or loans with a bank, trust company,...savings bank or savings and loan association whose home office is located in this state, with any insurance company authorized to do business in this state, with the United States government and its agencies, with respect to such real property and take any other action and execute any other document or instrument to the extent necessary or appropriate to effect any such loan, provide security therefor, carry out or modify the terms thereof, and effect any compromise or settlement of any such loan or of any claim with respect thereto; (b) to receive, hold and dispose of such real property, make and execute contracts, notes, deeds, mortgages, agreements and other instruments necessary and appropriate to acquire such property; and (c) to dispose of such real property so acquired, and make and execute contracts, deeds, agreements and other instruments necessary and appropriate to dispose of such property.

Notwithstanding any contrary provision or rule of law, no such husband or wife shall have the power to disaffirm, because of minority, any act or transaction which he or she is hereinabove empowered to perform or engage in, nor shall any defense based upon minority be interposed in any action or proceeding arising out of any such act or transaction.

. . . . (eff. Aug. 11, 1977 as amended)

<u>Section 3-102</u>. <u>Obligations Of Certain Minors For Hospital, Medical And Surgical Treatment And Care</u>

1. An obligation incurred by a married minor for hospital, medical and surgical treatment and care for such minor or such minor's children shall not be voidable because of minority. For the purpose of this section only,

129

subsequent judgment of divorce or annulment shall not alter the obligation previously incurred. (eff. Sept. 1, 1968).

Section 3-105.   Judicial Approval Of Certain Contracts For Services Of Infants; ...

1. A contract made by an infant or made by a parent or guardian of an infant, or a contract proposed to be so made, under which (a) the infant is to perform or render services as an actor, actress, dancer, musician, vocalist or other performing artist, or as a participant or player in professional sports, or (b) a person is employed to render services to the infant in connection with such services of the infant or in connection with contracts therefor, may be approved by the supreme court or the surrogate's court as provided in this section where the infant is a resident of this state or the services of the infant are to be performed or rendered in this state. If the contract is so approved the infant may not, either during his minority or upon reaching his majority, disaffirm the contract on the ground of infancy or assert that the parent or guardian lacked authority to make the contract. A contract modified, amended or assigned after its approval under this section shall be deemed a new contract.

2. a. Approval of the contract pursuant to this section shall not exempt any person from the requirements of...any law with respect to licenses, consents or authorizations required for any conduct, employment, use or exhibition of the infant in this state,...nor dispense with any other requirement of law relating to the infant.

b. No contract shall be approved which provides for an employment, use or exhibition of the infant, within or without the state, which is prohibited by law and could not be licensed to take place in this state.

c. No contract shall be approved unless (1) the written acquiescence to such contract of the parent or parents having custody, or other person having custody of the infant, is filed in the proceeding or (2) the court shall find that the infant is emancipated.

d. No contract shall be approved if the term during which the infant is to perform or render services or during which a person is employed to render services to the infant, including any extensions thereof by option or otherwise, extends for a period of more than three years from the date of approval of the contract.

....

e. If the court which has approved a contract pursuant to this section shall find that the well-being of the infant is being impaired by the performance thereof, it may, at any time during the term of the contract... either revoke its approval of the contract, or declare such approval revoked unless a modification of the contract which the court finds to be appropriate in the circumstances is agreed upon by the parties and the contract as modified is approved by order of the court. Application for an order pursuant to this paragraph may be made by the infant, or his parent or parents, or guardian,...or by the person having the care and custody of the infant.... Revocation of the approval of the contract shall not affect any right of action existing at the date of the revocation, except that the court may determine that a refusal to perform on the ground of impairment of the well-being of the infant was justified.

3. a. The court may withhold its approval of the contract until the filing of consent by the parent or parents entitled to the earnings of the infant, or of the infant if he is entitled to his own earnings, that a part of the infant's net earnings for services performed or rendered during the term of the contract be set aside and saved for the infant pursuant to the order of the court...until he attains his majority or until further order of the court. Such consent shall not be deemed to constitute an emancipation of the infant.

b. The court shall fix the amount or proportion of net earnings to be set aside as it deems for the best interests of the infant....

.... (eff. Sept. 1, 1974 - originally enacted in 1963)

Section 3-107. Certain Contracts Of Parents Or Guardians Respecting Employment Of Infants Not Enforceable Unless Approved

Where a contract providing for performance or rendering of services by an infant is one which the supreme court or surrogate's court has jurisidction to approve as provided in section 3-105 of this chapter, no parent or guardian of the infant with respect to whose services the contract is made shall, unless the contract is so approved, be liable on the contract either as a party or as a guarantor of its performance:

1. If the infant was a resident of the state at the time the contract was made or at the time of the event by reason of which liability is sought to be imposed, by reason of any disaffirmance, repudiation or breach of the contract or any term thereof, or any failure or refusal of the infant to perform, or

2. In any other case, by reason of any failure or refusal of the infant to perform or render services required or permitted by the contract to be performed or rendered in this state or any failure or refusal of the parent or guardian to cause such services to be rendered or performed. (eff. 1963)

Section 3-109. Payment Of Wages To Minor; When Valid

Where a minor is in the employment of a person other than his parent or guardian, payment to such minor of his wages is valid, unless such parent or guardian notify the employer in writing, within thirty days after the commencement of such service, that such wages are claimed by such parent or guardian, but whenever such notice is given at any time payments to the minor shall not be valid for services rendered thereafter. (eff. 1963)

131

Section 3-112. Limited Liability Of Parents Or Certain Legal Guardians
              Having Custody Of An Infant For Malicious And Destructive
              Acts Of Such Infant

Except as otherwise provided...the parent or legal guardian, other than
the state or a local social services department or a foster parent, having
custody of an infant over ten and less than eighteen years of age, shall, if
such infant willfully, maliciously or unlawfully damages or destroys real
or personal property or who with intent to deprive the owner of property or
to appropriate the same to himself or to a third person he knowingly enters
or remains unlawfully in a building and wrongfully takes, obtains or withholds
personal property from such building which personal property is owned or
maintained by another, be held liable for such damage or destruction in a
civil action brought in a court of competent jurisdiction. For the purposes
of this section the terms "enters or remains unlawfully" and "building" shall
have the same meaning as ascribed to such terms in...the penal law. In no
event, shall such liability under this section be in excess of the sum of
fifteen hundred dollars. It shall be a defense to any action brought here-
under that restitution has been made.... It shall also be a defense to an
action brought under this section that such child has become emancipated from
his parent or legal guardian prior to the occurrence of such damage. (eff.
July 31, 1981, as amended; originally enacted in 1979) .

NEW YORK EDUCATION LAW

Section 281. Loans And Extensions Of Credit To Infants

A contract hereafter made by an infant after he has attained the age of
sixteen years in relation to obtaining a loan or extension of credit from an
institution of the university of the state of New York in connection with such
infant's attendance upon a course of instruction offered by such institution,
or from a bank, trust company, industrial bank or national bank whose principal office is in this state for the purpose of defraying all or a portion of
the expenses of such infant's attendance upon a course of instruction in an
institution of the university of the state of New York or any other institution for higher education without this state which is a member of or
accredited by an accrediting agency recognized by the department, may not be
disaffirmed by him on the ground of infancy. (as amended, eff. Feb. 14, 1961,
originally enacted in 1959)

NEW YORK BUSINESS CORPORATION LAW:

Section 625: Infant Shareholders And Bondholders

(a) A corporation may treat an infant who holds shares or bonds of such
corporation as having capacity to receive and to empower others to receive
dividends, interest, principal and other payments and distributions, to vote
or express consent or dissent, in person or by proxy, and to make elections
and exercise rights relating to such shares or bonds, unless, in the case of
shares, the corporate officer responsible for maintaining the list of shareholders or the transfer agent of the corporation or, in the case of bonds,

the treasurer or paying officer or agent has received written notice that such holder is an infant.

(b)   An infant holder of shares or bonds of a corporation who has received or empowered others to receive payments or distributions, voted or expressed consent or dissent, or made an election or exercised a right relating thereto, shall have no right thereafter to disaffirm or avoid, as against the corporation, any such act on his part, unless prior to such receipt, vote, consent, dissent, election or exercise, as to shares, the corporate officer responsible for maintaining the list of shareholders or its transfer agent or, in the case of bonds, the treasurer or paying officer had received notice that such holder was an infant.

(c)   This section does not limit any other statute which authorizes any corporation to deal with an infant or limits the right of an infant to dis-affirm his acts.   (eff. 1963)

CAPACITY OF PARTIES: INFANTS AND INCOMPETENTS

NEW YORK CIVIL PRACTICE LAW AND RULES (C.P.L.R.)

Section 1201.   Representation Of Infant, Incompetent Person, Or Conservatee

Unless the court appoints a guardian ad litem, an infant shall appear by the guardian of his property or, if there is no such guardian, by a parent having legal custody, or, if there is no such parent, by another person or agency having legal custody, or, if the infant is married, by an adult spouse residing with the infant, a person judicially declared to be incompetent shall appear by the committee of his property,.... A person shall appear by his guardian ad litem if he is an infant and has no guardian of his property, parent, or other person or agency having legal custody, or adult spouse with whom he resides, or if he is an infant, person judicially declared to be in-competent, and the court so directs because of a conflict of interest or for other cause, or if he is an adult incapable of adequately prosecuting or defending his rights.   (as amended, eff. May 18, 1981) .

C.P.L.R. 1206 provides that a court must approve the settlement of any claim or lawsuit on behalf of an Infant or Incompetent, and Section 1207 provides the procedure by the court for approval of the disposition of the proceeds of any such claim or lawsuit.

See C.P.L.R. Section 1206. Disposition of proceeds of claim of infant, judicially declared incompetent or conservatee
and
C.P.R.L. Section 1207. Settlement of action or claim by infant, judi-cially declared incompetent or conservatee, by whom motion made; special proceeding notice; order of settlement

CAPACITY OF PARTIES: MARRIED WOMEN

NEW YORK GENERAL OBLIGATIONS LAW

Section 3-301. Powers Of Married Woman

1. A married woman has all the rights in respect to property, real or personal, and the acquisition, use, enjoyment and disposition thereof, and to make contracts in respect thereto with any person, including her husband, and to carry on any business, trade or occupation, and to exercise all powers and enjoy all rights in respect thereto and in respect to her contracts, and be liable on such contracts, as if she was unmarried.

2. All sums that may be recovered in actions or special proceedings by a married woman to recover damages to her person, estate or character shall be the separate property of the wife.

3. Judgment for or against a married woman, may be rendered and enforced, in a court of record, or not of record, as if she was single. A married woman may confess a judgment. (eff. 1963; originally enacted in 1835 and was contained in Code of Civil Procedure).

Section 3-305. Contract Of Married Woman Not To Bind Husband

A contract made by a married woman does not bind her husband or his property. (eff. 1963; originally enacted in 1860 and was contained in Domestic Relations Law)

CAPACITIES OF PARTIES
INFANTS

CASE NO. 23
STERNLIEB v. NORMANDIE NAT. SEC. CORP.

263 N. Y.   Jan. 1934

INTRODUCTION

Infants occasionally misrepresent their age to be over 18 (the age of majority) in order to induce the other party to contract with them. Such misrepresentation constitutes fraud. The legal question arises whether an infant who
commits such fraud can nevertheless disaffirm his contract. This leading
case illustrates the rule of law applicable in such cases. In 1974 New York
lowered the age of majority from 21 to 18.

Crane, J. Again we have the troublesome question arising from the repudiation by a young gentleman, just under twenty-one, of his contract of purchase. On the 21st day of September, 1929, the plaintiff purchased from the
defendant five shares of the capital stock of the Bank of United States and of
the Bankus Corporation, for which he paid $990. In his complaint he alleges
that he was under twenty-one years of age. After the stock had dropped in value until it was worthless, this young plaintiff further alleges that on the
14th day of September, 1932, he notified the defendant that he rescinded his
purchase, and that he was ready to tender and return the certificates.

In its answer the defendant as a defense alleges that the plaintiff falsely and fraudulently represented and warranted to the defendant before and at
the time of purchase he was over twenty-one years of age, and that the defendant relied upon these statements in parting with the stock.

That young men, nearly twenty-one years of age, actively engaged in business, can at will revoke any or all of their business transactions and obligations, thereby causing loss to innocent parties dealing with them, upon the
assumption or even the assurance that they were of age, has not appealed to
some courts, and has been adopted without much enthusiasm by others. This
State from the earliest days has followed the common-law doctrine, adopted
at a time when young men were not so actively engaged in trade and in lucrative
occupations as at present. The opportunities for making a living by barter
and sale were not so numerous for them as now.

At common law a male infant attains his majority when he becomes twenty-
one years of age, and all unexecuted contracts made by him before that date,
except for necessaries, while not absolutely void, are voidable at his election. In an action upon a contract made by an infant he is not estopped from
pleading his infancy by any representation as to his age made by him to induce another person to contract with him.... Neither could the infant be
sued for damages in tort by reason of any false representations made in inducing or procuring the contract. For his torts generally, where they have no
basis in any contract relation, an infant is liable, just as any other person
would be, but the doctrine is equally well settled that a matter arising
ex contractu, though infected with fraud, cannot be changed into a tort, in

order to charge an infant, by a change of the remedy.... The only difference between an executory and an executed contract appears to be, that in the former the infant may disaffirm at any time short of the period of the Statute of Limitations, unless by some act he has ratified the contract, whereas in the latter, he must disaffirm within a reasonable time after becoming of age, or his silence will be considered a ratification.

This case pertains to an executed contract for the purchase of stock which the plaintiff has disaffirmed within a reasonable time. The distinction which the appellant would have us make between these well-established authorities and the present case is the fact that the infant is here the plaintiff seeking relief from the courts and should do equity before obtaining relief. That is, while as a defendant the courts will protect him from further liability on his contracts, they will not aid him in getting back money or property which will give him profit or gain through his fraudulent representations regarding his age. This was the view taken by the Appellate Division of the Second Department in Falk v. MacMasters.

This court, however, has not gone so far. The nearest approach to the point is Rice v. Butler. In that case the infant was a plaintiff seeking to recover installments paid upon a bicycle which he offered to return. The court recognized the right of the infant to rescind his bargain and get back his money, insisting, however, that he must pay for the use of, or wear and tear on, the machine. The defendant was allowed to deduct this from the money paid by the infant.

The same principle was followed in Myers v. Hurley Motor Co., where it was held that a contract made by an infant, induced by his fraudulent representations of his age, may be disaffirmed by him and an action maintained to recover money paid under it. However, the infant must do equity and make restitution, not only of the profits and advantages which he has received if possible, but also for the use or deterioration of property, it is to be returned to the defendant. In that case, a young man, twenty years of age, represented that he was twenty-four, and contracted to buy a Hudson touring car, on which he had made certain installment payments. After becoming of age, he disaffirmed his contract and demanded the return of the money paid, offering to return the car. The Supreme Court held, while he was entitled to the relief asked, the defendant was also entitled to recoup out of the infant's money damages for deterioration of the car, or the value of its use. In Rice v. Butler (supra) there was no allegation or proof of false and fraudulent representations as to his age by the infant. In Myers v. Hurley Motor Co. (supra) the fraud was part of the defense. We do not see how the allegation of fraud justifies any distinction of principle. It is a mere element or feature of the case. The fundamental principle is the same, whether the infant be plaintiff or defendant. He may repudiate and rescind his contract upon becoming of age, whether he has made false representations regarding his years or not, and in any instance, the party with whom he had his dealings is entitled to recoup under certain circumstances.

That the false representation regarding age does not prevent rescission, even when the infant be the plaintiff, is the holding of the courts in the majority of our States.... That the infant is not liable in tort for false representations of age inducing a contract, see Slayton v. Barry....

Some of the state courts, however, have taken a different view, and find that fraudulent representations regarding age estop an infant from maintaining an action for relief. (Citing Kentucky, New Jersey and Tennessee Cases.)

Like so many questions of policy, there is much to be said upon both sides and the necessities of one period of time are not always those of another. The law, from time out of mind, has recognized that infants must be protected from their own folly and improvidence. It is not always flattering to our young men in college and in business, between the ages of eighteen and twenty-one, to refer to them as infants, and yet this is exactly what the law considers them in their mental capacities and abilities to protect themselves in ordinary transactions and business relationships. That many young people under twenty-one years of age are improvident and reckless is quite evident, but these defects in judgment are by no means confined to the young. There is another side to the question. As long as young men and women, under twenty-one years of age, having the semblance and appearance of adults, are forced to make a living and enter into business transactions, how are the persons dealing with them to be protected if the infant's word cannot be taken or recognized at law? Are business men to deal with young people at their peril? Well, the law is as it is, and the duty of this court is to give force and effect to the decisions as we find them. Some States have met the situation by legislation. (Citing Iowa, Kansas, Utah, and Washington.) Let us refer to the Iowa Code, as a fair example, taken from the case of Friar v. Rae-Chandler Co. (192 Iowa, 427, at p. 428):

"Sec. 3189. A minor is bound not only by contracts for necessaries, but also by his other contracts, unless he disaffirms them within a reasonable time after he attains his majority, and restores to the other party all money or property received by him by virtue of the contract, and remaining within his control at any time after his attaining his majority, except as otherwise provided.

"Sec. 3190. No contract can be thus disaffirmed in cases where, on account of the minor's own misrepresentations as to his majority, or from his having engaged in business as an adult, the other party had good reason to believe him capable of contracting."

We, therefore, conclude that the law of this State, in accordance with the trend of most of the authorities, is to the effect that the defense pleaded in the answer is insufficient and was properly stricken out by the Appellate Division.

The order should, therefore, be affirmed, with costs.

(Judgment for infant.)

DISCUSSION QUESTIONS

1.   According to the rule of law of this case, adults act at their peril when they contract with infants. In practice, do you think merchants who regularly sell to teen-age infants in the United States (approximately 15 million infants between 13-17) pass along their anticipated losses due to

disaffirmance by charging slightly higher prices? If so, do honest infants pay more because of dishonest infants?

2.   Automobile dealers and other merchants frequently require that an infant who buys "on time" have an adult guarantee payment by the infant. In such a case, the adult guarantor is liable on the infant's contract even if the infant exercises his right to disaffirm and thereby avoid liability. By what other ways can the business community minimize economic risk and loss when dealing with infants?

3.   This case cites the rule of law of Rice v. Butler which is followed today in New York. Does this rule help Normandie Nat. Sec. Corp. who dealt with Sternlieb. Why?

CAPACITY OF PARTIES

INFANTS

CASE NO. 24

KANE v. KANE et al.

13 App. Div. 544 Jan. 27, 1897

INTRODUCTION

Infants frequently enter into contracts with adults. The legal question arises as to (1) what requirement must be met before an infant can disaffirm his contract, (2) when he may disaffirm and (3) whether he may disaffirm without returning the property or money he has received from the other party. This case illustrates the rule of law applicable to real estate contracts entered into by infants.

(In this case a twenty year old infant, PATRICK M. KANE, borrowed $3,750 from an adult and gave him two real estate mortgages on real property owned by the infant as collateral. He spent and squandered the $3,750 while an infant. When Patrick reached his majority (then 21), he sought to disaffirm the two real estate mortgages on the ground that he was an infant at the time he executed the mortgages. At the trial conducted by the court-appointed referee, the adult contended that the infant ratified the mortgages after reaching his majority. After hearing all the evidence, the referee found that the infant had disaffirmed the mortgages and could legally do so without returning the money which he had spent and squandered. The adult appealed the decision to this court.)

HARDIN, P. J.   In Palmer v. Miller it was held that a mortgage executed by an infant is valid until some act is done by him to avoid it. Upon the hearing before the referee, it was clearly shown that Patrick was born on the 1st day of December, 1873, and arrived at his majority on the 1st day of December, 1894. It was thus made to appear that, at the time of the execution of the two mortgages held by the appellant, he was under age. It was also made clear by the evidence that, very soon after coming of age, he elected to disaffirm the mortgages, and gave notice thereof to the appellant. After such proof was given, the appellant took upon himself the burden of establishing a ratification of the mortgages subsequent to the time when Patrick became of age. In Henry v. Root it was said that the burden rests upon the party who seeks to establish a ratification after the infant so executing an instrument attains his majority....

In endeavoring to bear the burden of establishing the allegation of ratification, the appellant was sworn as a witness, and he called in support of his theory of the case two other witnesses, and insisted before the referee that there had been a promise, a ratification, and an approval of the mortgages.

To meet that issue, the defendant was sworn as a witness, and contradicted the testimony, to a large extent, delivered by the appellant. Upon the conflicting evidence presented to the referee, he has made a finding of fact adverse to the appellant. The referee saw the witnesses, their demeanor upon the hearing, and brought to mind all the circumstances attending the supposed ratification, and resolved the conflict in the evidence adverse to the appellant. It was within the prerogative of the referee to determine which of the witnesses he would give credit to. The appellant was interested as a party, and his evidence was open to criticism, cavil, and doubt; and the referee seems to have discredited the statements made by the appellant as a witness, and to have disbelieved the witnesses who were called to support his theory of the case; and a perusal of the evidence found in the appeal book leaves upon our mind the impression that the referee was warranted in reaching that conclusion upon the controverted question of fact.

We are not able to yield to the contention of the learned counsel for the appellant, that the finding of the referee is "clearly against the law and the weight of the evidence." According to the finding of the referee, Patrick had "spent and squandered all of the money that he had received of the defendant Radford" before arriving to full age; and according to the doctrine laid down in Green v. Green under such circumstances he was authorized to disaffirm the mortgages without returning the money.

In Dill v. Bowen, decided by the supreme court of Indiana in 1877 it was said:

"She had a right to disaffirm the deed, and recover the land back, without returning or offering to return the purchase money. Therefore she was guilty of no tort or legal wrong in disaffirming without restoring the purchase money. Having disaffirmed, the law imposes upon her no legal obligation to repay the money. * * * But, if the property has passed from his hands, the law imposes no obligation upon him to account."

In Beardsley v. Hotchkiss it was said:

"The defense of infancy is for the benefit and protection of the infant."

We find nothing in that case inconsistent with the principle which we have already adverted to.

In Hodges v. Hunt the question of a ratification was involved, and it was said:

"A new promise made by him (an infant) after he becomes of full age must possess all the ingredients of a complete agreement, to enable the creditor to recover."

In Mordecai v. Pearl it was said that, after the orders had been "effectually repudiated on the ground of infancy, they must be regarded, so far as they affect his legal rights, as though they never had any existence."

This case differs from Kincaid v. Kincaid, as that was a case where an infant bargained for property, and, on coming of age, received and used it, and sought to repudiate the obligation to pay for it.

The case in hand differs from Palmer v. Miller as in that case, after the infant arrived at majority, there was a fresh acknowledgement of the mortgage, which was held to be a ratification of the same.

In Walsh v. Powers the defense of infancy prevailed, because there was no finding of any act sufficient to work a ratification after the party came of age. We see nothing in the case that aids the contention of the appellant here....

(We are of the opinion that his (referee's) report should be sustained.)

1. In May, B, a 17 year old college student, through X Employment Agency, was introduced to D, the operator of a summer camp. B and D entered into a written agreement whereby D hired B as a camp counsellor during the summer vacation period at a salary of $500 per month. B also agreed in writing to pay X Employment Agency a certain commission for their services. In June, B discovered that he had failed one of his final exams, and he decided that, instead of working, he would attend college during the summer session. B disaffirmed both contracts.

(a) What rights do D and X Employment Agency have against B? Explain.

(b) Would your answer to (a) be the same if, when he entered into the contracts, B had fraudulently misrepresented his age as 18? Explain.

2. A, 17 years old and an orphan, had inherited the family house upon his father's death, and he continued to live there. A applied to B for a loan of $5,000. B, thinking A was of age, loaned the $5,000 to A, and A executed and delivered to B a mortgage on his house. A, after he reached the age of 18, immediately notified B that he disaffirmed the mortgage.

(a) Assume that A had spent the $5,000 on a vacation trip to Europe. Is A entitled to disaffirm the mortgage without tendering $5,000 to B? Explain.

(b) Assume that A had spent $1,000 on a vacation trip, $3,000 on a sports car, and had $1,000 left in his savings bank. What are B's rights against A? Explain.

(c) Assume that A had paid C $4,000 for the repair and renovation of his house, and had paid G, a grocer, $1,000 for necessary food until he reached the age of 18.

    (1) Is A entitled to disaffirm the contract for the purchase of food and to recover $1,000 from G? Explain.

    (2) Is A entitled to disaffirm the contract with C to repair the house and to recover $4,000 from C? Explain.

    (3) If A decided not to disaffirm his contracts with C and G, what are B's rights, if any, when A disaffirms the mortgage?

3. F, the father of a 17 year old son, A, sent his son to a boarding college where F paid A's expenses for board, clothing, and tuition.

(a) Assume that A decided to occupy his spare time, and accordingly contracted to take a two year correspondence course in radio and television maintenance with X Correspondence School. After A became 18, he continued for 6 months to receive the course materials, did the correspondence lessons, used the books sent him, and made six monthly payments. Then he notified X Correspondence School that he disaffirmed any further obligation under the contract.

In an action by X Correspondence School against A to recover the balance due under the contract, judgment for whom? Explain.

(b) Assume that while A was 17, his father suffered financial reverses, and A and F agreed that thereafter A was on his own. In order to return to college, A borrowed $5,000 from the college Student Aid Fund to defray his next year's expenses. The loan was payable at the end of 3 years. When A became 18 he immediately notified the college that he disaffirmed the loan agreement.

May the college enforce the loan agreement against A? Explain.

4. On his 17th birthday, A received a deed to Blackacre, a tract of farmland from his uncle as a gift. A cut down a number of trees suitable for making railroad ties. A sold Blackacre to B for $10,000, and the felled timber to C for $1,000. He spent the money, and immediately after his 18th birthday notified B and C that he disaffirmed the respective contracts. In the meantime, however, B had sold Blackacre to M, and C had sold the timber to N. Is A entitled to recover:

(a) Blackacre from M? Explain.

(b) the timber from N under common law? Explain.

(c) the timber from N under the Uniform Commercial Code? Explain.

5. A, 17 years old, bought a sports car for $3,000 on the installment plan. He had already paid $1,500 on the car, when he disaffirmed the contract on his 18th birthday. He offered to return the car and demanded the return of the $1,500 paid. The car is now worth only $2,000. What are the rights of the parties under:

(a) the majority rule? Explain.

(b) the minority rule? Explain.

6. Y, a minor, is studying to become a television repairman. He agrees to repair a television set belonging to O, a friend of the family, for $75 with a thirty-day parts and workmanship guaranty. Y does the work in such a negligent manner that the television set is ruined beyond repair.

(a) O sues Y for damages for breach of contract. Will he recover? Explain.

(b) O sues Y for the tort (wrong) of negligence. Will he recover? Explain.

143

NEW YORK CIVIL PRACTICE LAW AND RULES (C.P.L.R.)

Section 3002. Actions And Relief Not Barred For Inconsistency

....

(d) Action on Contract and to Reform. A judgment denying recovery in an action upon an agreement in writing shall not be deemed to bar an action to reform such agreement and to enforce it as reformed.

(e) Claim for Damages and Rescission. A claim for damages sustained as a result of fraud or misrepresentation in the inducement of a contract or other transaction, shall not be deemed inconsistent with a claim for rescission or based upon rescission. In an action for rescission or based upon rescission the aggrieved party shall be allowed to obtain complete relief in one action, including rescission, restitution of the benefits, if any, conferred by him as a result of the transaction, and damages to which he is entitled because of such fraud or misrepresentation; but such complete relief shall not include duplication of items of recovery. (eff. 1962)

Section 3004. Where Restoration Of Benefits Before Judgment Unnecessary

A party who has received benefits by reason of a transaction that is void or voidable because of fraud, misrepresentation, mistake, duress, infancy or incompetancy, and who, in an action or by way of defense or counterclaim, seeks rescission, restitution, a declaration or judgment that such transaction is void, or other relief, whether formerly denominated legal or equitable, dependent upon a determination that such transaction was void or voidable, shall not be denied relief because of a failure to tender before judgment restoration of such benefits; but the court may make a tender of restoration a condition of its judgment, and may otherwise in its judgment so adjust the equities between the parties that unjust enrichment is avoided. (eff. 1962)

Section 3005. Relief Against Mistake Of The Law

When relief against a mistake is sought in an action or by way of defense or counterclaim, relief shall not be denied merely because the mistake is one of law rather than one of fact. (eff. 1962)

Section 213. Actions To Be Commenced....Based On Mistake;...Based on Fraud

The following actions must be commenced within six years

....

6. an action based on mistake;

....

8. An action based upon fraud; the time within which the action must be commenced shall be computed from the time the plaintiff or the person under

whom he claims discovered the fraud, or could with reasonable diligence have discovered it. (eff. Sept. 1, 1975, as amended)

UNIFORM COMMERCIAL CODE: ARTICLE 2 - SALE OF GOODS

Section 2-403. Power To Transfer; Good Faith Purchaser of Goods;...

(1) A purchaser of goods acquires all title which his transferor had or had power to transfer except that a purchaser of a limited interest acquires rights only to the extent of the interest purchased. A person with voidable title has power to transfer a good title to a good faith purchaser for value. When goods have been delivered under a transaction of purchase the purchaser has such power even though

(a) the transferor was deceived as to the identity of the purchaser, or

(b) the delivery was in exchange for a check which is later dishonored, or

(c) it was agreed that the transaction was to be a "cash sale", or

(d) the delivery was procured through fraud punishable as larcenous under the criminal law....

Section 2-721. Remedies For Fraud

Remedies for material misrepresentation or fraud include all remedies available under this Article for non-fraudulent breach. Neither rescission or a claim for rescission of the contract for sale nor rejection or return of the goods shall bar or be deemed inconsistent with a claim for damages or other remedy.

Duress (coercion) and fraud could also impose criminal penalties. For example: See New York Penal Law 135.60: Coercion In The Second Degree under topic of Illegality

The term "fraud" is used in several sections of the New York Penal Law. See: Title K, "Offenses Involving Fraud", Sections 170-190.50 of the New York Penal Law.

Section 190.60.   Scheme To Defraud In The Second Degree

1.   A person is guilty of a scheme to defraud in the second degree when he (a) engages in a scheme constituting a systematic ongoing course of conduct with intent to defraud more than one person or to obtain property from more than one person by false or fraudulent pretenses, representations or promises, and (b) so obtains property from one or more of such persons.

2.   In any prosecution under this section, it shall be necessary to prove the identity of at least one person from whom the defendant so obtained property, but it shall not be necessary to prove the identity of any other intended victim.

Scheme to defraud in the second degree is a class A misdemeanor.

Section 190.65.   Scheme To Defraud In The First Degree

1.   A person is guilty of a scheme to defraud in the first degree when he (a) engages in a scheme constituting a systematic ongoing course of conduct with intent to defraud ten or more persons or to obtain property from ten or more persons by false or fraudulent pretenses, representations or promises, and (b) so obtains property from one or more of such persons.

2.   In any prosecution under this section, it shall be necessary to prove the identity of at least one person from whom the defendant so obtained property, but it shall not be necessary to prove the identity of any other intended victim.

Scheme to defraud in the first degree is a class E felony.

Note: Sections 190.60 and 190.65 of the New York Penal Law became effective on Jan. 1, 1977, and are derived from the federal crime of using the mails to defraud (18 U.S. Code 1341).

<u>REALITY OF ASSENT: FRAUD</u>

CASE NO. 25

RENO v. BULL

226 N. Y. 546   July 1919

<u>INTRODUCTION</u>

After a contract has been performed, the buyer may sue the seller to recover money damages claiming that the seller induced the buyer to enter into
the contract by committing fraud against the buyer. This case illustrates
(1) what a party must prove before a jury or court will find that fraud has
been committed, (2) how money damages are computed when fraud is proven, and
(3) the legal distinction between negligence and fraud.

McLAUGHLIN, J. Action to recover damages for fraud and deceit, by reason
of which it is claimed plaintiff was induced to purchase fifty shares, each of
the par value of $100, of the captial stock of the American Oriental Company,
a Maine corporation. Plaintiff had a verdict for $6,000, and from the judg-
ment entered thereon defendants appealed to the Appellate Division, where the
same was unanimously affirmed, and by permission they now appeal to this court.

The unanimous affirmance of the judgment conclusively establishes that
the findings of the jury are sustained by evidence. The judgment, therefore,
must be affirmed, unless errors, presented by proper exceptions, were committed
by the trial court which affect the substantial rights of the defendants.

After a careful consideration of the record, the briefs and argument of
respective counsel, I have reached the conclusion that there are at least two
errors of this character which are so fundamental that they necessitate the
reversal of the judgment. They are instructions given to the jury as to the
duty and obligations of the defendants and as to the measure of damages.

As to the duty and obligations of the defendants: At the time the stock
was purchased, they were, with others, directors of the corporation. It had a
plant, which cost several hundred thousand dollars, for refining crude oil,
located on San Francisco bay, in the state of California. The corporation was
organized with a capital stock of four million dollars, two million common and
two million preferred, and one million of the latter it was desirous of inducing the public to buy. To that end, it made an arrangement with Charles D.
Barney & Company, prominent bankers in New York and Philadelphia, to offer the
same for sale prior to the offering, Barney & Company prepared a circular, or
prospectus, signed by them, which consisted of a letter from one Ertz, the
president of the corporation, addressed to Barney & Company, which contained
statements as to the capacity of the plant, probable earnings of the corporation, crude oil supplied in the state of California, advantages in securing
trade in the Orient and large dividends that would be received by holders of
preferred stock. The circular also contained the names of the directors, the
advisory committee and other matters unnecessary to state. This circular was

adopted and approved by the directors of the corporation. The statements contained in the circular, which the plaintiff claimed were and which the jury have found to be false, were (a) that the plant was well built, fully completed and had a capacity of refining 2,000 barrels of crude oil per day; (b) that there was an abundance of crude oil in the state of California; and (c) that there was a profitable Oriental market for the sale of the refined products. In connection with these alleged false statements, it was also claimed that the defendants were liable, by reason of a statement made by Ertz, the president of the corporation, to the plaintiff at or immediately prior to the time he purchased the stock, to the effect that the corporation would begin business with $1,000,000 cash capital.

No evidence was offered at the trial, nor was the claim there made, or upon the argument before us, that the defendants or any of them had actual knowledge of the alleged false statements set forth in the circular or the statement made by the president, or that they had any connection with such statements other than as directors of the corporation, and all except one of them testified at the trial that they, at the time the circular was issued, believed the statements therein made to be true.

The action, as indicated, was to recover for fraud and deceit and to maintain it the plaintiff had to prove that the defendants, as directors, by adopting and authorizing Barney & Company to issue the circular, made the representations alleged; that such representations were false; that they knew they were false; that they were made for the purpose of deceiving the public, and that he, believing the same to be true, made the purchase and was thereby damaged; in other words, the plaintiff had to prove, as this court has recently said, "Representation, falsity, scienter, deception and injury." .... This rule is so well settled in this state that the citation of authorities seems almost unnecessary. The jury should have been so instructed. The trial court, however, in utter disregard of this rule, said to the jury that it was the duty of the defendants, when they, as directors of the corporation, approved of the circular, to know the truth of the facts stated therein and if they did not know whether such facts were true, they were bound to know if they had a reasonable opportunity to ascertain the same. He said, "It is their duty before they allow these representations to be made to the public...to know the facts... even though they believe the representations to be true...; if they had ample time to know...they are bound.... In other words, if although they did not know these facts and did not know them to be false, if they authorized the issuance of the prospectus, and authorized the statements to be made, then they are liable,...if in the exercise of ordinary care in the conduct of the business they would have been given means of knowing that they were false.... If they authorized a false statement to be made, when by common prudence and the exercise of ordinary care, they could have discovered that these representations were false, then they are just as liable as if they had actual personal knowledge that they were false:"

When the instructions thus given are subjected to the rule above stated, it at once becomes apparent that the same were erroneous. Erroneous, because there was substituted as the test of defendant's liability, negligence, instead of a purpose to deceive. Negligence and fraud are not synonymous terms: nor in legal effect are they equivalent terms. Fraud presupposes a willful purpose resorted to with intent to deprive another of his legal rights. It is positive in that the purpose concurs with the act, designedly and knowingly committed. Negligence, whatever be its grade, does not include a purpose to do a wrongful act. It may be some evidence of, but is not fraud.... Fraud always has its origin in a purpose, but negligence is an omission of duty minus the purpose.

In the instant case, the defendants, in approving the circular and authorizing Barney & Company to offer the stock for sale, acted solely for the corporation. They were not members of a syndicate to promote the sale, nor were they nor any of them, underwriters of the stock offered to the public. So far as they were concerned, the corporation alone was interested in the sale. Barney & Company was its agent and not the agent of the defendants.

The rule as to the measure of damages was not the one to be applied. The court said to the jury that if the plaintiff were entitled to recover, then he should be awarded "the difference between the value of the stock at the time it was sold to him...and the value of the stock as it would have been at the time if the representations were true. The purpose of an action for deceit is to indemnify the party injured. All elements of profit are excluded. The true measure of damage is indemnity for the actual pecuniary loss sustained as the direct result of the wrong. The plaintiff paid $5,000 for the stock purchased by him. If he were entitled to recover at all, it was the difference between that amount and the value of the stock which he received with interest from that time. He was not entitled to anything else.

My conclusion is that the judgments of the Appellate Division and the Trial Term should be reversed and a new trial ordered, with costs to abide event.

(Judgment for defendant.)

DISCUSSION QUESTION

1.   What other remedy does a victim of fraud have?

2.   If a victim of fraud wishes to disaffirm the contract, does he have to prove scienter?

REALITY OF ASSENT: MUTUAL MISTAKE

REMEDIES: REFORMATION OF CONTRACT

CASE NO. 26

AMEND v. HURLEY

293 N.Y. 587   December 1944

INTRODUCTION

When a written contract contains any provision as a result of mistakes made by both parties (mutual mistake), either party may ask the court to reform their written contract so that the correct provisions agreed to are included. The party who does not want the written contract reformed because the incorrect provisions are favorable to him will object to reformation of the contract on the legal ground that there was no mutual mistake but only unilateral mistake which does not legally justify reformation. This case illustrates what the legal requirements are and the burden of proof that must be met before a court will reform a written contract.

RIPPEY, J. George J. Hoffmann died June 10, 1937, then being the owner and proprietor of a sugar-weighing business in the city of New York which he had operated successfully and with large profits for more than thirty years under the trade name and style of "George J. Hoffmann & Company". For most of that time and at the time of his death, defendant was employed by Hoffmann on a yearly salary which included 37½% of the profits in the conduct of that business during the latter part of his employment. By the terms of his will, which was admitted to probate, Hoffmann left his whole estate to his wife, Anna E. Hoffmann, and named her executrix thereof.

From the time of Hoffmann's death, defendant actively sought to acquire and to operate his previous employer's business for himself alone and demonstrated no intention to continue to operate it for the estate. Matters reached a point when, on July 12, 1937, Mrs. Hoffmann had a conference with him with reference to his continuance of the business in behalf of the estate and he then notified her, definitely for the first time, that he would not act as manager of the business but was interested only in acquiring the business as his own. He then offered to pay her 50% of the profits of the business provided he should become the owner and should be allowed to run it entirely by himself, she to have no other interest. No agreement was reached at that conference between the parties and from that time on negotiations were carried forward principally between Joseph A. McNamara, attorney for Mrs. Hoffmann individually and for her husband's estate, and George W. Sheldon, a man of long practice and a member of one of the leading law firms of New York City, as attorney for Hurley.

A series of verbal conferences and written correspondence followed between the attorneys, who from time to time advanced various differing suggestions and proposals in behalf of their respective clients in an effort to reach an agreement, all without success. In that situation, it was agreed between the

150

attorneys on July 26, 1937, that McNamara should draft a proposed agreement and submit it to Sheldon for examination. That he did in typewritten form on the same day. In this draft, the termination of the agreement was fixed for June 30, 1945. McNamara, however, tentatively provided alternatively with other provisions for his client's benefit, in article X "that in the event of the death of the party of the first part (Mrs. Hoffmann) prior to July 1st, 1945, this agreement shall cease and terminate and all interest of the party of the first part thereunder come to an end as of the date of the death of the party of first part....The draft contained eleven separately numbered articles. After editing the draft to his satisfaction, Sheldon returned it to McNamara. Every one of the articles contained some changes, deletions, or additions in Sheldon's handwriting in ink, or, in some cases, a rider was attached, affecting not only the form but the substance of the article to which the same was applicable. When returned, it evidenced extensive and exhaustive examination by Sheldon and care on his part for the utmost of protection of his client's interests with carefully drawn provisions for his benefit which were not contained in McNamara's draft. There was no evidence that he had missed any opportunity to drive a good bargain for his client. Among other things, he drew lines through the entire part of article X quoted above and wrote opposite that part of the draft on the margin in large letters the word "No" and heavily underscored it. He made changes in the clauses relating to life insurance designed to protect Mrs. Hoffmann against losses under the contract. Thereupon the draft with its changes was sent to McNamara who retyped it verbatim with all changes and additions made by Sheldon, except in three minor particulars which did not change the wording, substance or effect of article X as re-prepared by Sheldon. Otherwise, neither in punctuation, words nor substance did the retyped instrument vary in any particular from the draft as edited by Sheldon. McNamara then presented the complete contract to Mrs. Hoffmann who discussed it at length with her attorney. She was not satisfied with the changes regarding life insurance protection against the death of Hurley before July 1, 1945, but finally acceded to the changes made by Sheldon and executed the final draft in duplicate on July 28, 1937. The agreement so executed was then delivered to Sheldon who presented it to his client who signed it in duplicate and one of the duplicate copies was given to McNamara....

Both parties fully performed the contract, without objection or question by either, until the death of Mrs. Hoffmann. The business under Hurley's operation continued to be profitable. Hurley, previous to her death, accounted for the profits and paid to Mrs. Hoffmann from the profits some $20,634. After her death he refused to perform further and this action was thereupon brought for specific performance.

The defense was a mistake on the part of Sheldon and fraud on the part of McNamara. Defendant claimed that his attorney inadvertently and mistakenly struck out from the McNamara draft the first sentence of article X, that McNamara knew this was inadvertently stricken out and failed to correct the mistake on copying the agreement in final form or to notify Sheldon of his mistake and that he, Hurley, did not read the final agreement when he signed it relying on Sheldon's statement that it was all right. Accordingly defendant has asked that the agreement be reformed so as to provide that it should terminate on the death of Mrs. Hoffmann.

The Trial Judge, who saw Sheldon, Hurley and McNamara on the witness stand

and heard them testify gave no credit to defendant's claim that the final written agreement did not express the true intention of the parties. The advantages of the trial court who saw and heard the witnesses should be considered and, when truth hangs upon the credibility of witnesses, his decision should be given the greatest weight....The trial court found that the evidence established that there never existed any verbal agreement between the parties, that the draft by McNamara was satisfactory to Sheldon in neither form nor substance, that his counter-proposals were reflected in the changes, deletions and additions which he made to the McNamara proposal, that McNamara accepted the counter-proposals, and that there was no meeting of the minds of the parties or any terms of agreement ever fixed until the formal written contract was executed. The Appellate Division, by a three to two vote, found to the contrary. We find that the weight of the evidence sustained the findings of the trial court. Defendant was a businessman of experience and competence and adept in the understanding and use of the English language. Not to have read the contract or to have had it read to him before signing, if that be a fact as he testified, furnishes no basis for his repudiation of any of its terms....

Before defendant can be granted reformation, he must establish his right to such relief by clear, positive and convincing evidence. Reformation may not be granted upon a probability nor even upon a mere preponderance of evidence, but only upon a certainty of error....The quality of the evidence in this case does not meet that test. Nor may the defendant secure reformation merely upon a showing that he or his attorney made a mistake. In the absence of fraud, the mistake shown "must be one made by both parties to the agreement so that the intentions of neither are expressed in it"....The court may not compel the plaintiffs to be bound by a contract which their principal never made....Since the right to reform the contract here is not claimed on the ground of mutual mistake, reliance is based on the alleged mistake of Sheldon and of defendant and the alleged fraud of McNamara in not disclosing to Sheldon his knowledge that the mistake was made. Both courts below have held that there was no fiduciary relation existing between McNamara on the one side and Sheldon and Hurley on the other. The trial court held upon the overwhelming weight of the evidence that the parties were "dealing at arm's length". There is no evidence that McNamara had any idea or knowledge that Sheldon had made a mistake. McNamara denies that he had either. To overcome that lack of evidence and the denial of McNamara and the inevitable consequence of the facts as established, the court would be compelled, to hold the contrary, to examine into the innermost recesses of McNamara's mind which, at least, would be a hazardous undertaking....Such a procedure may not here be undertaken in the face of the chain of events and the convincing facts. Were it otherwise "The law requires disclosure to be made only when there is a duty to make it, and this duty is not raised by the mere circumstance that the undisclosed fact is material, and is known to the one party, and not to the other, or by the additional circumstance that the party to whom it is known, knows that the other party is acting in ignorance of it"....It is not fraud for one party to say nothing on the subject where no confidential or fiduciary relation exists and where no false statement or acts to mislead the other are made....In the circumstances in this case, a finding of fraud may not be predicated upon McNamara's failure to speak, whether or not he had knowledge of Sheldon or to the defendant. Having accepted and acted on the written instrument, in the absence of fraud and deceit or mutual mistake, defendant was bound by its terms as the only existing agreement between the parties even though it did not contain some provision on which the parties may have agreed during the negotiations....

The judgment of the Appellate Division should be reversed and that of the Special Term affirmed, with costs in this court and in the Appellate Division.

(Judgment for plaintiff.)

DISCUSSION QUESTIONS

1.   How could Hurley have avoided the mistake he said he and his attorney made?

2.   What kind of provisions included in written contracts are most likely to be the object of an action to reform a contract? One example are provisions that refer to dollar amounts or dates which are mistakenly typed and which neither party discovers at the time of execution. Can you name other provisions?

3.   Was the mistake in the contract involved in this lawsuit a unilateral or mutual mistake? Why?

4.   What legal tests must be met before a court will reform a contract when mistake is alleged to have been made in the written contract?

AUSTIN INSTRUMENT, INC., v. LORAL CORPORATION

29 N.Y. 2d 124   July 1971

INTRODUCTION

Sometimes a seller asks a buyer to amend their contract to provide for
increases in prices of goods which remain to be delivered under their contract. Where a buyer reluctantly agrees to pay increased prices to insure
delivery, the buyer may successfully use economic duress as a defense to
avoid liability for the increase in prices he agreed to if certain conditions
are met as is illustrated by this leading case on the subject of economic
duress.

Chief Judge FULD. The defendant, Loral Corporation, seeks to recover
payment for goods delivered under a contract which it had with plaintiff
Austin Instrument, Inc., on the ground that the evidence establishes, as a
mater of law, that it was forced to agree to an increase in price on the
items in question under circumstances amounting to economic duress.

In July of 1965, Loral was awarded a $6,000,000 contract by the Navy for
the production of radar sets. The contract contained a schedule of deliveries,
a liquidated damages clause applying to late deliveries and a cancellation
clause in case of default by Loral. The latter thereupon solicited bids for
some 40 precision gear components needed to produce the radar sets, and
awarded Austin a subcontract to supply 23 such parts. That party commenced
delivery in early 1966.

In May, 1966, Loral was awarded a second Navy contract for the production of more radar sets and again went about soliciting bids. Austin bid
on all 40 gear components but, on July 15, a representative from Loral informed Austin's president, Mr. Krauss, that his company would be awarded the
subcontract only for those items on which it was low bidder. The Austin
officer refused to accept an order for less than all 40 of the gear parts
and on the next day he told Loral that Austin would cease deliveries of the
parts due under the existing subcontract unless Loral consented to substantial increases in the prices provided for by that agreement--both retro-
actively for parts already delivered and prospectively on those not yet
shipped--and placed with Austin the order for all 40 parts needed under
Loral's second Navy contract. Shortly thereafter, Austin did, indeed, stop
delivery. After contacting 10 manufacturers of precision gears and finding
none who could produce the parts in time to meet its commitments to the Navy,
Loral acceded to Austin's demands; in a letter dated July 22, Loral wrote to
Austin that "We have feverishly surveyed other sources of supply and find that
because of the prevailing military exigencies, were they to start from
scratch as would have to be the case, they could not even remotely begin to
deliver on time.... Accordingly, we are left with no choice or alternative
to meet your conditions."

Loral thereupon consented to the price increases insisted upon by Austin
under the first subcontract and the latter was awarded a second subcontract

and the latter was awarded a second subcontract making it the supplier of all 40 gear parts for Loral's second contract with the Navy. Although Austin was granted until September to resume deliveries, Loral did, in fact, receive parts in August and was able to produce the radar sets in time to meet its commitments to the Navy on both contracts. After Austin's last delivery under the second subcontract in July, 1967, Loral notified it of its intention to seek recovery of the price increases.

On September 15, 1967, Austin instituted this action against Loral to recover an amount in excess of $17,750 which was still due on the second subcontract. On the same day, Loral commenced an action against Austin claiming damages of some $22,250--the aggregate of the price increases under the first subcontract--on the ground of economic duress. The two actions were consolidated and, following a trial, Austin was awarded the sum it requested and Loral's complaint against Austin was dismissed on the ground that it was not shown that "it could not have obtained the items in question from other sources in time to meet its commitment to the Navy under the first contract." A closely divided Appellate Division affirmed.... There was no material disagreement concerning the facts; as Justice STEUER stated in the course of his dissent below, "the facts are virtually undisputed, nor is there any serious question of law. The difficulty lies in the application of the law to these facts.".....

The applicable law is clear and, indeed, is not disputed by the parties. A contract is voidable on the ground of duress when it is established that the party making the claim was forced to agree to it by means of a wrongful threat precluding the exercise of his free will.... The existence of economic duress or business compulsion is demonstrated by proof that "immediate possession of needful goods is threatened"...or, more particularly, in cases such as the one before us, by proof that one party to a contract has threatened to breach the agreement by withholding goods unless the other party agrees to some further demand.... However, a mere threat by one party to breach the contract by not delivering the required items, though wrongful, does not in itself constitute economic duress. It must also appear that the threatened party could not obtain the goods from another source of supply and that the ordinary remedy of an action for breach of contract would not be adequate."

We find without any support in the record the conclusion reached by the courts below the Loral failed to establish that it was the victim of economic duress. On the contrary, the evidence makes out a classic case, as a matter of law, os such duress.

It must be remembered that Loral was producing a needed item of military hardware. Moreover, there is authority for Loral's position that nonperformance by a subcontractor is not an excuse for default in the main contract.... In light of all this, Loral's claim should not be held insufficiently supported because it did not request an extension from the Government.

Loral, as indicated above, also had the burden of demonstrating that it could not obtain the parts elsewhere within a reasonable time, and there can be no doubt that it met this burden. The 10 manufacturers whom Loral contracted comprised its entire list of "approved vendor" for precision gears, and none was able to commence delivery soon enough. As Loral was producing a highly

sophisticated item of military machinery requiring parts made to the strictest
engineering standards, it would be unreasonable to hold that Loral should have
gone to other vendors, with whom it was either unfamiliar or dissatisfied, to
procure the needed parts. As Justice STEUER noted in his dissent, Loral "contacted all the manufacturers whom it believed capable of making these parts"...,
and this was all the law requires.

It is hardly necessary to add that Loral's normal legal remedy of accepting
Austin's breach of the contract and then suing for damages would have been inadequate under the circumstances, as Loral would still have had to obtain the
gears elsewhere with all the concomitant consequences mentioned above. In other
words, Loral actually had no choice, when the prices were raised by Austin, except to take the gears at the "coerced" prices and then sue to get the excess
back.

Austin's final argument is that Loral, even if it did enter into the contract under duress, lost any rights it had to a refund of money by waiting
until July, 1967, long after the termination date of the contract, to disaffirm
it. It is true that one who would recover monies allegedly paid under duress
must act promptly to make his claim known.... In this case, Loral delayed
making its demand for a refund until these days after Austin's last delivery on
the second subcontract. Loral's reason--for waiting until that time--is that it
feared another stoppage of deliveries which would again put it in an untenabale
situation. Considering Austin's conduct in the past, application by Austin of
further business compulsion still existed until all of the parts were delivered.

In sum, the record before us demonstrates that Loral agreed to the price
increases in consequence of the economic duress employed by Austin. Accordingly,
the matter should be remanded to the trial court for a computation of its
damages.

DISCUSSION QUESTION

1. How can a seller avoid this successful defense being raised at a later date
by a buyer when the two parties agree to an increase in price?

156

REALITY OF ASSENT - FRAUD, MISREPRESENTATION
DURESS, MISTAKE, UNDUE INFLUENCE

1. S owned five acres of land in Wilton, New York, on which were two springs of mineral water and machinery to bottle the mineral water. S sold the real property to B for $15,000 representing that the water was natural mineral water and could be bottled or sold as it flowed from the ground. He also represented that the daily natural flow of water from the two springs was 4,200 gallons.

B entered into possession and purchased and installed modern machinery for the bottling and distribution of the mineral water. He soon discovered that the water was not natural mineral water, but fresh water to which certain chemicals had been added, and that the daily flow did not exceed 160 gallons. Meanwhile, B had expended $4,500 in the installation and operation of machinery, cost of new machinery and for labor paid.

What remedy or remedies, if any, are available to B:

(a) under common law? Explain.

(b) under New York law? Explain.

2. On April 1 S, a dealer in mining stocks, sold B 10,000 shares of Alaska Uranium Ltd. at $1 per share knowingly misrepresenting that the Corporation had proven uranium deposits in its Alaska tract. B paid for the stock on April 1, and on April 15, on the advice of friends, he had the Corporation investigated and found that it never had any prospects of uranium but that it had just discovered a copper vein on the tract and was putting it into production. On the following February B received a check from the Corporation for its one cent per share dividend and deposited it. One month later B regretted his purchase.

(a) In an action by B against S to disaffirm the contract, judgment for whom? Explain.

(b) In an action by B against S to recover damages based on fraud, judgment for whom? Explain.

(c) Is B entitled to disaffirm and sue for damages at the same time under New York Civil Practice Law and Rules Section 3002(e)? Explain.

(d) In an action by B against Alaska Uranium Ltd. to recover damages based on fraud, judgment for whom? Explain.

3. M Corporation, a well-known radio and televisiion manufacturer had several odd lots of discontinued models which it desired to clear out. M, the president, invited D, the owner of the D Discount Chain to come in and examine the different models and make M an offer for the entire lot. The sets were segregated from the regular inventory. Fifteen radios which were not discontinued models were inadvertently included in this segregated group. D was unaware that M did not intend to include the fifteen radios in the group.

D made M an offer of $9,000 for the entire lot, which represented a sharp reduction in price from the normal sales price. Being unaware of the error, M accepted the offer. M would not have accepted D's offer had it known the fifteen current models were included.

Upon learning of the error M Corporation refused to perform and alleged mistake as a defense. D Discount Chain sued M Corporation for breach of contract.

Judgment for whom? Explain.

4. C was bequeathed an oil painting by his childless aunt. C was not favorably disposed toward the painting because it reminded him that his aunt had left her entire estate (except the painting) to the Society for the Prevention of Cruelty to Animals. When C's best friend, B, admired it, C offered to sell it to him for $10. B accepted, paid the $10 and took the painting.

The painting was plainly an original and bore the signature "Ad Schreyer", but neither C nor B had ever heard of the painter.

Several weeks later, B gleefully informed C that he inquired about the artist and had learned that the painting was worth $7,500.

C thereupon tendered B $10 and demanded the return of the "Schreyer." B refused and C brought suit to recover the painting.

(a) Judgment for whom? Explain.

(b) Would your answer to (a) be the same if B had known, at the time he bought the painting, that Ad Schreyer was a famous artist and that the painting was far more valuable than realized? Explain.

5. A Shipping Company transported a cargo of jute for I Trading Corporation from Pakistan to New York. On arrival in New York A refused to release the cargo unless I paid $3,000 for demurrage, in addition to the agreed freight charges. A claimed that when its vessel arrived in Pakistan, the cargo was not ready for loading and that, as a result, there was a 3 days' delay in loading. I cabled its representative in Pakistan and was informed that the delay in loading was caused by the failure of the Captain of the vessel to obtain the necessary papers to enter the port, and not through the fault of I.

158

I tendered payment of the freight charges and suggested that the claim for demurrage be deferred until the cause of the delay could be established. A arbitrarily rejected the suggestion and again advised I that it would not release the jute unless the demurrage charges were paid. I then informed A that it was under contract to deliver the jute to a customer within two days, and that unless it delivered on time, not only would I suffer a very substantial loss on that contract, but would also lose a very valuable account. A remained adamant. Thereupon, I paid the freight and demurrage charges, the latter upon protest.

Assume the facts concerning the delay to be as claimed by I's representative in Pakistan. Is there any legal theory upon which I may recover the demurrage charge of $3,000 it paid to A? Explain.

6.   A gave the following message to W Telegraph Co. to be sent to B:

"Will sell 800 M laths two ten net cash."

In error, W Telegraph Co. sent the following message to B:

"Will sell 800 M laths two net cash."

B wired:

"Accept your telegraphic offer on laths."

Shortly thereafter, A informed B of the error made by the telegraph company Nevertheless, B insisted upon delivery of the 800 M laths at $2.00 per M. A thereupon delivered at that price.

A then brought action against the W Telegraph Co. to recover the difference between the $2.00 per M price and $2.10 per M for 800 M laths, claiming that due to its negligence, he had become bound by contract to sell at $2.00 per M, instead of at $2.10, as he intended.

The W Telegraph Co. contended that A was not obliged to sell at $2.00 per M because there had been no meeting of the minds and no contract.

(a)   Judgment for whom? Explain.

(b)   Would your answer to (a) be the same if the telegram delivered by the defendant read:

"Will sell 800 M laths at one ten net cash."? Explain.

1. In the event the purchaser seeks to rescind a contract for the purchase
    of land because of the seller's misrepresentation (as contrasted with
    seeking damages for the tort of fraud), the plaintiff (purchaser)

    a. Need not show knowledge of falsity on the defendant's part (seller)
        in order to recover.
    b. Need not show reliance upon the misrepresentation on his part in
        order to recover.
    c. Can resort to the Statute of Frauds in order to obtain a rescission
        of the contract.
    d. Will prevail only if there was misrepresentation in the execution
        which renders the contract void.

2. Williams induced Jackson to enter into an employment contract by
    deliberately telling Jackson certain material facts which Williams knew
    were not true. If there are no other relevant facts, on what legal
    grounds is the contract voidable?

    a. Undue influence.
    b. Fraud.
    c. Duress.
    d. Unilateral mistake of fact.

3. A contract was created by a false representation of a material fact. The
    fact was known to be false by the person making the representation, and
    there was an intent to deceive the party who relied on the representation
    to his detriment. This contract is voidable on the basis of

    a. Undue influence.
    b. Fraud.
    c. Duress.
    d. Negligence.

4. In the process of negotiating the sale of his manufacturing business to
    Grand, Sterling made certain untrue statements which Grand relied upon.
    Grand was induced to purchase the business for $10,000 more than its
    true value. Grand is not sure whether he should seek relief based upon
    misrepresentation or fraud. Which of the following is a correct
    statement?

    a. If Grand merely wishes to rescind the contract and get his money
        back, misrepresentation is his best recourse.
    b. In order to prevail under the fraud theory, Grand must show that
        Sterling intended for him to rely on the untrue statements; whereas
        he need not do so if he bases his action on misrepresentation.
    c. Both fraud and misrepresentation require Grand to prove that
        Sterling knew the statements were false.
    d. If Grand chooses fraud as his basis for relief, the Statute of
        Frauds applies.

5. Master Corporation, a radio and television manufacturer, invited Darling Discount Chain to examine several odd lots of discontinued models and make an offer for the entire lot. The odd lots were segregated from the regular inventory but inadvertently included 15 current models. Darling was unaware that Master did not intend to include the 15 current models in the group. Darling made Master an offer of $9,000 for the entire lot, which represented a large discount from the normal sales price. Unaware of the error, Master accepted the offer. Master would not have accepted had it known of the inclusion of the 15 current models. Upon learning of the error, Master alleged mistake as a defense and refused to perform. Darling sued for breach of contract. Under the circumstances, what is the status of the contract?

   a. There is no contract since Master did not intend to include the 15 current models in the group of radios to be sold.
   b. The contract is voidable because of a unilateral mistake.
   c. The contract is voidable because of a mutual mistake.
   d. There is a valid and binding contract which includes the 15 current model radios.

6. The element which makes fraud or deceit an intentional tort is

   a. The materiality of the misrepresentation.
   b. Detrimental reliance.
   c. Actual reliance by the aggrieved party upon the misrepresentation.
   d. Scienter or knowledge of falsity.

7. Madison advertised for the submission of bids on the construction of a parking lot. Kilroy submitted a bid of $112,000. There were nine other bids. Kilroy's bid was $45,000 less than the next lowest bid. The discrepancy was due to the omission of a $46,000 item on the part of Kilroy's staff. Madison accepted the bid and demands either performance or damages from Kilroy. Kilroy is

   a. Bound by the acceptance at $112,000.
   b. Not bound by the acceptance but only if Madison knew of the mistake.
   c. Not bound by the acceptance if the mistake should have been known by Madison.
   d. Not bound by the bid submitted because there was no subjective meeting of the minds.

8. Smith, an executive of Apex Corporation, became emotionally involved with Jones. At the urging of Jones, and fearing that Jones would sever their relationship, Smith reluctantly signed a contract which was grossly unfair to Apex. Apex's best basis to rescind the contract would be

   a. Lack of express authority.
   b. Duress.
   c. Undue influence.
   d. Lack of consideration.

ILLEGALITY

Over the years, New York State has enacted statutes which provide certain contract provisions to be contrary to public policy, and has declared such contract provisions to be unlawful, illegal, void, and/or unenforceable. In addition, some statutes place prohibitions against certain contract provisions and against certain trade practices, and in some instances the statute imposes a criminal penalty. These statutory provisions cover numerous areas of the law. A representative sample of some of these statutory provisions, divided by the following subtopics, follows:

1. Wagering Contracts
2. Larceny
3. Coercion
4. Commercial Bribing
5. Usury
6. Licensing Statutes
7. Unconscionable Contracts and Unconscionable Clauses
8. Exculpatory Clauses
9. Contracts In Restraint Of Trade
10. False Advertising
11. False Advertising and Consumer Protection
12. Trade Practices - relating to Miscellaneous Consumer Transactions
13. Sunday Laws

1. WAGERING CONTRACTS

NEW YORK GENERAL OBLIGATIONS LAW

Section 5-401. Illegal Wagers, Bets and Stakes

All wagers, bets or stakes, made to depend upon any race, or upon any gaming by lot or chance, or upon any lot, chance, casualty or unknown or contingent event whatever, shall be unlawful. (eff. Sept. 1, 1967; derived from Penal Law)

Section 5-411. Contracts On Account Of Money Or Property Wagered, Bet Or Staked Are Void

All contracts for or on account of any money or property, or thing in action wagered, bet or staked, as provided in section 5-401, shall be void. (eff. Sept. 1, 1967; derived from Penal Law)

GOVERNMENT CONTROL RELATING TO GAMBLING AND WAGERING

RACING, PARI-MUTUEL WAGERING AND BREEDING LAW

Section 101.   New York State Racing And Wagering Board

There is hereby created within the executive department the New York
state racing and wagering board, which board shall have general jurisdiction
over all horse racing activities and all pari-mutuel betting activities,
both on-track and off-track, in the state and over the corporation, associations, and persons engaged therein . . .   (eff. 1982)

Section 104.   Prohibition Of Wagering By Certain Officials, Employees And Minors

. . . No association or corporation which is licensed or franchised by
the board shall permit any person who is actually and apparently under
eighteen years of age to bet on a horse race conducted by it nor shall such
person to be permitted bo bet at an establishment of a regional corporation
conducting off-track betting. (eff. 1982)

Section 213.   Licenses For Participants And Employees At Race Meetings

1. For the purpose of maintaining a proper control over race meetings
conducted pursuant to . . . this chapter the state racing and wagering
board shall license persons only as owners, which term shall be deemed to
include part owners and lessees, trainers, assistant trainers and jockeys,
jockey agents, stable employees, and such other persons as the board may by
rule prescribe at running races and at steeplechases and hunts. . . .
(eff. 1982)

Section 216.   Penalty For Unlawful Racing And Betting

All racing or trials of speed between horses or other animals for
any bet, stake or reward, except such as is allowed by this article or by
special laws, is a public nuisance; and every person acting or aiding therein,
or making or being interested in such bet, stake or reward is guilty of a
misdemeanor and upon conviction is punishable by imprisonment in the county
jail or penitentiary for a period of not more than one year; and in addition
to the penalty prescribed therefor he forfeits to the people of this state
all title or interest in any animal used with his privity in such race or
trial of speed, and in any sum of money or other property betted or staked
upon the result thereof. (eff. 1982).

Note: These sections were previously contained in the Unconsolidated Laws.

NEW YORK CITY OFF-TRACK BETTING CORPORATION LAW

Section 601. Declaration Of Policy And Statement Of Purposes

It is hereby found, determined and declared:

...

2.   That the New York State off-track pari-mutuel betting commission, established by such law, was authorized to approve the operation of off-track pari-mutuel betting systems by public benefit corporations in participating municipalities;

3.   That the operation of an off-track pari-mutuel betting system by a public benefit corporation in New York City, in accordance with the provision of the New York State off-track pari-mutuel betting law, is deemed to be a matter of state concern and a public purpose which cannot be adequately attained except by the powers of government, and that such public benefit corporation in the exercise of the powers conferred upon it by this article, will perform a governmental function.

Section 603.   New York City Off-Track Betting Corporation
Section 604.   Powers Of The Corporation
Section 605.   Policing Of Off-Track Betting

2.   LARCENY

NEW YORK PENAL LAW

Section 155.05.   Larceny; Defined

1.   A person steals property and commits larceny when, with intent to deprive another of property or to appropriate the same to himself or to a third person, he wrongfully takes, obtains or withholds such property from an owner thereof.

2.   Larceny includes a wrongful taking, obtaining or withholding of another's property, with the intent prescribed in subdivision one of this section, committed in any of the following ways:

(a)   By conduct heretofore defined or known as common law larceny by trespassory taking, common law larceny by trick, embezzlement or obtaining property be false pretenses;

(b)   By acquiring lost property.

A person acquires lost property when he exercises control over property of another which he knows to have been lost or mislaid, or to have been delivered under a mistake as to the identity of the recipient or the nature or amount of the property, without taking reasonable measures to return such property to the owner;

(c) By committing the crime of issuing a bad check, as defined in section 190.05;

(d) By false promise.

A person obtains property by false promise when, pursuant to a scheme to defraud, he obtains property of another by means of representation, express or implied, that he or a third person will in the future engage in particular conduct, and when he does not intend to engage in such conduct or, as the case may be, does not believe that the third person intends to engage in such conduct.

...

(e) By extortion....(eff. 1965, derived from several prior sections of the Penal Law, some originally derived in 1892 and thereafter).

3. COERCION

NEW YORK PENAL LAW

Section 135.60. Coercion In The Second Degree

A person is guilty of coercion in the second degree when he compels or induces a person to engage in conduct which the latter has a legal right to abstain from engaging in, or to abstain from engaging in conduct in which he has a legal right to engage, by means of instilling in him a fear that, if the demand is not complied with, the actor or another will:

1. Cause physical injury to a person; or

2. Cause damage to property; or

3. Engage in other conduct constituting a crime; or

4. Accuse some person of a crime or cause criminal charges to be instituted against him; or

5. Expose a secret or publicize an asserted fact, whether true or false, tending to subject some person to hatred, contempt or ridicule; or

6. Cause a strike, boycott or other collective labor group action injurious to some person's business; except that such a threat shall not be deemed coercive when the act or omission compelled is for the benefit of the group in whose interest the actor purports to act; or

165

7. Testify or provide information or withhold testimony or information with respect to another's legal claim or defense; or

8. Use or abuse his position as a public servant by performing some act within or related to his official duties, or by failing or refusing to perform an official duty, in such manner as to affect some person adversely; or

9. Perform any other act which would not in itself materially benefit the actor but which is calculated to harm another person materially with respect to his health, safety, business, calling, career, financial condition, reputation or personal relationships.

.... (eff. 1965, derived from prior sections of the Penal Law)

NOTE: Coercion consists of compelling a person by intimidation to commit or refrain from committing an act, and includes extortion. Extortion is a form of coercion in which the act compelled is the payment of money. (See Penal Law Section 155.05 under Larceny.

4. COMMERCIAL BRIBING

NEW YORK PENAL LAW

Section 180.00. Commercial Bribing In The Second Degree

A person is guilty of commercial bribing in the second degree when he confers, or offers or agrees to confer, any benefit upon any employee, agent or fiduciary without the consent of the latter's employer or principal, with intent to influence his conduct in relation to his employer's or principal's affairs.

Commercial bribing in the second degree is a class A misdemeanor. (eff. Sept. 1, 1976; derived from prior sections of the Penal Law; amended eff. Sept. 1, 1983).

Section 180.03. Commercial Bribing In The First Degree

A person is guilty of commercial bribing in the first degree when he confers, or offers or agrees to confer, any benefit upon any employee, agent or fiduciary without the consent of the latter's employer or principal, with intent to influence his conduct in relation to his employer's or principal's affairs, and when the value of the benefit conferred or offered or agreed to be conferred exceeds one thousand dollars, and causes economic harm to the employer or principal in an amount exceeding $250.

Commercial bribing in the first degree is a class E felony. (eff. Sept. 1, 1976; derived from prior sections of the Penal Law; amended eff. Sept. 1, 1983).

166

Section 180.05. Commercial Bribe Receiving In The Second Degree

An employee, agent or fiduciary is guilty of commercial bribe receiving in the second degree when, without the consent of his employer or principal, he solicits, accepts or agrees to accept any benefit from another person upon an agreement or understanding that such benefit will influence his conduct in relation to his employer's or principal's affairs.

Commercial bribe receiving in the second degree is a class B misdemeanor. (eff. Sept. 1, 1976; derived from prior sections of the Penal Law).

5. USURY: CHARGING OF AN ILLEGAL RATE OF INTEREST

NEW YORK GENERAL OBLIGATIONS LAW

Section 5-501. Rate Of Interest; Usury Forbidden

1. The rate of interest, as computed pursuant to this title, upon the loan or forbearance of any money, goods, or things in action, except as provided in subdivisions five and six of this section or as otherwise provided by law, shall be six per centum per annum unless a different rate is prescribed in section fourteen-a of the banking law.... (eff. Dec. 1, 1980, as amended; derived from prior sections.

NEW YORK BANKING LAW

Section 14-a. Rate of Interest; Banking Board To Adopt Regulations

1. The maximum rate of interest provided for in section 5-501 of the general obligations law shall be sixteen per centum per annum.

2. The rate of interest as so prescribed under this section shall include as interest any and all amounts paid or payable, directly or indirectly, by any person, to or for the account of the lender in consideration for the making of a loan or forbearance as defined by the banking board.... (eff. Dec. 1, 1980, as amended)

NEW YORK CIVIL PRACTICE LAW AND RULES (C.P.L.R.)

Section 5004. Rate Of Interest

Interest shall be at the rate of nine per centum per annum, except where otherwise provided by statute. (eff. June 25, 1981, as amended).

Section 5-511.   Usurious Contract Void

1. All bonds, bills, notes, assurances, conveyances, all other contracts or securities whatsoever...
and all deposits of goods or other things whatsoever, whereupon or whereby there shall be reserved or taken, or secured or agreed to be reserved or taken, any greater sum, or greater value, for the loan or forbearance of any money, goods or other things in action, than is prescribed in section 5-501, shall be void, except that the knowingly taking, receiving, reserving or charging such a greater sum or greater value by a savings bank, a savings and loan association or a federal savings and loan association shall only be held and adjudged a forfeiture of the entire interest which the loan or obligation carries with it or which has been agreed to be paid thereon. If a greater sum or greater value has been paid, the person paying the same or his legal representative may recover from the savings bank, the savings and loan association or the federal savings and loan association twice the entire amount of the interest thus paid.

2. Except as provided in subdivision one, whenever it shall satisfactorily appear by the admissions of the defendant, or by proof, that any bond, bill, note, assurance, pledge, conveyance, contract, security or any evidence of debt, has been taken or received in violation of the foregoing provisions, the court shall declare the same to be void, and enjoin any prosecution thereon, and order the same to be surrendered and cancelled. (eff. July 1, 1969, as amended; enacted 1963)

Section 5-513.   Recovery Of Excess

Every person who, for any such loan or forbearance, shall pay or deliver any greater sum or value than is allowed to be received pursuant to section 5-501, and his personal representatives, may recover in an action against the person who shall have taken or received the same, and his personal representatives, the amount of the money so paid or value delivered, above the rate aforesaid. (eff. July 1, 1969, as amended; enacted 1963)

Section 5-515.   Borrower Bringing An Action Need Not Offer To Repay

Whenever any borrower of money, goods or things in action, shall begin an action for the recovery of the money, goods or things in action taken in violation of the foregoing provisions of this title, it shall not be necessary for him to pay or offer to pay any interest or principal on the sum or thing loaned; nor shall any court require or compel the payment or deposit of the principal sum or interest, or any portion thereof, as a condition of granting relief to the borrower in any case of usurious loans forbidden by the foregoing provisions of this title. (eff. 1963; originally derived from General Business Law 1837)

Section 5-519. <u>Return Of Excess A Bar To Further Penalties</u>

Every person who shall repay or return the money, goods or other things so taken, accepted or received, or the value thereof, shall be discharged from any other or further forfeiture or penalty which he may have incurred under sections 5-511 or 5-513, by taking or receiving the money, goods or other thing so repaid, or returned, as aforesaid. (eff. July 1, 1965 as amended; originally derived from General Business Law)

Section 5-524. <u>Taking Security Upon Certain Property For Usurious Loans</u>

A person who takes security, upon any household furniture, sewing machines, plate or silverware in actual use, tools or implements of trade, wearing apparel or jewelry, for a loan or forbearance of money, or for the use or sale of his personal credit, conditioned upon the payment of a greater rate than the rate prescribed by the banking board pursuant to section four-teen-a of the banking law, or, if no rate has been so prescribed, six per centum per annum, or who as security for such loan, use or sale of personal credit as aforesaid, makes a pretended purchase of such property from any person, upon the like condition, and permits the pledgor to retain the possession thereof is guilty of a misdemeanor. (eff. May 15, 1968, as amended; derived from Penal Law)

Section 5-521. <u>Corporations Prohibited From Interposing Defense Of Usury</u>

1. No corporation shall hereafter interpose the defense of usury in any action. The term corporation, as used in this section, shall be construed to include all associations, and jointstock companies having any of the powers and privileges of corporations not possessed by individuals or partnerships.

2. The provisions of subdivision one of this section shall not apply to a corporation, the principal asset of which shall be the ownership of a one or two family dwelling, where it appears either that the said corporation was organized and created, or that the controlling interest therein was acquired, within a period of six months prior to the execution, by said corporation of a bond or note evidencing indebtedness, and a mortgage creating a lien for said indebtedness on the said one or two family dwelling; provided, that as to any such bond, note or mortgage executed by such a corporation and effective prior to April sixth, nineteen hundred fifty-six, the defense of usury may be interposed only in an action or proceeding instituted for the collection, enforcement or foreclosure of such note, bond or mortgage.

Any provision of any contract, or any separate written instrument executed prior to, simultaneously with or within sixty days after the delivery of any moneys to any borrower in connection with such indebtedness, whereby the defense of usury is waived or any such corporation is estopped from asserting it, is hereby declared to be contrary to public policy and absolutely void....(eff. June 7, 1974, as amended; enacted 1963)

169

Section 6-f.   Alternative Mortgage Instruments Made By Banks, Trust
Companies, Savings Banks, Savings and Loan Associations and
Credit Unions

1.   Notwithstanding any inconsistent provision of this chapter or any
other law of this state, the banking board is authorized to adopt such rules
or regulations as shall permit banks, trust companies, foreign banking corporations licensed to maintain a branch or agency in this state, savings
banks, savings and loan associations and credit unions to make residential
mortgage loans which provide for (a) periodic readjustments of the rate of
interest charged for the loan or successive terms of the loan or (b) terms
of loan which are shorter than the term of the mortgage or (c) repayment of
the principal amount of the loan by regular payments which are not equal in
amount throughout the term of the mortgage or (d) any combination of paragraphs (a), (b) and (c) above, subject to the provisions of subdivision two of
this section.

2.   Any rules or regulations which are adopted by the banking board pursuant to subdivision one of this section:

(a)   shall provide for disclosures and notices to the borrower with
respect to the terms and conditions of the loan and the mortgage, and the
banking board may require the adoption of uniform disclosure and notice forms
for this purpose;

(b)   shall provide for the conditions governing renewals of the term
of the loan; ....(eff. Dec. 1, 1980, as amended)

NEW YORK PENAL LAW

Section 190.40.   Criminal Usury In The Second Degree

A person is guilty of criminal usury in the second degree when, not being
authorized or permitted by law to do so, he knowingly charges, takes or
receives any money or other property as interest on the loan or forbearance
of any money or other property, at a rate exceeding twenty-five per centum per
annum or the equivalent rate for a longer or shorter period.

Criminal usury in the second degree is a class E felony. (eff. Sept. 1,
1976, as amended)

NEW YORK GENERAL OBLIGATIONS LAW

Section 5-1301.   How Interest Calculated

Whenever, in any statute, act, deed, written or verbal contract, or in
any public or private instrument whatever, any certain rate of interest is or

shall be mentioned, and no period of time is stated for which such rate is to be calculated, interest shall be calculated at the rate mentioned, by the year, in the same manner as if the words "per annum" or "by the year" had been added to such rate. (eff. 1963, derived from General Business Law)

In addition to the above statutes, limitations and restrictions are placed on interest charges for specific types of consumer transactions. A representative selection of statutes enacted in New York State regulating interest and other credit charges involving consumers follows.

NEW YORK PERSONAL PROPERTY LAW

Section 404. Credit Service Charge Limitation

1. A seller may, in a retail instalment contract or obligation, contract for and, if so contracted for, the holder thereof may charge, receive and collect a credit service charge computed on the principal balance of the contract or obligation from the date thereof to and including the date when the final instalment is payable, at the rate or rates agreed to by the buyer.

...

4. The credit service charge shall be inclusive of all charges incident to investigating and making the contract or obligation, and for the extension of the credit provided for in the contract or obligation, and no fee, expense or other charge whatsoever shall be taken, received, reserved or contracted for except as otherwise provided in this article. (eff. Dec. 1, 1980, as amended)

Section 46-f. Limit On Interest And Other Charges

Except as provided in article nine of the banking law, no person shall directly or indirectly receive or accept, whether by discount or otherwise, for the use and sale of his personal credit or for making or continuing any advance or loan of money (1) in anticipation of earnings assigned outright, or (2) on the security of an assignment of any earnings assigned as security, a greater sum than at the rate of eighteen per centum per annum on the amount of such loan or advance, either as a bonus, interest or otherwise, or under the guise of a charge for investigating the status of a person applying for such loan or advance, or drawing of papers or other service in connection with such loan or advance, except such charges as are not permitted by section 5-531 of the general obligation law. Any assignment, whether outright or as security, which is made wholly or partly in consideration of or as security for a loan or advance which violates this section, shall be void, and invalid for any purpose whatsoever. Every person, firm, corporation, director, agent, officer or member thereof who shall violate any provision of this section, directly or indirectly, or assent to such violation shall be guilty of a misdemeanor. (eff. 1950)

See, also, Assignments for other statutes involving Wage Assignments.

6. LICENSING STATUTES

NEW YORK REAL PROPERTY LAW

Section 442-d. Actions For Commission; License Prerequisite

No person, copartnership or corporation shall bring or maintain an action in any court of this state for the recovery of compensation for services rendered, in any place in which this article is applicable, in the buying, selling, exchanging, leasing, renting, or negotiating a loan upon any real estate without alleging and proving that such person was a duly licensed real estate broker or real estate salesman on the date when the alleged cause of action arose.

The practice of a profession which requires a license is governed by statute. In New York State, many of the licensing statutes regulating some of the well known professions are found in the New York State Education Law; the practice of law is regulated by the New York State Judiciary Law. A representative selection of some of the statutory provisions for a few of the well known professions such as medicine, dentistry, public accountancy, and law follows:

NEW YORK EDUCATION LAW

Section 6501. Admission To A Profession (Licensing)

Admission to practice of a profession in this state is accomplished by a license being issued to a qualified applicant by the education department. To qualify for a license an applicant shall meet the requirements prescribed in the article for the particular profession. (eff. Sept. 1, 1971, derived from prior sections of the Education Law)

Section 6503. Practice Of A Profession

Admission to the practice of a profession (1) entitles the licensee to practice the profession as defined in the article for the particular profession, (2) entitles the individual licensee to use the professional title as provided in the article for the particular profession, and (3) subjects the licensee to the procedures and penalties for professional misconduct as prescribed in this article....(eff. Sept. 1, 1971, as amended)

172

Section 6509. Definitions Of Professional Misconduct

Each of the following is professional misconduct, and any licensee found guilty of such misconduct... shall be subject to the penalties prescribed ...

(1) Obtaining the license fraudulently,

(2) Practicing the profession fraudulently, beyond its authorized scope, with gross incompetence, with gross negligence on a particular occasion or negligence or incompetence on more than one occasion,

(3) Practicing the profession while the ability to practice is impaired by alcohol, drugs, physical disability, or mental disability.

(4) Being habitually drunk or being dependent on, or a habitual user of narcotics, barbituates, amphetamines, hallucinogens, or other drugs having similar effects,

(5)(a) Being convicted of committing an act constituting a crime...

...

(6) Refusing to provide professional service to a person because of such person's race, creed, color, or national origin,

(7) Permitting, aiding or abetting an unlicensed person to perform activities requiring a license,

(8) Practicing the profession while the license is suspended, or wilfully failing to register or notify the department of any change of name or mailing address,...(eff. July 1, 1980, as amended).

Section 6512. Unauthorized Practice A Crime

1. Anyone not authorized to practice under this title who practices or offers to practice or holds himself out as being able to practice in any profession in which a license is a prerequisite to the practice of the acts, or who practices any profession as an exempt person during the time when his professional license is suspended, revoked or annulled, or who aids or abets an unlicensed person to practice a profession, or who fraudulently sells, files, furnishes, obtains, or who attempts fraudulently to sell, file, furnish or obtain any diploma, license, record or permit purporting to authorize the practice of a profession, shall be guilty of a class E felony.

....(eff. Sept. 1, 1979, as amended)

Section 6513. Unauthorized Use Of A Professional Title A Crime

1. Anyone not authorized to use a professional title regulated by this title, and who uses such professional title, shall be guilty of a class A misdemeanor...(eff. July 24, 1976, as amended).

Section 6515. Restraint Of Unlawful Acts

Where a violation of this title is alleged to have occurred, the attorney general or,...the corporation counsel may apply to the supreme court within the judicial district in which such violation is alleged to have occurred for an order enjoining or restraining commission or continuance of the unlawful acts complained of. The court shall have jurisdiction of the proceedings and shall have power to grant such temporary relief or re-straining order as it deems just and proper. In any such proceeding it shall be unnecessary to allege or prove that an adequate remedy at law does not exist or that irreparable damage would result if such order were not granted. The remedy provided in this section shall be in addition to any other remedy provided by law or to the proceedings commenced against a licensee under this title. (eff. July 24, 1976, as amended)

Section 6522. Practice Of Medicine And Use Of Title "Physician"

Only a person licensed or otherwise authorized under this article shall practice medicine or use the title "physician". (eff. Sept. 1, 1971, as amended)

Section 6524. Requirements For a Professional License [as Medical Doctor]

To qualify for a license as a physician, an applicant shall fulfull the following requirements:

(1) Application: file an application with the department;

(2) Education: have received an education, including a degree of doctor of medicine, "M.D.", or doctor of osteopathy, "D.O.", or equivalent degree in accordance with the commissioner's regulations;

(3) Experience: have experience satisfactory to the board and in accordance with the commissioner's regulations;

(4) Examination: pass an examination satisfactory to the board and in accordance with the commissioner's regulations;

(5) Age: be at least twenty-one years of age;

(6) Citizenship: be a United States citizen, or file a declaration of intention to become a citizen, unless such requirement is waived, in accordance with the commissioner's regulations;

(7) Character: be of good moral character as determined by the department;.... (eff. Sept. 1, 1971, as amended)

Section 6602. Practice Of Dentistry And Use Of Title "Dentist"

Only a person licensed or otherwise authorized to practice under this article shall practice dentistry or use the title "dentist". (eff. Sept. 1, 1971, as amended)

Section 7401. Definition Of Practice Of Public Accountancy

The practice of the profession of public accountancy is defined as holding one's self out to the public, in consideration of compensation received or to be received, offering to perform or performing for other persons, services which involve signing, delivering or issuing or causing to be signed, delivered or issued any financial, accounting or related statement or any opinion on, report on, or certificate to such statement if, by reason of the signature, or the stationery or wording employed, or otherwise, it is indicated or implied that the practitioner has acted or is acting, in relation to said financial, accounting or related statement, or reporting as an independent accountant or auditor or as an individual having or purporting to have expert knowledge in accounting or auditing. (eff. Sept. 1, 1971, as amended)

Section 7402. Practice Of Public Accountancy And Use Of Title "Certified Public Accountant" or "Public Accountant"

Only a person licensed or otherwise authorized to practice under this article shall practice public accountancy and use the title "certified public accountant" or the designation "C.P.A." or "public accountant" or any other derivative or designation provided in section seventy-four hundred eight. (eff. Sept. 1, 1971, as amended)

Section 7404. Requirements For A License As A Certified Public Accountant

1. To qualify for a license as a certified public accountant, an applicant shall fulfill the following requirements:

(1) Application: file an application with the department;

(2) Education: have received an education, including a bachelor's

or higher degree based on a program in accountancy, in accordance with the commissioner's regulations;

(3) Experience: have experience satisfactory to the board and in accordance with the commissioner's regulations;

(4) Examination: pass a written examination satisfactory to the board and in accordance with the commissioner's regulations and the requirement with respect to such examination may not be waived;

(5) Age: be at least twenty-one years of age;

(6) Citizenship: meet no requirements as to United State citizenship;

(7) Character: be of good moral character as determined by the department;....(eff. Sept..1, 1971, as amended).

Section 7408. Special Provisions

1. Nothing contained in this article shall be deemed to prohibit two or more certified public accountants or two or more public accountants, or any combination thereof, from forming a partnership; provided, however, that no partnership shall use the words "certified public accountants" or the letters "C.P.A.'s" in connection with its name unless each partner of such partnership, resident or engaged within the United States in practice is in good standing as a certified public accountant of one or more of the states or political subdivisions of the United States, and each partner thereof resident or engaged in practice within the state is licensed under this article. ....(eff. April 1, 1976, as amended).

NEW YORK JUDICIARY LAW

Section 460. Examination And Admission Of Attorneys

A citizen of the state, of full age, applying to be admitted to practice as an attorney or counselor in the courts of record of this state, must be examined and licensed to practice as prescribed in this chapter. Race, creed, color, national origin or sex shall constitute no cause for refusing any person examination or admission to practice. (eff. March 24, 1963, as amended.

Section 478. Practicing Or Appearing As Attorney-At-Law Without Being Admitted And Registered

It shall be unlawful for any natural person to practice or appear as an attorney-at-law or as an attorney and counselor-at-law for a person other than himself in a court of record in this state or in any court in the city of New York, or to furnish attorneys or counsel or an attorney and counsel to render legal services, or to hold himself out to the public as being entitled to practice law as aforesaid, or in any other manner, or to assume to be an attorney or counselor-at-law, or to assume, use, or advertise the title of lawyer,....[without having taken the oath and affirmation required by the Judiciary Law].... (eff. June 5, 1980, as amended)

Section 484. None But Attorneys To Practice In The State

No natural person shall ask or receive, directly or indirectly, compensation for appearing for a person other than himself as attorney in any court or before any magistrate, or for preparing deeds, mortgages, assignments, discharges, leases or any other instruments affecting real estate, wills, codicils, or any other instrument affecting the disposition of property after death, or decedent's estates, or pleadings of any kind in any action brought before any court of record in this state, or make it a business to practice for another as an attorney in any court or before any magistrate unless he has been regularly admitted to practice, as an attorney or counselor, in the courts of record in the state;.... (eff. March 30, 1981, as amended)

Section 486. Practice Of Law By Attorney Who Has Been Disbarred, Suspended, Or Convicted Of A Felony

Any person whose admission to practice as an attorney and counselor-at-law has been revoked or who has been removed from office as attorney and counselor-at-law or, being an attorney and counselor-at-law, has been convicted of a felony or has been suspended from practice and has not been duly and regularly reinstated, who does any act forbidden by the provisions of this article to be done by any person not regularly admitted to practice law in the courts of record of this state, unless the judgment, decree or order suspending him shall permit such act, shall be guilty of a misdemeanor. (eff. Sept. 1, 1967, derived from the Penal Law)

7. UNCONSCIONABLE CONTRACTS AND UNCONSCIONABLE CLAUSES

UNIFORM COMMERCIAL CODE (SALE OF GOODS)

Section 2-302. Unconscionable Contract Or Clause

(1) If the court as a matter of law finds the contract or any clause of the contract to have been unconscionable at the time it was made the court may refuse to enforce the contract, or it may enforce the remainder of the contract without the unconscionable clause, or it may so limit the application of any unconscionable clause as to avoid any unconscionable result.

(2) When it is claimed or appears to the court that the contract or any clause thereof may be unconscionable the parties shall be afforded a reasonable opportunity to present evidence as to its commercial setting, purpose and effect to aid the court in making the determination.

NEW YORK REAL PROPERTY LAW

Section 235-c. Unconscionable Lease Or Clause

1. If the court as a matter of law finds a lease or any clause of the lease to have been unconscionable at the time it was made the court may refuse to enforce the lease, or it may enforce the remainder of the lease without the unconscionable clause, or it may so limit the application of any unconscionable clause as to avoid any unconscionable result.

2. When it is claimed or appears to the court that a lease or any clause thereof may be unconscionable the parties shall be afforded a reasonable opportunity to present evidence as to its setting, purpose and effect to aid the court in making the determination. (eff. 1976)

8. EXCULPATORY CLAUSES IN CONTRACTS

Several **contract** provisions exempting a party from liability for damages caused by the party's negligence have been declared void as against public policy and wholly unenforceable. A representative selection of such statutes are included with the full text, while others are merely listed by section number and title.

NEW YORK GENERAL OBLIGATIONS LAW

Section 5-321. Agreements Exempting Lessors From Liability For Negligence Void And Unenforceable

Every covenant, agreement or understanding in or in connection with or collateral to any lease of real property exempting the lessor from liability for damages for injuries to person or property caused by or resulting from the negligence of the lessor, his agents, servants or employees, in the operation or maintenance of the demised premises or the real property containing the demised premises shall be deemed to be void as against public policy and wholly unenforceable. (eff. 1963; derived from Real Property Law Section 234; originally enacted 1937)

Section 5-322. Agreements Exempting Caterers And Catering Establishments From Liability For Negligence Void And Unenforceable

Every covenant, agreement or understanding in or in connection with or collateral to any contract entered into with a caterer or catering establishment exempting the said caterer or catering establishment from liability for damages caused by or resulting from the negligence of the caterer or catering establishment, his agents, servants, employee or patrons at the affair contracted therefor, shall be deemed to be void as against public policy and wholly unenforceable. (eff. June 14, 1966)

Section 5-322.1. Agreements Exempting Owners And Contractors From Liability For Negligence Void And Unenforceable; Certain Cases

Section 5-323. Agreements Exempting Building Service Or Maintenance Contractors From Liability For Negligence Void And Unenforceable

Section 5-324. Agreements By Owners, Contractors, Subcontractors Or Suppliers To Indemnify Architects, Engineers And . . .

Section 5-325. Garages And Parking Places; Agreements Exempting From Liability For Negligence Void

1. No person who conducts or maintains for hire or other consideration a garage, parking lot or other similar place which has the capacity for the housing, storage, parking, repair or servicing of four or more motor vehicles, as defined by the vehicle and traffic law, may exempt himself from liability for damages for injury to person or property resulting from the negligence of such person, his agents or employees, in the operation of any such vehicle, or in its housing, storage, parking, repair or servicing, or in the conduct or maintenance of such garage, parking lot or other similar place, and except as hereinafter provided, any agreement so exempting such person shall be void.

2. Damages for loss or injury to property may be limited by a provision in the storage agreement limiting the liability in case of loss or damage by theft, fire or explosion and setting forth a specific liability per vehicle, which shall in no event be less than twenty-five thousand dollars, beyond which the person owning or operating such garage or lot shall not be liable; provided, however, that such liability may on request of the person delivering such vehicle be increased, in which event increased rates may be charged based on such increased liability. (as amended, eff. 60 days after Aug. 8, 1983).

Section 5-326. Agreements Exempting Pools, Gymnasiums, Places Of
               Public Amusement Or Recreation And Similar Establish-
               ments From Liability For Negligence Void And Unen-
               forceable

Every covenant, agreement or understanding in or in connection with, or
collateral to, any contract, membership application, ticket of admission or
similar writing, entered into between the owner or operator of any pool,
gymnasium, place of amusement or recreation, or similar establishment and the
user of such facilities, pursuant to which such owner or operator receives a
fee or other compensation for the use of such facilities, which exempts the
said owner or operator from liability for damages caused by or resulting
from the negligence of the owner, operator or person in charge of such
establishment, or their agents, servants or employees, shall be deemed to be
void as against public policy and wholly unenforceable. (eff. Sept. 1, 1976)

Section 5-331. Certain Covenants And Restrictions In Conveyances And
               Other Agreements Affecting Real Property Void As
               Against Public Policy

Any promise, covenant or restriction in a contract, mortgage, lease,
deed or conveyance or in any other agreement affecting real property, heretofore or hereafter made or entered into, which limits, restrains, prohibits
or otherwise provides against the sale, grant, gift, transfer, assignment,
conveyance, ownership, lease, rental, use or occupancy of real property to
or by any person because of race, creed, color, national origin, or ancestry,
is hereby declared to be void as against public policy, wholly unenforceable,
and shall not constitute a defense in any action, suit or proceeding.
....(eff. 1964, as amended)

9. CONTRACTS IN RESTRAINT OF TRADE

NEW YORK GENERAL BUSINESS LAW

Section 340. Contracts Or Agreements For Monopoly Or In Restraint Of
              Trade Illegal And Void

1. Every contract, agreement, arrangement or combination whereby

A monopoly in the conduct of any business, trade or commerce or in the
furnishing of any service in this state, is or may be established or maintained, or whereby

Competition or the free exercise of any activity in the conduct of any
business, trade or commerce or in the furnishing of any service in this state
is or may be restrained or whereby

For the purpose of establishing or maintaining any such monopoly or

unlawfully interfering with the free exercise of any activity in the conduct
of any business, trade or commerce or in the furnishing of any service in
this state any business, trade or commerce or the furnishing of any service is
or may be restrained, is hereby declared to be against public policy, illegal
and void.

2.   Subject to the exceptions hereinafter provided in this section, the
provisions of this article shall apply to licensed insurers, licensed
insurance agents, licensed insurance brokers, licensed independent adjusters
and other persons and organizations subject to the provisions of the insurance law, to the extent not regulated by provisions of article eight of the
insurance law;...

3.   The provisions of this article shall not apply to cooperative
associations, corporate or otherwise, of farmers, gardeners, or dairymen,
including live stock farmers and fruit growers, nor to contracts, agreements
or arrangements made by such associations, nor to bona fide labor unions.

4.   The labor of human beings shall not be deemed or held to be a
commodity or article of commerce as such terms are used in this section and
nothing herein contained shall be deemed to prohibit or restrict the right
of workingmen to combine in unions, organizations and associations, not
organized for the purpose of profit.

5.   An action to recover damages caused by a violation of this section
must be commenced within four years after the cause of action has accrued.
The state, or any political subdivision or public authority of the state,
or any person who shall sustain damages by reason of any violation of this
section, shall recover three-fold the actual damages sustained thereby, as
well as costs not exceeding ten thousand dollars, and reasonable attorneys'
fees.... (eff. July 1, 1975, as amended; originally enacted 1909.

10. FALSE ADVERTISING

NEW YORK GENERAL BUSINESS LAW

Section 350.   False Advertising Unlawful

False advertising in the conduct of any business, trade or commerce or
in the furnishing of any service in this state is hereby declared unlawful.
(eff. Sept. 1, 1963; originally enacted 1899)

Section 350-a.   False Advertising

The term "false advertising" means advertising, including labeling, which
is misleading in a material respect; and in determining whether any advertising is misleading, there shall be taken into account, (among other things) not

only representations made by statement, word, design, device, sound or any combination thereof, but also the extent to which the advertising fails to reveal facts material in the light of such representations with respect to the commodity to which the advertising relates under the conditions prescribed in said advertisement, or under such conditions as are customary or usual. (eff. Sept. 1, 1963)

Section 350-d. Construction

. . .

3. Any person who has been injured by reason of any violation of section three hundred fifty or three hundred fifty-a of this article may bring an action in his own name to enjoin such unlawful act or practice and to recover his actual damages or fifty dollars, whichever is greater. The court may, in its discretion, increase the award of damages to an amount not to exceed three times the actual damages up to one thousand dollars, if the court finds the defendant willfully or knowingly violated this section. The court may award reasonable attorney's fees to a prevailing plaintiff. (eff. June 19, 1980, as amended)

NEW YORK PENAL LAW

Section 190.20. False Advertising

A person is guilty of false advertising when, with intent to promote the sale or to increase the consumption of property or services, he makes or causes to be made a false or misleading statement in any advertisement or publishes any advertisement in violation of chapter three of the act of congress entitled "Truth in Lending Act" and the regulations thereunder, as such act and regulations may from time to time be amended, addressed to the public or to a substantial number of persons; except that, in any prosecution under this section, it is an affiramtive defense that the allegedly false or misleading statement was not knowingly or recklessly made or caused to be made.

False advertising is a class A misdemeanor. (eff. July 1, 1969, as amended - originally enacted in 1909)

11.FALSE ADVERTISING AND CONSUMER PROTECTION

NEW YORK GENERAL BUSINESS LAW

Section 349. Deceptive Acts And Practices Unlawful

(a) Deceptive acts or practices in the conduct of any business, trade or commerce or in the furnishing of any service in this state are hereby declared unlawful.

(b)   Whenever the attorney general shall believe from evidence satisfactory to him that any person, firm, corporation or association or agent or employee thereof has engaged in or is about to engage in any of the acts or practices stated to be unlawful he may bring an action in the name and on behalf of the people of the state of New York to enjoin such unlawful acts or practices and to obtain restitution of any moneys or property obtained directly or indirectly by any such unlawful acts or practices.   In such action preliminary relief may be granted under article sixty-three of the civil practice law and rules.

...

(d)   In any such action it shall be a complete defense that the act or practice is, or if in interstate commerce would be, subject to and complies with the rules and regulations of, and the statutes administered by, the federal trade commission or any official department, division, commission, or agency of the United States as such rules, regulations or statutes are interpreted by the federal trade commission or such department, division, commission or agency or the federal courts.

(e)   Nothing in this section shall apply to any television or radio broadcasting station or to any publisher or printer of a newspaper, magazine or other form of printed advertising, who broadcasts, publishes, or prints the advertisement.

...

(g)   This section shall apply to all deceptive acts or practices declared to be unlawful, whether or not subject to any other law of this state, and shall not supersede, amend or repeal any other law of this state under which the attorney general is authorized to take any action or conduct any inquiry.

(h)   In addition to the right of action granted to the attorney general pursuant to this section, any person who has been injured by reason of any violation of this section may bring an action in his own name to enjoin such unlawful act or practice and to recover his actual damages or fifty dollars, whichever is greater.   The court may, in its discretion, increase the award of damages to an amount not to exceed three times the actual damages up to one thousand dollars, if the court finds the defendant willfully or knowingly violated this section.   The court may award reasonable attorney's fees to a prevailing plaintiff.   (eff. June 19, 1980, as amended; originally enacted 1970)

12.   TRADE PRACTICES RELATING TO MISCELLANEOUS CONSUMER TRANSACTIONS

LEASE FOR RESIDENTIAL APARTMENT:

NEW YORK REAL PROPERTY LAW

Section 235-b. Warranty Of Habitability

1.   In every written or oral lease or rental agreement for residential premises the landlord or lessor shall be deemed to covenant and warrant that the premises so leased or rented and all areas used in connection therewith in common with other tenants or residents are fit for human habitation and for the uses reasonably intended by the parties and that the occupants of such premises shall not be subjected to any conditions which would be danger-ous, hazardous or detrimental to their life, health or safety. When any such condition has been caused by the misconduct of the tenant or lessee or persons under his direction or control, it shall not constitute a breach of such covenants and warranties.

2.   Any agreement by a lessee or tenant of a dwelling waiving or modify-ing his rights as set forth in this section shall be void as contrary to public policy.

3.   In determining the amount of damages sustained by a tenant as a result of a breach of the warranty set forth in this section, the court;

(a)   need not require any expert testimony, and

(b)   shall, to the extent the warranty is breached or cannot be cured by reason of a strike or other labor dispute which is not caused primarily by the individual landlord or lessor and such damages are attributable to such strike, exclude recovery to such extent, except to the extent of the net savings, if any, to the landlord or lessor by reason of such strike or labor dispute allocable to the tenant's premises, provided, however, that the landlord or lesser has made a good faith attempt, where practicable, to cure the breach. (eff. June 30, 1983, as amended; originally enacted in 1975).

CONTRACTS FOR HEALTH CLUB SERVICES:

NEW YORK GENERAL BUSINESS LAW

Article 30 - HEALTH CLUB SERVICES

Section 620-631. (SEE NEXT PAGE).

184

Section 620. Legislative Intent

....

2. The legislature declares that the purpose of this article is to safe-guard the public and the ethical health club industry against deception and financial hardship, and to foster and encourage competitiion, fair dealing, and prosperity in the field of health club services by prohibiting or re-stricting false or misleading advertising, erroneous contract terms, harmful financial practices, and other unfair, deceptive and discriminatory practices which have been conducted by some health club operators. (eff. Jan. 1, 1979)

Section 622. Escrow Required

All moneys received by a seller pursuant to a contract for services for use by a buyer of a health club prior to the full operation of such health club shall be placed in escrow.... (eff. Jan. 1, 1979)

Section 623. Contract Restrictions

1. No contract for services shall require payment by the person re-ceiving service or the use of the facilities of a total amount in excess of one thousand two hundred dollars, provided, however, that this subdivision shall not apply to contracts relating solely to the use of tennis, platform tennis or racquet ball facilities.

2. No contract for services shall provide for a term longer than thirty-six months. No contract for services shall require payments or financing by the buyer over a period in excess of thirty-seven months from the date the contract is entered into, nor shall the term of any such contract be measured by or be for the life of the buyer. Provided, however, that the services to be rendered to the buyer under the contract may extend over a period not to exceed three years from the date the contract is entered into with the right to renew, at the option of the buyer for a like period. The buyer may have thirty days after the expiration to renew the contract. The installment pay-ments shall be in substantially equal amounts exclusive of the down payment and shall be required to be made at substantially equal intervals, not to exceed one month.

3. No contract for services may contain any provisions whereby the buyer agrees not to assert against the seller or any assignee or transferee of the health club services contract any claim or defense arising out of the health club services contract.

4. No contract for services may require the buyer to execute a promis-sory note or series of promissory notes which, when negotiated, cuts off as to third parties a defense which the buyer may have against the seller.

5. No contract may be assigned by one health club to another health club not located on the same premises without written consent of the buyer. (eff. Jan. 1, 1979)

<u>Section 624</u>.   <u>Rights Of Cancellation Of Contracts For Services</u>

1.   Every contract for services at a planned health club or a health club under construction shall, at the option of the buyer, be voidable in the event that the health club and the services to be provided pursuant to such contract are not available within one year from the date the contract is executed by the buyer.

2.   Every contract for services shall provide that such contract may be cancelled within three business days after the date of receipt by the buyer of a copy of the written contract.   Notice of cancellation shall be delivered by certified or registered United States mail at the address specified in the contract.   Such contract shall contain the following written notice in at least ten point bold type: CONSUMERS RIGHT TO CANCELLATION.   YOU MAY CANCEL THIS CONTRACT WITHOUT ANY PENALTY OR FURTHER OBLIGATION WITHIN THREE (3) DAYS FROM THIS DATE......   Notice of cancellation shall be in writing subscribed by the buyer and mailed by registered or certified United States mail to the seller at the address specified in such form.   Such notice shall be accompanied by the contract forms, membership cards and any other documents or evidence of membership previously delivered to the buyer.   All moneys paid pursuant to such contract shall be refunded within fifteen business days of receipt of such notice of cancellation....   Such contract shall contain the following notice captioned in at least ten point bold type: ADDITIONAL RIGHTS TO CANCELLATION.

You may also cancel this contract for any of the following reasons:

If upon a doctor's order, you cannot physically receive the services because of significant physical disability for a period in excess of six months.

If you die, your estate shall be relieved of any further obligation for payment under the contract not then due and owing.

If you move your residence more than twenty-five miles from any health club operated by seller.

If the services cease to be offered as stated in the contract.

All moneys paid pursuant to such contract cancelled for the reasons contained in this subdivision shall be refunded within fifteen days of receipt of such notice of cancellation; provided however that the seller may retain the expenses incurred and the portion of the total price representing the services used or completed, and further provided that the seller may demand the reasonable cost of goods and services which the buyer has consumed or wishes to retain after cancellation of the contract.   In no instance shall the seller demand more than the full contract price from the buyer.   If the buyer has executed any credit or loan agreement to pay for all or part of health club services, any such negotiable instrument executed by the buyer shall also be returned within fifteen days.   (eff. Jan. 1, 1979)

Section 625. Assignment Of Contract For Services: See Assignments

Section 626. Deceptive Acts Prohibited

It is hereby declared to be an unfair and deceptive trade practice and unlawful for a seller to:

1. Misrepresent directly or indirectly in its advertising, promotional materials, or in any manner the size, location, facilities or equipment of its studio, or place of business or the number or qualifications of its personnel;

....

4. Misrepresent the location or locations at which its services will be offered;

5. Misrepresent the nature of its courses, training devices, methods or equipment or the number, qualifications, training, or experience of its personnel, whether by means of endorsements or otherwise;

6. Misrepresent the nature and extent of any personal services, guidance, assistance, or other attention the business will provide for consumers;

....

8. Misrepresent in any manner by the seller or his assignee the buyer's right to cancel under this article. (eff. Jan. 1, 1979)

Section 627. Contracts Void And Unenforceable

1. Any contract for services which does not comply with the applicable provisions of this article shall be void and unenforceable as contrary to public policy.

2. Any waiver by the buyer of the provisions of this article shall be deemed void and unenforceable by the seller as contrary to public policy. (eff. Jan. 1, 1979)

Section 628. Private Right Of Action

1. Any buyer damaged by a violation of this article may bring an action for recovery of damages. Judgment may be entered in an amount not to exceed three times the actual damages plus reasonable attorney fees.

2. Nothing in this article shall be construed so as to nullify or impair any right or rights which a buyer may have against a seller at common law, by statute, or otherwise. (eff. Jan. 1, 1979)

Section 629. Violations

Any seller or his assignee who violate any provision of this article, or who shall counsel, aid or abet such violation shall be liable for a civil fine of not more than twenty-five hundred dollars for each violation. The provisions of this article are not exclusive and do not relieve the seller or his assignees or the contracts subject to this article from compliance with all other applicable provisions of law.

DEBT COLLECTION PRACTICES:

NEW YORK GENERAL BUSINESS LAW

ARTICLE 29-H - DEBT COLLECTION PROCEDURES

Sec.
600. Definitions
601. Prohibited Practices
602. Violations and penalties
603. Severability

Section 600. Definitions

As used in this article, unless the context or subject matter otherwise requires:

1. "Consumer claim" means any obligation of a natural person for the payment of money or its equivalent which is or is alleged to be in default and which arises out of a transaction wherein credit has been offered or extended to a natural person, and the money, property or service which was the subject of the transaction was primarily for personal, family or household purposes. The term includes an obligation of a natural person who is a co-maker, endorser, guarantor or surety as well as the natural person to whom such credit was originally extended.

2. "Debtor" means any natural person who owes or who is asserted to owe a consumer claim.

3. "Principal creditor" means any person, firm, corporation or organization to whom a consumer claim is owed, due or asserted to be due or owed, or any assignee for value of said person, firm, corporation or organization. (eff. Sept. 1, 1973)

Section 601. Prohibited Practices

No principal creditor, as defined by this article, or his agent shall:

1. Simulate in any manner a law enforcement officer, or a representative of any governmental agency of the state of New York or any of its political subdivisions; or

2. Knowingly collect, attempt to collect, or assert a right to any collection fee, attorney's fee, court cost or expense unless such charges are justly due and legally chargeable against the debtor; or

3. Disclose or threaten to disclose information affecting the debtor's

reputation for credit worthiness with knowledge or reason to know that the information is false; or

4. Communicate or threaten to communicate the nature of a consumer claim to the debtor's employer prior to obtaining final judgment against the debtor. The provisions of this subdivision shall not prohibit a principal creditor from communicating with the debtor's employer to execute a wage assignment agreement if the debtor has consented to such an agreement; or

5. Disclose or threaten to disclose information concerning the existence of a debt known to be disputed by the debtor without disclosing that fact; or

6. Communicate with the debtor or any member of his family or household with such frequency or at such unusual hours or in such a manner as can reasonably be expected to abuse or harass the debtor; or

7. Threaten any action which the principal creditor in the usual course of his business does not in fact take; or

8. Claim, or attempt to threaten to enforce a right with knowledge or reason to know that the right does not exist; or

9. Use a communication which simulates in any manner legal or judicial process or which gives the appearance of being authorized, issued or approved by a government, governmental agency, or attorney at law when it is not. (eff. Sept. 1, 1973)

Section 602. Violations and Penalties

1. Except as otherwise provided by law, any person who shall violate the terms of this article shall be guilty of a misdemeanor, and each such violation shall be deemed a separate offense.

2. The attorney general or the district attorney of any county may bring an action in the name of the people of the state to restrain or prevent any violation of this article or any continuance of any such violation. (eff. Sept. 1, 1973)

NEW YORK GENERAL BUSINESS LAW

ARTICLE 34 - CREDITOR BILLING ERRORS

Sec.
701. Definitions.
702. Application.
703. Notice of error and response.
704. Permissible procedures by creditor.
705. Statement to contain instructions for notification of error.
706. Notice to consumer of this act.
707. Penalties.

Section 703. Notice Of Error And Response

If a creditor, having transmitted to a consumer a statement of the consumer's account, receives from the consumer...within thirty days of the mailing of said statement, a written notice,...by registered or certified mail, return receipt requested, setting forth sufficient information to enable the creditor to identify the consumer and the account, the amount and transaction shown in the statement which the consumer in good faith believes to be a billing error, and the facts providing the basis for the consumer's belief that the statement is in error; the creditor shall:

1. Not later than thirty days after receipt of the notice, mail a written acknowledgment to the consumer; and

2. Not later than ninety days after receipt of the notice and prior to taking any action to collect the amount believed by the consumer to be a billing error, (a) make appropriate corrections in the account of the consumer and mail to the consumer a written notice stating that the amount believed to be in error has been corrected and will be shown on the next statement mailed to the consumer or (b) send a written notice to the consumer setting forth the reasons why the creditor believes the account of the consumer was correctly shown in the statement; and

3. Not communicate unfavorable credit information concerning the consumer to any person, including but not limited to credit bureaus or credit reporting agencies, based upon the consumer's failure to pay the amount believed by him to be a billing error, until the creditor has complied with this section. (eff. Nov. 1, 1973)

Section 707. Penalties

Any creditor, having received a notice from a consumer as provided in section seven hundred three of this act, who fails to comply with the requirements of that section:

1. If such an amount is not in fact a billing error, forfeits any rights to collect from the consumer any finance charge or other charge imposed by the creditor in connection with the amount so specified, from the date of the mailing of such notice to the date the creditor complies with section seven hundred three of this act; and

2. If such amount is in fact a billing error, is liable to the consumer in an amount equal to the sum of:

(a) the actual damages sustained by the consumer as a result of the failure of the creditor to comply with such section;

(b) twice the amount of the billing error shown in the statement of the consumer's account except that liability under this paragraph shall not be greater than one hundred dollars; and

(c) in the case of any successful action to enforce the foregoing liability, the costs of the action together with a reasonable attorney's fee as determined by the court.

3. If such amount is in fact a billing error but the creditor shows by a preponderance of evidence that the violation was not intentional and resulted from bona fide error made despite the maintenance of procedures reasonably adopted to avoid any such error, the creditor shall be liable to the consumer only to the extent of the actual damages sustained by the consumer as a result of the failure of the creditor to comply with such section and the costs of any action brought to enforce collection of such erroneous bill together with a reasonable attorney's fee as determined by the court. (eff. Nov. 1, 1973)

NEW YORK GENERAL BUSINESS LAW

Article 25 - Fair Credit Reporting Act

380.   Short title.
380-a.   Definitions.
380-b.   Permissible dissemination of reports.
380-c.   Preparation and/or procurement of investigative consumer reports.
380-d.   Disclosure to consumers.
380-e.   Methods and conditions of disclosure to consumers.
380-f.   Procedure for resolving disputes.
380-g.   Public record information.
380-h.   Restrictions on investigative consumer reports.
380-i.   Requirements on users of consumer reports.
380-j.   Prohibited information.
380-k.   Compliance procedures.
380-l.   Civil liability for willful noncompliance.
380-m.   Civil liability for negligent noncompliance.
380-n.   Jurisdiction of courts; limitation of actions.
380-o.   Obtaining information under false pretenses; penalty.
380-p.   Unauthorized disclosures by officers or employees; penalty.
380-q.   Disclosure of medical information.
380-r.   Disclosures to governmental agencies.
380-s.   Severability.

Section 380-b. Permissible Dissemination Of Reports

(a) A consumer reporting agency may furnish a consumer report under the following circumstances and no other:

(1) In response to the order of a court having jurisdiction to issue such an order, or

(2) In accordance with the written instructions of the consumer to whom it relates, or

(3) To a person whom it has reason to believe intends to use the

information (i) in connection with a credit transaction involving the consumer on whom the information is to be furnished and involving the extension of credit to, or review or collection of an account of, the consumer, or (ii) for employment purposes, or (iii) in connection with the underwriting of insurance involving the consumer, or (iv) in connection with a determination of the consumer's eligibility for a license or other benefit granted by a governmental instrumentality required by law to consider an applicant's financial responsibility or status, or (v) to a person in connection with a business transaction involving the consumer where the user has a legitimate business need for such information.

(b) No person shall request a consumer report, other than an investigative consumer report, in connection with an application made after the effective date of this article, for credit, employment or insurance, unless the applicant is first informed in writing or in the same manner in which the application is made that (i) a consumer report may be requested in connection with such application, and (ii) that applicant upon request will be informed whether or not a consumer report was requested, and if such report was requested, informed of the name and address of the consumer reporting agency that furnished the report.... (eff. Jan. 1, 1978)

Section 380-c. Preparation And/Or Procurement Of Investigative Consumer Reports

(a) No person may procure or cause to be prepared an investigative consumer report on any consumer unless such person:

(1) has first provided the consumer with notice of the procurement or preparation as described in subdivision (b) of this section, and

(2) has first received from the consumer an authorization for preparation or procurement of such investigative consumer report as described in subdivision (c) of this section, provided, however, that the notice and authorization specified by this section shall not be required for an investigative consumer report to be used in connection with an investigation of an employee by such employee's present employer involving an employment purpose for which the employee has not specifically applied.

(b) The notice required by this section shall be in writing if a written application is made by the consumer, or may be in writing or oral in all other circumstances. Such notice shall inform the consumer that:

(1) an investigative consumer report may be requested on the consumer, and

(2) the consumer upon written request will be informed whether or not an investigative consumer report was requested, and if such report was requested, the name and address of the consumer reporting agency to whom the request was made. Upon the furnishing to the consumer of the name and address of the consumer reporting agency to whom the request was made the

192

consumer shall also be informed he may inspect and receive a copy of such report by contacting such agency.... (eff. Jan. 1, 1978)

Section 380-d. Disclosure To Consumers

(a) Every consumer reporting agency shall, upon request and proper identification of any consumer, clearly and accurately disclose to the consumer:

(1) all information in its files at the time of the request concerning such consumer; and

(2) the sources of the information;...

(3) the recipients of any consumer report on the consumer which it has furnished;

(i) for employment purposes within the two-year period preceding the request, and

(ii) for any other purpose within the six month period preceding the request.

....

(c) ...All consumers shall be specifically advised that if they have been denied credit in the past thirty days they are entitled to receive a written copy of their complete file, at no charge whatsoever, should they choose to request such a copy. (eff. June 15, 1981, as amended)

Section 380-e. Methods And Conditions Of Disclosure To Consumers

(a) A consumer reporting agency shall make the disclosures required under section three hundred eighty-d of this article during normal business hours and on reasonable notice.

(b) The disclosure required under section three hundred eighty-d of this article shall be made to the consumer by one or more of the following methods:

(1) in person if he appears in person and furnishes proper identification, in which case the consumer shall be permitted a personal visual inspection of his file and, if he so requests, shall be furnished a copy of his entire file or any part thereof,

(2) by telephone if he has made a written request, the proper identification, for telephone disclosure and the toll charge, if any, for the telephone call is prepaid by or charged directly to the consumer, and at the time of the disclosure by telephone the consumer shall be advised of the right to receive a complete written disclosure of the information pertaining to him, or

(3) by mailing a copy or transcription of all information in the

consumer's file to him, if he has made a written request with proper identification.

(c)   Every consumer reporting agency shall provide trained personnel to
explain to the consumer any information furnished to him either by personal
interview or telephone communication, and information furnished by mail must
be accompanied by an explanation of such information if provided in code or
trade terminology.

....

(e)(1)   A consumer reporting agency shall make all disclosures authorized
under section three hundred eighty-d of this article without charge to any
person who receives a notification of adverse action pursuant to section
three hundred eighty-i of this article, or receives notification from a debt
collection agency affiliated with such consumer reporting agency stating the
consumer's credit rating may be or has been adversely affected if, within
thirty days of receipt of such notification, the consumer makes a request for
such disclosure.   A written statement by a consumer indicating that he has
been denied credit in the past thirty days or has been contacted by a debt
collection agency as described in this paragraph is sufficient to require the
disclosure without charge.

(2)   In all other cases where such disclsoure is requested, the
consumer reporting agency may impose a reasonable charge for such disclosure,
provided that such charges are indicated to the consumer prior to making
disclosure....(eff. June 15, 1981, as amended)

Section 380-f.   Procedure For Resolving Disputes

(a)   If a consumer disputes any item of information contained in his
file, and such dispute is directly conveyed to the consumer reporting agency
by the consumer, the consumer reporting agency shall promptly re-investigate
and record the current status of such information, unless it has reasonable
grounds to believe that the dispute by the consumer is frivolous, and it
shall promptly notify the consumer of the result of its investigation, its
decision on the status of the information and his rights pursuant to this
section.   The presence of contradictory information in a consumer's file shall
not, in and of itself, constitute reasonable grounds for believing the dispute is frivolous.

(b)   If, after conducting the re-investigation required by subdivision
(a) of this section, the consumer reporting agency finds that an item is in
error or that it can no longer be verified, it shall:

(1)   promptly expunge the item and otherwise correct the file,

(2)   refrain from reporting the item in subsequent consumer reports,

(3)   clearly and conspicuously disclose to the consumer his rights
to make a request for notification and upon request of the consumer, promptly
notify any person designated by the consumer who has received information

194

regarding the item during the previous year that an error existed, and shall furnish such person with the corrected information, and

....

(c)   If, after conducting a re-investigation pursuant to this section, the consumer reporting agency is unable to resolve any remaining differences between the statements made by its sources and the consumer, it shall:

(1)   promptly indicate in the file that the item is disputed,

(2)   permit the consumer to file a statement concerning the nature of the dispute, which statement may be limited by the agency to not more than one hundred words if such agency provides the consumer with assistance in writing a clear summary of the dispute,

(3)   include the consumer's statement of the dispute in all subsequent credit reports containing the information in question, and

(4)   clearly note in all subsequent consumer reports that the item is disputed by the consumer.

(d)   Notwithstanding any other provision of this section, if any item disputed and reinvestigated is found to be in error or can no longer be verified, upon completion of the reinvestigation of all items disputed, the agency shall promptly mail the consumer a corrected written copy of the file, reflecting any changes, with an explanation of any code used, at no charge to the consumer. (eff. June 15, 1981, as amended)

Section 380-i.   Requirements On Users Of Consumer Reports

(a)   Whenever credit or insurance for personal, family or household purposes is denied, or the charge for such credit or insurance is increased, either wholly or partly because of information contained in a consumer report, the user of the report shall:

(1)   advise the consumer against whom such adverse action has been taken of such action,

(2)   supply the name and address of the consumer reporting agency making the report, and

(3)   inform the consumer of his right to inspect and receive a copy of such report by contacting the consumer reporting agency.

(b)   In addition to the requirements of subdivision (a) of this section, the user of any such report for purpose of evaluating an application for credit shall furnish to the consumer the reasons for any adverse action in relation to such application in conformance with the requirements of the federal equal credit opportunity act (P.L. 93-435, 15 USC 1691 et seq) as that statute may from time to time be amended.

(c)   Every user of a consumer report or an investigative consumer report

195

shall be prohibited from disseminating any such report to any other person unless such other person has a legitimate business need for the information in connection with a business transaction involving the consumer. (eff. Jan. 1, 1978)

Section 380-j. Prohibited Information

(a) No consumer reporting agency shall report or maintain in the file on a consumer, information:

    (1) relative to an arrest or a criminal charge unless there has been a criminal conviction for such offense, or unless such charges are still pending,

    (2) relative to a consumer's race, religion, color, ancestry or ethnic origin, or

    (3) which it has reason to know is inaccurate,
        ....

(d) No consumer reporting agency shall issue a consumer report which lists a person as having been denied credit if the sole reason for such denial is lack of sufficient information to grant credit, unless the report states that the denial was for such reason.

(e) Consumer reporting agencies shall maintain reasonable procedures designed to assure maximum possible accuracy of the information concerning the individual about whom the report relates.

(f)(1) Except as authorized under paragraph two of this subdivision, no consumer reporting agency may make any consumer report containing any of the following items of information.

    (i) bankruptcies which, from date of adjudication of the most recent bankruptcy, antedate the report by more than fourteen years;

    (ii) judgments which, from date of entry, antedate the report by more than seven years or until the governing statute of limitations has expired, whichever is the longer period; or judgments which, from date of entry, having been satisfied within a five year period from such entry date, shall be removed from the report five years after such entry date;

    (iii) paid tax liens which, from date of payment, antedate the report by more than seven years or,....

    (iv) accounts placed for collection or charged to profit and loss which antedate the report by more than seven years; or accounts placed for collection or charged to profit and loss, which have been paid and which antedate the report by more than five years;

    (v) records of conviction of crime which, from date of disposition, release, or parole, antedate the report by more than seven years;

(vi) information regarding drug or alcoholic addiction where the last reported incident relating to such addiction antedates the consumer report or investigative consumer report by more than seven years;

(vii) information relating to past confinement in a mental institution where the date of last confinement antedates the report by more than seven years; or

(viii) any other adverse information which antedates the report by more than seven years.

(2) The provisions of this subdivision shall not apply to:

(i) a credit transaction involving, or which may reasonably be expected to involve, a principal amount of fifty thousand dollars or more;

(ii) the underwriting of life insurance involving, or which may reasonably be expected to involve, a face amount of fifty thousand dollars or more; or

(iii) the employment of any individual at an annual salary which equals, or which may reasonably be expected to equal twenty-five thousand dollars, or more. (eff. Jan. 1, 1981, as amended)

Section 380-m. Civil Liability For Negligent Noncompliance

Any consumer reporting agency or user of information who or which is negligent in failing to comply with any requirement imposed under this article with respect to any consumer is liable to that consumer in an amount equal to the sum of:

(a) Any actual damages sustained by the consumer as a result of an failure;

(b) In the case of any successful action to enforce any liability under this section, the costs of the action together with reasonable attorney's fees as determined by the court. (eff. Jan. 1, 1978)

Note: Section 380-1. "Civil Liability For Willful Noncompliance" also provides punitive damages to be imposed.

Section 380-o. Obtaining Information Under False Pretense; Penalty

1. Any person who knowingly and willfully obtains information concerning a consumer from a consumer reporting agency under false pretenses shall, upon conviction, be fined not more than five thousand dollars or imprisoned not more than one year, or both.

2. Any person who knowingly and willfully introduces, attempts to introduce or causes to be introduced, false information into a consumer reporting agency's files for the purpose of wrongfully damaging or wrongfully enhancing the credit information of any individual shall, upon conviction, be fined not more than five thousand dollars or imprisoned not more than one year, or both. (as amended, eff. Jan. 1, 1984)

Section 380-p. Unauthorized Disclosures By Officers Or Employees;
               Penalty

[provides same penalty upon an officer or employee of a consumer
reporting agency as in section 380-o "Obtaining Information Under False
Pretenses"].

RESTRICTIONS REGARDING CREDIT CARDS AND TRUTH-IN-LENDING

NEW YORK GENERAL BUSINESS LAW

Section 512. Limitation Of Liability For Unauthorized Use Of A Credit
              Card

1. A provision which imposes liability upon a holder for a cash advance
or loan or for the purchase or lease of property or services obtained by the
unauthorized use of a credit card shall not be enforceable to the extent that
it imposes a greater liability upon the holder than is imposed under the provisions of the act of congress entitled "Truth in Lending Act" and the regulations thereunder as such act and regulations may from time to time be
amended. (eff. July 2, 1971)

Section 515. Issuance Of Credit Cards

1. Notwithstanding any other provision of law, no person shall issue a
credit card in violation of the provisions of an act of congress entitled
"Truth in Lending Act" and the regulations thereunder, as such act and regulations may from time to time be amended.

2. The issuance of a credit card in violation of the provisions of subdivision one of this section shall constitute a misdemeanor. (eff. July 2,
1971, as amended)

Section 517. Statements Of Account

No agreement between the issuer and the holder shall contain any provision that a statement sent by the issuer to the holder shall be deemed
correct unless objected to within a specified period of time. Any such
provision is against public policy and shall be of no force or effect. (eff.
June 1, 1977)

RETAIL INSTALLMENT SALES CONTRACTS

NEW YORK PERSONAL PROPERTY LAW

ARTICLE 10 - RETAIL INSTALMENT SALES ACT
Sec.
401.   Definitions.
402.   Provisions of retail instalment contracts and obligations
402A. Merchandise certificates and obligations therefor.
403.   Restrictions on retail instalment contracts and obligations.

198

404. Credit service charge limitation.
405. Delivery of copy of contract or obligation; buyer's acknowledgment.
406. Notice of assignment; payments.
407. Statements of account; receipts.
408. Credit upon anticipation of payments.
409. Refinancing.
410. Add-ons and consolidations of retail instalment contracts and obligations.
411. Terms of purchase by financing agency.
412. Cancellation.
413. Retail instalment credit agreements.
414. Penalties.
415. Exceptions.
416. Waiver.
417. Severability.
418. Short title.
419. Refund credit on cancellation of accident and health insurance or prepayment of contract.
420. Guaranties to sellers of liabilities of buyers under retail instalment contracts.
421. Security interests in other property.
422. Claim for deficiency after default and repossession.

Section 402. Provisions Of Retail Instalment Contracts And Obligations

1. A retail instalment contract or obligation shall be dated and in writing; the printed portion thereof shall be in at least eight point type.

2. A contract or obligation shall contain the entire agreement of the parties with respect to the goods and services, including any promise, whether made in writing or orally, by the seller, made as an inducement to the buyer to become a party to the contract or which is part of the contract or which is made incidental to negotiations between the seller and the buyer with respect to the sale of the goods or services that are the subject of the contract,...and:

(a) Both at the top of the contract or obligation and directly above the space reserved for the signature of the buyer, the words RETAIL INSTALMENT CONTRACT or RETAIL INSTALMENT OBLIGATION, as the case may be, in at least ten point bold type; and

(b) A notice in at least eight point bold type reading as follows: NOTICE TO THE BUYER: 1. Do not sign this agreement before you read it or if it contains any blank space. 2. You are entitled to a completely filled in copy of this agreement. 3. Under the law, you have the right to pay off in advance the full amount due and under certain conditions to obtain a partial refund of the credit service charge.

...

6-a. A provision in a contract or obligation which provides for the payment of attorney's fees or the costs of attorney's services incurred in a legal action or proceeding for collection shall be null and void.

6-b. A provision in a contract or obligation which provides for waiver of the right to impose any counterclaim or offset arising out of a breach of that contract or obligation by the seller shall be void and unenforceable.

7. All of the terms of an obligation need not be contained in a single document but if they are not then there shall be an original document executed by the parties containing provisions making it applicable to purchases of goods or services, which may not exceed a cash sale price of one hundred seventy-five dollars on each purchase, to be made by the buyer from time to time from a retail seller, which document, together with other written statements relating to the sale of such goods or services shall constitute a retail instalment obligation and shall contain the entire agreement of the parties. In such cases, the original document shall contain those items required to be disclosed by the act of congress entitled "Truth in Lending Act" and the regulations thereunder, as such act and regulations may from time to time be amended and shall further contain:

   (i) a legend as provided in paragraph (a) of subdivision two hereof,

   (ii) a notice to the buyer as provided in paragraph (b) of subdivision two hereof,

   (iii) the names of the seller and the buyer.

   (iv) the place of business of the seller and the residence or place of business of the buyer as specified by the buyer,

   (v) the number of instalment payments, and

   (vi) the amount or rate of the credit service charge applicable to purchases thereunder.

At the time of each purchase under such document, the seller shall give the buyer statements which shall contain at the top thereof a legend in at least eight-point bold type: PART OF A RETAIL INSTALMENT OBLIGATION and an adequate description of the goods, accessories and services sold or furnished (including the make and model, if any, in the case of goods customarily sold by make and model) and shall further contain those items required to be disclosed by the act of congress entitled "Truth in Lending Act" .... If the seller does not deliver to the buyer at the time of each purchase under such original document a statement in compliance with the act of congress entitled "Truth in Lending Act" ... the seller shall promptly thereafter, ... within ten days from the date of such purchase, deliver, mail or cause to be mailed to the buyer at his address shown on the seller's records, such statement. Unless the seller does so, the buyer shall have an unconditional right to cancel such purchase and to receive an immediate refund of any payments made and re-delivery of all goods traded in to the seller on account of or in contemplation of such purchase; upon the written request of the buyer the seller shall prove the accuracy of the calculation in such statement .... (eff. Dec. 1, 1980, as amended; amended eff. June 6, 1983).

Section 413. Retail Instalment Credit Agreements

1. A retail instalment credit agreement shall be dated and in writing
and the printed portion thereof shall be in at least eight point type. No
retail instalment credit agreement shall be signed by the buyer when it
contains blank spaces to be filled in after it had been signed by the buyer.
The seller, before he shall be able to avail himself of the rates authorized
by subdivision three of this section, shall deliver to the buyer a copy of
the credit agreement executed by the seller.

...

3. (a) A seller may, in a retail instalment credit agreement, contract
for and, if so contract for, the seller or holder thereof may charge, receive
and collect the service charge authorized by this article. The service
charge shall not exceed the rates agreed upon by the seller and the buyer
computed, for the purposes of this section, on the outstanding indebtedness
from month to month or if the service charge so computed is less than seventy
cents for any month, seventy cents.

...

5. The service charge shall include all charges incident to investigating and making the retail instalment credit agreement and for the extension
of credit thereunder. No fee, expense, delinquency, collection or other
charge whatsoever shall be taken, received, reserved or contracted for by the
seller under or holder of a retail instalment credit agreement except as
provided in this section and except that the credit agreement may provide
for the payment of attorney's fees not exceeding twenty per centum of the
amount due and payable under the credit agreement if it is referred to an
attorney not a salaried employee of the seller or holder for collection; and
provided further that when credit cards are issued in connection with a retail
instalment credit agreement, the retail instalment credit agreement may in
addition provide for an annual fee for membership in the credit card plan,
which fee shall not be deemed a service charge or interest for any purpose of
law.

10. No retail instalment credit agreement shall contain any provision by
which:

(a) In the absence of the buyer's default, the holder may, arbitrarily and without reasonable cause, accelerate the maturity of any part or
all of the amount owing thereunder,

(b) A power-of-attorney is given to confess judgment in this state,
or an assignment of wages is given;

(c) The buyer waives any right of action against the seller or
holder of the agreement, or other person acting on his behalf, for any illegal
act committed in the collection of payments under the agreement;

...

(e) The buyer relieves the seller from liability for any legal
remedy which the buyer may have against the seller under the agreement or
otherwise;

201

(f) The buyer waives any right to a trial by jury in any action or proceeding arising out of the agreement.

Any such prohibited provision shall be void but shall not otherwise affect the validity of the contract.

. . .

13. (a) Subject to the limitation contained in paragraph (b) of this subdivision, the holder of a retail instalment credit agreement (including for purposes of this subdivision a financing agency which enters into a credit agreement with a retail buyer as provided in subdivision eleven of this section) shall be subject to all claims (other than tort claims) and defenses arising out of the buyer's purchase of goods and services to be paid in accordance with the credit agreement if (1) the buyer has made a good faith attempt to obtain satisfactory resolution of a disagreement or problem relative to the sale from the seller; (2) the amount of the initial transaction exceeds fifty dollars; and (3) the place where the initial transaction occurred was in the same state as the mailing address previously provided by the buyer or was within one hundred miles from such address, except that the limitations set forth in subparagraphs (2) and (3) of this paragraph with respect to a buyer's right to assert claims and defenses against the holder shall not be applicable to any transaction in which the seller (A) is the same person as the holder; (B) is controller by the holder; (C) is under direct or indirect common control with the holder; (d) is a franchised dealer of the holder's products or services; or (e) has obtained the order for such sale through a mail solicitation made by or participated in by the holder in which the buyer is solicited to enter into such transactions by using the credit agreement with the holder.

(b) The amount of claims or defenses asserted by the buyer may not exceed the amount of indebtedness owing to the holder with respect to such transaction at the time the buyer first notifies the holder or seller of such claim or defense.... (eff. 1980, as amended)

Section 414. Penalties

1. Any person who shall wilfully violate any provision of this article shall be guilty of a misdemeanor and upon conviction shall be punished by a fine not exceeding five hundred dollars.... (eff. 1961, as amended)

Section 416. Waiver

Any waiver by the buyer of the provisions of this article shall be unenforceable and void. (eff. 1957)

See also Sections 301-315 of the Personal Property Law: "Article 9 - Motor Vehicle Retail Instalment Sales Act."

In collecting money judgments, certain exemptions and restrictions are provided by statute. A representative selection of such statutes enacted in New York State follows:

NEW YORK CIVIL PRACTICE LAW AND RULES (C.P.L.R)

Section 5205. Personal Property Exempt From Application To The Satisfaction Of Money Judgments

(a) Exemption for personal property. The following personal property when owned by any person is exempt from applicable to the satisfaction of a money judgment except where the judgment is for the purchase price of the exempt property or was recovered by a domestic, laboring person or mechanic for work performed by that person in such capacity.

1. all stoves kept for use in the judgment debtor's dwelling house and necessary fuel therefor for sixty days; one sewing machine with its appurtenances;

2. the family bible, family pictures, and school books used by the judgment debtor or in the family; and other books, not exceeding fifty dollars in value, kept and used as part of the family or judgment debtor's library;

3. a seat or pew occupied by the judgment debtor or the family in a place of public worship;

4. domestic animals with the necessary food for those animals for sixty days,...all necessary food actually provided for the use of the judgment debtor or his family for sixty days;

5. all wearing apparel, household furniture, one mechanical, gas or electric refrigerator, one radio receiver, one television set, crockery, tableware and cooking utensils necessary for the judgment debtor and the family;

6. a wedding ring; a watch not exceeding thirty-five dollars in value; and

7. necessary working tools and implements, including those of a mechanic, farm machinery, team, professional instruments, furniture and library, not exceeding six hundred dollars in value,...provided, however, that the articles specified in this paragraph are necessary to the carrying on of the judgment debtor's profession or calling.

...

(d) Income Exemptions. The following personal property is exempt from application to the satisfaction of a money judgment, except such part as a court determines to be unnecessary for the reasonable requirements of the judgment debtor and his dependents:

1. ninety per cent of the income or other payments from a trust the principal of which is exempt under subdivision (c);

2. ninety per cent of the earnings of the judgment debtor for his personal services rendered within sixty days before, and at any time after, an income execution is delivered to the sheriff or a motion is made to secure the application of the judgment debtor's earnings to the satisfaction of the judgment; and

3. payments pursuant to an award in a matrimonial action, for the support of a wife, where the wife is the judgment debtor, or for the support of a child, where the child is the judgment debtor; where the award was made by a court of the state, determination of the extent to which it is unnecessary shall be made by that court.

...

(g) Security deposit exemption. Money deposited as security for the rental of real property to be used as the residence of the judgment debtor or the judgment debtor's family; and money deposited as security with a gas, electric, water, steam, telegraph or telephone corporation, or a municipality rendering utility services, for services to judgment debtor's residence or the residence of judgment debtor's family, are exempt from application to the satisfaction of a money judgment.

(h) The following personal property is exempt from application to the satisfaction of money judgment, except such part as a court determines to be unnecessary for the reasonable requirements of the judgment debtor and his dependents:

1. any and all medical and dental accessions to the human body and all personal property or equipment that is necessary or proper to maintain or assist in sustaining or maintaining one or more major life activities or is utilized to provide mobility for a person with a permanent disability; and

2. any guide dog or hearing dog, as those terms are defined in section one hundred eight of the agriculture and markets law, or any animal trained to aid or assist a person with a permanent disability and actually being so used by such person, together with any and all food or feed for any such dog or other animal. (eff. May 13, 1980, as amended)

<u>Section 5206.</u> <u>Real Property Exempt From Application To The Satisfaction</u>
<u>Of Money Judgments</u>

(a) Exemption of homestead. Property of one of the following types, not exceeding ten thousand dollars in value above liens and encumbrances, owned and occupied as a principal residence, is exempt from application to the satisfaction of a money judgment, unless the judgment was recovered wholly for the purchase price thereof:

1. a lot of land with a dwelling thereon,

2. shares of stock in a cooperative apartment corporation,

3. units of a condominium apartment, or

4. a mobile home.

But no exempt homestead shall be exempt from taxation or from sale for nonpayment of taxes or assessments.... (eff. June 26, 1980, as amended)

Section 5231. Income Execution

(a) Form. An income execution shall specify,...the name and address of the person from whom the judgment debtor is receiving or will receive money; the amount of money, the frequency of its payment and the amount of the installments to be collected therefrom; and shall contain a notice to the judgment debtor that he shall commence payment of the installments specified to the sheriff forthwith and that, upon his default, the execution will be served upon the person from whom he is receiving or will receive money.

(b) Issuance. Where a judgment debtor is receiving or will receive more than eighty-five dollars per week from any person, an income execution for installments therefrom of not more than ten percent thereof may be issued and delivered to the sheriff of the county in which the judgment debtor resides or, where the judgment debtor is a non-resident, the county in which he is employed.... (eff. May 13, 1975, as amended)

CONSUMER TRANSACTIONS - ATTORNEYS FEES

General Obligations Law

Section 5-327. Consumers' Right To Recover Attorney's Fees In Actions Arising Out Of Consumer Contracts

1. As used in this section, the following terms shall have the following meanings:
    (a) "Consumer contract" means a written agreement entered into between a creditor or seller as one party with a natural person who is the debtor or buyer as the second party, and the money, other personal property or services which are the subject of the transaction are primarily for personal, family or household purposes;
2. Whenever a consumer contract provides that the creditor or seller may recover attorney's fees and expenses incurred as the result of a breach of any contractual obligation by the debtor or buyer, it shall be implied that the creditor or seller shall pay the attorney's fees and expenses of the debtor or buyer incurred as the result of a breach of any contractual obligation by the creditor or seller, or in the successful defense of any action arising out of the contract commenced by the creditor or seller. Any limitations on attorney's fees recoverable by the creditor or seller shall also be applicable to attorney's fees recoverable by the debtor or buyer under this section. Any waiver of this section shall be void as against public policy. (eff. June 13, 1983).

13. "SUNDAY LAWS"

NEW YORK GENERAL BUSINESS LAW

Section 5. Labor Prohibited On Sunday

All labor on Sunday is prohibited, excepting the works of necessity and charity. In works of necessity or charity is included whatever is needful during the day for the good order, health or comfort of the community. (eff. Sept. 1, 1967 - originally enacted in 1909, and was previously contained in Penal Law.)

Section 6. Persons Observing Another Day As A Sabbath

It is a sufficient defense to a prosecution for work or labor on the first day of the week that the defendant uniformly keeps another day of the week as holy time, and does not labor on that day, and that the labor complained of was done in such manner as not to interrupt or disturb other persons observing the first day of the week as holy time. (eff. Sept. 1, 1967 - originally enacted in 1909, and was previously contained in Penal Law).

Section 8. Trades, Manufactures, And Mechanical Employments Prohibited On Sunday

All trades, manufacturers, agricultural or mechanical employments upon the first day of the week are prohibited, except that when the same are works of necessity they may be performed on that day in their usual and orderly manner, so as not to interfere with the repose and religious liberty of the community. (eff. Sept. 1, 1967 - originally enacted in 1909, and was previously contained in Penal Law).

Section 11. Serving Civil Process On Sunday

All service or execution of legal process, of any kind whatever, on the first day of the week is prohibited, except in criminal proceedings or where service or execution is specially authorized by statute. Service or execution of any process upon said day except as herein permitted is absolutely void for any and every purpose whatsoever. (eff. May 15, 1972, as amended).

CASE NO. 28
CIOFALO v. VIC TANNEY GYMS, INC.

10 N.Y. 2d 294   October 1961

INTRODUCTION

Many kinds of businesses that enter into contracts with the public include a provision in the contract designed to limit or eliminate liability in
the event the customer sustains physical injury and/or economic loss as a
result of use of the company's product or services whether such injury and/or
loss is sustained on or off the comapny's premises. Courts are frequently
asked to determine whether such a provision is legal or a violation of state
statute or a violation of what courts declare "the public policy of the state".
The following case illustrates the rule of law applied to private gyms at the
time this case was decided. However, subsequently, New York enacted a statute
which declared such contract provisions void as indicated in the discussion
questions that follow this case.

FROESSEL, J. This action by plaintiff wife for personal injuries, and by
plaintiff husband for medical expenses and loss of services, stems from injuries which the wife sustained as the result of a fall at or near the edge of a
swimming pool located on defendant's premises. Plaintiff claimed that because
of excessive slipperiness and lack of sufficient and competent personnel she
was caused to fall and fractured her left wrist.

At the time of the injury, plaintiff wife was a "member" or patron of the
gymnasium operated by defendant, and in her membership contract she had agreed
to assume full responsibility for any injuries which might occur to her in or
about defendant's premises, "including but without limitation, any claims for
personal injuries resulting from or arising out of the negligence of" the defendant.

In addition to denying the material allegations of the complaint, defendant's answer set forth as an affirmative defense the provision of the contract
above referred to. Defendant moved for summary judgment, and plaintiffs, by
cross motion, moved to strike said defense, their attorney contending in an
affidavit that the exculpatory clause is void as against public policy. Summary judgment was granted in favor of defendant, and the Appellate Division has
affirmed.

Although exculpatory clauses in a contract, intended to insulate one of
the parties from liability resulting from his own negligence, are closely
scrutinized, they are enforced, but what a number of qualifications. Whether
or not such provisions, when properly expressed, will be given effect depends
upon the legal relationship between the contracting parties and the interest of
the public therein. Thus such a provision has been held void when contained in
the contract of carriage of a common carrier * * * unless a reduced fare was
charged * * * ; or in the contract of a public utility under a duty to furnish
telephone service * * * ; or when imposed by the employer as a condition of

employment * * *.

On the other hand, where the intention of the parties is expressed in sufficiently clear and unequivocal language * * *, and it does not come within any of the aforesaid categories where the public interest is directly involved a provision absolving a party from his own neglignet acts will be given effect. This was the situation in Kirshenbaum v. General Outdoor Adv. Co. ...a landlord and tenant relationship; in Graves v. Davis...involving a contract for towage by the owners of a tug; and in the so-called contractor cases * * *. In situations such as these, "public policy does not condemn the immunity clause voluntarily agreed upon by these parties" * * *.

Of course, contracts may not be construed to exempt parties from the consequences of their own negligence in the absence of express language to that effect * * *. In none of these cases was it necessary for us to decide the larger question of whether the exculpatory agreement should be stricken as void since we found that the language employed by the parties did not express in unequivocal terms their intention to relieve the defendant of the liability for his own negligence.

The wording of the contract in the instant case expresses as clearly as language can the intention of the parties to completely insulate the defendant from liability for injuries sustained by plaintiff by reason of defendant's own negligence, and, in the face of the allegation of the complaint charging merely ordinary negligence, such agreement is valid.

Here there is no special legal relationship and no overriding public interest which demand that this contract provision, voluntarily entered into by competent parties, should be rendered ineffectual. Defendant, a private corporation, was under no obligation or legal duty to accept plaintiff as a "member" or patron. Having consented to do so, it had the right to insist upon such terms as it deemed appropriate. Plaintiff, on the other hand, was not required to assent to unacceptable terms, or to give up a valuable legal right, as a condition precedent to obtaining employment or being able to make use of the services rendered by a public carrier or utility. She voluntarily applied for membership in a private organization, and agreed to the terms upon which this membership was bestowed. She may not repudiate them now.

The judgment appealed from should be affirmed, without costs.

(Judgment for defendant.)

DISCUSSION QUESTIONS

1.   In 1976 New York State enacted the General Obligations Law 5-326 which is set forth in this book. What is the effect of this statute? What kinds of businesses are listed in this statute?
2.   How would General Obligations Law 5-326 alter this decision?
3.   Why did New York enact this statute which results in less "freedom of contract" between parties?
4.   How does the decision in this case differ from the decisions in the Weinberg case (No. 11) and the Gross case (No. 29)?

ILLEGALITY: EXCULPATORY CLAUSES

CASE NO. 29

GROSS v. SWEET

424 N.Y.S. 2d 365   November 1979

INTRODUCTION

Contracts frequently contain clauses called exculpatory clauses which provide that one party is excused from all liability if the other party suffers any physical injury or economic loss caused by the first party. If injury or loss occurs and an action is commenced to recover damages, the defendant will assert the defense that he is not liable because of the exculpatory clause in the contract. The following case illustrates how the courts view exculpatory clauses in general and what tests must be met before a court will enforce an exculpatory clause and deny recovery to an injured party. New York and almost all states have enacted statutes declaring exculpatory clauses void in certain contracts. See the New York statutes in this book.

FUCHSBERG, Judge.

We hold that, in the circumstances of this case, a release signed by the plaintiff as a precondition for his enrollment in defendant's parachute jumping course does not bar him from suing for personal injuries he allegedly incurred as a result of defendant's negligence.

Plaintiff Bruce Gross, wishing to learn how to parachute, enrolled in the Stormville Parachute Center Training School, a facility owned and operated by the defendant William Sweet for the purpose of offering instruction in the sport. The ensuing events are essentially undisputed. As a prerequisite for admission into the course, Gross had to pay a fee and sign a form entitled "Responsibility Release". He was then given the standard introductory lesson, which consisted of approximately one hour of on-land training, including oral instruction as well as several jumps off a two and a half foot table. Plaintiff then was equipped with a parachute and flown to an altitude of 2,800 feet for his first practice jump. Upon coming in contact with the ground on his descent, plaintiff suffered serious personal injuries.

The suit is grounded on negligence, breach of warranty and gross negligence. In the main, plaintiff claims that defendant failed to provide adequate training and safe equipment, violated certain rules and procedures promulgated by the Federal Aviation Administration governing the conduct of parachute schools and failed to warn him sufficiently of the attendant dangers.

Defendant pleaded the release plaintiff had signed and moved for summary judgment, contending that the terms of the release exculpated the defendant from any liability. Plaintiff, in turn, cross-moved to strike this affirmative defense contending, primarily, that the terms of the release did not specifically bar a suit for personal injuries negligently caused by the defendant. He also urged that, as a matter of policy, the release should not be enforceable as between a student and his teacher, a relationship in which one of the parties holds himself out as qualified and responsible to provide training in a skill and the other party relies on this expertise, particularly in the context of an activity in which the degree of training necessary for safe participation is much greater than might be apparent to a novice. Alternatively, plaintiff argues that the release in any event does not excuse defendant's violation of the Federal Aviation Administration's regulations governing parachute jumping schools and student parachutists, one of which allegedly required that a medical certificate be furnished as a prerequisite to enrollment in a parachute jumping course. Defendant's failure to request one, plaintiff asserts, bore critically on his situation because, despite his having informed defendant that several years earlier an orthopedic pin had been inserted in his leg, he was accepted as a student though, as the school must have known, landing in a parachute puts special stress on one's legs.

However, Special Term granted defendant's motion, denied plaintiff's cross motion and dismissed the complaint. On plaintiff's appeal from that order, a divided Appellate Division reversed, reinstated the complaint and granted plaintiff's motion to dismiss the affirmative defense. The appeal is now before us on a certified question: "Was the order of this Court, which reinstated the complaint and granted plaintiff's motion to dismiss the affirmative defense of release, correct as a matter of law?" Our answer is that it was.

We begin with the proposition, too well settled to invoke any dispute, that the law frown upon contracts intended to exculpate a party from the consequences of his own negligence and though, with certain exceptions, they are enforceable, such agreements are subject to close judicial scrutiny....To the extent that agreements purport to grant exemption for liability for willful or grossly negligent acts they have been viewed as wholly void....And so, here, so much of plaintiff's complaint as contains allegations that defendant was grossly negligent, may not be barred by the release in any event. But we need not explore further this possibility for we conclude the complaint in its entirety withstands the exculpatory agreement.

Nor need we consider plaintiff's request that we ignore the release on the grounds that the special relationship of the parties and the public interest involved forbids its enforcement. While we have, for example, had occasion to invalidate such provisions when they were contained in the contract between a passenger and a common carrier...or in a contract between a customer and a public utility under a duty to furnish telephone service...or when imposed by an employer as a condition of employment...the circumstances here do not fit within any of these relationships. And, though we note that a recent statute renders void agreements purporting to exempt from liability for negligence those engaged in a variety of businesses that serve the public (e.g., landlords (General Obligations Law, 5-321); caterers (5-322); building service or maintenance contractors (5-323); those who maintain garages or parking garages (5-325); or pools, gymnasiums or places of public amusement or recreation (5-326)), defendant's occupation does not fall within any of these classes either. We also decline, at this point, plaintiff's invitation that we proceed further to consider what effect, if any, the alleged contravention of Federal regulations may have on the relationship of the parties or the public interest involved. Such questions need not be reached in view of our holding that the wording of the exculpatory agreement does not preclude plaintiff's suit for negligence.

As the cases make clear, the law's reluctance to enforce exculpatory provisions of this nature has resulted in the development of an exacting standard by which courts measure their validity. So, it has been repeatedly emphasized that unless the intention of the parties is expressed in unmistakable language, an exculpatory clause will not be deemed to insulate a party from liability for his own negligent acts....Put another way, it must appear plainly and precisely that the "limitation of liability extends to negligence or other fault of the party attempting to shed his ordinary responsibility....

Not only does this stringent standard require that the drafter of such an agreement make its terms unambiguous, but it mandates that the terms be understandable as well. Thus, a provision that would exempt its drafter from any liability occasioned by his fault should not compel resort to a magnifying glass and lexicon....Of course, this does not imply that only simple or monosyllabic language can be used in such clauses. Rather, what the law demands is that such provisions be clear and coherent....

By and large, if such is the intention of the parties, the fairest course is to provide explicitly that claims based on negligence are included....That does not mean that the word "negligence" must be employed for courts to give effect to an exculpatory agreement; however, words conveying a similar import must appear....

We are, of course, cognizant of the fact that the general rule of strict judicial construction has been somewhat liberalized in its application to exoneration clauses in indemnification agreements, which are usually "negotiated at arm's length between * * * sophisticated business entities" and which can be viewed as merely "allocating the risk of liability to third parties between themselves, essentially through the employment of insurance"....In such cases, the law, reflecting the economic realities, will recognize an agreement to relieve one party from the consequences of his negligence on the strength of a broadly worded clause framed in less precise language than would normally be required, though even then it must evince the "unmistakable intent of the parties"....

The case before us today obviously does not fit within this exception to the strict legal standard generally employed by the courts of this State under which exculpatory provisions drawn in broad and sweeping language have not been given effect. For example, agreements to release from "any and all responsibility or liability of any nature whatsoever for any loss of property or personal injury occurring on this trip"...or to "waive claim for any loss to personal property, or for any personal injury while a member of (a)club"...have not barred claims based on negligence....Moreover, in Boll v. Sharp & Dohme... we held not sufficiently unambiguous a release form in which a blood donor was required to agree that defendants were not "in any way responsible for any consequences * * * resulting from the giving of such blood or from any of the tests, examinations or procedures incident thereto", and further "release(d) and discharge(d) more (defendants) from all claims and demands whatsoever * * * against them or any of them by reason of any matter relative or incident to donation of blood"....The donor was thus allowed to sue in negligence for injuries he sustained when, on the completion of the blood donation, he fainted and fell to the floor.

With all this as background, the language of the "Responsibility Release" in the case before us, must be viewed as no more explicit than that in Boll. In its entirety, it reads: "I, the undersigned, hereby, and by these covenants, do waive any and all claims that I, my heirs, and/or assignees may have against Nathaniel Sweet, the Stormville Parachute Center, the Jumpmaster and the Pilot who shall operate the aircraft when used for the purpose of parachute jumping for any personal injuries or property damage that I may sustain or which may arise out of my learning, practicing or actually jumping from an aircraft. I also assume full responsibility for any damage that I may do or cause while participating in this sport".

Assuming that this language alerted the plaintiff to the dangers inherent in parachute jumping and that he entered into the sport with apprehension of the risks, it does not follow that he was aware of, much less intended to accept, any enhanced exposure to injury occasioned by the carelessness of the very persons on which he depended for his safety. Specifically, the release nowhere expresses any intention to exempt the defendant from liability for injury or property damages which may result from his failure to use due care either in his training methods or in his furnishing safe equipment. Thus, whether on a running reading or a careful analysis, the agreement could most reasonably be taken merely as driving home the fact that the defendant was not to bear any responsibility for injuries that ordinarily and inevitably would occur, without any fault of the defendant, to those who participate in such a physically demanding sport.

In short, instead of specifying to prospective students that they would have to abide any consequences attributable to the instructor's own carelessness, the defendant seems to have preferred the use of opaque terminology rather than suffer the possibility of lower enrollment. But, while, with exceptions not pertinent to this case, the law grudgingly accepts the proposition that men may contract away their liability for negligently caused injuries, they may do so only on the condition that their intention be expressed clearly and in "unequivocal terms"....

Accordingly, the certified question is answered in the affirmative, and the order of the Appellate Division reversing the grant of summary judgment, reinstating the complaint and dismissing the defense based on the release should be affirmed.

(Judgment for plaintiff.)

DISCUSSION QUESTION

1. How could the defendant have written the exculpatory clause to bar recovery by the injured plaintiff?
2. How does the decision in this case differ from the decisions in the Weinberg case (No. 11) and the Vic Tanney case (No. 28)?

ILLEGALITY: EFFECT ON PARTY'S RIGHTS
CASE NO. 30
UNION EXCHANGE NAT. BANK v. JOSEPH

231 N.Y. 250   May 1921

INTRODUCTION

Sometimes a party enters into a contract to pay money in exchange for the other party's promise not to bring criminal charges. Thereafter, a court may be asked by one of the parties to enforce the contract or to declare the contract void because it was entered into under duress (to avoid criminal prosecution). In such a case the court will apply the rule of law, illustrated in this leading case, that if the purpose of the contract was to prevent criminal prosecution the court will neither enforce nor declare void any such contract--but will leave the parties where it finds them. Thus, the victim of duress, who is a wrongdoer by entering into such a contract, is without a legal remedy.

CARDOZO, J. Plaintiff sues upon a promisory note. Defendant answers that there was duress, and counterclaims for the recovery of payments already made. No question is before us in respect of the adequacy of the answer considered as a defense. The point to be determined is the validity of the counterclaim.

The substance of the counterclaim is this: The defendant's brother-in-law, one Bloch, was bankrupt and the plaintiff's debtor. The plaintiff informed the defendant that Bloch was guilty of criminal misappropriation of its funds, and threatened to arrest him and send him to prison unless it received the defendant's notes for the amount of the indebtedness. The pressure thereby exerted overpowered and constrained his will. He excuted the notes to save his brother-in-law from jail, and to save his sister, Bloch's wife, from the shame of her husband's disgrace, and the loss of her sole support. The note in suit is one of a series on which payments have been made. The defendant asks judgment that the payments be returned.

We think the defendant, if a victim of duress, was at the same time a wrongdoer when he stifled a charge of crime. In such circumstances the law will leave the parties where it finds them.... Neither is permitted to recover from the other. The contract is not helped by the suggestion that, for all that appears, Bloch may have been innocent. That issue, beyond doubt, would be irrelevant if prosecution had begun.... We are asked to hold otherwise where prosecution is merely threatened. Some cases do, indeed, give effect to that distinction. The prosecution once initiated, they say, must be left to take its course; the prosecution merely threatened, may be bought off, if directed against innocence.... We think it has not been law in this state since the ruling of this court in Haynes v. Rudd (supra). There the plaintiff gave his note under duress to stifle a prosecution threatened, but not begun. We approved a charge that "an agreement to suppress the evidence of a crime alleged to have been committed" was a illegal as one "to suppress the evidence or refrain from prosecuting a crime which had been in fact committed."

213

The principle thus vindicated is simple and commanding. There is to be no traffic in the privilege of invoking the public justice of the state. One may press a charge or withhold it as one will. One may not make action or inaction dependent on a price.... The state has, indeed, no interest to be promoted by the prosecution of the innocent.... That consideration, if it were controlling, is as applicable to agreements to discontinue as to agreements to abstain. The state has an interest, however, in preserving to complainants the freedom of choice, the incentives to sincerity, which are the safeguards and the assurance of the prosecution of the guilty.

(The court concluded that the defendant could not recover payments made to the plaintiff and that the plaintiff could not recover any additional payments from the defendant.)

ILLEGALITY: COMMERCIAL BRIBERY

CASE NO. 31

McCONNELL, v. COMMONWEALTH PICTURES CORPORATION

7 N.Y. 2d 465   March 31, 1960

INTRODUCTION

A commission contract provides that one party will pay the other party a
specified commission for business obtained. The legal question arises whether
a party is legally entitled to collect his commission when he commits commercial bribery to obtain business. This case illustrates the rule of law and its
rationale which is applicable to commercial bribery cases.

DESMOND, Chief Judge.

The appeal is by defendant from so much of an Appellate Division, First
Department, order as affirmed that part of a Special term order which struck
out two defenses in the answer.

Plaintiff sues for an accounting. Defendant had agreed in writing that if
plaintiff should succeed in negotiating a contract with a motion   picture producer whereby defendant would get the distribution rights for certain motion
pictures, defendant would pay plaintiff $10,000 on execution of the contract
between defendant and the producer, and would thereafter pay plaintiff a stated
percentage of defendant's gross receipts from distribution of the pictures.
Plaintiff negotiated the distribution rights for defendant and defendant paid
plaintiff the promised $10,000 but later refused to pay him the commissions or
to give him an accounting of profits.

Defendant's answer contains two affirmative defenses the sufficiency of
which we must decide. In these defenses it is asserted that plaintiff, without
the knowledge of defendant or of the producer, procured the distribution rights
by bribing a representative of the producer and that plaintiff agreed to pay
and did pay to that representative as a bribe the $10,000 which defendant paid
plaintiff. The courts below (despite a strong dissent in the Appellate Division) held that the defenses were insufficient to defeat plaintiff's suit.
Special Term's opinion said that, since the agreement sued upon--between plaintiff and defendant-- was not in itself illegal, plaintiff's right to be paid for
performing it could not be defeated by a showing that he had misconducted himself in carrying it out. The court found a substantial difference between this
and the performance of an illegal contract. We take a different view. Proper
and consistent application of a prime and long-settled public policy closes
the doors of our courts to those who sue to collect the rewards of corruption.

New York's policy has been frequently and emphatically announced in the
decisions. "It is the settled law of this State (and probably of every other
State) that a party to an illegal contract cannot ask a court of law to help
him carry out his illegal object, nor can such a person plead or prove in any

215

court a case in which he, as a basis for his claim, must set forth his illegal purpose' ... The money plaintiff sues for was the fruit of an admitted crime and "no court should be required to serve as paymaster of the wages of crime' ... And it makes no difference that defendant has no title to the money since the court's concern 'is not with the position of the defendant' but with the question of whether 'a recovery by the plaintiff should be denied for the sake of public interests', a question which is one 'of public policy in the administration of the law' .... That public policy is the one described in Riggs v. Palmer: "No one shall be permitted to profit by his own fraud, or to take advantage of his own wrong, or to found and claim upon his own iniquity, or to acquire property by his own crime. These maxims are dictated by public policy, have their foundation in universal law administered in all civilized countries, and have nowhere been superseded by statutes.' ...

We must either repudiate those statements of public policy or uphold these challenged defenses. It is true that some of the leading decisions ... were in suits on intrinsically illegal contracts but the rule fails of its purpose unless it covers a case like the one at bar. Here, as in Stone v. Freeman and Carr v. Hoy (supra), the money sued for was (assuming the truth of the defenses) "the fruit of an admitted crime." To allow this plaintiff to collect his commissions would be to let him "profit by his own fraud, or to take advantage of his own wrong, or to found (a) claim upon his own iniquity, or to acquire property by his own crime".... The issue is not whether the acts alleged in the defenses would constitute the crime of commercial bribery under section 439 of the Penal Law, Consol, Laws, c.40, although it appears that they would. "A seller cannot recover the price of goods sold where he has paid a commission to an agent of the purchaser ... neither could the agent recover the commission, even at common law and before the enactment of section 384--r of the Penal Law (now section 439)" ... The Sirkin opinion has been cited with approval by this court in Merchants' Line v. Baltimore & Ohio R. Co., and Morgan Munitions Supply Co. v. Studebaker Corp. In unmistakable terms it forbids the courts to honor claims founded on commercial bribery. (Note: see penal law 180.00, 180.05 pages 166-167.)
We are not working here with narrow questions of technical law. We are applying fundamental concepts of morality and fair dealing not to be weakened by exceptions. So far as precedent is necessary, we can rely on Sirkin v. Fourteenth Street Store. App. Div. and Reiner v. North American Newspaper Alliance. Sirkin is the case closest to ours and shows that, whatever be the law in other jurisdictions, we in New York deny awards for the corrupt performance of contracts even though in essence the contracts are not illegal. Sirkin had sued for the price of goods sold and delivered to defendant. Held to be good was a defense which charged that plaintiff seller had paid a secret commission to an agent of defendant purchaser. There cannot be any difference in principle between that situation and the present one where plaintiff (it is alleged) contracted to buy

motion-picture rights for defendant but performed his convenant only by bribing the seller's agent. In the Reiner case (supra), likewise, the plaintiff had fully performed the services required by his agreement with the defendant but was denied a recovery because his performance had involved and included "fraud and deception" practiced not on defendant but on a third party. It is beside the point that the present plaintiff on trial might be able to prove a prima facie case without the bribery being exposed. On the whole case (again assuming that the defenses speak the truth) the disclosed situation would be within the rule of our precedents forbidding court assistance to bribers.

It is argued that a reversal here means that the doing of any small illegality in the performance of an otherwise lawful contract will deprive the doer of all rights, with the result that the other party will get a windfall and there will be great injustice. Our ruling does not go as far as that. It is not every minor wrongdoing in the course of contract performance that will insulate the other party from liability for work done or goods furnished. There must at least be a direct connection between the illegal transaction and the obligation sued upon. Connection is a matter of degree. Some illegalities are merely incidental to the contract sued on .. . . We cannot now, any more than in our past decisions, announce what will be the results of all the kinds of corruption, minor and major, essential and peripheral. All we are doing here is labeling the conduct described in these defenses as gross corruption depriving plaintiff of all right of access to the courts of New York State. Consistent with public morality and settled public policy, we hold that a party will be denied recovery even on a contract valid on its face, if it appears that he has resorted to gravely immoral and illegal conduct in accomplishing its performance.

Perhaps this application of the principle represents a distinct step beyond Sirkin and Reiner (supra) in the sense that we are here barring recovery under a contract which in itself is entirely legal. But if this be an extension, public policy supports it. We point out that our holding is limited to cases in which the illegal performance of a contract originally valid takes the form of commercial bribery or similar conduct and in which the illegality is central to or a dominant part of the plaintiff's whole course of conduct in performance of the contract . . .

(Judgment for defendant.)

DISCUSSION QUESTIONS
1. Does this case stand for the proposition that if a party uses any illegal means to perform his obligations under a contract he will not be able to enforce the contract against the other party?
2. In the court of original jurisdiction Commonwealth's counterclaim against McConnell was "brushed aside" and dismissed. Commonwealth never appealed this dismissal. If it had appealed, what do you think the Court of Appeals would have held?

ILLEGALITY: LIQUIDATED DAMAGE CLAUSES

CASE NO. 32

SEIDLITZ v. AUERBACH

230 N.Y. 167   Dec. 1920

INTRODUCTION

Parties to a contract frequently include a liquidated damage clause in their contract. This clause states the agreed amount of damages that one party will pay the other in the event a breach subsequently occurs. A liquidated damage clause must meet two tests before a court will declare it valid and enforce it: (1) actual damages must be difficult to measure or determine and (2) the amount agreed to in the liquidated damage clause must be reasonable in relation to the anticipated loss that will occur upon breach of the contract. If the foregoing tests are not met, a court will declare the liquidated damage clause void and unenforceable as a penalty. This case illustrates the applicable rule of law involving the legality of a liquidated damage clause.

ANDREWS, J. In 1914 the Arco Realty Company leased to Fox, Temple and Kalek the premises No. 104 and 106 West One Hundred and Sixteenth Street, New York, to be used as a theatre. It was agreed that the buildings then existing should be torn down and one proper for this purpose should be erected by the lessor in their place. The lease contained numerous express conditions "all and everyone of which the tenant covenants with the landlord to keep and perform." Some of these conditions were comparatively of slight importance; as, for instance, that requiring the tenant to keep the sidewalks free from ice and snow and not to allow waste to accumulate. Others are more vital. Again, the damages caused by the breach of certain conditions were susceptible of accurate valuation, such as that the tenants should obtain a liability insurance policy of $10,000 and pay the premiums. This the parties themselves understood for they agreed that if not paid by the tenants they might be paid by the landlord, in which case they would become due as additional rent. The lease then provided that the tenants had paid to the landlord $7,500, later reduced to $7,065.25, "As security for the faithful performance by the tenant of all the covenants and agreements herein contained and to indemnify the landlord against loss by reason of any such default; and as the damages which the landlord would sustain in the event of a default by the tenant hereunder would not be susceptible of ascertainment, it is hereby convenanted and agreed between the landlord and tenant that in the event of any such default the damages sustained by the said landlord be and they are hereby fixed and liquidated at the amount of Seven Thousand Five Hundred dollars in payment of which the landlord shall retain the said sum of Seven Thousand Five Hundred dollars so deposited as aforesaid, without any deduction or offset whatever." There was a further provision that if default was made in the payment of the rent or upon the continued breach of the other covenants, the landlord might re-enter the premises and remove all persons therefrom by summary proceedings or otherwise; and at his option might relet the premises as agent of the tenant and receive the rents therefor. But in the event of re-entry or of termination of the lease by summary proceedings or otherwise, the tenant shall remain liable for his rent until the time when this lease would have expired.

The landlord did tear down the buildings and constructed a theatre and the tenants afterwards entered into possession. The lease, with the security deposited thereunder, was later assigned to the plaintiff and the property itself, with the deposit and all rights under the lease, was transferred to the defendants. On March 6th, 1917, one month's rent was not paid. Summary proceedings were begun and on March nineteenth the plaintiff was evicted. On April tenth the defendants contracted to sell the demised premises to one Stern and on the fourteenth they actually conveyed the same to the latter "free from all incumbrances." A few days later this action was begun to recover the security deposited under the lease, less the landlords' actual damage. It was defended on the ground that the deposit was fixed and liquidated damages for breaches of the covenants of the lease; that many of such covenants had been broken and that, therefore, the sum deposited might be retained by the defendants. As a counterclaim it was also alleged that because of the breaches by the plaintiff of the covenants the defendants have been damaged to the extent of $7,500.

The trial court directed a verdict in favor of the plaintiff for the sum of $6,764.19, the amount of the security in the defendants' possession at the time of the trial, less their actual damages as proved by them. On appeal the Appellate Division reversed this judgment and dismissed the complaint on the theory that the security was deposited as liquidated damages. We think this disposition of the case was erroneous.

As has been said, the lease contained many covenants of varying importance on the part of the lessees. As to some a loss occasioned by a breach were ascertainable with certainty and necessarily would be inconsiderable. It appeared on the trial that the premium for liability insurance was $17.01. As to the other covenants the damage that might result were uncertain. Still the meaning of the agreement as to the deposit of the $7,500 is clear. It was deposited as security for the performance of each of these covenants. In the event of default in the case of any one of them the damages are said to be liquidated at the sum of $7,500. A default does not mean a breach of all of them. Nor can it mean the breach of that one of them which may seem the most important. The language is too specific to admit of any such construction as was given in Brownold v. Rodbell. Nor, as their answer shows, is such its proper construction as understood by the defendants. This being so, it is immaterial which covenant was in fact broken. In determining whether the amount of the deposit is to be treated as liquidated damages or as penalty the agreement is to be interpreted as of its date not as of its breach....It is also true that a stipulation to forfeit a certain sum for the breach of any of the terms of the contract cannot be separated and a part treated as penalty and the remainder as liquidated damages....With these principles in mind the great weight of authority is to the effect that where a contract contains a number of covenants of different degrees of importance and the loss resulting from the breach of some of them will be clearly disproportionate to the sum sought to be fixed as liquidated damages, especially where the loss in some cases is readily ascertainable, the sum so fixed will be treated as a penalty. The strength of a chain is that of its weakest link.

Whether a sum is to be treated as liquidated damages or as a penalty

219

depends upon the intent of the parties to a contract as disclosed by the situation and by the terms of the instrument....Generally whenever the damages flowing from a breach of a contract can be easily established or where the damages fixed are plainly disproportionate to the injury the stipulated sum will be treated as a penalty. So where a strict construction would result in absurdity. There must be some attempt to proportion these damages to the actual loss. The parties must not lose sight of the principle of compensation. It is impossible to believe that the lessor and the lessees here intended that the sum of $7,500 should be treated alike as liquidated damages for the breach of a covenant involving the payment of many thousand dollars of rent and of a covenant involving the payment of an insurance premium of $17. This conclusion in the case before us is fortified by other provisions in the agreement. If the $7,500 is liquidated damages it would at once be due were the tenants dispossessed for the non-payment of rent. In such a case it would fix the amount of their liability....Yet it is agreed that after dispossession they shall remain liable for any deficiency which may result from reletting the premises to the end of the term of the lease. The two clauses are consistent only if the $7,500 is regarded as security. The landlord is not entitled both to retain this sum and to enforce this liability.

If then the $7,500 is to be treated as a penalty the landlords are entitled to retain only such part of it as will make them good for such damages as they have sustained by reason of the tenant's defaults. It was conceded that there remained in the defendants' hands of the $7,500 the sum of $7,065.25. From this the trial judge deducted $214.59 damages for minor breaches of the contract, unpaid rent for March, 1917, and unpaid rent for April to April fourteenth, the date on which the landlords conveyed the premises by a full covenant deed to one Stern, making no mention of the lease.

The result must be that the judgment of the Appellate Division should be reversed and that of the trial court affirmed, with costs in the Appellate Division and this court.

(Judgment for plaintiff tenant.)

DISCUSSION QUESTIONS

1. Liquidated damage clauses are frequently included in contracts to state the amount of damages to be paid for each day of delay beyond the date set forth for performance. What daily rate for each day of delay would you consider "reasonable" if a builder agreed to construct, complete and deliver a commercial building for $1,000,000 on July 1?

2. What factors would you consider to determine if the amount of liquidated damages is "reasonable"?

ILLEGALITY: RESTRICTIVE COVENANTS

CASE NO. 33

KARPINSKI v. INGRASCI

28 N.Y. 2d 45   February 1971

INTRODUCTION

Employment contracts often contain a restrictive covenant pursuant to which an employee agrees not to compete with his employer for a specified time in a specified geographical area after employmant is terminated. The legal question arises (1) whether such a restrictive covenant is legal, (2) what requirements must be met for a restrictive covenant to be enforceable, (3) the extent to which the court will do judicial surgery to enforce an otherwise unreasonable restrictive covenant and (4) the extent to which an ex-employer can obtain injunctive relief and liquidated damages against his ex-employee who breaches the restrictive covenant. This leading case illustrates the applicable rules of law.

Chief Judge FULD. This appeal requires us to determine whether a covenant by a professional man not to compete with his employer is enforceable and, if it is, to what extent.

The plaintiff, Dr. Karpinski, an oral surgeon, had been carrying on his practice alone in Auburn--in Cayuga County--for many years. In 1953, he decided to expand and, since nearly all of an oral surgeon's business stems from referrals, he embarked upon a plan to "cultivate connections" among dentists in the four nearby Counties of Tompkins, Seneca, Cortland, and Ontario. The plan was successful, and by 1962 twenty per cent of his practice consisted of treating patients referred to him by dentists located in those counties. In that year, after a number of those dentists had told him that some of their patients found it difficult to travel from their homes to Auburn, the plaintiff decided to open a second office in central -located Ithaca. He began looking for an assistant and, in the course of his search, met the defendant, Dr. Ingrasci, who was just completing his training in oral surgery at the Buffalo General Hospital and was desirous of entering private practice. Dr. Ingrasci manifested an interest in becoming associated with Dr. Karpinski and, after a number of discussions, they reached an understanding; the defendant was to live in Ithaca, a locale with which he had no prior familiarity, and there work as an employee of the plaintiff.

A contract, reflecting the agreement, was signed by the defendant in June, 1962. It was for three years and, shortly after its execution, the defendant started working in the office which the plaintiff rented and fully equipped at his own expense. The provision of the contract with which we are concerned is a covenant by the defendant not to compete with the plaintiff. More particularly, it recited that the defendant:

"promises and covenants that while this agreement is in effect and forever thereafter, he will never practice dentistry and/or Oral

221

Surgery in Cayuga, Cortland, Seneca, Tompkins or Ontario counties execpt: (a) In association with (plaintiff) or (b) If the (plaintiff) terminates the agreement and employs another oral surgeon."

In addition, the defendant agreed, "in consideration of the...terms of employment, and of the experience gained while working with" the plaintiff, to execute a $40,000 promissory note to the plaintiff, to become payable if the defendant left the plaintiff and practiced "denstistry and/or Oral Surgery" in the five enumerated counties.

When the contract expired, the two men engaged in extended discussions as to the nature of their continued association--as employer and employee or as partners. Unable to reach an accord, the defendant, in February, 1968, left the plaintiff's employ and opened his own office for the practice of oral surgery in Ithaca a week later. The dentists in the area, thereupon, began referring their patients to the defendant rather than to the plaintiff, and in two months the latter's practice from the Ithaca area dwindled to almost nothing and he closed the office in that city. In point of fact, the record discloses that about 90% of the defendant's present practice comes from referrals from dentists in the counties specified in the restrictive covenant, the very same dentists who had been referring patients to the plaintiff's Ithaca office when the defendant was working there.

The plaintiff, alleging a breach of the restrictive covenant, seeks not only an injunction to enforce it but also a judgment of $40,000 on the note. The Supreme Court, after a nonjury trial, dicided in favor of the plaintiff and granted him both an injunction and damages as requested. On appeal, however, the Appellate Division reversed the resulting judgment and dismissed the complaint, it was the court's view that the covenant was void and unenforceable on the ground that its restriction against the practice of both dentistry and oral surgery was impermissibly broad.

There can be no doubt that the defendant violated the terms of the covenant when he opened his own office in Ithaca. But the mere fact of breach does not, in and of itself, resolve the case. Since there are "powerful considerations of publid policy which militate against sanctioning the loss of a man's livelihood," the courts will subject a covenant by an employee not to compete with his former employer to an "overriding limitation of 'reasonableness'".... Such covenants by physicians are, if reasonable in scope, generally given effect.... "It is a firmly established doctrine", it has been noted, "that a member of one of the learned professions, upon becoming assistant to another member thereof, may, upon a sufficient consideration, bind himself not to engage in the practice of his profession upon the termination of his contract of em‑ployment, within a reasonable territorial extent, as such agreement is not in restraint of trade or against public policy....

Each case must, of course, depend, to a great extent, upon its own facts. It may well be that, in some instances, a restriction not to conduct a profession or a business in two counties or even in one, may exceed permissable limits. But, in the case before us, having in mind the character and size of the counties involved, the area restriction imposed is manifestly reasonable. The five small rural counties which it encompasses comprise the very areas from which the plaintiff obtained his patients and in which the defendant would be in direct competition with him. Thus, the covenant's coverage coincides precisely with "the territory over which the practice extends", and this is proper and permissible.... In brief, the plaintiff made no attempt to extend his influence beyond the area from which he drew his patients, the defendant being perfectly free to practice as he chooses outside the five specified counties.

Nor may the covenant be declared invalid because it is unlimited as to time, forever restricting the defendant from competing with the plaintiff. It is settled that such a covenant will not be stricken merely because it "contains no time limit or is expressly made unlimited as to time".... "According to the weight of authority as applied to contracts by physicians, surgeons and others of kindred profession," the court wrote in Foster..."relief for violation of these contracts will not be denied merely because the agreement is unlimited as to time, where as to area the restraint is limited and reasonable." In the present case, the defendant opened an office in Ithaca, in competition with the plaintiff, just one week after his employment had come to an end. Under the circumstances presented, we thoroughly agree with the trial judge that it is clear that nearly all of the defendant's practice was, and would be, directly attributable to his association with his former employer.

This brings us to the most troublesome part of the restriction imposed upon the defendant. By the terms of the contract, he agreed not to practice "dentistry and/or Oral Surgery" in competition with the plaintiff. Since the plaintiff practices only "oral surgery," and it was for the practice of that limited type of "dentistry" that he had employed the defendant, the Appellate Division concluded that the plaintiff went beyond permissible limits when he obtained from the defendant the covenant that he would not engage in any "dentistry" whatsoever. The restriction, as formulated, is, as the Appellate Division concluded, too broad; it is not reasonable for a man to be excluded from a profession for which he has been trained when he does not compete with his former employer by practicing it.

The plaintiff seeks to justify the breadth of the covenant by urging that, if it had restricted only the defendant's practice of oral surgery and permitted him to practice "dentistry"--that is, to hold himself out as a dentist generally--the defendant would have been permitted, under the Education Law... to do all the work which an oral surgeon could. We have no sympathy with this argument; the plaintiff was not privileged to prevent the defendant from working in an area of dentistry in which he would not be in competition with him. The plaintiff would have all the protection he needs if the restriction were to be limited to the practice of oral surgery, and this poses the question as to the court's power to "sever" the impermissible from the valid and uphold the covenant to the extent that it is reasonable.

Although we have found no decision in New York directly in point, cases in this court support the existence of such a power.... Moreover, a number of out-of-state decision, and they are supported by authoritative texts and commentators, explicitly recognize the court's power of severance and divisibility in order to sustain the covenant insofar as it is reasonable. As Professor Blake put it (73 Harv. L. Rev., at pp 674-675), "If in balancing the equities the court decides that his (the employee's) activity would fit within the scope of a reasonable prohibition, it is apt to make use of the tool of severance, paring an unreasonable restraint down to appropriate size and enforcing it." In short, to cull from the Washington Supreme Court's opinion in Wood v. May..."we find it just and equitable to protect appellant (employer) by injunction to the extent necessary to accomplish the basic purpose of the contract insofar as such contract is reasonable." Accordingly, since his practice is solely as an oral surgeon, the plaintiff gains all the injunctive protection to which he is entitled if effect be given only to that part of the covenant which prohibits the defendant from practicing oral surgery.

The question arises, however, whether injunctive relief is precluded by the fact that the defendant's promissory note for $40,000 was to become payable if he breached the agreement not to compete. We believe not. The mere inclusion in a covenant of a liquidated damages provision does not automatically bar the grant of an injunction.... As this court wrote in the Diamond March Co. case.... "It is a question of intention, to be deduced from the whole instrument and the circumstances; and if it appear that the performance of the covenant under consideration in this case may not reasonably be read to render "the liquidated damages provision...the sole remedy.".... On the other hand, it would be grossly unfair to grant the plaintiff, in addition to an injunction, the full amount of damages ($40,000) which the parties apparently contemplated for a total breach of the covenant, since the injunction will halt any further violation. The proper approach is that taken in Wirth.... The court, there faced with a similar situation, granted the injunction sought and, instead of awarding the amount of liquidated damages specified, remitted the matter for determination of the actual damages suffered during the period of the breach.

The hardship necessarily imposed on the defendant must be borne by him in view of the plaintiff's rightful interest in protecting the valuable practice of oral surgery which he built up over the course of many years. The defendant is, of course, privileged to practice "dentistry" generally in Ithaca or continue to practice "oral surgery" anywhere in the United States outside of the five small rural counties enumerated. The covenant, part of a contract carefully negotiated with no indication of fraud or overbearing on either side, must be enforced, insofar as it reasonably and validly may, according to its terms. In sum, then, the plaintiff is entitled to an injunction barring the defendant from practicing oral surgery in the five specified counties and to damages actually suffered by him in the period during which the defendant conducted such a practice in Ithaca after leaving the plaintiff's employ.

(Judgment for plaintiff.)

DISCUSSION QUESTION

1. What factors determine what is a "reasonable time" and a "reasonable geographical area" when a restrictive covenant is analyzed by courts?

ILLEGALITY: RESTRICTIVE COVENANTS

CASE NO. 34

GELDER MEDICAL GROUP v. WEBBER

394 N.Y.S. 2d 867   May 1977

INTRODUCTION

Restrictive covenants are frequently included in employment contracts where both employer and employee are members of a licensed profession, such as medicine, law, or public accounting. The following case addresses the question of whether or not an employer must act in good faith before he can enforce the restrictive covenant against his ex-employee when the employer discharges the employee.

BREITEL, Chief Judge.

In an action by a medical partnership for a permanent injunction to enforce a restrictive covenant not to compete, defendant physician appeals. He had been expelled as a partner pursuant to the partnership agreement....

At issue is whether a partner who has been forced out of a partnership as permitted by the partnership agreement may be held to his covenant not to compete within a restricted radius of 30 miles for a five-year period.

There should be an affirmance. Having joined a partnership governed by articles providing for the expulsion without cause of a member on terms that are not oppressive, and including a reasonable restrictive covenant, defendant may not complain of its enforcement.

The Gelder Medical Group, a partnership engaged in practicing medicine and surgery in Sidney, New York, was first formed in 1956. Some 17 years later, defendant Dr. Webber, then 61 years old and a newcomer to Sidney, a village of 5,000 population, was admitted to the small partnership following a one-year trial period in which he was employed by the group as a surgeon. Previously, after having entered the field of surgery, he had drifted from one professional association to another in two different provinces of Canada and in at least four different States of this country in the northeast and midwest. He came to the group from Columbus, Indiana.

As had the other members of the group who had joined since its inception, and critical to plaintiff's complaint, Dr. Webber had agreed that he "will not for five years after any (voluntary or involuntary) termination of his association with said Gelder Medical Group, practice his profession within a radius of 30 miles of the Village of Sidney, as a physician or surgeon * * * without the consent, in writing, of said Gelder Medical Group." The partnership agreement also provided a procedure for the involuntary withdrawal of partners. Thus, it was, in pertinent part, provided that "In the event that any member is requested to resign or withdraw from the group by a majority vote of the other members of the group, such notice shall be effective immediately and his share of the profits to the date of termination shall be computed and he shall be paid in full to the date of termination of his employment pursuant to his agree-with the association."

Dr. Webber's association turned out to be unsatisfactory to his partners. His conduct, both professional and personal, assertedly became abrasive and objectionable to his partners and their patients, a cause of "intolerable" embarrassment to the group. Revealing is a letter of a psychiatrist who, after his formal termination, examined Dr. Webber a number of times on the referral of the partnership. In the psychiatrist's words, Dr. Webber initially "appeared clinically with what would be termed an adjustment reaction of adult life with anxiety and depression". While the psychiatrist concluded that the adjustment reaction soon cleared, he summed up his description of Dr. Webber as a perfectionist who was a "rather idealistic sincere, direct, frank individual who quite possibly could be perceived at times as being somewhat blunt." In fact, Dr. Webber, in one of his affidavits, conceded, commendably, that he is probably "more of a perfectionist and idealist than he should be."

Although during the association difficulties were from time to time discussed with Dr. Webber, the unhappy relationship persisted. In October, 1973, the discord culminated with the group's unanimous decision to terminate Dr. Webber's association with the partnership. After Dr. Webber refused to withdraw voluntarily, the group, in writing, formally notified him of the termination. It was effective immediately, and, on the basis of an accounting, Webber was paid $18,568.41 in full compliance with the articles of agreement which, it is notable, provided for voluntary or involuntary termination on substantially the same terms. But that did not end the unpleasantness.

In about two months, the expelled partner, disregarding the restrictive covenant, resumed his surgical practice as a single practitioner in Sidney. The group, to protect its practice, promptly brought this action to enjoin Dr. Webber's violation of the restrictive covenant and obtained a temporary injunction. Dr. Webber instituted his own action for a declaratory judgment and for damages in allegedly wrongfully expelling him. The actions were consolidated.

The plain meaning and intended effect of the restrictive covenant and the provisions for expulsion are not now in dispute. Dr. Webber urges, however, that the court superimpose a good faith requirement on the partnership's right to expel and to enforce the restrictive covenant. Also urged is the inevitable argument that the restrictive covenant is unreasonable under the circumstances.

The applicable law is straightforward. Covenants restricting a professional, and in particular a physician, from competing with a former employer or associate are common and generally acceptable....As with all restrictive covenants, if they are reasonable as to time and area, necessary to protect legitimate interests, not harmful to the public, and not unduly burdensome, they will be enforced....

226

Similarly common and acceptable are provisions in a partnership agreement
to provide for the withdrawal or expulsion of a partner. While there is no
common-law or statutory right to expel a member of a partnership, partners may
provide, in their agreement, for the involuntary dismissal, with or without
cause, of one of their number....

Turning to the Gelder Group agreement, no acceptable reason is offered for
limiting the plainly stated provisions for expulsion, freely subscribed to by
Dr. Webber when he joined the group, and none is perceived. When, as here, the
agreement provides for dismissal of one of their number on the majority vote of
the partners, the court may not frustrate the intention of the parties at least
so long as the provisions for dismissal work no undue penalty or unjust forfeiture, overreaching, or other violation of public policy....

Assuming, not without question, that bad faith might limit the otherwise
absolute language of the agreement, the record does not reveal bad faith.
Embarrassing situations developed, affecting the physicians and their patients,
as a result of Dr. Webber's conduct, however highly motivated his conduct might
have been. It was as important, therefore, in the group's eyes, as anything
affecting survival of the group that it be disassociated from the new member's
conflict-producing conduct. Indeed, at the heart of the partnership concept is
the principle that partners may choose with whom they wish to be associated....

Even if bad faith on the part of the remaining partners would nullify the
right to expel one of their number, it does not follow that under an agreement
permitting expulsion without cause the remaining partners have the burden of
establishing good faith. To so require would nullify the right to expel without cause and frustrate the obvious intention of the agreement to avoid bitter
and protracted litigation over the reason for the expulsion. Obviously, no
expulsion would ever occur without some cause, fancied or real, but the agreement provision is addressed to avoiding the necessity of showing cause and
litigating the issue. On the other hand, if an expelled partner were to allege
and prove bad faith going to the essence, a different case would be presented.
As with any contractual agreement, in the time-honored language of the law,
there is an implied term of good faith....In his affidavits Dr. Webber has not
shown even a suggestion of evil, malevolent, or predatory purpose in the expulsion. Hence, he raises no triable issue on this score.

Insofar as the restrictive covenant is concerned, its reasonableness must
be measured by the circumstances and context in which enforcement is sought....
The Gelder Group, named after its founder and long dominant manager, was
founded more than 20 years ago. Dr. Gelder and his associates, before Dr. Webber's advent, had spent years, great effort, and money in its development,
including ownership of the building in which it operated. It was not unreasonable, in admitting new members to the partnership, that voluntary withdrawal or
involuntary expulsion should be coupled with a restrictive covenant. In the
small Village of Sidney, it was not unreasonable to extend the covenant to a
radius of 30 miles of the village, and it was certainly quite reasonable to
limit the noncompetition term to five years.

In this case the covenant applies to a man whose career had been spent,
during the same time the Gelder Group was built up, in repeatedly changing

professional associations within a range of thousands of miles. Until his arrival in Sidney he had no roots there, and, if he had developed any, they were shallow and originated largely because of his association with the Gelder Group.

There is, and it is significant, no evident harm brought to the public by enforcing the covenant. Dr. Webber is, obviously, not the only physician in Sidney; defendant himself submits there are at least a half dozen others serving the small village and its environs. Even crediting his contention, which does not go unchallenged, that he is the village's only surgeon, there is every indication surgeons are available in nearby Binghamton and Oneonta, cities presumably capable of supporting surgical facilities more sophisticated than those of modest Sidney. Moreover, Dr. Webber points out in his affidavit that, by arrangement, surgeons came from Binghamton to Sidney.

Hence, defendant's attempts to free himself from the covenant not to compete, which, it is notable, will expire by its own provisions in less than two years, must be rejected. It is true, as the group stated in its letter of termination to Dr. Webber, that the termination was a tragedy which it regretted. But the expulsion clause was designed to function when the conflict between the group and one of its members was insoluble, and the necessity for its use must always be unfortunate. Such use is free of fault to remedy an intolerable situation, a situation which would not be less intolerable because the "blame" for its occasion could be pointed in one direction rather than another.

(Judgment for plaintiff.)

DISCUSSION QUESTION

1. What specific language could Dr. Webber have added to the original language in the restrictive covenant which would have allowed him to compete under certain circumstances with his ex-employer?

ILLEGALITY: RESTRICTIVE COVENANTS

CASE NO. 35

AM BROADCASTING COMPANIES v. WOLF

438 N.Y.S. 2d 482   April 1981

INTRODUCTION

Employment contracts with celebrities often contain a restrictive
covenant which provides that the employee cannot work for a competitor of the
employer if the employment contract is not renewed and that the employee must
engage in good faith negotiations with the employer for a renewal or extension
of the employment contract. Such restrictive covenants usually provide that
if the employee breaches the restrictive covenant, the employer is entitled to
injunctive relief to restrain the employee from working for a competitor. This
case illustrates the tests that must be met before a court will enforce a
restrictive covenant and the public policy underlying the rule of law.

COOKE, Chief Judge.

This case provides an interesting insight into the fierce competition in the
television industry for popular performers and favorable ratings. It requires
legal resolution of a rather novel employment imbroglio.

The issue is whether plaintiff American Broadcasting Companies, Incorporated (ABC), is entitled to equitable relief against defendant Warner Wolf, a
New York City sportscaster, because of Wolf's breach of a good faith negotiation provision of a now expired broadcasting contract with ABC. In the present
circumstances, it is concluded that the equitable relief sought by plaintiff--
which would have the effect of forcing Wolf off the air--may not be granted.

I.

Warner Wolf, a sportscaster who has developed a rather colorful and unique
on-the-air personality, had been employed by ABC since 1976. In February, 1978
ABC and Wolf entered into an employment agreement which, following exercise of
renewal option, was to terminate on March 5, 1980. The contract contained a
clause, known as a good-faith negotiation and first-refusal provision, that is
at the crux of this litigation: "You agree, if we so elect, during the last
ninety (90) days prior to the expiration of the extended term of this agreement
to enter into good faith negotiations with us for the extension of this agreement on mutually agreeable terms. You further agree that for the first forty-
five (45) days of this renegotiation period, you will not negotiate for your
services with any other person or company other than WABC-TV or ABC. In the
event we are unable to reach an agreement for an extension by the expiration
of the extended term hereof, you agree that you will not accept, in any market
for a period of three (3) months following expiration of the extended term of
this agreement, any offer of employment as a sportscaster, sports news reporter

229

commentator, program host, or analyst in broadcasting (including television, cable television, pay televsion and radio) without first giving us, in writing, an opportunity to employ you on substantially similar terms and you agree to enter into an agreement with us on such terms." Under this provision, Wolf was bound to negotiate in good faith with ABC for the 90-day period from December 6, 1979 through March 4, 1980. For the first 45 days, December 6 through January 19, the negotiation with ABC was to be exclusive. Following expiration of the 90-day negotiating period and the contract on March 5, 1980, Wolf was required, before accepting any other offer, to afford ABC a right of first refusal; he could comply with this provision either by refraining from accepting another offer or by first tendering the offer to ABC. The first-refusal period expired on June 3, 1980 and on June 4 Wolf was free to accept any job opportunity, without obligation to ABC.

Wolf first met with ABC executives in September, 1979 to discuss the terms of a renewal contract. Counterproposals were exchanged, and the parties agreed to finalize the matter by October 15. Meanwhile, unbeknownst to ABC, Wolf met with representatives of CBS in early October. Wolf related his employment requirements and also discussed the first refusal-good faith negotiation clause of his ABC contract. Wolf furnished CBS a copy of that portion of the ABC agreement. On October 12, ABC officials and Wolf met, but were unable to reach agreement on a renewal contract. A few days later, on October 16 Wolf again discussed employment possibilities with CBS.

Not until January 2, 1980 did ABC again contact Wolf. At that time, ABC expressed its willingness to meet substantially all of his demands. Wolf rejected the offer, however, citing ABC's delay in communicating with him and his desire to explore his options in light of the impending expiration of the 45-day exclusive negotiation period.

On February 1, 1980, after termination of that exclusive period, Wolf and CBS orally agreed on the terms of Wolf's employment as sportscaster for WCBS-TV, a CBS-owned affiliate in New York. During the next two days, CBS informed Wolf that it had prepared two agreements and divided his annual compensation between the two: one covered his services as an on-the-air sportscaster, and the other was an off-the-air production agreement for sports specials Wolf was to produce. The production agreement contained an exclusivity clause which barred Wolf from performing "services of any nature for" or permitting the use of his "name, likeness, voice or endorsement by, any person, firm or corporation" during the term of the agreement, unless CBS consented. The contract had an effective date of March 6, 1980.

Wolf signed the CBS production agreement on February 4, 1980. At the same time, CBS agreed in writing, in consideration of $100 received from Wolf, to hold open an offer of employment to Wolf as sportscaster until June 4, 1980, the date on which Wolf became free from ABC's right of first refusal. The next day, February 5, Wolf submitted a letter of resignation to ABC.

Representatives of ABC met with Wolf on February 6 and made various offers and promises that Wolf rejected. Wolf informed ABC that they had delayed negotiations with him and downgraded his worth. He stated he had no future with the company. He told the officials he had made a "gentleman's agreement" and would leave ABC on March 5. Later in February, Wolf and ABC agreed that Wolf would continue to appear on the air during a portion of the first-refusal period, from March 6 until May 28.

ABC commenced this action on May 6, 1980, by which time Wolf's move to CBS had become public knowledge. The complaint alleged that Wolf, induced by CBS breached both the good-faith negotiation and first-refusal provisions of his contract with ABC. ABC sought specific enforcement of its right of first refusal and an injunction against Wolf's employment as a sportscaster with CBS.

After a trial, Supreme Court found no breach of the contract, and went on to note that, in any event, equitable relief would be inappropriate. A divided Appellate Division, while concluding that Wolf had breached both the good-faith negotiation and first-refusal provisions, nonetheless affirmed on the ground that equitable intervention was unwarranted. There should be an affirmance.

II.

Initially, we agree with the Appellate Division that defendant Wolf breached his obligation to negotiate in good faith with ABC from December, 1979 through March, 1980. When Wolf signed the production agreement with CBS on February 4, 1980, he obligated himself not to render services "of any nature" to any person, firm or corporation on and after March 6, 1980. Quite simply, then, beginning on February 4 Wolf was unable to extend his contract with ABC; his contract with CBS precluded him from legally serving ABC in any capacity after March 5. Given Wolf's existing obligation to CBS, any negotiations he engaged in with ABC, without the consent of CBS, after February 4 were meaningless and could not have been in good faith.

At the same time, there is no basis in the record for the Appellate Division's conclusion that Wolf violated the first-refusal provision by entering into an oral sportscasting contract with CBS on February 4. The first-refusal provision required Wolf, for a period of 90 days after termination of the ABC agreement, either to refrain from accepting an offer of employment or to first submit the offer to ABC for its consideration. By its own terms, the right of first refusal did not apply to offers accepted by Wolf prior to the March 5 termination of the ABC employment contract. It is apparent, therefore, that Wolf could not have breached the right of first refusal by accepting an offer during the term of his employment with ABC. Rather, his conduct violates only the good-faith negotiation clause of the contract. The question is whether this breach entitled ABC to injunctive relief that would bar Wolf from continued employment at CBS. To resolve this issue, it is necessary to trace the principles of specific performance applicable to personal service contracts.

III.

-A-

Courts of equity historically have refused to order an individual to perform a contract for personal services....Originally this rule evolved because of the inherent difficulties courts would encounter in supervising the performance of uniquely personal efforts....During the Civil War era, there emerged a more compelling reason for not directing the performance of personal services: the Thirteenth Amendment's prohibition of involuntary servitude. It has been strongly suggested that judicial compulsion of services would violate the express command of that amendment....For practical, policy and constitutional reasons, therefore, courts continue to decline to affirmatively enforce employment contracts.

Over the years, however, in certain narrowly tailored situations, the law fashioned other remedies for failure to perform an employment agreement. Thus, where an employee refuses to render services to an employer in violation of an existing contract, and the services are unique or extraordinary, an injunction may issue to prevent the employee from furnishing those services to another person for the duration of the contract....Such "negative enforcement" was initially available only when the employee had expressly stipulated not to compete with the employer for the term of the engagement....Later cases permitted injunctive relief where the circumstances justified implication of a negative covenant....In these situations, an injunction is warranted because the employee either expressly or by clear implication agreed not to work elsewhere for the period of his contract. And, since the services must be unique before negative enforcement will be granted, irreparable harm will befall the employer should the employee be permitted to labor for a competitor....

-B-

After a personal service contract terminates, the availability of equitable relief against the former employee diminishes appreciably. Since the period of service has expired, it is impossible to decree affirmative or negative specific performance. Only if the employee has expressly agreed not to compete with the employer following the term of the contract, or is threatening to disclose trade secrets or commit another tortious act, is injunctive relief generally available at the behest of the employer....Even where there is an express anticompetitive covenant, however, it will be rigorously examined and specifically enforced only if it satisfies certain established requirements....Indeed, a court normally will not decree specific enforcement of an employee's anticompetitive covenant unless necessary to protect the trade secrets, customer lists or good will of the employer's business, or perhaps when the employer is exposed to special harm because of the unique nature of the employee's services....And, an otherwise valid covenant will not be enforced if it is unreasonable in time, space or scope or would operate in a harsh or oppressive manner.... There is, in short, general judicial disfavor of anticompetitive covenants contained in employment contracts....

Underlying the strict approach to enforcement of these covenants is the notion that, once the term of an employment agreement has expired, the general public policy favoring robust and uninhibited competition should not give way merely because a particular employer wishes to insulate himself from competition....Important, too, are the "powerful considerations of public policy which militate against sanctioning the loss of a man's livelihood"....At the same time, the employer is entitled to protection from unfair or illegal conduct that causes economic injury. The rules governing enforcement of anticompetitive covenants and the availability of equitable relief after termination of employment are designed to foster these interests of the employer without impairing the employee's ability to earn a living or the general competitive mold of society.

-C-

Specific enforcement of personal service contracts thus turns initially upon whether the term of employment has expired. If the employee refuses to perform during the period of employment, was furnishing unique services, has expressly or by clear implication agreed not to compete for the duration of the contract and the employer is exposed to irreparable injury, it may be appropriate to restrain the employee from competing until the agreement expires. Once the employment contract has terminated, by contrast, equitable relief is potentially available only to prevent injury from unfair competition or similar tortious behavior or to enforce an express and valid anticompetitive covenant. In the absence of such circumstances, the general policy of unfettered competition should prevail.

IV.

Applying these principles, it is apparent that ABC's request for injunctive relief must fail. There is no existing employment agreement between the parties; the original contract terminated in March, 1980. Thus, the negative enforcement that might be appropriate during the term of employment is unwarranted here. Nor is there an express anticompetitive covenant that defendant Wolf is violating, or any claim of special injury from tortious conduct such as exploitation of trade secrets. In short, ABC seeks to premise equitable relief after termination of the employment upon a simple, albeit serious, breach of a general contract negotiation clause. To grant an injunction in that situation would be to unduly interfere with an individual's livelihood and to inhibit free competition where there is no corresponding injury to the employer other than the loss of a competitive edge. Indeed, if relief were granted here, any breach of an employment contract provision relating to renewal negotiations logically would serve as the basis for an open-ended restraint upon the employee's ability to earn a living should he ultimately choose not to extend his employment. Our public policy, which favors the free exchange of goods and services through established market mechanisms, dictates otherwise.

Equally unavailing is ABC's request that the court create a noncompetitive covenant by implication. Although in a proper case an implied-in-fact covenant not to compete for the term of employment may be found to exist, anticompetitive covenants covering the postemployment period will not be implied. Indeed, even an express covenant will be scrutinized and enforced only in accordance with established principles.

This is not to say that ABC has not been damaged in some fashion or that Wolf should escape responsibility for the breach of his good-faith negotiation obligation. Rather, we merely conclude that ABC is not entitled to equitable relief. Because of the unique circumstances presented, however, this decision is without prejudice to ABC's right to pursue relief in the form of monetary damages, if it be so advised.

Accordingly, the order of the Appellate Division should be affirmed.

233

CASE NO. 36

PURCHASING ASSOCIATES, INC., v. WEITZ

13 N Y 2d 267   December 1963

INTRODUCTION

Contracts for the sale of a business and employment contracts frequently contain restrictive covenants which provide that the seller of the business or employee will not compete with the buyer/employer during a specified time and within a specified geographical area. Such contracts usually provide that if the party breaches the restrictive covenant, then the other party can obtain injunctive relief (court order which restrains the breaching party from continuing to violate the restrictive covenant under penalty of fine or prison or both) and liquidated damages for the breach of the restrictive covenant.

This case illustrates (1) when a court will enforce a restrictive covenant, (2) what requirements must be met before a court will enforce a restrictive covenant and (3) when a court will declare a restrictive covenant void and unenforceable.

FULD, J. This appeal requires us to determine whether the covenant made by the defendant not to compete with the plaintiff is enforceable.

The defendant Morton Weitz was engaged for some years in data processing work in New York City as an employee of Grayson-Robinson Stores, a retail chain. In April of 1961, he and two other men formed a partnership known as Purchasing Associates to carry on the business of purchasing routine supplies for business organizations on a fee basis. About a month and a half later, on June 6, a contract was executed between that partnership and Associated Sales Analysts, Inc., whereby the former agreed in terms to "sell" its assets to the plaintiff, a newly formed wholly owned subsidiary of Associated, which was to engage, among other things, in the data processing business. Under this contract, the defendant and his copartners were to receive all of the net profits realized by the plaintiff in the years 1962, 1963 and 1964 as payment for their interests in the former partnership.

On June 13, 1961, the defendant entered into an employment contract with the plaintiff. By its terms, the plaintiff agreed to employ the defendant for two years, beginning October 1, 1961, at an annual salary of $18,000, plus $2,000 a year for expenses, and, for his part, the defendant agreed that for a period of two years from the date of the termination of his employment he would not "within a 300-mile radius" of New York City "directly or indirectly own...be employed or participate in the management, operation or control of, or be connected in any manner with, any business of the type and character of business engaged in by (his employer)...at the time of such termination". In October of 1962, following a disagreement with his employer, the defendant resigned from his job and thereafter organized Datamor Associates, Inc., which is also engaged in the data processing business.

The plaintiff thereupon brought this action to compel compliance with the terms of the restrictive covenant and to enjoin the defendant from engaging in such data processing business within the area and for the period specified in the covenant. Its complaint, neither describing the covenant as one ancillary to the "sale" of a business nor characterizing the defendant's services as "special, unique or extraordinary," alleged that the defendant, as a part of his services, "learned the operation and conduct of the business of the plaintiff," "became familiar with all of the trade secrets of (the) plaintiff and of (its) business methods" and "intends to use the knowledge...methods and trade secrets" thus acquired "in violation of the restrictive covenant contained in (the) agreement". The defendant not only denied these allegations but questioned the enforceability of the covenant.

Following a trial without a jury, the court, although holding that "there are no trade secrets involved," granted the plaintiff the relief sought. It was the court's view that the restrictive covenant was enforceable on two grounds--first, that the defendant's services were "'special, unique and of extraordinary character"' and, second, that the covenant was made "in connection with the sale of a business". The Appellate Division affirmed the judgment and, as already noted, we granted leave to appeal.

At one time, a covenant not to compete, basically an agreement in restraint of trade, was regarded with high disfavor by the courts and denounced as being "against the benefit of the commonwealth.... It later became evident, however, that there were situations in which it was not only desirable but essential that such covenants not to compete be enforced.

Where, for instance, there is a sale of a business, involving as it does the transfer of its good will as a going concern, the courts will enforce an incidental covenant by the seller not to compete with the buyer after the sale.... This rule is grounded, most reasonably, on the premise that a buyer of a business should be permitted to restrict his seller's freedom of trade so as to prevent the latter from recapturing and utilizing, by his competition, the good will of the very business which he transferred for value.... This court has applied the "sale of a business" rationale where an owner, partner or major stockholder of a commercial enterprise has sold his interest for an immediate consideration which was, in part, payment for the good will of the business, in terms of "continuity of place" and "continuity of name".... The sole limitation on the enforceability of such a restrictive covenant is that the restraint imposed be "reasonable," that is, not more extensive, in terms of time and space, than is reasonably necessary to the buyer for the protection of his legitimate interest in the enjoyment of the asset bought....

Also enforceable is a covenant given by an employee that he will not compete with his employer when he quits his employ, and the general limitation of "reasonableness", to which we have just referred, applies equally to such a covenant.... However, since in the case of such a covenant the element of good will, or its transfer, is not involved and since there are powerful considerations of public policy which militate against sanctioning the loss of a man's livelihood, the courts have generally displayed a much stricter attitude with respect to covenants of this type.... Thus, a covenant by which an employee simply agrees, as a condition of his employment, not to compete with his employer after they have severed relations is not only subject to the overriding limitation of "reasonableness" but is enforced only to the extent necessary to prevent the employee's use or disclosure of his former employer's trade secrets, processes of formulae...or his solicitation of, or disclosure of any information concerning, the other's customers.... If, however, the employee's services are deemed "special, unique or extra-ordinary", then, the covenant may be enforced by injunctive relief, if "reasonable," even though the employment did not involve the possession of trade secrets or confidential customer lists....

With these principles in mind, we turn to the record before us to determine if the present restrictive covenant permits enforcement as either one ancillary to the sale of a business or one made in connection with a contract of employment. In our view, it does not.

Although the plaintiff had the defendant sign a paper labeled "contract of sale", the present transaction may not be considered the sale of a "business" involving the transfer of its "good will". We must look behind and beyond the label to ascertain the true nature of the transaction. What it really was, was a hiring of the defendant as an employee, plus the consequent elimination of the very short-lived partnership as a competitor. To view the deal by which the plaintiff accomplished his dual purpose as a "sale" would be to exalt form over substance. More, to judge the defendant's restrictive covenant by the rules governing covenants in "sale" situations would tend to undermine the teaching of the cases that it is contrary to this State's public policy to enforce restrictive covenants in employment agreements unless the special circumstances noted above exist....

It may well be, as the defendant claims, that the transaction took the form it did for tax purposes but, whether that be so or not, it is manifest that the defendant conveyed nothing to the plaintiff. He certainly could not have transferred any data processing customers or good will in the data processing business because, as the record itself demonstrates, neither he nor his partnership was in that business and had no customers at the time of the deal. He was merely a salaried employee of Grayson-Robinson. Thus, the only thing which the defendant "gave" the plaintiff was his services as an employee and, accordingly, there was here no more of a transfer of "good will" than is present in any employment situation. The enforceability of the defendant's restrictive covenant is, therefore, necessarily governed by the rules applicable to covenants made in connection with contracts of employment.

When so viewed, it is clear that it is not enforceable. Since there is a finding below that no trade secrets are involved and since no claim is advanced that customers have been pirated or customer lists used, the plaintiff may prevail only if the defendant's services are "unique" or "extraordinary". More must, of course, be shown to establish such a quality than that the employee excels at his work or that his performance is of high value to his employer. It must also appear that his services are of such character as to make his replacement impossible or that the loss of such services would cause the employer irreparable injury....

We search the record before us in vain for any evidence which even points in such a direction. On the contrary, not only is there neither mention in the complaint nor proof upon the trial that the defendant's services are or were considered "unique" or "extraordinary" but, when the defendant sought to establish the "ordinary" nature of his work by eliciting testimony concerning the availability of others with the same skills, he was actually prevented from so doing by an objection from the plaintiff.

Since, then, there is no evidence to support a finding either that the defendant's services are "unique" or that the transaction under consideration constitutes a "sale" of the kind envisaged by the court when it announced the rule to govern the enforcement of restrictive covenants ancillary to the sale of a business, it follows that no basis exists for enjoining the defendant from pursuing his occupation.

The order appealed from should be reversed, with costs in all courts, and the complaint dismissed.

(Judgment for defendant.)

ILLEGALITY: RESTRICTIVE COVENANTS

CASE NO. 37

POST v. MERRILL LYNCH ETC.

421 N.Y.S. 2d 847   Oct. 1979

INTRODUCTION

Employment contracts frequently contain restrictive covenants prohibiting competition by the ex-employee. Such agreements usually provide that the ex-employee who breaches the "no competition" agreement also forfeits pension benefits previously earned while an employee. The legal question arises whether the court will enforce or declare void and unenforceable a forfeiture provision where an employee has been discharged by his employer and the ex-employee then competes with his former employer. The following case illustrates that the rule of law depends in part upon whether the employee resigns or is fired.

WACHTLER, Judge.

The narrow issue presented by this appeal from a grant of summary judgment for the defendant is the efficacy of a private pension plan provision permitting the employer to forfeit pension benefits earned by an employee who competes with the employer after being involuntarily discharged.

We begin with the premise that "powerful considerations of public policy... militate against sanctioning the loss of a man's livilihood".... So potent is this policy that covenants tending to restrain anyone from engaging in any lawful vocation are almost uniformly disfavored and are sustained only to the extent that they are reasonably neccessary to protect the legitimate interests of the employer and not unduly harsh or burdensome to the one restrained....

Merrill Lynch employed Post and Maney as account executives at its Rochester offices beginning April 20, 1959 and May 15, 1961, respectively. Both men elected to be paid a salary and to participate in the firm's pension and profit-sharing plans rather that take a straight commission, which would have returned approximately twice the amount they earned in salary during the period in question.

The employment of both plaintiffs by Merrill Lynch terminated August 30, 1974. On September 4, 1974 both began working for Bache & Company, admittedly a competitor of Merrill Lynch, in Rochester. Merrill Lynch learned about their new employment in September, 1974.

Fifteen months after their termination, and following repeated inquiries by the plaintiffs into the status of their pensions, the plaintiffs were informed by Merrill Lynch that all of their rights in the company-funded pension plan had been forfeited pursuant to a provision of the plan which permitted forfeiture in the event that an employee directly or indirectly competed with the firm.

Plaintiffs brought this action against Merrill Lynch for conversion and breach of contract, to recover amounts allegedly owed them on account of the pension plan and for punitive damages. They aver that they were discharged by Merrill Lynch without cause. Merrill Lynch does not, for the purpose of this motion, dispute plaintiff's version, contending, rather, that for this purpose the reason for termination is irrelevant.

The Appellate Division granted Merrill Lynch's motion for summary judgment and dismissed the complaint, relying principally on the Appellate Division decision in Kristt v. Whelan,...to sustain the validity of the forfeiture provision. As the Appellate Division in Kristt held: "It is no unreasonable restriction of the liberty of a man to earn his living if he may be relieved of the restriction by forfeiting a contract right or by adhering to the provisions of his contract (citations omitted). The provision for forfeiture here involved did not bar plaintiff from other employment. He had the choice of preserving his rights under the trust by refraining from competition with (his former employer) or risking forfeiture of such rights by exercising his right to compete with (him)."

Now, in determining the effect to be accorded a forfeiture-for-competition provision in an employees' pension, we are for the first time invited to distinguish between voluntary and involuntary termination of employment of the affected employee. Examinination of our cases discloses no prior instance in which enforcement of such a forfeiture clause has been sought in circumstances where the employment has been terminated by the employer without cause. Rather, as in Kristt, they have involved claims by an employee who sought pension benefits from his former employer despite having voluntarily left the employer and joined forces with a competitor. In such situations effect has been given to the forfeiture-for-competition provision, and the employee's claim has been rejected.

Not only do we find no dispositive judicial precedent in our State where the employee has been terminated by the employer without cause. Now we also must take into account the declaration of a strong public policy against forfeiture of employee benefits manifested by the Employee Retirement Income Security Act of 1974.... Indeed, had the relevant provisions of ERISA been in effect at the time of termination of these appellants' employment, its mandatory provisions might well have been dispositive in this case and have precluded the forfeiture countenanced by the court below.

Impelled as we are then by what powerfully articulated congressional policy, and confronted with no decisions which command a contrary result, we now conclude that our own policies--those in favor of permitting individuals to work where and for whom they please, and against forfeiture--preclude the enforcement of a forfeiture-for-competition clause where the termination of employment is involuntary and without cause.

In the case at bar we note that the particular provision in the pension plan was not drawn explicitly to cover employees whose employment had been involuntarily terminated; it indiscriminately mandates forfeiture by any

"Participant who enters employment or engages directly or indirectly in any business deemed by the Committee to be competitive". Therefore we need not consider now what would have been our decision had the draftsman of this pension plan manifested an unmistakable intention to impose the heavy penalty of forfeiture for engaging in competition even after discharge of an employee without cause.

Acknowledging the tension between the freedom of individuals to contract, and the reluctance to see one barter away his freedom, the State enforces limited restraints on an employee's employment mobility where a mutuality of obligation is freely bargained for by the parties. An essential aspect of that relationship, however, is the employer's continued willingness to employ the party covenanting not to compete. Where the employer terminates the employment relationship without cause, however, his action necessarily destroys the mutuality of obligation on which the covenant rests as well as the employer's ability to impose a forfeiture. An employer should not be permitted to use offensively an anti-competition clause coupled with a forfeiture provision to economically cripple a former employee and simultaneously deny other potential employers his services.

Under the circumstances of the case at bar it would be unconscionable to tolerate a forfeitrue, precipitated as it is by the unwarranted action of the employer. We find, therefore, that in the case of an involuntary discharge, the rule stated in Kristt v. Whelan...supra does not apply. Further, we hold, that where an employee is involuntarily discharged by his employer without cause and thereafter enters into competition with his former employer, and where the employer, based on such competition, would forfeit the pension benefits earned by his former employee, such a forfeiture is unreasonable as a matter of law and cannot stand.

(Judgment for plaintiffs-ex-employees.)

DISCUSSION QUESTIONS

1. If Merrill Lynch discharged these two employee _for cause_, do you think the court would have declared the forfeiture of pension benefits clause valid and enforceable? Why?

2. Would the forfeiture of benefits clause be enforceable under the Employee Retirement Income Security Act of 1974 (ERISA) which today covers millions of American employees?

ILLEGALITY

CASE NO. 38

STATE OF NEW YORK v. AVCO FINANCIAL SERVICE OF NEW YORK INC.

50 N.Y. 2d 383   June 5, 1980

INTRODUCTION

Contracts between business firms and consumers occasionally contain provisions that the seller retains a lien on the consumer goods until paid in full. Such contracts occasionally provide that the consumer grant the seller a lien on all other personal property owned by the consumer as additional collateral for the unpaid purchase price. The following case discusses the legal question of whether such a provision is "unconscionable" and what tests are applied by the court to determine whether a provision is unconscionable and therefore void and unconscionable.

New York law permits the Attorney General of the State of New York to bring a proceeding against a party to enjoin fraudulent practices.

FUCHSBERG, Judge.

The Attorney-General, acting on a consumer complaint, instituted this special proceeding under subdivision 12 of section 63 of the Executive Law to enjoin respondent Avco's use of a security clause in a loan agreement form. The petition alleged that the clause was illegal and void as against public policy on the theory that it constituted an impermissible waiver of the personal property exemption afforded a judgment debtor under CPLR 5205 (subd. (a)). We... hold that it is not illegal and that the determination of unconscionability was improperly made without any opportunity for an evidentiary presentation as to the commercial and bargaining context in which the clause appears.

The clause at issue is one regularly inserted by Avco, a finance company, in its loan agreements. Its terms unmistakably provide: "This loan is secured by * * * all household goods, furniture, appliances, and consumer goods of every kind and description owned at the time of the loan secured hereby, or at the time of any refinance or renewal thereof, or cash advanced under the loan agreement secured hereby, and located about the premises at the Debtor's residence (unless otherwise stated) or at any other location to which the goods may be moved."

It is not denied that this language must be understood to create a security interest in items of personal property which include the ones made exempt from the reach of a judgment creditor by CPLR 5205 (subd. (a)). From its inception, this statute--along with its venerable antecedents--has embodied the humanitarian policy that the law should not permit the enforcement of judgments to such a point that debtors and their families are left in a state of abject deprivation....

241

It is well recognized, however, that simply because the law exempts such property from levy and sale upon execution by a judgment creditor does not mean that the exemption statute was intended to serve the far more paternalistic function of restricting the freedom of debtors to dispose of these possessions as they wish....No statute precludes exempt property from being sold; nor is there any which expressly interdicts the less drastic step of encumbering such property. So, for example, while contractual waivers of a debtor's statutory exemptions are usually held to be void...the law has not forbidden a debtor to execute a mortgage upon the property so protected and thus create a lien which may be foreclosed despite the property's exempt status....The clause here permits no more and, hence, cannot be said to contravene the exemption statute.

The Attorney-General nevertheless argues that the clause should be invalidated under the doctrine of unconscionability. The contention, as accepted by the majority of the Appellate Division, is that "the inequality of bargaining position and the granting to the creditor of enforcement rights greater than those which the law confers upon a judgment creditor armed with execution, lead inevitably to the conclusion that the absence of choice on the part of the debtor left him with no recourse but to grant to his creditor rights which, in good conscience, the law should not enforce"....The clause is also alleged to be unconscionable in that its broad terms create security interests even in items not sold or financed by Avco and function mainly as an in terrorem device to spur repayment.

In this connection, we note initially that the statute under which this proceeding was brought (Executive Law, Sect. 63, subd. 12) lists "unconscionable contractual provisions" as a type of "fraudulent" conduct against which the Attorney-General is authorized to move. Furthermore, an application for injunctive or other relief under this provision is one which may properly look to the exercise of a sound judicial discretion....But the petition here provided no opportunity for the operation of such discretion on the issue of unconscionability since it alleged only that the clause per se was "illegal" and "void as against public policy and contrary to law", theories which, as we have seen, are not consonant with established law. Indeed, the only ground presented
....   was that the clause violated CPLR 5205 (subd. (a)); the petitioner never raised an unconscionability argument until it arrived at the Appellate Division.

As a general proposition, unconscionability, a flexible doctrine with roots in equity...requires some showing of "an absence of meaningful choice on the part of one of the parties together with contract terms which are unreasonably favorable to the other party"....The concept, at least as defined in the Uniform Commercial Code--which both parties seem to agree governs the transactions at issue here--is not aimed at "disturbance of allocation of risks because of superior bargaining power" but, instead, at "the prevention of oppression and unfair surprise"....To that extent at least it hailed a further retreat of caveat emptor.

By its nature, a test so broadly stated is not a simple one, nor can it be mechanically applied....So, no doubt precisely because the legal concept of unconscionability is intended to be sensitive to the realities and nuances of the bargaining process, the Uniform Commercial Code goes on to provide: "When it is claimed or appears to the court that the contract or any clause thereof

242

may be unconscionable the parties shall be afforded a reasonable opportunity to present evidence as to its commercial setting, purpose and effect to aid the court in making the determination" (Uniform Commercial Code, Sect. 2-302, subd. 2).

That such evidence may be crucial is made plain too by the drafters' own explication of unconscionability as "whether * * * the clauses involved are so one-sided as to be unconscionable under the circumstances existing at the time of the making of the contract"....And, in the light of this dependency upon the particular circumstances surrounding a transaction, courts and commentators have consistently construed subdivision 2 of section 2-302 to mandate at least the opportunity for an evidentiary hearing....

Specifically, at no point did the Attorney-General by affidavits from borrowers or otherwise make any factual showing as to such matters as, for instance, deception of borrowers as to the clause's content or existence...or the presence of language difficulties or illiteracy affecting its execution, or any other reasons that would have made it unlikely that consent was freely and knowingly given...all within the embrace of what is sometimes referred to as "procedural unconscionability"....Nor, for that matter, in light of the limited scope of its petition, was there occasion to delve into, much less attempt to prove, the now belated assertion of so-called "substantive unconscionability"....

Accordingly, the order of the Appellate Division should be reversed and the petition should be dismissed, without costs, with leave to the petitioner to commence a new proceeding, if it be so advised.

1. S agreed to pay M a 5% "commission" on all purchases M made from S on behalf of M's employer, X. Corp. M then ordered $1,500 of goods from S for X Corp. S then paid M the agreed "commission" of $75. After the goods were delivered, X Corp. learned of the "kickback scheme" between S and M and refused to pay S.

In an action by S against X Corp. to recover $1,500, the agreed price and reasonable value of the goods, judgment for whom? Explain.

2. General Drug Corporation was interested in the promotion in the state legislature of a certain bill designed to prohibit misrepresentations describing brand name drugs as superior to those described generically where the chemical composition and quality are identical. It agreed to pay A, an attorney, $7,500 for his services in drawing the proposed legislation, procuring its introduction in the legislature and making an argument for its passage before the legislative committee to which it would be referred. A rendered these services and submitted his bill for payment which General Drug Corporation refused to pay on the ground that it was an illegal contract.

In an action by A against General Drug Corporation to recover $7,500, judgment for whom? Explain.

3. A and B, an accounting firm operating nationally over a long period of years with branch offices in all major cities and coverage of all major industrial areas in the United States, acquired the entire practice and goodwill of X and Y, another accounting firm operating nationally and with branch offices in all major cities. The price was to be paid in ten annual installments. The agreement provided that the five major partners of X and Y, both individually and as members of the accounting firm, were not to engage in practice anywhere in the United States for three years.

(a) Is the agreement enforceable? Explain.
(b) Assume the agreement is enforceable. Are A and B entitled to obtain money damages and an injunction against any of the partners who breach the agreement? Explain.

4. W, a teller, admittedly misappropriated $5,000 of the funds of his employer, the Merchants Bank. The bank president informed J, W's brother-in-law, that unless arrangements for restitution were made, the bank would have W arrested and sent to jail. J believed the bank would carry out its threat. To save his brother-in-law from jail and to save his sister, W's wife, from the shame of her husband's disgrace and the loss of her sole support, J executed and delivered to the bank 5 notes for $1,000 each. He paid two of the notes, but defaulted in the payment of the three others. Merchants Bank brings action against J on the notes to recover the sum of $3,000.

(a) Judgment for whom? Explain.

(b) Assume that J alleged the above facts in his answer to the action and counterclaimed for the recovery of the $2,000 he paid the bank. Judgment for whom on the counterclaim? Explain.

1. A contract effecting an unreasonable restraint of trade is invalid or
    void as against public policy, but a contract containing a covenant not
    to compete is valid if it is

    a. In writing.
    b. Filed with the attorney General.
    c. Reasonable as to area and time.
    d. For services.

2. Philpot purchased the King Pharmacy from Golden. The contract contained
    a promise by Golden that he would not engage in the practice of pharmacy
    for one year from the date of the sale within one mile of the location of
    King Pharmacy. Six months later Golden opened the Queen Pharmacy within
    less than a mile of King Pharmacy. Which of the following is a correct
    statement?

    a. Golden has not breached the above covenant since he did not use his
        own name or the name King in connection with the new pharmacy.
    b. The covenant is reasonable and enforceable.
    c. The contract is an illegal restraint of trade and illegal under
        federal antitrust laws.
    d. The covenant is contrary to public policy and is illegal and void.

PERFORMANCE; DEFECTIVE PERFORMANCE; SUBSTANTIAL PERFORMANCE;
IMPOSSIBILITY OF PERFORMANCE; CONDITIONS; BREACH OF CONTRACT;
DAMAGES, REMEDIES

NEW YORK GENERAL OBLIGATIONS LAW

Section 5-1311. Uniform Vendor And Purchaser Risk Act

1. Any contract for the purchase and sale or exchange of realty shall
be interpreted, unless the contract expressly provides otherwise, as
including an agreement that the parties shall have the following rights and
duties:

a. When neither the legal title nor the possession of the subject
matter of the contract has been transferred to the purchaser:

(1) if all or a material part thereof is destroyed without
fault of the purchaser or is taken by eminent domain, the vendor cannot
enforce the contract, and the purchaser is entitled to recover any portion
of the price that he has paid; but nothing herein contained shall be deemed
to deprive the vendor of any right to recover damages against the purchaser
for any breach of contract by the purchaser prior to the destruction or
taking;

(2) if an immaterial part thereof is destroyed without fault
of the purchaser or is taken by eminent domain, neither the vendor nor the
purchaser is thereby deprived of the right to enforce the contract; but there
shall be, to the extent of the destruction or taking, an abatement of the
purchase price.

b. When either the legal title or the possession of the subject
matter of the contract has been transferred to the purchaser, if all or any
part thereof is destroyed without fault of the vendor or is taken by eminent
domain, the purchaser is not thereby relieved from a duty to pay the price,
nor is he thereby entitled to recover any portion thereof that he has paid;
but nothing herein contained shall be deemed to deprive the purchaser of any
right to recover damages against the vendor for any breach of contract by
the vendor prior to the destruction or taking. (eff. 1963 - originally
enacted in 1936, and was previously contained in Real Property Law)

UNIFORM COMMERCIAL CODE: ARTICLE 2: SALE OF GOODS

A representative selection of some of the numerous statutory provisions
contained in Article 2 of the Uniform Commercial Code dealing with performance
of the contract, defective performance, impossibility of performance,
conditions, breach of contract, damages, and remedies is included herewith.

To include all applicable sections with the full text of each section is
beyond the scope of this book for use of students studying The Law of

Business Contracts, and would be more appropriate for a course in the Law of Sales or Mercantile Transactions.

Therefore, only some of the more currently applicable sections for use of students studying the Law of Business Contracts have been included. Some of the statutory provisions have been included with the full or partial text, while for some statutes, only the titles of the particular sections have been listed.

Section 2-209. Modification, Rescission And Waiver

(1) An agreement modifying a contract within this Article needs no consideration to be binding.

(2) A signed agreement which excludes modification or rescission except by a signed writing cannot be otherwise modified or rescinded, but except as between merchants such a requirement on a form supplied by the merchant must be separately signed by the other party.

(3) The requirements of the statute of frauds section of this Article ... must be satisfied if the contract as modified is within its provisions.

(4) Although an attempt at modification or rescission does not satisfy the requirements of subsection (2) or (3) it can operate as a waiver.

(5) A party who has made a waiver affecting an executory portion of the contract may retract the waiver by reasonable notification received by the other party that strict performance will be required of any term waived, unless the retraction would be unjust in view of a material change of position in reliance on the waiver.

Section 2-311. Options And Cooperation Respecting Performance

...

(2) Unless otherwise agreed specifications relating to assortment of the goods are at the buyer's option and except as otherwise provided... specifications or arrangements relating to shipment are at the seller's option.

(3) Where such specification would materially affect the other party's performance but is not seasonably made or where one party's cooperation is necessary to the agreed performance of the other but is not seasonably forthcoming, the other party in addition to all other remedies

(a) is excused for any resulting delay in his own performance; and

(b) may also either proceed to perform in any reasonable manner or after the time for a material part of his own performance treat the failure to specify or to cooperate as a breach by failure to deliver or accept the goods.

Section 2-601. Buyer's Rights On Improper Delivery

Subject to the provisions of this Article on breach in installment contracts (Section 2-612) and unless otherwise agreed under the sections on contractual limitations of remedy (Section 2-718 and 2-719), if the goods or the tender of delivery fail in any respect to conform to the contract, the buyer may

      (a) reject the whole; or

      (b) accept the whole; or

      (c) accept any commercial unit or units and reject the rest

Section 2-602. Manner And Effect Of Rightful Rejection

(1) Rejection of goods must be within a reasonable time after their delivery or tender. It is ineffective unless the buyer seasonably notifies the seller....

Section 2-606. What Constitutes Acceptance Of Goods

(1) Acceptance of goods occurs when the buyer

      (a) after a reasonable opportunity to inspect the goods signifies to the seller that the goods are conforming or that he will take or retain them in spite of their non-conformity; or

      (b) fails to make an effective rejection...but such acceptance does not occur until the buyer has had a reasonable opportunity to inspect them; or

      (c) does any act inconsistent with the seller's ownership;...

(2) Acceptance of a part of any commercial unit is acceptance of that entire unit.

Section 2-607. Effect Of Acceptance; Notice Of Breach; Burden of Establishing Breach After Acceptance;...

(1) The buyer must pay at the contract rate for any goods accepted.

(2)   Acceptance of goods by the buyer precludes rejection of the goods accepted....

(3)   Where a tender has been accepted

(a)   the buyer must within a reasonable time after he discovers or should have discovered any breach notify the seller of breach or be barred from any remedy; and

...

(4)   The burden is on the buyer to establish any breach with respect to the goods accepted.

....

Section 2-608.   Revocation Of Acceptance In Whole Or In Part

Section 2-609.   Right To Adequate Assurance Of Performance

See, ASSIGNMENTS

Section 2-610.   Anticipatory Repudiation

When either party repudiates the contract with respect to a performance not yet due the loss of which will substantially impair the value of the contract to the other, the aggrieved party may

(a)   for a commercially reasonable time await performance by the repudiating party; or

(b)   resort to any remedy for breach (Section 2-703 or Section 2-711), even though he has notified the repudiating party that he would await the latter's performance and has urged retraction; and

(c)   in either case suspend his own performance or proceed in accordance with the provisions of this Article on the seller's right to identify goods to the contract notwithstanding breach or to salvage unfinished goods (Section 2-704).

Section 2-611.   Retraction Of Anticipatory Repudiation

(1)   Until the repudiating party's next performance is due he can retract his repudiation unless the aggrieved party has since the repudiation cancelled or materially changed his position or otherwise indicated that he considers the repudiation final.

(2)   Retraction may be by any method which clearly indicates to the

aggrieved party that the repudiating party intends to perform, but must include any assurance justifiably demanded under the provisions of this Article (Section 2-609).

(3) Retraction reinstates the repudiating party's rights under the contract with due excuse and allowance to the aggrieved party for any delay occasioned by the repudiation.

Section 2-612. "Installment Contract"; Breach

(1) An "installment contract" is one which requires or authorizes the delivery of goods in separate lots to be separately accepted, even though the contract contains a clause "each delivery is a separate contract" or its equivalent.

(2) The buyer may reject any installment which is non-conforming if the non-conformity substantially impairs the value of that installment and cannot be cured....

(3) Whenever non-conformity or default with respect to one or more installments substantially impairs the value of the whole contract there is a breach of the whole. But the aggrieved party reinstates the contract if he accepts a non-conforming installment without seasonably notifying of cancellation or if he brings an action with respect only to past installments or demands performance as to future installments.

Section 2-613. Casualty To Identified Goods

Where the contract requires for its performance goods identified when the contract is made, and the goods suffer casualty without fault of either party before the risk of loss passes to the buyer,...then

(a) if the loss is total the contract is avoided; and

(b) if the loss is partial or the goods have so deteriorated as no longer to conform to the contract the buyer may nevertheless...at his option either treat the contract as avoided or accept the goods with due allowance from the contract price for the deterioration or the deficiency in quantity but without further right against the seller.

Section 2-614. Substituted Performance

(1) Where without fault of either party the agreed berthing, loading, or unloading facilities fail or an agreed type of carrier becomes unavailable or the agreed manner of delivery otherwise becomes commercially impracticable but a commercially reasonable substitute is available, such substitute performance must be tendered and accepted.

(2) If the agreed means or manner of payment fails because of domestic or foreign governmental regulation, the seller may withhold or stop delivery

unless the buyer provides a means or manner of payment which is commercially a substantial equivalent. If delivery has already been taken, payment by the means or in the manner provided by the regulation discharges the buyer's obligation unless the regulation is discriminatory, oppressive or predatory.

Section 2-615. Excuse By Failure Of Presupposed Conditions

Except so far as a seller may have assumed a greater obligation and subject to the preceding section on substituted performance:

(a) Delay in delivery or non-delivery in whole or in part by a seller who complies with paragraphs (b) and (c) is not a breach of his duty under a contract for sale if performance as agreed has been made impracticable by the occurrence of a contingency the non-occurrence of which was a basic assumption on which the contract was made or by compliance in good faith with any applicable foreign or domestic governmental regulation or order whether or not it later proves to be invalid.

(b) Where the causes mentioned in paragraph (a) affect only a part of the seller's capacity to perform, he must allocate production and deliveries among his customers but may at his option include regular customers not then under contract as well as his own requirements for further manufacture. He may so allocate in any manner which is fair and reasonable.

(c) The seller must notify the buyer seasonally that there will be delay or non-delivery and, when allocation is required under paragraph (b), of the estimated quota thus made available for the buyer.

Section 2-616. Procedure On Notice Claiming Excuse

Section 2-701. Remedies For Breach Of Collateral Contracts Not Impaired

Remedies for breach of any obligation or promise collateral or ancillary to a contract for sale are not impaired by the provisions of this Article.

Section 2-703. Seller's Remedies In General

Where the buyer wrongfully rejects or revokes acceptance of goods or fails to make a payment due on or before delivery or repudiates with respect to a part or the whole, then with respect to any goods directly affected and, if the breach is of the whole contract...then also with respect to the whole undelivered balance, the aggrieved seller may

(a) withhold delivery of such goods;

...

(d) resell and recover damages as hereafter provided...

251

(e)   recover damages for non-acceptance...or in a proper case the price...

(f)   cancel

Section 2-708.   Seller's Damages For Non-Acceptance Or Repudiation

(1)   ...the measure of damages for non-acceptance or repudiation by the buyer is the difference between the market price at the time and place for tender and the unpaid contract price together with any incidental damages..., but less expenses saved in consequence of the buyer's breach.

(2)   If the measure of damages provided in subsection (1) is inadequate to put the seller in as good a position as performance would have done then the measure of damages is the profit...which the seller would have made from full performance by the buyer,....

Section 2-709.   Action For The Price

(1)   When the buyer fails to pay the price as it becomes due the seller may recover, together with any incidental damages under the next section, the price

(a)   of goods accepted or of conforming goods...and

(b)   of goods identified to the contract if the seller is unable after reasonable effort to resell them....

....

Section 2-710.   Seller's Incidental Damages

Incidental damages to an aggrieved seller include any commercially reasonable charges, expenses or commissions incurred in stopping delivery, in the transportation, care and custody of goods after the buyer's breach, in connection with return or resale of the goods or otherwise resulting from the breach.

Section 2-711.   Buyer's Remedies In General;...

(1)   Where the seller fails to make delivery or repudiates or the buyer rightfully rejects or justifiably revokes acceptance then with respect to any goods involved, and with respect to the whole if the breach goes to the whole contract...the buyer may cancel and whether or not he has done so may in addition to recovering so much of the price as has been paid

(a)   "cover" and have damages under the next section as to all the goods affected whether or not they have been identified to the contract; or

(b)   recover damages for non-delivery as provided in this Article...

(2)   Where the seller fails to deliver or repudiates the buyer may also

(a)   if the goods have been identified recover them as provided in this Article...; or

(b)   in a proper case obtain specific performance or replevy the goods as provided in this Article....

. . . .

Section 2-712.   "Cover"; Buyer's Procurement Of Substitute Goods

Section 2-713.   Buyer's Damages For Non-Delivery Or Repudiation

(1)   ...the measure of damages for non-delivery or repudiation by the seller is the difference between the market price at the time when the buyer learned of the breach and the contract price...

. . . .

Section 2-714.   Buyer's Damages For Breach In Regard To Accepted Goods

(1)   Where the buyer has accepted goods and given notification...he may recover as damages for any non-conformity of tender the loss resulting in the ordinary course of events from the seller's breach as determined in any manner which is reasonable.

. . . .

(3)   In a proper case any incidental and consequential damages under the next section may also be recovered.

Section 2-715.   Buyer's Incidental And Consequential Damages

(1)   Incidental damages resulting from the seller's breach include expenses reasonably incurred in inspection, receipt, transportation and care and custody of goods rightfully rejected, any commercially reasonable charges, expenses or commissions in connection with effecting cover and any other reasonable expense incident to the delay or other breach.

(2)   Consequential damages resulting from the seller's breach include

(a)   any loss resulting from general or particular requirements and needs of which the seller at the time of contracting had reason to know and which could not reasonably be prevented by cover or otherwise; and

(b)   injury to person or property proximately resulting from any breach of warranty.

Section 2-716.   Buyer's Right To Specific Performance Or Replevin

(1) Specific performance may be decreed where the goods are unique or in other proper circumstances.

(2) The decree for specific performance may include such terms and conditions as to payment of the price, damages, or other relief as the court may deem just.

(3) The buyer has a right of replevin for goods identified to the contract if after reasonable effort he is unable to effect cover for such goods or the circumstances reasonably indicate that such effort will be unavailing or if the goods have been shipped under reservation and satisfaction of the security interest in them has been made or tendered.

Section 2-717.   Deduction Of Damages From The Price

The buyer on notifying the seller of his intention to do so may deduct all or any part of the damages resulting from any breach of the contract from any part of the price still due under the same contract.

Section 2-718.   Liquidation Or Limitation Of Damages;...

(1) Damages for breach by either party may be liquidated in the agreement but only at an amount which is reasonable in the light of the anticipated or actual harm caused by the breach, the difficulties of proof of loss, and the inconvenience or nonfeasibility of otherwise obtaining an adequate remedy. A term fixing unreasonably large liquidated damages is void as a penalty.

(2) Where the seller justifiably withholds delivery of goods because of the buyer's breach, the buyer is entitled to restitution of any amount by which the sum of his payments exceeds

(a) the amount of which the seller is entitled by virtue of terms liquidating the seller's damages in accordance with subsection (1), or

(b) in the absence of such terms, twenty per cent of the value of the total performance for which the buyer is obligated under the contract or $500, whichever is smaller.

(3) The buyer's right to restitution under subsection (2) is subject to offset to the extent that the seller establishes

(a) a right to recover damages under the provisions of this Article other than subsection (1), and

(b)   the amount or value of any benefits received by the buyer directly or indirectly by reason of the contract.

. . . .

Section 2-719.   Contractual Modification Or Limitation Of Remedy

(1)   Subject to the provisions of subsections (2) and (3) of this section and of the preceding section on liquidation and limitation of damages.

(a)   the agreement may provide for remedies in addition to or in substitution for those provided in this Article and may limit or alter the measure of damages recoverable under this Article, as by limiting the buyer's remedies to return of the goods and repayment of the price or to repair and replacement of non-conforming goods or parts; and

(b)   resort to a remedy as provided is optional unless the remedy is expressly agreed to be exclusive, in which case it is the sole remedy.

(2)   Where circumstances cause an exclusive or limited remedy to fail of its essential purpose, remedy may be had as provided in this Act.

(3)   Consequential damages may be limited or excluded unless the limitation or exclusion is unconscionable. Limitation of consequential damages for injury to the person in the case of consumer goods is prima facie unconscionable but limitation of damages where the loss is commercial is not.

Section 2-720.   Effect Of "Cancellation" Or "Rescission" On Claims For Antecedent Breach

Unless the contrary intention clearly appears, expressions of "cancellation" or "rescission" of the contract or the like shall not be construed as a renunciation or discharge of any claim in damages for an antecedent breach.

Section 2-721.   Remedies For Fraud

Remedies for material misrepresentation or fraud include all remedies available under this Article for non-fraudulent breach. Neither rescission or a claim for rescission of the contract for sale nor rejection or return of the goods shall bar or be deemed inconsistent with a claim for damages or other remedy.

Note: See, also Reality of Assent

Section 2-312. <u>Warranty Of Title And Against Infringement; Buyer's Obligation Against Infringement</u>

(1) Subject to subsection (2) there is in a contract for sale a warranty by the seller that (a) the title conveyed shall be good, and its transfer rightful; and (b) the goods shall be delivered free from any security interest or other lien or encumbrance of which the buyer at the time of contracting has no knowledge. . . .

Section 2-313. <u>Express Warranties By Affirmation, Promise, Description, Sample</u>

(1) Express warranties by the seller are created as follows: (a) Any affirmation of fact or promise made by the seller to the buyer which relates to the goods and becomes part of the basis of the bargain creates an express warranty that the goods shall conform to the affirmation or promise. (b) Any description of the goods which is made part of the basis of the bargain creates an express warranty that the goods shall conform to the description. (c) Any sample or model which is made part of the basis of the bargain creates an express warranty that the whole of the goods shall conform to the sample or model. . . .

Section 2-314. <u>Implied Warranty: Merchantability; Usage Of Trade</u>

(1) Unless excluded or modified (2-316), a warranty that the goods shall be merchantable is implied in a contract for their sale if the seller is a merchant with respect to goods of that kind. Under this section the serving for value of food or drink to be consumed either on the premises or elsewhere is a sale. (2) Goods to be merchantable must be at least such as (a) pass without objection in the trade under the contract description; and . . .
(c) are fit for the ordinary purposes for which such goods are used; and
(d) run, within the variations permitted by the agreement, of even kind, quality and quantity within each unit and among all units involved; and
(e) are adequately contained, packaged, and labeled as the agreement may require; and (f) conform to the promises or affirmations of fact made on the container or label if any. (3) Unless excluded or modified (2-316) other implied warranties may arise from course of dealing or usage of trade.

Section 2-315. <u>Implied Warranty: Fitness For Particular Purpose</u>

Where the seller at the time of contracting has reason to know any particular purpose for which the goods are required and that the buyer is relying on the seller's skill or judgment to select or furnish suitable goods, there is unless excluded or modified under the next section, an implied warranty that the goods shall be fit for such purpose.

Section 2-316. <u>Exclusion Or Modification Of Warranties</u>

(1) Words or conduct relevant to the creation of an express warranty and words or conduct tending to negate or limit warranty shall be construed wherever reasonable as consistent with each other; but subject to the provisions of this Article on parol or extrinsic evidence (2-202) negation or limitation is inoperative to the extent that such construction is unreasonable. . . .
(4) Remedies for breach of warranty can be limited in accordance with the provisions of this Article on liquidation or limitation of damages and on contractual modification of remedy (2-718 and 2-719)

WARRANTY AND THE CONSUMER

GENERAL BUSINESS LAW: Section 198-a. <u>Warranties</u>

(a) As used in this section: (1) "Consumer" means the purchaser, other than for purposes of resale, of a motor vehicle normally used for personal, family, or household purposes . . .

(b) If a new motor vehicle does not conform to all applicable express warranties during the first eighteen thousand miles of operation or during the period of two years following the date of original delivery of the motor vehicle to such consumer, whichever is the earlier date, the consumer shall during such period report the nonconformity, defect or condition to the manufacturer, its agent or its authorized dealer. If the notification is received by the manufacturer's agent or authorized dealer, the agent or dealer shall within seven days forward written notice thereof to the manufacturer by certified mail, return receipt requested. The manufacturer, its agent or its authorized dealer shall correct said nonconformity, defect or condition at no charge to the consumer, notwithstanding the fact that such repairs are made after the expiration of such period of operation or such two year period.

(c) If, within the period specified in subd. (b) of this section, the manufacturer, or its agents or authorized dealers are unable to repair or correct any defect or condition which substantially impairs the value of the motor vehicle to the consumer after a reasonable number of attempts, the manufacturer at the option of the consumer, shall replace the motor vehicle with a comparable motor vehicle, or accept return of the vehicle from the consumer and refund to the consumer the full purchase price including all sales tax, license fees, registration fees and any similar governmental charges, less a reasonable allowance for the consumer's use of the vehicle in excess of the first twelve thousand miles of operation and a reasonable allowance for any damage not attributable to normal wear or improvements. . . .

(d) It shall be presumed that a reasonable number of attempts have been undertaken to conform a motor vehicle to the applicable express warranties, if:

(1) the same nonconformity, defect or condition has been subject to repair four or more times by the manufacturer or its agents or authorized dealers within the first eighteen thousand miles of operation or during the period of two years following the date of original delivery of the motor vehicle to a consumer, whichever is the earlier date, but such nonconformity, defect or condition continues to exist; or (2) the vehicle is out of service by reason of repair of nonconformity, defect or condition for a cumulative total of thirty or more days during either period, whichever is the earlier date.
. . .

(g) If a manufacturer has established an informal dispute settlement procedure which complies in all respects with the provisions of part seven hundred three of title sixteen of the code of federal regulations the provisions of subdivision (c) of this section concerning refunds or replacement shall not apply to any consumer who has not first resorted to such procedure.

(h) In no event shall a consumer who has resorted to an informal dispute settlement procedure be precluded from seeking the rights or remedies available by law.

(i) Any agreement entered into by a consumer for the purchase of a new motor vehicle which waives, limits or disclaims the rights set forth in this section shall be void as contrary to public policy. Said rights shall inure to a subsequent transferee of such motor vehicle.

(j) Any action brought pursuant to this section shall be commenced within four years of the date of original delivery of the motor vehicle to the consumer.

(k) A court may award reasonable attorney's fees to a prevailing plaintiff.
(eff. Sept. 1, 1983).

CONDITIONS AND SUBSTANTIAL PERFORMANCE

CASE NO. 39

JACOB & YOUNGS v. KENT

230 N.Y. 239   Jan. 1921

INTRODUCTION

A party to a contract breaches his contract when he does not <u>fully</u> perform his obligations under the contract. If the breach of contract is <u>material</u>, the victim of the breach may lawfully <u>reject</u> the tendered performance and hold the other party liable for damages for breach of contract. However, if the breach of contract is <u>trivial</u>, the victim of the breach <u>must accept</u> the tendered performance (called "substantial performance") while being entitled to recover money damages for the <u>trivial</u> breach. This leading case illustrates what factors a court analyzes to determine if the breach is material or trivial and thus whether substantial performance has been tendered. Furthermore, this case analyzes the factors which determine whether the damages awarded to the victim of the breach will be (a) the cost of the correcting the breach or (b) the difference in value between substantial performance and full performance.

CARDOZO, J.   The plaintiff built a country residence for the defendant at a cost of upwards of $77,000, and now sues to recover a balance of $3,483.46, remaining unpaid. The work of construction ceased in June, 1914, and the defendant then began to occupy the dwelling. There was no complaint of defective performance until March, 1915. One of the specifications for the plumbing work provides that "all wrought iron pipe must be well galvanized, lap welded pipe of the grade known as 'standard pipe' of Reading manufacture." The defendant learned in March, 1915, that some of the pipe, instead of being made in Reading, was the product of other factories. The plaintiff was accordingly directed by the architect to do the work anew. The plumbing was then encased within the walls except in a few places where it had to be exposed. Obedience to the order meant more than the substitution of other pipe. It meant the demolition at great expense of substantial parts of the completed structure. The plaintiff left the work untouched, and asked for a certificate that the final payment was due. Refusal of the certificate was followed by this suit.

The evidence sustains a finding that the omission of the prescribed brand of pipe was neither fraudulent nor willful. It was the result of the oversight and inattention of the plaintiff's subcontractor. Reading pipe is distinguished from Cohoes pipe and other brands only by the name of the manufacturer stamped upon it at intervals of between six and seven feet. Even the defendant's architect, though he inspected the pipe upon arrival, failed to notice the discrepancy. The plaintiff tried to show that the brands installed, though made by other manufacturers, were the same in quality, in appearance, in market value and in cost as the brand stated in the contract--that they were, indeed, the same thing, though manufactured in another place. The evidence was excluded, and a verdict directed for the defendant. The Appellate Division reversed, and granted a new trial.

258

We think the evidence, if admitted, would have supplied some basis for the inference that the defect was insignificant in its relation to the project. The courts never say that one who makes a contract fills the measure of his duty by less than full performance. They do say, however, that an omission, both trivial and innocent, will sometimes be atoned for by allowance of the resulting damage, and will not always be the breach of a condition to be followed by a forfeiture.... The decisions in this state commit us to the liberal view, which is making its way, nowadays, in jurisdictions slow to welcome it. Where the line is to be drawn between the important and the trivial cannot be settled by a formula: "In the nature of the case precise boundaries are impossible" (2 Williston on Contracts, sec. 841). The same omission may take on one aspect or another according to its setting. Substitution of equivalents may not have the same significance in fields of art on the one side and in those of mere utility on the other. Nowhere will change be tolerated, however, if it is so dominant or pervasive as in any real or substantial measure to frustrate the purpose of the contract.... There is no general license to install whatever, in the builder's judgment, may be regarded as "just as good".... The question is one of degree, to be answered, if there is doubt, by the trier of the facts and, if the inferences are certain, by the judges of the law. We must weigh the purpose to be served, the desire to be gratified, the excuse for deviation from the letter, the cruelty of enforced adherence. Then only can we tell whether literal fulfillment is to be implied by law as a condition. This is not to say that the parties are not free by apt and certain words to effectuate a purpose that performance of every term shall be a condition of recovery. That question is not here. This is merely to say that the law will be slow to impute the purpose, in the silence of the parties, where the significance of the default is grievously out of proportion to the oppression of the forfeiture. The willful transgressor must accept the penalty of his transgression.... For him there is no occasion to mitigate the rigor of implied conditions. The transgressor whose default is unintentional and trivial may hope for mercy if he will offer atonement for his wrong.

In the circumstances of this case, we think the measure of the allowance is not the cost of replacement, which would be great, but the difference in value, which would be either nominal or nothing. Some of the exposed sections might perhaps have been replaced at moderate expense. The defendant did not limit his demand to them, but treated the plumbing as a unit to be corrected from cellar to roof. In point of fact, the plaintiff never reached the stage at which evidence of the extent of the allowance became necessary. The trial court had excluded evidence that the defect was unsubstantial, and in view of that ruling there was no occasion for the plaintiff to go farther with an offer to proof. We think, however, that the offer, if it had been made, would not of necessity have been defective because directed to difference in value. It is true that in most cases the cost of replacement is the measure.... The owner is entitled to the money which will permit him to complete, unless the cost of completion is grossly and unfairly out of proportion to the good to be attained. When that is true, the measure is the difference in value. Specifications call, let us say, for a foundation built of granite quarried in Vermont. On completion of the building, the owner learns that through the blunder of a subcontractor part of the foundation has been built of granit of the same quality quarried in New Hampshire. The measure of allowance is not the cost of reconstruction. "There may be omissions of that which could not afterwards be supplied exactly as called for by the contract without taking down the building to its foundations, and at the same time the omission may not affect the value of the building for use or otherwise, except so slightly as to be hardly appreciable." The rule that gives a remedy in cases of substantial performance with compensation for defects of trivial or inappreciable importance, has been developed by the courts as an instrument of justice. The measure of the allowance must be shaped to the same end.

(Judgment for plaintiff builder)

DISCUSSION QUESTIONS

1. The court held that the home buyer was entitled to damages from the builder based on the difference of value "which would be either nominal or nothing". Do you think the court would have so held if the omission of the prescribed brand of pipe was either fraudulent or willful? In such a case, would the court have given the home buyer the "cost of correction" no matter how expensive?

2. May a contracting party legally protect himself against the result of this case by including a contract provision to the effect that each and every term and requirement to be performed is a material condition and any breach will entitle the other party to reject the tendered performance? Will a court automatically enforce such a clause or simply consider the as <u>one</u> factor, among others, to determine if a particular breach is a material breach or a trivial breach?

CONDITIONS AND DEFECTIVE PERFORMANCE

CASE NO. 40

BELLIZZI v. HUNTLEY

3 N.Y. (2d) 112   July 1957

INTRODUCTION

This case illustrates the general rule of law that when a court must decide which rule to apply when awarding damages--the difference in value or the
cost of correction--it will consider whether the particular breach is material
or trivial. To determine if a breach is material, the court will consider
among other factors, whether the tendered performance is suitable, usable,
useful and safe for the other party. If not, the court will apply the general
rule of law that a party who breaches his contract must pay the cost of correction rather than the difference in value.

DYE, J. The defendant-respondent, a real estate developer, on or about
August 19, 1950, contracted to sell to the plaintiff-appellant a lot designated
as No. 235 in its development and to build a house thereon in accordance with
its demonstration model known as "The 1951 Kent" which, among other features,
had an attached garage with an access driveway substantially at street level.
When the construction work was commenced, the defendant encountered rock close
to the surface and, instead of excavating same, as might have been done without
too much trouble at the time, it placed the house thereon, with the result that
from the entrance of the garage to the street, a distance of 43 feet, there was
a difference in elevation of 9 feet and 8 inches. This amounted to a 22-$\frac{1}{2}$%
grade, which is so steep that the driveway cannot be used safely and convenient-
ly. As a matter of fact, the evidence shows that a grade of 12% is considered
the permissive maximum. While the plans are silent as to the grade of the
driveway, the defendant does not now claim that the grade of the existing driveway is reasonable or that plaintiff has no cause for complaint. It defends
against plaintiff's claim for damages on the sole ground that the trial court
erred when it excluded evidence offered by it as to the value of the property
and should not have refused to charge that the measure of damages "is the difference between the value of the building as constructed and its value had it
been constructed conformably to the contract or the cost of repairs, whichever
is the lesser." Instead, the trial court charged in substance that the measure
of damage is "the fair and reasonable cost to remedy the defect in this controversy or to get a reasonably usable driveway."

The Appellate Division adopted the defendant's contention largely in reliance on Jacob & Youngs v. Kent.... In that case, we had applied the "difference in value" rule simply because the proof failed to show any substantial
damage or loss in value, since the wrought iron galvanized pipe, as furnished,
was substantially the same in quality, weight, market price, serviceability
and appearance as pipe of "Reading" manufacture called for in the contract
specifications and that the cost of replacing same with the "Reading" pipe as
specified "would be great, but the difference in value...would be either nomi-

261

nal or nothing"; in other words, replacement of the pipe, under the circumstances in that case, would have constitued economic waste.

However, this litigation poses an entirely different kind of breach, the consequence of which is to burden plaintiff with an unusable, unsafe and unsightly driveway. While it is unfortunate that the defendant elected to build the garage at an unsuitable elevation in order to avoid the cost of excavating unforeseen rock and that to correct the defect will now cost, much more than initially, nonetheless, that loss should not fall on the innocent owner whose protests made at the time were cut off by the president of the defendant corporation with assurances not to worry, that when finished the grade would not exceed 10% and that the plaintiff would be happy when he got into his home.

The "difference in value" rule in defective performance of construction contracts seems to be applied only when it would be unfair to apply the general rule.... In a case such as the present (when the variance is so substantial as to render the finished building partially unusable and unsafe, the measure of damage is "the market price of completing or correcting the performance"....). It is only "If the defect is not thus remediable, damages are based on the difference between the value of the defective structure and that of the structure if properly completed.".... This rule we have long applied....

Here, there is uncontradicted evidence that the dangerous and unsatisfactory driveway can be corrected. When that is done, the plaintiff will have received no more than he was entitled to under his contract and the defendant will have given no more than it obligated itself to furnish.

(Judgment for plaintiff home owner.)

DISCUSSION QUESTIONS

1. According to this case, when will a court apply the difference in value rule in defective performance of construction contracts?

CONDITIONS AND SUBSTANTIAL PERFORMANCE

CASE NO. 41

JUNGMANN v. ATTERBURY

249 N.Y. 119   July 1928

INTRODUCTION

A contract for the sale of goods involving international shipment of goods or shipment over a great distance will often specify that the seller must give the buyer notice (by cable of telegram) on the date shipment is made in order to allow the buyer to make arrangements to receive and possibly resell the goods. The legal question arises whether the seller's failure to give such notice constitutes a __material__ breach which entitles the buyer to reject the tendered performance? This case illustrates circumstances under which a court may hold that giving "notice" is a __condition__ __precedent__ to enforcing a contract against the other party.

LEHMAN, J.   In February, 1923, the plaintiff entered into a written contract with the defendant for the sale of thirty tons of casein. The contract contained a clause: "Shipment: May-June from Europe. Advice of shipment to be made by cable immediately goods are dispatched." Fifteen tons of casein were shipped on June 9th, 1923. No notice of shipment was given to the defendant. Tender of this shipment by the plaintiff was refused by the defendant on June 20th. On June 21st the defendant wrote to the plaintiff that the plaintiff "failed to make any May delivery under the contract and also failed to advise us of shipment as required to do by your contract." The plaintiff declined an offer of the defendant "to take this shipment as the June quota on your contract and call the contract filled." On June 26th the plaintiff shipped the remaining fifteen tons of casein. The defendant received no advice of shipment "by cable" immediately after the goods were shipped. It did receive a letter from the plaintiff dated June 23rd that the plaintiff had received advice by cable that these fifteen tons would be shipped per steamship Magnolia sailing on June 26th, and another letter from the plaintiff on "which sailed on June 26th with the balance of your order on board, we will deliver to you the full 30 tons of Casein in conformity with our contract." On the arrival of the steamship Magnolia the plaintiff tendered to the defendant the thirty tons of casein. The defendant refused the tender.

Upon the demand of the defendant the parties agreed to the insertion in the contract of the clause, "Advice of shipment to be made by cable immediately goods are dispatched." Concedely until the goods shipped on June 9th arrived, no notice of any kind was given to the defendant that they had been shipped. Notice that the remainder of the goods was shipped on June 26th was given by letter from the plaintiff, not by cable. It is said that since the defendant received notice when the steamship Magnolia sailed with fifteen tons that upon its arrival the plaintiff would tender to the defendant the entire thirty tons, the defendant is in no worse position that if it had received the stipulated "advice of shipment by cable immediately the goods are dispatched." Even if that be true, the fact remains that the plaintiff was obligated under its contract to see that defendant obtained advice of shipment by cable. That it failed to do. It may be that the defendant would have been satisfied to enter into a contract which required the plaintiff only to notify the defendant of intention to make delivery a definite time before actual delivery. It stipulated for another kind of notice. It may have believed that certainty of delivery would be greater if it received advice of actual shipment by cable. We may not weigh the benefit it might receive from other notice. The plaintiff may not recover upon its contract without proof that it has performed all conditions precedent required of it.... The plaintiff is barred from recovery here by failure to give notice according to the terms of the contract.

(Judgment for defendant buyer.)

DISCUSSION QUESTION

1. Many contracts state that "time is of the essence". Why is such a clause included? Do courts strictly enforce this clause to entitle a party to reject tendered performance or simply consider this clause one factor, among others, to determine if a party may reject tendered performance?

CONDITIONS AND IMPOSSIBILITY OF PERFORMANCE

CASE NO. 42

TOMPKINS v. DUDLEY

25 N.Y. 272   Sept. 1862

INTRODUCTION

Under the terms of a building contract, an independent building contractor is engaged to construct, complete and deliver a structure pursuant to certain plans and specifications. Progress payments are usually made to the building contractor as the work progresses. Sometimes the structure is destroyed <u>before</u> completion due to circumstances beyond the control of the building contractor, such as fire, flood, earthquake or other natural disaster. The legal question arises whether he may keep them. This leading case illustrates the rule of law still followed today.

Davies, J.   On the 31st of August, 1857, Cornelius Chambers, by a written contract, agreed to make, erect, build and furnish for the plaintiffs a school-house, according to the certain plans and specifications, and to furnish the materials for the sum of $678.50. The school-house was to be completed on the 1st day of October, 1857. The defendants guaranteed the performance of the contract on the part of the builder. The building was not completed on the 1st day of October, and it was burned down on the night of the 5th of October. The judge who tried the cause found, as matter of fact, that the contract was substantially performed by Chambers, but that the building was not entirely completed according to the specifications, there remaining to be done a small amount of painting and the hanging of the window blinds, and that the same had not been formally accepted nor the key delivered on the 5th of October. This action is brought to recover the money paid on account to Chambers as the building progressed, and for the damages which the plaintiffs have sustained by reason of the non-completion of the contract, the fulfillment of which was guaranteed by the defendants. It is undeniable that the school-house was not completed, nor delivered and accepted by the plaintiffs at the time of its destruction. They had a right to insist upon the completion of the contract according to its terms, and the builder did not allege or pretend that he had completed it. A substantial compliance with the terms of the contract will not answer when the contractor, as in this case, admits and conceded that the work was incomplete; he was still in possession, engaged in its completion. According to the testimony, about $60 was yet to be expended on the building. Had the builder completed the building and complied with his contract at the time of the destruction of the school-house? I am constrained to say he had not. He was not only to complete it in accordance with its terms, but was to deliver it over to the plaintiffs thus finished, or offer to deliver it, before his whole duty was performed. Now it is undeniable that the builder did not do this. A portion of the work was yet to be done; the builder was still in possession, and actually engaged in the work of completion at the time of its destruction.

The builder, in the present case, by his own contract, created a liability and incurred a duty, which the defendant guaranteed he should perform, and which he has not performed. In justification of such non-performance, he alleges the destruction of the building by fire and inevitable accident, without any fault on his part. The law is well settled, that this is no legal justification for the non-performance of the contract. This subject was most carefully considered and elaborately discussed in the case of Harmony v. Bingham and it was then held by this court, that when a party is prevented by the act of God from discharging a duty created by the law, he is excused; but when he engages unconditionally, by express contract, to do an act, performance is not excused by inevitable accident or other unforeseen contingency not within his control. Edwards, J., says: "This rule has been uniformly followed, and that, too, even in cases in which its applications has been considered by the court as attended with great hardships." Ruggies, J., said: "It is a well settled rule of law, that when a party, by his own fault and folly that he did not thereby expressly provide against contingencies and exempt himself from responsibility in certain events; and in such a case, therefore, that is, in the instance of an absolute and general contract, the performance is not excused by an inevitable accident or other contingency, although not foreseen by or within the control of the party."

I arrive at the conclusion that the law is well settled that the defense interposed by the defendants constitutes no justifications to Chambers, the builder, for the non-performance of his contract with the plaintiffs, and that, having guaranteed for and adequate consideration, expressed therein, its performance, they are liable to respond to the plaintiffs for the damages which they have sustained by reason of such non-performance.

(Judgment for plaintiffs.)

DISCUSSION QUESTIONS

1.   How can a building contractor protect himself against the economic loss imposed by the rule of law?

2.   Would an "Act of God" clause in a contract legally excuse non-performance or late performance because of "natural disasters" such as fire, explosion and earthquake?

3.   In addition to an "Act of God" clause, contracts frequently list other events which legally excuse non-performance or late performance, such as strike, riot and civil commotion. What other similar events can you think of including in a contract to legally excuse non-performance or late performance?

CONDITIONS: OBJECTIVE TEST OF SATISFACTION

CASE NO. 43

DUPLEX SAFETY BOILER CO., v. C. HENRY GARDEN et al.

101 N.Y. 387   Feb. 1866

INTRODUCTION

Contracts frequently provide that the party receiving performance is not
obligated to pay unless "satisfied". Courts frequently are asked to decide
which legal test is applied to determine if performance is "satisfactory" -
the objective test or the subjective test. This case illustrates when the
objective test is used while also identifying those types of contracts where
the subjective test is applied by the courts.

Danforth, J. The plaintiff sued to recover $700, the agreed price, as it
alleged, for materials furnished and work done for the defendants at their
request. The defense set up was that the work was done under a written contract for the alteration of certain boilers, and to be paid for only when the
defendants "were satisfied that the boilers as changed were a success." Upon
the trial it appears that the agreement between the parties was contained in
letters, by the first of which the defendants said to plaintiff: "You may
alter our boilers, changing all the old sections for your new pattern;
changing our fire front, raising both boilers enough to give ample fire space;
you doing all disconnecting and connecting, also all necessary mason work, and
turning boilers over to us ready to steam up. Work to be done by tenth of
May next. For above changes we are to pay you $700, as soon as we are satis-
fied that the boilers as changed are a success, and will not leak under a
pressure of one hundred pounds of steam."

The plaintiff answered, "accepting the proposition," and as the evidence
tended to show, and as the jury found, completed the required work in all
particulars by the 10th of May, 1881, at which time the defendants began and
thereafter continued the use of the boilers.

The contention on the part of the appellants is that the plaintiff was entitled to no compensation, unless the defendants "were satisfied that the
boilers as repaired were a success, and that this question was for the defendants alone to determine," thus making their obligation depend upon the mental
condition of the defendants, which they alone could disclose. Performance
must of course accord with the terms of the contract, but if the defendants
are at liberty to determine for themselves when they are satisfied, there
would be no obligation, and consequently no agreement which could be enforced.
It cannot be presumed that the plaintiff entered upon its work with this
understanding, nor that the defendants supposed they were to be the sole
judge in their own cause. On the contrary, not only does the law presume for
services rendered, renumeration shall be paid, but here the parties have so
agreed. The amount and manner of compensation are fixed; time of payment is
alone uncertain. The boilers were changed. Were they, as changed, satisfactory to the defendants?
In the case before us the work required was specified, and was completed;

the defendants made it available and continued to use the boilers without objection or complaint. If there was full performance on the plaintiff's part, nothing more could be required, and the time for payment had arrived; for "that which the law will say a contracting party ought in reason to be satisfied with, that the law will say he is satisfied with."

Another rule has prevailed, where the object of a contract was to gratify taste, serve personal convenience, or satisfy individual preference. In either of these cases the person for whom the article is made, or the work done, may properly determine for himself - if the other party so agrees- whether it shall be accepted. Such instances are cited by the appellants. One who makes a suit of clothes,... or undertakes to fill a particular place as agent... mold a bust...or paint a portrait...may not unreasonably be expected to be bound by the opinion of his employer, honestly entertained. A different case is before us, and in regard to it, no error has been shown.

(Judgment affirmed for plaintiff).

DISCUSSION QUESTION

1.   Since the objective test to determine if performance is "satisfactory" is whether a "reasonable man" would be satisfied with the tendered performance -and not the party paying for the tendered performance - how could a buyer legally protect himself so he does not have to pay for the tendered performance unless he (rather than a "reasonable man") is personally satisfied? For example, could a buyer provide that the product must work for a specified time before a final payment becomes due?

CONDITIONS: SUBJECTIVE TEST OF SATISFACTION

CASE NO. 44

APPELGATE v. MACFADDEN CORP.

214 App. Div. 221   Oct. 1925

INTRODUCTION

Employment contracts frequently provide that an employer may discharge an employee if the employer is not "satisfied" with the services rendered. This case illustrates when and why the courts apply the subjective test to determine if the employee's services are "satisfactory".

Merrell, J.: The action was brought to recover the sum of $12,000 damages alleged to have been sustained by the plaintiff by reason of his wrongful discharge by the defendant from its employ. The contract between the parties whereby the plaintiff was employed by the defendant was in writing. The defendant is a newspaper publishing corporation and employed the plaintiff "as Editor of the Saturday feature section and to have charge of the Rotogravure section" of the defendant's newspaper. The contract, a copy of which is annexed to the complaint, recites that "Whereas, Mr. Appelgate is an editor possessing unique and original ability, "and the employer desired to secure his exclusive services, the said Appelgate desiring to secure and accept employment with the defendant, "First. The Employer does hereby employ the Employee to render his services as Editor of the Saturday feature section and to have charge of the Rotogravure Section of the newspaper to be published by the MacFadden Newspaper Publishing Corporation exclusively.... It is further provided "that the Employee will work for and devote his entire time, skill, attention and energy to the Employer exclusively," and that "it being conceded by the Employee that his services are special, unique and extraordinary." In the 4th paragraph of the contract it is provided: "Fourth. The Employee shall faithfully execute to the satisfaction of the Employer all instructions in respect to his duties given by his Employer."

The plaintiff alleges that the contract in question was entered into between the parties on July 28, 1924, and that pursuant thereto and on or about August 4, 1924, the plaintiff entered upon his duties as editor of the Saturday feature section and took charge of the rotogravure section of the newspaper published by the defendant, and continued to perform such duties until on or about November 7, 1924, and duly performed all the terms and conditions on the part of the plaintiff to be performed under the said agreement; that on or about said last-mentioned date the defendant wrongfully and without just cause therefor discharge the plaintiff to plaintiff's damage in the sum of $12,000.

A perusal of the contract discloses that the parties regarded the services of the plaintiff for which the defendant contracted as of the character commonly known as unique. The contract itself recites that "Mr. Appelgate is an editor possessing unique and original ability." Plaintiff was hired as "Editor of the Saturday feature section and to have charge of the Rotogravure Section" of the defendant's newspaper. There can be no doubt that the parties understood that the plaintiff was to render services involving "art, taste, fancy and judgment"....

In a contract for services involving fancy taste and judgment, the question whether the fancy, taste or judgment of the employer is arbitrary or unreasonable does not arise, the question being whether the claimed dissatisfaction was feigned or genuine."

In Crawford v. Mail & Express Publishing Co. the plaintiff was employed as an editor to write at least two columns a week on the progress of the world or other appropriate subjects for publication in The Mail and Express, and in his contract with the defendant agreed that his services would be satisfactory to the defendant, and that in case they were not he should receive on week's notice. In discussing the absence of limitation upon the exercise by the employer of its judgment as to what was satisfactory to it, the Court of Appeals said "But, on the part of the publishers of The Mail & Express, it is very clear that they did not intend to be bound for a period longer than his services proved satisfactory, and that they expressly reserved the right to discharge him upon a week's notice. It is also apparent from a reading of the contract that the employment was not intended to be that of an ordinary servant to perform work, labor and services of an ordinary business or of a commercial nature. He was not called upon to perform the work of an ordinary reporter, writing up the general news of the day, but contracted to prepare articles on the progress of the world or other appropriate subjects in the line of the policy of the paper for the purpose, as expressed, of promoting the general interests of the paper, of aiding in its circulation and the obtaining of advertisements, by improving the quality of its contents. The evident design was that the articles should be interesting and attractive, involving art, taste, fancy and judgment. There is no provision in the contract in any manner limiting the publishers in the exercise of their judgment as to what is satisfactory, but if his services are unsatisfactory for any reason they are given the right to terminate the employment upon a week's notice, at any time they so elect."

In Diamond v. Mendelsohn the contract required the employee to "perform the duties of foreman competently and energetically to the best of his abilities and complete satisfaction of his employers." Mr. Justice CLARKE of this court, now its presiding justice, in writing in that case said: "There is no doubt that under the terms of this written contract (above stated) it lay within the power of the defendants to discharge the plaintiff because he did not perform his duties to their complete satisfaction and that it would not be proper to submit to a jury the question whether they ought to have been satisfied."

It, therefore, seems very clear to me that the only question to be determined upon the trial was as to whether the dissatisfaction pleaded by the defendant as ground for the discharge of the plaintiff was real or feigned. If the dissatisfaction was a mere whim of the employer, then, of course, it was not justified in terminating the contract, but if, in fact, the defendant was dissatisfied with the special and unique services rendered by the plaintiff as editor, then the defendant was justified in discharging him. The contract with the plaintiff clearly involved personal taste, fancy, and judgment, and when the employer become dissatisfied with the services of the character specified which its employee was to render, it had the right to discharge him and was not called upon to give reasons therefor.

The order appealed from should be reversed.

(Judgment for defendant employer.)

DISCUSSION QUESTIONS

1. What kind of provision in an employment contract would legally protect an employee if the employer insists on an employment contract provision giving the employer the right to discharge the employee if the employer concludes subjectively and in good faith that the employee's services are not "satisfactory"? For example, could parties define "satisfactory services" in objective terms such as "sales volume", "net profit", etc.

2. Some highly paid corporate executives negotiate a severance pay clause in employment contract based on length of employment in event of discharge for "unsatisfactory performance" to provide economic consolation. Would you advise an employer - client of yours to agree to a "severance pay" clause?

3. Give examples of an employer acting in bad faith when discharging an employee?

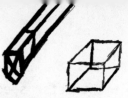

ESSAY QUESTIONS

<u>PERFORMANCE; DEFECTIVE PERFORMANCE; SUBSTANTIAL PERFORMANCE; IMPOSSIBILITY</u>
<u>OF PERFORMANCE; CONDITIONS; BREACH OF CONTRACT; DAMAGES; REMEDIES</u>

1. O, the sole owner of a multinational manufacturing business with factories throughout the world, entered into a written contract with E, whereby O hired E "as manager of the Paris factory for a term of five years, at a salary of $150,000 per year." At the end of three years E was notified that his services would no longer be required.

Would E have a cause of action for damages for breach of contract if his employment was terminated because of:

(a) O's death? Explain.

(b) E's permanent disability which prevented him from doing his job? Explain.

(c) The Paris factory burned down, and O decided not to rebuild? Explain.

(d) The French government imposed a heavy tax on the business which cut the profit in half? Explain.

Assume that the employer was O Corp., a corporation in which O was president and majority stockholder, all other facts remaining the same.

Would E have a cause of action for damages for breach of contract if his employment was terminated because of:

(e) O's death? Explain.

(f) The sale of all the stock of O Corp. to X? Explain.

(g) The voluntary dissolution of O Corp. and the liquidation of its business, pursuant to the stockholders decision? Explain.

2. C, a building contractor, entered into a written contract with A, the owner of real estate. The contract required C to build a public garage for A upon A's land at a cost of $75,000, payments to be made in installments as the work progressed, the work to be finished by October 1. On September 10, when the work was almost completed, C having already spent $55,000 on labor and materials, and A having made installment payments of $50,000, the building was totally destroyed by a fire of undetermined origin.

(a) Is C excused from his obligation to build the garage? Explain.

(b) Who bears the loss of the partly finished building? Explain.

(c) Is A entitled to recover the $50,000 paid before completion? Explain.

(d) How may A and C protect themselves from loss in this situation?

3. Assume that the contract in the previous question was to put a new roof

on an existing garage owned by A at a price of $10,000 payable on completion of work. When the work was half done, a fire destroyed the building completely.

(a) Is C entitled to a recovery against A? Explain.

(b) Is A liable to C for C's loss of profits on the unfinished part of the job? Explain.

(c) Who bears the loss of the building? Explain.

4. S, a cotton merchant, had 50 bales of cotton in his warehouse. B, a prospective buyer, inspected the bales in the warehouse, and entered into a contract with S to buy the bales at a price of $500 per bale. Delivery was to be made by S at B's factory in two weeks. Two days before the delivery date S's warehouse and the cotton were destroyed by fire. B demanded that S deliver another 50 bales of similar grade, and upon S's refusal, sued S for breach of contract. Judgment for whom? Explain.

5. (a) B, after visiting S's farm and inspecting two particular parcels of land sown to wheat, entered into a written agreement with S to purchase at a fixed and stated price the entire wheat crop to be harvested from the two particular and specified parcels of land. The agreement was expressly one to purchase the specific wheat crops indicated, and not simply an agreement to buy a given quantity of wheat from S. Subsequently the crops on the two specified parcels were destroyed by blight before harvest time. S notified B of such destruction prior to the agreed delivery date. Shortly after the date for delivery, B brought suit against S for breach of contract, claiming failure to perform under the agreed terms. S pleaded in defense that his contractual obligation had been discharged by reason of impossibility of performance due to destruction of specified wheat.

Judgment for whom? Explain.

(b) Assume the same agreement as in (a), with the following changes in developments. The crops were destroyed by blight, but before harvest time S sold the two specified parcels of land to X, together with the crops growing thereon. Legal title was duly conveyed to X. Prior to the agreed date for delivery of the wheat to B, S notified B of the sale of the land and the crops thereon and that the sale would make it impossible to perform his agreement. Shortly after the agreed delivery date, B brought suit against S for breach of contract, claiming failure to perform under the agreed terms. S pleaded in defense that his contractual obligation had been discharged by reason of impossibility of performance due to the transfer of the land and crops to X.

Judgment for whom? Explain.

6. O, sole proprietor of a small business, hired E by written agreement as his secretary for the period of one year at a salary of $18,000 to be paid

273

in monthly installments. At the end of the third month O died. The executor of O's estate terminated E's employment and refused to pay the third month's installment on the contract. Would you set up any amount as a liability of the estate for the claim? Explain the legal principles involved.

7.   A, a CPA who was engaged in practice without any partners or associates, was retained by C to audit his accounts and prepare a report including his professional opinion for submission to a prospective purchaser of C's business. When the field work was about half completed A became seriously ill, and was unable to complete the engagement. The prospective buyer lost interest and the sale of the business fell through.

(a)   C sues A for breach of his contract. Judgment for whom? Explain.

(b)   A sues C for his fee for the work he was able to complete. Judgment for whom? Explain.

8. C contracted to build a house for A according to A's architect's specifications at a total price of $250,000, payable in stages as the work progressed. The final payment of $10,000 was to be made when C obtained a certificate from the architect that the work had been done according to the detailed specifications. C, as was customary, subcontracted out various parts of the work to contractors who were specialists in excavation, brick-work, electricity, flooring, etc. When the house was finished the architect refused to issue a certificate of completion because the flooring was done in maple instead of oak as required by the specifications. The difference in value because of the variation was $1,000. It turned out that D, the flooring subcontractor, had deliberately used the maple flooring to reduce the cost of his contract with C, and so make a larger profit. C did not know or consent to the substitution. A refused to make the final payment of $10,000, and C, who had already paid D, refused to replace the floors with oak wood. C now sues A for $10,000.

(a) Has C committed a material breach of the contract? Explain.

(b) Are A's damages measured by the cost of removing the maple floors and replacing them with oak floors? Explain.

(c) Is C entitled to be paid $10,000 less the damages incurred by A? Explain.

(d) Has C a claim for damages against D? If so, for how much? Explain.

9. The City of A is serviced by two railroads, X and Y, which operate separate freight yards. S entered into a contract with B, a merchant in the City of A, to sell to B 100 bales of cotton waste "shipment to be made by X Railroad during the month of June", at a price of $10,000 which was to include the freight charges. S shipped 50 bales on June 10 by X Railroad prepaying the freight to the City of A.

(a) Is B entitled to refuse to take the 50 bales on the ground that he ordered 100? Explain.

(b) Did S breach the contract by shipping only 50 bales? Explain.

(c) If S shipped another 50 bales on July 10, would B be obligated to accept the two shipments? Explain.

Assume that S tried to ship 100 bales on June 10 via X Railroad, but that the shipment was refused due to a strike of X Railroad's engineers. S, the following day, shipped the 100 bales, via Y Railroad, freight prepaid, to the City of A, and B was notified of their arrival, but he refused to accept the shipment.

(d) Was B justified in refusing the shipment? Explain.

275

Assume that B accepted the shipment from Y Railroad.

(e) Would S's defective performance justify B in refusing to pay for the goods? Explain.

(f) Would S's defective performance render S liable to B for the additional transportation costs to move the goods from Y's terminal to B's warehouse as compared with the costs from X's terminal? Explain.

10. X Corp. wishing to dispose of its surplus warehouse offered it for sale for $500,000 cash. B informed X Corp. that he would pay the price asked. A contract of sale was executed by the parties and B paid down 10% of the price to X Corp. The closing was set for 4 weeks later, at which time B was to pay the balance by certified check, and X Corp. was to deliver the deed. The contract provided that X Corp. would retain the down-payment as liquidated damages if B defaulted. At the time of closing B told X Corp. that his arrangements to borrow the balance of the purchase price had not been completed and he requested an additional two weeks to complete the arrangements. X Corp. refused and stated it was cancelling the contract and retaining the down-payment.

(a) Did B's failure to pay on time constitute a material breach of the contract? Explain.

(b) If B raises the money in two weeks, is he entitled to a decree of specific performance of the contract against X Corp.? Explain.

Assume that X Corp. granted B an additional 6 weeks to raise the money, but notified him that it would grant no further extensions. At the end of 6 weeks B had still been unable to raise the money, and X Corp. notified him that it was cancelling the contract. A month later X Corp. sold the warehouse to C for $550,000.

(c) Is B now entitled to recover his $50,000 down payment? Explain.

Assume that when B originally negotiated for the purchase, X Corp., had little confidence in B's ability to raise the money. Accordingly, the parties agreed on the contract containing a clause reading "Time is of the essence in this contract." At the closing, X Corp. was unable to tender clear title to B since the day before The State Tax Department had notified them that an additional unpaid franchise tax constituted a lien on the warehouse. X Corp. requested a delay of 3 days to pay the tax and satisfy the lien. B, who had repented of his bargain, refused any extension, tendered his certified check for the balance, and demanded clear title. When X Corp. was unable to comply, B said he was cancelling the contract.

(d) Is B entitled to the return of his down-payment? Explain.

(e) Is X Corp. liable in damages to B for B's cost of conducting a title search? Explain.

11. D, a famous interior decorator and music lover, ordered a custom made, high fidelity, stereophonic, console radio-phonograph from the Pure Tone Phonograph Company. D maintained a lavish apartment which he used as a showcase to impress his wealthy clientele. In making the contract D insisted that the set meet his personal approval, and the contract guaranteed personal satisfaction. Skilled craftsmen worked for months on the set and even rivals of Pure Tone considered it one of the finest products ever produced. D, however, was not satisfied. He didn't like the finish nor did he find the tone to be as outstanding as he wished. He, therefore, refused to accept the set unless it was refinished and substantial improvements made in the tone quality.

Pure Tone, stating that the set was the best that could be made, refused to make the changes and sued D for breach of contract.

Will Pure Tone prevail? Explain.

12. E hired S as his full-time assistant to review and analyze the financial aspects of E's prospective real estate investments. S's hiring came after working with E on similar projects on a part-time basis for several years and resulted because of E being well satisfied with S's work and experience in the field.

The lengthy employment agreement prepared by E's attorney and signed by the parties provides that employment is to terminate after three years unless the contract is renewed. It also provides, in part:

> "It is distinctly understood and agreed that the services to be rendered by S hereunder must meet E's approval, and E shall be sole judge as to the adequacy of the services. If at any time E is in any way dissatisfied with any of the services, he is free to terminate the services."

S, who left an excellent position to accept employment with E, had not read the clause in the contract set out above. He was, therefore, shocked when two months after starting his new job E referred to the contract clause and requested S to leave his employ. S has commenced a suit for damages against E, alleging breach of the contract.

(a) Was the contract clause allowing E to terminate the agreement effective even though S did not read it? Explain.

(b) If a contract existed and the contract clause allowing E to terminate the agreement was effective, would E be liable for breach of contract if a jury found:

    (1) that E was not in fact dissatisfied with S's services but that the real motivation for firing was E's plan to retire from business and he, therefore, no longer required help. Explain.

    (2) that E was dissatisfied with some of the conclusions S reached

but that any reasonable man would disagree with E and find
S's work proper and satisfactory. Explain.

13. On July 9, P, president of X Corporation, with the approval of the board
of directors, engaged A, a certified public accountant, to conduct a special
interim review of the Corporation's financial statements for the nine months
ended September 30, and to render his report on November 30. A proceeded at
reasonable speed, but on November 10 he complained to P that the Corporation's staff was so inefficient and uncooperative that it might be impossible
to meet the deadline. P said "Don't worry. I'll fix that." A went on with
his work, but the staff of the Corporation showed no improvement. Despite
A's reasonable efforts, the report was not ready until December 12. P,
acting on behalf of the Corporation, refused to accept the report or pay for
the accounting services since delivery of the report by November 30 was a
condition of the contract and now it did not serve its intended purpose. A
sues X Corporation for breach of contract.

Judgment for whom? Explain.

MULTIPLE CHOICE
   QUESTIONS

PERFORMANCE: DEFECTIVE PERFORMANCE, SUBSTANTIAL PERFORMANCE:
   CONDITIONS: BREACH OF CONTRACT: DAMAGES: REMEDIES

1. Barnes agreed to purchase from Damion 1,000 shares of
   Excelsior Photo, Inc., stock at $100 per share. Barnes was
   interested in obtaining control of Excelsior, whose stock
   was very closely held. The stock purchase agreement contained
   the following clause: "The contract is subject to my
   (Barnes') obtaining more than 50% of the shares outstanding
   of Excelsior Photo stock." In this situation

   a. The contract is not binding on Damion because it lacks
      consideration on Barnes' part, i.e., unless he obtained
      more than 50%, he is not liable.
   b. The contract is subject to an express condition precedent.
   c. Specific performance would not be available to Barnes if
      Damion refuses to perform.
   d. While the contract is executory, Damion cannot transfer
      good title to a third party who takes in good faith.

2. Ames and Bates have agreed that Bates will sell a parcel of
   land to Ames for $10,000 if the land is rezoned from residen-
   tial to industrial use within six months of the agreement.
   Bates agreed to use his best efforts to obtain the rezoning,
   and Ames agreed to make a $2,000 goodfaith deposit with Bates
   two weeks after the date of the agreement. What is the
   status of this agreement?

   a. No contract resulted because the event is contingent.
   b. The agreement is probably unenforceable because Bates
      would be required to attempt to influence governmental
      action.
   c. The parties have entered into a bilateral contract
      subject to a condition.
   d. Ames is not obligated to make the deposit at the agreed
      time even though Bates has by then made an effort to
      procure a rezoning.

3. Ambrose undertook to stage a production of a well-known play.
   He wired Belle, a famous actress, offering her the lead at
   $1,000 per week (for six evening performances per week) for
   six weeks from the specified opening night, plus $1,000 for
   a week of rehearsal prior to opening. The telegram also
   said, "Offer ends in three days." Assuming a contract
   between Ambrose and Belle is made and that Belle did not
   perform after the third week of the six-week run

   a. If Belle was able to perform, a court would probably
      order specific performance.
   b. If Belle became unable to perform because of illness,
      Belle could hold Ambrose to his contract if she arranged
      for the appearance of a substitute star of at least
      equal fame and ability.
   c. If Belle became ill and it appeared that she would miss a

279

substantial number of performances, Ambrose might terminate the contract but would be liable for payment for performances previous given.

    d. Belle's refusal to perform would not have constituted a breach of contract if Ambrose had been declared bankrupt.

4. Keats Publishing Company shipped textbooks and other books for sale at retail to Campus Bookstore. An honest dispute arose over Campus' right to return certain books. Keats maintained that the books in question could not be returned and demanded payment of the full amount. Campus relied upon trade custom which indicated that many publishers accepted the return of such books. Campus returned the books in question and paid for the balance with a check marked "Account Paid in Full to Date." Keats cashed the check. Which of the following is a correct statement?

    a. Keats is entitled to recover damages.
    b. Keats' cashing of the check constituted an accord and satisfaction.
    c. The pre-existing legal duty rule applies and Keats is entitled to full payment for all the books.
    d. The custom of the industry argument would have no merit in a court of a law.

5. The Johnson Corporation sent its only pump to the manufacturer to be repaired. It engaged Travis, a local trucking company, both to deliver the equipment to the manufacturer and to redeliver it to Johnson promptly upon completion of the repair. Johnson's entire plant was inoperative without this pump, but the trucking company did not know this. The trucking company delayed several days in its delivery of the repaired pump to Johnson. During the time it expected to be without the pump, Johnson incurred $5,000 in lost profits. At the end of that time Johnson rented a replacement pump at a cost of $200 per day. As a result of these facts, what is Johnson entitled to recover from Travis?

    a. The $200 a day cost incurred in renting the pump.
    b. The $200 a day cost incurred in renting the pump plus the lost profits.
    c. Actual damages plus punitive damages.
    d. Nothing because Travis is not liable for damages.

6. The remedy of specific performance is available where the subject matter of the contract involves
    a. Services.
    b. Goods with a price of $500 or more.
    c. Fraud.
    d. Land.

7. A contract will be enforceable even if the party seeking to avoid performance alleges and proves
    a. Innocent misrepresentation.
    b. Fraud.
    c. Mutual mistake of material fact.
    d. Extreme hardship.

NEW YORK GENERAL OBLIGATIONS LAW

Section 13-101. Transfer Of Claims

Any claim or demand can be transferred, except in one of the following cases:

1. Where it is to recover damages for a personal injury;

2. Where it is founded upon a grant, which is made void by a statute of the state; or upon a claim to or interest in real property, a grant of which, by the transferrer, would be void by such a statute;

3. Where a transfer thereof is expressly forbidden by a statute of the state, or of the United States, or would contravene public policy. (eff. 1963; originally enacted in 1941, and was previously contained in Personal Property Law Section 41(1).

Section 13-105. Effect Of Transfer Of Claim Or Demand

Where a claim or demand can be transferred, the transfer thereof passes an interest, which the transferee may enforce by an action or special proceeding, or interpose as a defense or counter-claim, in his own name, as the transferrer might have done; subject to any defense or counter-claim, existing against the transferrer, before notice of the transfer, or against the transferee. But this section does not apply, where the rights or liabilities of a party to a claim or demand, which is transferred, are regulated by special provision of law; nor does it vary the rights or liabilities of a party to a negotiable instrument, which is transferred. (eff. 1963; originally enacted in 1941, and was previously contained in Personal Property Law 41(3).

Section 13-109. Definition Of "Transfer"

As used in section 13-101, 13-303, 13-105 and 13-107, the term "transfer" includes sale, assignment, conveyance, deed and gift. (eff. 1963).

Section 5-1107. Written Assignment; see Consideration

Section 2-210. Delegation Of Performance; Assignment Of Rights

(1) A party may perform his duty through a delegate unless otherwise agreed or unless the other party has a substantial interest in having his original promisor perform or control the acts required by the contract. No delegation of performance relieves the party delegating of any duty to perform or any liability for breach.

(2) Unless otherwise agreed all rights of either seller or buyer can be assigned except where the assignment would materially change the duty of the other party or increase materially the burden or risk imposed on him by his contract, or impair materially his chance of obtaining return performance. A right to damages for breach of the whole contract or a right arising out of the assignor's due performance of his entire obligation can be assigned despite agreement otherwise.

(3) Unless the circumstances indicate the contrary a prohibition of assignment of "the contract" is to be construed as barring only the delegation to the assignee of the assignor's performance.

(4) An assignment of "the contract" or of "all my rights under the contract" or an assignment in similar general terms is an assignment of rights and unless the language or the circumstances (as in an assignment for security) indicate the contrary, it is a delegation of performance of the duties of the assignor and its acceptance by the assignee constitutes a promise by him to perform those duties. This promise is enforceable by either the assignor or the other party to the original contract.

(5) The other party may treat any assignment which delegates performance as creating reasonable grounds for insecurity and may without prejudice to his rights against the assignor demand assurances from the assignee (Section 2-609)

Section 2-609. Right To Adequate Assurance Of Performance

(1) A contract for sale imposes an obligation on each party that the other's expectation of receiving due performance will not be impaired. When reasonable grounds for insecurity arise with respect to the performance of either party the other may in writing demand adequate assurance of due performance and until he receives such assurance may if commercially reasonable suspend any performance for which he has not already received the agreed return.

(2) Between merchants, the reasonableness of grounds for insecurity and the adequacy of any assurance offered shall be determined according to commercial standards.

(3) Acceptance of any improper delivery or payment does not prejudice the aggrieved party's right to demand adequate assurance of future performance.

(4)   After receipt of a justified demand failure to provide within a reasonable time not exceeding thirty days such assurance of due performance as is adequate under the circumstances of the particular case is a repudiation of the contract.

UNIFORM COMMERCIAL CODE: ARTICLE 9:   SECURED TRANSACTIONS

Section 9-206.   Agreement Not To Assert Defenses Against Assignee;...

(1)   Subject to any statute or decision which establishes a different rule for buyers or lessees of consumer goods, an agreement by a buyer or lessee that he will not assert against an assignee any claim or defense which he may have against the seller or lessor is enforceable by an assignee who takes his assignment for value, in good faith and without notice of a claim or defense, except as to defenses of a type which may be asserted against a holder in due course of a negotiable instrument under the Article on Commercial Paper (Article 3).   A buyer who as part of one transaction signs both a negotiable instrument and a security agreement makes such an agreement.

...

Section 9-318.   Defenses Against Assignee; Modification Of Contract After Notification Of Assignment; Term Prohibiting Assignment Ineffective; Identification And Proof Of Assignment

(1)   Unless an account debtor has made an enforceable agreement not to assert defenses or claims arising out of a sale as provided in Section 9-206 the rights of an assignee are subject to

(a)   all the terms of the contract between the account debtor and assignor and any defense or claim arising therefrom; and

(b)   any other defense or claim of the account debtor against the assignor which accrues before the account debtor receives notification of the assignment.

(2)   So far as the right to payment of a part thereof under an assigned contract has not been fully earned by performance, and notwithstanding notification of the assignment, any modification of or substitution for the contract made in good faith, in accordance with reasonable commercial standards and without material adverse effect upon the assignee's rights under or the assignor's ability to perform the contract, is effective against an assignee unless the account debtor has otherwise agreed but the assignee acquires corresponding rights under the modified or substituted contract.   The assignment may provide that such modification or substitution is a breach by the assignor.

(3)   The account debtor is authorized to pay the assignor until the account debtor receives notification that the amount due or to become due has been assigned and that payment is to be made to the assignee.   A notification which does not reasonably identify the rights assigned is ineffective.   If

requested by the account debtor, the assignee must seasonably furnish reasonable proof that the assignment has been made and unless he does so the account debtor may pay the assignor.

(4)   A term in any contract between an account debtor and an assignor is ineffective if it prohibits assignment of an account or prohibits creation of a security interest in a general intangible for money due or to become due or requires the account debtor's consent to such assignment or security interest. (as amended, eff. July 2, 1978).

ASSIGNMENTS: CONSUMER PROTECTION

Over the years, the New York State legislature has enacted different statutes, placing restrictions on the assignment of certain contracts as well as prohibiting certain types of contracts which forbid assignments.

The following statutes are representative of legislative policy in New York State.

NEW YORK PERSONAL PROPERTY LAW

Section 431.   Restriction On Assignment Of Obligation(Door-to-Door Sales)

1.   A seller shall not negotiate, transfer, sell or assign any note or other evidence of indebtedness to a finance company or other third party prior to midnight of the fifth business day following the day the contract was signed or the goods or services were purchased.

2.   The assignee of any note or evidence of indebtedness shall be subject to all claims and defenses of the buyer against the seller arising from the sale notwithstanding any agreement to the contrary, but the assignee's liability under this subdivision shall not exceed the amount owing to the assignee at the time the claim or defense is asserted against the assignee. Rights of the buyer under this section can be asserted affirmatively against or as a matter of defense to or set-off against a claim by the assignee. (eff. Sept. 1, 1976).

Note: The above (Section 431) is part of the Door-To-Door Sales Protection Act of the New York Personal Property Law. See Formation of Contracts, for some of the other sections.

Section 403.   Restrictions On Retail Instalment Contracts And Obligations

1.   No contract or obligation shall require or entail the execution of any note or series of notes by the buyer, which when separately negotiated, will cut off as to third parties any right of action or defense which the buyer may have against the seller.

2.   No contract or obligation shall contain any provision by which:

(a)   The buyer agrees not to assert against an assignee a claim or

284

defense arising out of the sale, but it may contain such a provision as to an assignee who acquires the contract or obligation on the sale of a boat, where the principal balance at the time of sale exceeds five thousand dollars, and to whom the buyer has not mailed written notice of the facts giving rise to the claim or defense within ten days after such assignee mails to the buyer, at his address shown on the contract or obligation, notice of the assignment.

. . .

4.   Except as provided in paragraph (a) of subdivision two of this section, the assignee of a retail instalment contract or obligation shall be subject to all claims and defenses of the buyer against the seller arising from the sale notwithstanding any agreement to the contrary, but the assignee's liability under this subdivision shall not exceed the amount owing to the assignee at the time the claim or defense is asserted against the assignee. (eff. Dec. 1, 1980, as amended).

Section 406.   Notice Of Assignment; Payments (Retail Installment Sale).

Unless the buyer has notice of actual or intended assignment of a contract, obligation, or credit agreement payment thereunder made by the buyer to the last known holder of such contract, obligation or credit agreement shall be binding upon all subsequent holders or assignees.   (eff. 1957).

Note: The above (sections 403 and 406) are part of the Retail Installment Sales Act of the New York Personel Property Law.   See Illegality for some of the other sections.

NEW YORK GENERAL BUSINESS LAW

Section 625.   Assignment Of Contracts For Services (Health Clubs).

1.   No assignee who takes a note or other obligation as consideration for a contract containing the disclosure requirements of section six hundred twenty-four of this article shall fail to honor the consumer's right of cancellation as provided in this article.

2.   No creditor holding a note or other obligation, to which a consumer has obligated himself in order to purchase a contract shall fail to honor the consumer's right of cancellation under this article if:

(a)   the creditor is a person related to the seller of services; or

(b)   the seller prepares documents used in connection with the loan; or

(c)   the creditor supplies forms to the seller used by the consumer in obtaining the loan; or

(d)   the creditor makes twenty or more loans in any calendar year, the proceeds of which are used in transactions with the same seller or with a person related to the same seller; or

        (e)   the consumer is referred to the creditor by the seller; or

        (f)   the creditor, directly or indirectly, pays the seller any consideration whether or not it is in connection with the particular transactions; or

        (g)   the creditor participated in or was connected with the sale.

3. No assignee of a contract shall fail to give notice of the assignment to the consumer. A notice of assignment shall be in writing addressed to the consumer at the address shown on the contract and shall identify the contract. (eff. Jan. 1, 1979).

Note: The above (section 625) is part of the Health Club Services Article of the New York General Business Law. See Illegality for some of the other sections.

NEW YORK PERSONAL PROPERTY LAW

ASSIGNMENT OF EARNINGS (Article 3A)
(Sections 46 - 49-b)

Section 46. Definitions

In this article unless the context or subject matter otherwise requires:

1. "Assignment" means any assignment of or order for payment of any earnings, whether given outright or as security. "Assignment" shall not include a payroll deduction, nor any part of earnings required by law to be withheld in payment of taxes, nor such sums as may be deducted by the employer for payment to a labor union or to a trust fund for the benefit of employees, pursuant to agreement in writing either with the employee or with a labor union of which the employee is a member.

. . .

3. "Earnings" means any salary, wages, commissions, or other compensation for services. "Future earnings" means earnings which become payable by an employer, to the assignor or persons claiming under him, after the execution of the instrument of assignment.

. . .

6. "Assignor" means one who executes an assignment.

7. "Assignee" means one to whom any sum is payable under an assignment.

. . . (eff. 1950).

<u>Section 46-c.</u>   <u>Formal Requisites Of Assignments Of Less Than One</u>
                      <u>Thousand Dollars And Of Assignments Securing Certain</u>
                      <u>Guarantees Amounting To Fifteen Hundred Dollars Or Less</u>

No assignment of future earnings, securing or relating to any indebtedness aggregating less than one thousand dollars, shall be valid for any purpose whatsoever unless:

(a)   such assignment shall be contained in a separate written instrument in which all printed matter is in at least eight point type and which shall have written or printed thereon in a size equal to at least ten point bold type the following title: "Assignment of Wages, Salary, Commissions or other Compensation for Services," and shall have written or printed at the bottom thereof just above the place reserved for the signature of the assignor in a size equal to at least ten point bold type the following: "This is an Assignment of Wages, Salary, Commissions or Other Compensation For Services";

(b)   such assignment shall, either in its text or in a writing permanently attached thereto, identify specifically and describe fully the transaction to which it relates, said description to include the name and address of the assignee, the identity of the merchandise sold or services rendered or other basis of the indebtedness secured by, or consideration given for the assignment, and the date on and place at which payments are to be made; and on the face or back of the instrument there shall be a summary of sections forty-six-c, forty-six-e, forty-six-f, forty-seven-e, forty-eight, forty-eight-a, forty-eight-b, forty-eight-c and forty-nine of the personal property law;

(c)   such assignment, if given as security, is security only for the transaction or series of transactions identified specifically and described therein, or a renewal thereof, and no other valid and legally enforceable assignment exists in connection with the same transaction or series of transactions;   ... (as amended, eff. Sept. 1, 1974 - originally enacted in 1942).

<u>Section 46-e.</u>   <u>Personal Execution Of Assignment By Assignor; Delivery</u>
                      <u>Of Copies Of Papers</u>

No assignment of future earnings shall be valid for any purpose whatever unless such assignment is personally executed by the assignor. A copy thereof and of any papers attached thereto together with a copy or copies of any papers executed by the assignor pertaining to the transaction or series of transactions described in the assignment shall be delivered to the assignor before such assignment is filed with the employer. (as amended, eff. Sept. 1, 1974).

<u>Section 49-b.</u>   <u>Income Deduction By Court Order In Support Cases</u>

....

2. The limitations and regulations of section forty-six to forty-eight-a, personal property law, do not apply to assignment of, or order for, monies

287

due or payable, the entitlement to which is based upon remuneration for employment, past or present, for the support of children under the age of twenty-one, and/or spouse, and/or former spouse, when such assignments or orders are made to comply with a court order of support. Notwithstanding sections forty-six to forty-eight-a, personal property law, an assignment of or order for monies due or payable to be paid for the support of a person's children under the age of twenty-one, spouse, or former spouse in compliance with an order of a court for the support of his or her children under the age of twenty-one, spouse, or former spouse takes priority over any other assignment or garnishment of monies due or payable, except as to those deductions made mandatory by law or hereinafter made mandatory, including labor union dues.

... (eff. June 2, 1981, as amended)

NEW YORK CIVIL PRACTICE LAW AND RULES (C.P.L.R.)

Section 5252. <u>Dismissal Or Lay Off Of Employee To Avoid Compliance With Wage Assignment Or Income Execution</u>

1. No employer shall discharge or lay off an employee because one or more wage assignments or income executions have been served upon such employer against the employee's wages or because of the pendency of any action or judgment against such employee for nonpayment of any alleged contractual obligation.

2. An employee may institute a civil action for damages for wages lost as a result of a violation of this section within ninety days after such violation. Damages recoverable shall not exceed lost wages for six weeks and in such action the court also may order the reinstatement of such discharged employee. Not more than ten per centum of the damages recovered in such action shall be subject to any claims, attachments or executions by any creditors, judgment creditors or assignees of such employee. (eff. Jan. 1, 1978, as amended; originally enacted in 1966).

THIRD PARTY BENEFICIARIES

CASE NO. 45

SEAVER v. RANSOM

224 N.Y. 233   Oct. 1918

INTRODUCTION

The legal question arises whether a third party-who is <u>not</u> a party to a contract-can enforce a contract made between two other parties which is intended for the benefit of the third party. This leading case traces the history of the subject and analyzes the four classes of cases where a third party beneficiary can enforce a contract.

POUND, J. Judge Beman and his wife were advanced in years. Mrs. Beman was about to die. She had a small estate consisting of a house and lot in Malone and little else. Judge Beman drew his wife's will according to her instructions. It gave $1,000 to plaintiff, $500 to one sister, plaintiff's mother, and $100 each to another sister and her son, the use of the house to her husband for life, remainder to the American Society for the Prevention of Cruelty to Animals. She named her husband as residuary legatee and executor. Plaintiff was her niece, thirty-four years old, in ill health, sometimes a member of the Beman household. When the will was read to Mrs. Beman she said that it was not as she wanted it; she wanted to leave the house to plaintiff. She had no other objection to the will, but her strength was waning and although the judge offered to write another will for her, she said she was afraid she would not hold out long enough to enable her to sign it. So the judge said if she would sign the will he would leave plaintiff enough in his will to make up the difference. He avouched the promise by his uplifted hand with solemnity and his wife then executed the will. When he came to die it was found that his will made no provision for the plaintiff.

Contracts for the benefit of third persons have been the prolific source of judicial and academic discussion (Williston, Contracts for the Benefit of a Third Person 16 Harvard Law Review, 767; Corbin, Contracts for the Benefit of Third Persons, 27 Yale Law Review, 1008.) The general rule, both in law and equity...was that privity between a plaintiff and a defendant is necessary to the maintenance of an action on the contract. The consideration must be furnished by the party to whom the promise was made. The contract cannot be enforced against the third party and, therefore, it cannot be enforced by him. On the other hand, the right of the beneficiary to sue on a contract made expressly for his benefit has been fully recognized in many American jurisdictions, either by judicial decision or by legislation, and is said to be "the prevailing rule in this country.".... It has been said that the establishment of this doctrine has been gradual, and is a victory of practical utility over theory, of equity over technical subtlety (Brantly on Contracts (2d ed.), p. 253.) The reasons for this view are that it is just and practical to permit the person for whose benefit the contract is made to enforce it against one whose duty it is to pay. Other jurisdictions still adhere to the present

English rule that a contract cannot be enforced by or against a person who is not a party. In New York the right of the beneficiary to sue on contracts made for his benefit is not clearly or simply defined. It is at present confined, first, to cases where there is a pecuniary obligation running from the promisee to the beneficiary; "a legal right founded upon some obligation of the promisee in the third party to adopt and claim the promise as made for his benefit.".... Secondly, to cases where the contract is made for the benefit of the wife..., or child of a party to the contract. The close relationship cases go back to the early King's Bench case (1677), long since repudiated in England.... The natural and moral duty of the husband or parent to provide for the future of wife or child sustains the action on the contract made for their benefit. "This is the farthest the cases in this state have gone," says Cullen, J., in the marriage settlement case of Borland v. Welch....

The right of the third party is also upheld in, thirdly, the public contract cases...where the municipality seeks to protect its inhabitants by covenants for their benefit and, fourthly, the cases where, at the request of a party to contract, the promise runs directly to the beneficiary although he does not furnish the consideration.... It may be safely said that a general rule sustaining recovery at the suit of the third party would include but few classes of cases not included in these groups, either categorically or in principle.

The desire of the childless aunt to make provision for a beloved and favorite niece differs imperceptibly in law or in equity from the moral duty of the parent to make testamentary provision for a child. The contract was made for the plaintiff's benefit. She alone is substantially damaged by its breach. The representatives of the wife's estate have no interest in enforcing it specifically. It is said in Buchanan v. Tilden that the common law imposes moral and legal obligations upon the husband and the parent not measured by the necessaries of life. It was, however, the love and affection or the moral sense of the husband and the parent that imposed such obligations in the cases cited rather than any commonlaw duty of husband and parent to wife and child. If plaintiff had been a child of Mrs. Beman, legal obligation would have required no testamentary provision for her, yet the child could have enforced a covenant in her favor identical with the covenant of Judge Beman in this case.... The constraining power of conscience is not regulated by the degree of relationship alone. The dependent or faithful niece may have a stronger claim than the affluent or unworthy son. No sensible theory of moral obligation denies arbitrarily to the former what would be conceded to the latter. We might consistently either refuse or allow the claim of both, but I cannot reconcile a decision in favor of the wife in Buchanan v. Tilden based on the moral obligations arising out of near relationship with a decision against the niece here on the ground that the relationship is to remote for equity's kin. No controlling authority depends upon so absolute a rule.

The equities are with the plaintiff and they may be enforced in this action, whether it be regarded as an action for damages or an action for specific performance to convert the defendants into trustees for plaintiff's benefit under the agreement.

(Judgment affirmed for plaintiff.)

<u>DISCUSSION QUESTIONS</u>

1.   Was the niece a third party creditor beneficiary or a third party donee beneficiary or a third party incidental beneficiary?

2.   If the niece were not a relative but only a "very dear friend", do you think the court would have allowed recovery based on the court's reasoning in this case?

ASSIGNMENT OF CONTRACTS

CASE NO. 46

NASSAU HOTEL CO. v. BARNETT

162 App. Div. 381   May 1914

INTRODUCTION

Contracts are frequently made between business companies and an individual pursuant to which the individual is to render personal services such as the management of the business. The legal question arises (1) whether an individual may lawfully assign the contract to another party, such as a corporation in which he is a substantial stockholder and (2) what rights the other party to the contract has when such an assignment is made.

McLAUGHLIN, J:

Plaintiff owns a hotel at Long Beach, L.I., and on the 21st of November, 1912, it entered into a written agreement with the individual defendants Barnett and Barse to conduct the same for a period of years. On April fourteenth following, the agreement was modified and incorporated into another one of that date between the same parties, which is the only one that need be considered. Shortly after this agreement was signed, Barnett and Barse organized the Barnett & Barse Corporation with a capital stock of $10,000, and then assigned the agreement to it. Immediately following the assignment the corporation went into possession and assumed to carry out its terms. The plaintiff thereupon brought this action to cancel the agreement and to recover possession of the hotel and furniture therin, on the ground that the agreement was not assignable. (The lower court held the contract was not assignable and the defendant appealed.)

The only question presented is whether the agreement is assignable. It provided, according to the allegations of the complaint, that the plaintiff leased the property to Barnett and Barse with all its equipment and furniture for a period of three years, with a privilege of five successive renewals of three years each. It expressly provided "That said Lessees shall forthwith, upon becoming possessed of the Hotel situated upon the premises herein-before decribed, its furniture and equipment, become responsible for the operation of the said hotel and for the upkeep and maintenance thereof, and of all its furniture and equipment, in accordance with the terms of this agreement, and the said Lessees shall have the exclusive possession, control and management thereof.... The said Lessees hereby covenant and agree that they will operate the said hotel, at all times, in a first class, businesslike manner, keep the same open for at least six (6) months of each year, ..." and "in lieu of rental the Lessor and Lessees hereby covenant and agree, that the gross receipts of such operation shall be, as received, divided between the parties hereto as follows" (a) Nineteen percent (19%) to the Lessor.... In the event of the failure of the Lessees well and truly to perform the covenants and agreements herein contained" they should be liable in the sum of $50,000, as

292

liquidated damages; that "in consideration and upon condition that the said Lessees shall well and faithfully perform all the covenants and agreements by them to be performed without evasion or delay, the said Lessor, for itself, and its successors, covenants and agrees that the said Lessees, their legal representative and assigns, may, at all times during said term and the renewals thereof, peaceable have and enjoy the said demised premises;" and that "this agreement shall inure to the benefit of and bind the respective parties hereto, their personal representatives, successors and assigns."

The complaint further alleges that the agreement was entered into by plaintiff in reliance upon the financial responsibility of Barnett and Barse, their personal character, and especially the experience of Barnett in conducting hotels; that though he at first held a controlling interest in the Barnett & Barse Corporation, he has since sold all his stock to the defendant Barse, and has no interest in the corporation and no longer devotes any time or attention to the management or operation of the hotel.

I am clearly of the opinion that the agreement in question was personal to Barnett and Barse and could not be assigned by them without the plaintiff's consent. By its terms the plaintiff not only intrusted them with the care and management of the hotel and its furnishings, valued, according to the allegations of the complaint at more than $1,000,000, but agreed to accept as rental or compensation a percentage of the gross receipts. Obviously the receipts depended to a large extent upon the management and the care of the property, upon the personal character and responsibility of the persons in possession. When the whole agreement is read, it is apparent that the plaintiff relied in making it upon the personal covenants of Barnett and Barse. They were financially responsible. As already said, Barnett had had a long and successful experience in managing hotels, which was undoubtedly an inducing cause for plaintiff's making the agreement in question and for personally obligating them to carry out its terms.

It is suggested that because there is a clause in the agreement to the effect that it should "inure to the benefit of and bind the respective parties hereto, their personal representatives, successors and assigns." Barnett and Barse had a right to assign it to the corporation. But the intention of the parties is to be gathered not from one clause, but from the entire instrument...and when it is thus read it clearly appears that Barnett and Barse were to personally carry out the terms of the agreement, and did not have a right to assign it. This follows from the language used, which shows that a personal trust or confidence was reposed by the plaintiff in Barnett and Barse when the agreement was made.

In Arkansas Smelting Co v. Belden Co. Mr. Justice Gray, in delivering the opinion of the court, said: "The rule upon this subject, as applicable to the case at bar, is well expressed in a recent English treatise. 'Rights arising out of contract cannot be transferred if they are coupled with liabilities, or if they involve a relation of personal confidence such that the party whose agreement conferred those rights must have intended them to be exercised only by him in whom he actually confided.' Pollock on Contracts (4th ed.) 425."

This rule was applied in New York Bank Note Co. v. Hamilton Bank Note

Co., the court holding that the plaintiff, the assignee, was not only technical-
ly but substantially a different entity from its predecessor, and that the
defendant was not obliged to intrust its money collected on the sale of the
presses to the responsibility of an entirely different corporation from that
with which it had contracted, and that the contract could not be assigned to
the plaintiff without the assent of the other party to it.

The reason which underlies the basis of the rule is that a party has the
right to the benefit contemplated from the character, credit and substance of
him with whom he contracts...and in such case he is not bound to recognize
either an assignment of the contract the principal....

(Judgment for plaintiff affirmed.)

DISCUSSION QUESTION

1.   How could Barnett and Barse have provided a lawful assignment of the contract to their corporation?

2.   Assuming assignment was expressly provided for in the original contract,
would Barnett and Barse be personally liable for breach of the contract by the
assignee corporation?

ESSAY QUESTIONS :   THIRD PARTY BENEFICIARIES

AND

ASSIGNMENTS

1. S, who owned a retail shoe store, decided to sell the business. The assets of the business consisted of a one-story building worth $100,000, merchandise worth $50,000, accounts receivable of $10,000, fixtures worth $30,000 and good will estimated at $50,000. He owed various wholesalers a total of $20,000 for shoes bought by him on credit. He offered to sell all these assets to B for $220,000 cash, provided B would also agree to assume payment of the $20,000 owed for merchandise. B agreed, and a written contract was drawn up embodying these terms. The deal was closed, and upon payment of $220,000 by B, S signed deeds and bills of sale for all the assets listed. C, who is one of the wholesalers to whom S owed $5,000, called upon S for payment. S informed him that B was to pay. C sued S and B for $5,000.

(a) B defended on the ground that he had made no contract with C. Is the defense valid? Explain.

(b) S defended on the ground that B had agreed to pay. Is the defense valid? Explain.

Assume that the court entered judgment against S and B for $5,000 as a joint liability.

(c) If S paid $2,500 and B $2,500 has either any claim against the other? Explain.

(d) Would your answer to (a) be the same, if B had paid $240,000 for the assets, but had not agreed to pay the $20,000 owed to S's creditors? Explain.

2. In the previous question, assume that S wished to make a present to his wife, W, of one-half the sales value of the business, and that B agreed to pay for the business in two installments. Accordingly, B agreed with S to "pay $110,000 to S upon taking over the store, and $110,000 to W two years later." W was not one of the parties to the contract. Two years elapse and B has not paid W.

(a) Has W a cause of action against B for the $110,000 promised to her? Explain.

(b) Would the one year Statute of Frauds be a defense to B if the agreement between S and B were oral? Explain.

3. D Inc., a manufacturing corporation, was in financial difficulty. D, the majority stockholder of D Inc. told the president of the corporation "I will furnish whatever moneys are necessary to run the business up to $25,000. If you have to advertise, do so. I will advance the money. Spend it as though

295

you've got it." Thereafter, D Inc. entered into a contract with C, who operated an advertising agency, under which C rendered certain advertising services to D Inc. at the agreed price of $5,000. Upon D Inc. becoming bankrupt, C demands payment from D.

(a) Is C entitled to enforce D's promise as a third party beneficiary? Explain.

(b) Would D be liable to C as a guarantor of D Inc.'s debts? Explain.

(c) Would D be liable to C if his promise had been contained in a letter to D Inc.? Explain.

4. S, a manufacturer of electrical appliances, entered into a written contract in December with B, a wholesale dealer, under which S agreed to deliver to B 200 electric broilers each month during the next year at $100 each. The broilers were to be paid for 60 days after each delivery. B sold his business to C the following June and assigned to C his contract with S as part of the same transaction. C agreed to assume all of B's past and future obligations under the contract with S. C notified S of the purchase of the business and assumption agreement in July. S refused to make delivery to C.

(a) Is S justified in refusing to deliver the July shipment to C? Explain.

(b) If S delivers the broilers to C, but C fails to pay for them, what are S's right's against C and B? Explain.

(c) If B owed S $20,000 for broilers delivered in June before the business was sold to C, has S any rights against C? Explain.

(d) Assume on the sale of the business that B assigned the contract to C but C did not assume B's obligations under it. Would S have any rights against B or C, if C refused to take any broilers in July? Explain.

(e) Would your answer to (a) be the same if the $100 price under the original contract had been a special low price to induce B, an established wholesaler and sales agent, to become the sole distributor of the broilers in New York State, and B had undertaken to use the best efforts of himself and his organization to promote the sale of the broilers among the retail dealers with whom he had established contacts, and thus to develop a New York market? Explain.

5. T owns and operates a gas station and restaurant on a highway about a mile from a beautiful, but undeveloped, lake region. R, seeing the value of the lake region as a potential resort area, purchases several acres of lake front property. He then enters into a contract with M, a building contractor, to have him construct an elaborate hotel and ten beautiful cottages. T, learning of these facts from a conversation with R, expands his restaurant and gas station facilities in contemplation of a substantial increase in business. Subsequently, R decides not to go ahead with his plans, but instead to breach

the contract with M. He promptly notifies M not to commence construction and M complies. T, learning of the change in plans, sues R for breach of contract. He claims that he (T) is a third party beneficiary under the contract between R and M and upon R's breach, he is entitled to recover damages from R for the costs he incurred in expanding his business and the profits he would have made had the contract been performed by R.

(a) Can T recover from R? Explain.

(b) List and define the three kinds of third pary beneficiaries.

6. In question 1, assume that S, on closing the contract with B, signed a document reading as follows: "May 1, For value received, I hereby transfer to B all my right, title and interest in and to the following accounts receivable owed to me:

(1) From D, $5,000 due June 1.

(2) From E, $2,000 presently due.

(3) From F, $3,000 due July 1.

(a) If D pays S $5,000 on June 3, without knowledge of the assignment, what are B's rights against S and D? Explain.

(b) If B immediately notifies E of the assignment, and then E pays S $2,000, what are B's rights against S and E? Explain.

(c) If B notifies E of the assignment, but E does not pay because he is insolvent, what are B's rights against S? Explain.

(d) Assume that B notifies F of the assignment on June 15 and F fails to pay on the due date. B then sues F for $3,000, and F interposes as a defense that the goods sold to him by S, out of which transaction the debt arose, were defective, and worth only $1,000. What are B's rights against S and F? Explain.

(e) Assume that in (d), F interposes as a defense that he paid $3,000 on June 10 to X, to whom S had assigned the same debt on June 1. What are B's rights against S, F, and X? Explain.

(f) In (c) and (d) above, what steps could B have taken to ensure the collectibility of the debts? Explain.

1. Walsh owns and operates a gas station and restaurant on a highway nearby a beautiful undeveloped lake region. Clark, interested in developing the area, purchased several acres of lake-front property and contracted with Mahoney, a building contractor, to construct an elaborate hotel and ten beautiful cottages. After learning these facts from Clark, Walsh expanded his restaurant and gas station in contemplation of a substantial increase in business. Subsequently, Clark changed his plans and breached his contract with Mahoney. Clark promptly notified Mahoney not to commence construction, and Mahoney complied with Clark's instruction.

   Walsh is now suing Clark for breach of contract. Walsh claims that he is a third party beneficiary under the contract between Clark and Mahoney and entitled to damages for the cost of expanding his business and the profits he would have earned had the contract been performed. In his suit against Clark, Walsh will

   a. Win in that he is third party creditor beneficiary.
   b. Lose in that he is a third party incidental beneficiary.
   c. Win in that he is a donee beneficiary.
   d. Win in that Clark and Mahoney have acted fraudulently.

2. Charles Lands offered to sell his business to Donald Bright. The assets consisted of real property, merchandise, office equipment, and the rights under certain contracts to purchase goods at an agreed price. In consideration for receipt of the aforementioned assets Bright was to pay $125,000 and assume all business liabilities owed by Lands. Bright accepted the offer and a written contract was signed by both parties. Under the circumstances the contract

   a. Represents an assignment of all the business assets and rights Lands owned and a delegation of whatever duties Lands was obliged to perform.
   b. Must be agreed to by all of Lands' creditors and the parties who had agreed to deliver goods to Lands.
   c. Frees Lands from all liability to his creditors once the purchase is consummated.
   d. Is too indefinite and uncertain to be enforced.

3. Matson loaned Donalds $1,000 at 8% interest for one year. Two weeks before the due date, Matson called upon Donalds and obtained his agreement in writing to modify the terms of the loan. It was agreed that on the due date Donalds would pay $850 to Cranston to who Matson owed that amount, and pay the balance plus interest to his son Arthur, to whom he wishes to make a gift. Under the modified terms of the loan, Cranston and/or Arthur have what legal standing?

   a. Cranston is a creditor beneficiary and Arthur is a donee beneficiary.
   b. Cranston has the right to prevent Matson's delegation if he gives timely notice.
   c. If Cranston is to be able to proceed against Donalds, he must have

received notice of Donald's promise to pay him the $850 prior to the due date.

    d.   Arthur is an incidental beneficiary.

4. Higgins contracted to pay $3,500 to Clark for 44 thirty-day accounts receivables that arose in the course of Clark's office equipment leasing business. Higgins subsequently paid the $3,500. What is the legal status of this contract?

    a.   The contract is within the Statute of Frauds.
    b.   If Higgins failed to notify the debtors whose accounts were purchased, they will, upon payment in good faith to Clark, have no liability to Higgins.
    c.   The contract in question is illegal because it violates the usury laws.
    d.   Higgins will be able to collect against the debtors free of the usual defenses which would be assertable against Clark, e.g., breach of contract.

5. Fennell and McLeod entered into a binding contract whereby McLeod was to perform routine construction services according to Fennell's blueprints. McLeod assigned the contract to Conerly. After the assignment

    a.   Fennell can bring suit under the doctrine of anticipatory breach.
    b.   McLeod extinguishes all his rights and duties under the contract.
    c.   McLeod extinguishes all his rights but is <u>not</u> relieved of his duties under the contract.
    d.   McLeod still has all his rights but is relieved of his duties under the contract.

6. Monroe purchased a ten-acre land site from Acme Land Developers, Inc. He paid 10% at the closing and gave his note for the balance secured by a 20-year mortgage. Three years later, Monroe found it increasingly difficult to make payments on the note and finally defaulted. Acme Land threatened to accelerate the loan and foreclose if he continued in default. It told him either to get the money or obtain an acceptable third party to assume the obligation. Monroe offered the land to Thompson for $1,000 less than the equity he had in the property. This was acceptable to Acme and at the closing Thompson paid the arrearage, executed a new mortgage and note, and had title transferred to his name. Acme surrendered Monroe's note and mortgage to him. The transaction in question is a (an)

    a.   Assignment and delegation.
    b.   Third party beneficiary contract.
    c.   Novation.
    d.   Purchase of land subject to a mortgage.

INTERPRETATION; RULES OF CONSTRUCTION; PAROL EVIDENCE RULE

UNIFORM COMMERCIAL CODE: ARTICLE 2: SALE OF GOODS

The following material includes several sections of Articles 1 and 2 which contain rules of interpretation and general rules of construction that are applied, in addition to several statutes in Article 2 specifically governing interpretation of contract provisions, rules of construction, and the parol evidence rule governing contracts for the sale of goods.

Section 1-103. Supplementary General Principles Of Law Applicable

Unless displaced by the particular provisions of this Act, the principles of law and equity, including the law merchant and the law relative to capacity to contract, principal and agent, estoppel, fraud, misrepresentation, duress, coercion, mistake, bankruptcy, or other validating or invalidating cause shall supplement its provisions.

Section 1-106. Remedies To Be Liberally Administered

(1) The remedies provided by this Act shall be liberally administered to the end that the aggrieved party may be put in as good a position as if the other party had fully performed but neither consequential or special nor penal damages may be had except as specifically provided in this Act or by other rule of law.

Section 1-203. Obligation Of Good Faith

Every contract or duty within this act imposes an obligation of good faith in its performance or enforcement.

Section 1-204. Time; Reasonable Time; "Seasonably"

(1) Whenever this Act requires any action to be taken within a reasonable time, any time which is not manifestly unreasonable may be fixed by agreement.

(2) What is a reasonable time for taking any action depends on the nature, purpose and circumstances of such action.

(3) An action is taken "seasonably" when it is taken at or within the time agreed or if no time is agreed at or within a reasonable time.

Section 1--205. Course Of Dealing And Usage Of Trade

(1) A course of dealing is a sequence of previous conduct between the

300

parties to a particular transaction which is fairly to be regarded as establishing a common basis of understanding for interpreting their expressions and other conduct.

(2) A usage of trade is any practice or method of dealing having such regularity of observance in a place, vocation or trade as to justify an expectation that it will be observed with respect to the transaction in question. The existence and scope of such a usage are to be proved as facts. If it is established that such a usage is embodied in a written trade code or similar writing the interpretation of the writing is for the court.

(3) A course of dealing between parties and any usage of trade in the vocation or trade in which they are engaged or of which they are or should be aware give particular meaning to and supplement or qualify terms of an agreement.

(4) The express terms of an agreement and an applicable course of dealing or usage of trade shall be construed whereever reasonable as consistent with each other; but when such construction is unreasonable express terms control both course of dealing and usage of trade and course of dealing controls usage of trade.

(5) An applicable usage of trade in the place where any part of performance is to occur shall be used in interpreting the agreement as to that part of the performance.

(6) Evidence of a relevant usage of trade offered by one party is not admissible unless and until he has given the other party such notice as the court finds sufficient to prevent unfair surprise to the latter.

Section 2--208. <u>Course Of Performance Or Practical Construction</u>

(1) Where the contract for sale involves repeated occasions for performance by either party with knowledge of the nature of the performance and opportunity for objection to it by the other, any course of performance accepted or acquiesced in without objection shall be relevant to determine the meaning of the agreement.

(2) The express terms of the agreement and any such course of performance, as well as any course of dealing and usage of trade, shall be construed whenever reasonable as consistent with each other; but when such construction is unreasonable, express terms shall control course of performance and course of performance shall control both course of dealing and usage of trade (Section 1--205) ....

Section 2-301. <u>General Obligations Of Parties</u>

The obligation of the seller is to transfer and deliver and that of the buyer is to accept and pay in accordance with the contract.

Section 2-308. Absence Of Specified Place For Delivery

Unless otherwise agreed

(a) The place for delivery of goods is the seller's place of business or if he has none his residence; but

(b) in a contract for sale of identified goods which to the knowledge of the parties at the time of contracting are in some other place, that place is the place for delivery....

Section 2-309. Absence Of Specific Time Provisions; Notice of Termination

(1) The time for shipment or delivery or any other action under a contract if not provided in this Article or agreed upon shall be a reasonable time.

(2) Where the contract provides for successive performances but is indefinite in duration it is valid for a reasonable time but unless otherwise agreed may be terminated at any time by either party.

(3) Termination of a contract by one party except on the happening of an agreed event requires that reasonable notification be received by the other party and an agreement dispensing with notification is invalid if its operation would be unconscionable.

PAROL EVIDENCE RULE

Section 2- 202. Final Written Expression; Parol Or Extrinsic Evidence

Terms with respect to which the confirmatory memoranda of the parties agree or which are otherwise set forth in a writing intended by the parties as a final expression of their agreement with respect to such terms as are included therein may not be contradicted by evidence of any prior agreement or of a contemporaneous oral agreement but may be explained or supplemented

(a) by course of dealing or usage of trade (Section 1-205) or by course of performance (Section 2-208); and

(b) by evidence of consistent additional terms unless the court finds the writing to have been intended also as a complete and exclusive statement of the terms of the agreement.

PAROL EVIDENCE RULE

CASE NO. 47

REYNOLDS v. ROBINSON

110 N.Y. 564   Oct. 1888

INTRODUCTION

The parol evidence rule is one of the most important rules of law. The parol evidence rule provides that if two parties enter into a written contract which is the "final expression of their agreement", then neither party can offer evidence at a trial of any oral or written agreement made either before or at the time the parties entered into their written contract which contradicts their written contract. However, the parol evidence rule does <u>not</u> bar either party from introducing evidence at a trial 1. to prove the contract was entered into as a result of one party committing fraud against the other, 2. to explain an <u>ambiguity</u> in the contract, 3. to prove that condition had to be met <u>before</u> the contract became effective (called condition precedent), or 4. that the parties entered into another contract <u>subsequently</u> to modify their written contract.

This case illustrates one of there four instances when parol evidence is admissible at a trial.

This action was brought to recover damages for a breach of an alleged contract for the purchase, by plaintiff, and sale by defendants, of a quantity of lumber.

The finding of the referee, which is supported by evidence, to the effect that the contract for the purchase and sale of the lumber on credit, contained in the correspondence between the parties, proceeded upon a contemporaneous oral understanding that the obligation of the defendants to sell and deliver was contingent upon their obtaining satisfactory reports from the commercial agencies as to the pecuniary responsibility of the plaintiff, brings the case within an exception to the general rule that a written contract cannot be varied by parol evidence, or rather it brings the case within the rule, now quite well established, that parol evidence is admissible to show that a written paper which, in form, is a complete contract, of which there has been a manual tradition, was, nevertheless, not to become a binding contract until the performance of some condition precedent resting in parol. Upon this ground, we think the evidence of the parol understanding, and also that the reports of the agencies were unsatisfactory; was properly admitted by the referee and sustained his report, and that the General Term erred in reversing his judgment. It is perhaps needless to say that such a defense is subject to suspicion, and that the rule stated should be cautiously applied to avoid mistake or imposition, and confined strictly to cases clearly within its reason.

(Judgment for Defendant seller)

<u>DISCUSSION QUESTION</u>: Why was the parol evidence rule adopted by courts?

1. S and B discussed the sale and purchase of certain stock. They then signed the following contract:

"February 3

S agrees to sell 100 shares of X Corp. stock to B for $50 a share, delivery of the stock to be made on March 5. B agrees to pay cash on delivery of the stock properly endorsed for transfer.

(Signed)   S

(Signed)   B."

B refused to perform, S sues B for damages. Would the court, on the trial, allow B, over S's objection, to testify:

(a)   that during the negotiations S falsely informed B that the stock had paid a dividend of $5 per share last year? Explain.

(b)   that, during the negotiations, S had threatened to prosecute B's son for the embezzlement of funds while B's son was in S's employ? Explain.

(c)   that the parties had discussed the sale of Y Corp. stock, and that neither had intended to make a contract dealing with X Corp. stock? Explain.

(d)   that, in the negotiations, S had promised B that he would give B 30 days after delivery to pay? Explain.

(e)   that, two weeks later, they had orally agreed to cancel the contract? Explain.

(f)   that, at the time of signing the contract, B had told S that before the agreement became operative, he (B) was going to investigate X Corp., and if he were not satisfied as to its financial condition the contract was to be cancelled, and that S had agreed to this? Explain.

PAROL EVIDENCE RULE

1. The parol evidence rules does not apply to

    a. Prior oral agreements which would normally have been included in
        the written contract.
    b. Oral agreements relating to and made contemporaneously with the
        written contract.
    c. Written agreements intended by the parties as the final expression
        of their agreement of the terms included in the written contract.
    d. Written agreements which were obtained by fraud.

2. The parol evidence rule

    a. Requires that certain types of contracts be in writing.
    b. Precludes the use of oral testimony to show that a written contract
        was fraudulently obtained.
    c. Eliminates the requirement of consideration if the rule is satisfied.
    d. Does not prohibit a subsequent oral modification of a written
        contract.

3. Walker and White entered into a written contract involving the purchase
    of certain used equipment by White. White claims that there were oral
    understandings between the parties which are included as a part of the
    contract. Walker pleads the parol evidence rule. The rule applies to

    a. Subsequent oral modifications of the written contract by the parties.
    b. Additional consistent terms even if the contract was not intended
        as a complete and exclusive listing of all terms of the agreement.
    c. A contemporaneous oral understanding of the parties which contradicts
        the terms of a written contract intended as the final expression of
        the agreement between the parties.
    d. Evidence in support of the oral modification based upon the perform-
        ance by Walker.

4. The parol evidence rule prohibits contradiction of a written contract
    through the proof of

    a. A previous oral contract.
    b. A subsequent written contract.
    c. The meaning or clarification of the contract's terms.
    d. A subsequent oral contract.

5. Austin is attempting to introduce oral evidence in court to explain or
    modify a written contract he made with Wade. Wade has pleaded the parol
    evidence rule. In which of the following circumstances will Austin not
    be able to introduce the oral evidence?

    a. The contract contains an obvious ambiguity on the point at issue.
    b. There was a mutual mistake of fact by the parties regarding the
        subject matter of the contract.
    c. The modification asserted was made several days after the written

contract had been executed.

   d. The contract indicates that it was intended as the "entire contract" between the parties and the point is covered in detail.

6. Marsh and Lennon entered into an all-inclusive written contract involving the purchase of a tract of land. Lennon claims that there was a contemporaneous oral agreement between the parties which called for the removal by Marsh of several large rocks on the land. Marsh relies upon the parol evidence rule to avoid having to remove the rocks. Which of the following is correct?

   a. The parol evidence rule does not apply to contemporaneous oral agreements.

   b. Since the Statute of Frauds was satisfied in respect to the contract for the purchase of the land, the parol evidence rule does not apply.

   c. Since the oral agreement does not contradict the term of the written contract, the oral agreement is valid despite the parol evidence rule.

   d. The parol evidence rule applies and Lennon will be precluded from proving the oral promise in the absence of fraud.

7. Elrod is attempting to introduce oral evidence in court to explain or modify a written contract he made with Weaver. Weaver has pleaded the parol evidence rule. In which of the following circumstances will Elrod <u>not</u> be able to introduce the oral evidence?

   a. The modification asserted was made several days after the written contract had been executed.

   b. The contract indicates that it was intended as the "entire contract" between the parties, and the point is covered in detail.

   c. There was a mutual mistake of fact by the parties regarding the subject matter of the contract.

   d. The contract contains an obvious ambiguity on the point at issue.

8. With respect to written contracts, the parol evidence rule applies

   a. Exclusively to the purchase or sale of goods.
   b. To subsequent oral modifications.
   c. Only to prior or contemporaneous oral modifications.
   d. To modifications by prior written or oral agreements.

D.D.C.A.D.D

STATUTE OF LIMITATIONS

The Statute of Limitations is the name given to a collection of statutes which provide the time within which an action or proceeding may be commenced. If an action or proceeding is not commenced within the applicable statute of limitations, the action or proceeding cannot be maintained, and may be dismissed by the court if the statute of limitations is raised as an affirmative defense.

NEW YORK GENERAL OBLIGATIONS LAW

Section 17-101. Acknowledgment Or New Promise Must Be In Writing

An acknowledgment or promise contained in a writing signed by the party to be charged thereby is the only competent evidence of a new or continuing contract whereby to take an action out of the operation of the provisions of limitations of time for commencing actions under the civil practice law and rules other than action for the recovery of real property. This section does not alter the effect of a payment of principal or interest. (eff. 1963)

Section 17-103. Agreements Waiving The Statute Of Limitation

1. A promise to waive, to extend, or not to plead the statute of limitation applicable to an action arising out of a contract express or implied in fact or in law, if made after the accrual of the cause of action and made, either with or without consideration, in a writing signed by the promisor or his agent is effective, according to its terms, to prevent interposition of the defense of the statute of limitations in an action or proceeding commenced within the time that would be applicable if the cause of action had arisen at the date of the promise, or within such shorter time as may be provided in the promise.

2. A promise to waive, to extend, or not to plead the statute of limitation may be enforced as provided in this section by the person to whom the promise is made or for whose benefit it is expressed to be made or by any person who, after the making of the promise, succeeds or is subrogated to the interest of either of them.

3. A promise to waive, to extend, or not to plead the statute of limitation has no effect to extend the time limited by statute for commencement of an action or proceeding for any greater time or in any other manner than that provided in this section, or unless made as provided in this section.

4. This section

a. does not change the requirements or the effect with respect to the statute of limitation, of an acknowledgment or promise to pay, or a payment or part payment of principal or interest, or a stipulation made in an action or proceeding;

b. does not affect the power of the court to find that by reason of conduct of the party to be charged it is inequitable to permit him to interpose the defense of the statute of limitation; and

c. does not apply in any respect to a cause of action to foreclose a mortgage of real property or a mortgage of a lease of real property, or to a cause of action to recover a judgment affecting the title to or the possession, use or enjoyment of real property, or a promise or waiver with respect to any statute of limitation applicable thereto. (eff. 1963, as amended)

NEW YORK CIVIL PRACTICE LAW AND RULES (C.P.L.R.)

Section 203. Methods Of Computing Periods Of Limitation Generally

(a) Accrual of cause of action and interposition of claim. The time within which an action must be commenced, except as otherwise expressly prescribed, shall be computed from the time the cause of action accrued to the time the claim is interposed.... (eff. Sept. 1, 1970, as amended)

....

Following is a representative sample of some of the titles and subtitles of the applicable statute of limitations sections. In addition, portions of C.P.L.R. 213 (dealing primarily with contracts) are included.

Section 211. Actions To Be Commenced Within Twenty Years

(a) On a Bond...

(b) On a money judgment...

(c) By state for real property...

(d) By grantee of state for real property...

Section 213. Actions To Be Commenced Within Six Years....

The following actions must be commenced within six years:

1. an action for which no limitation is specifically prescribed by law;

2. an action upon a contractual obligation or liability express or implied, **except as provided in section two hundred thirteen-a of this article or article 2 of the uniform commercial code;**

...

4. an action upon a bond or note, the payment of which is secured by a mortgage upon real property, or upon a bond or note and mortgage so secured, or upon a mortgage of real property, or any interest therein;

                                    ...
    6. an action based upon mistake;
                                    ...
    8. an action based upon fraud; the time within which the action must
be commenced shall be computed from the time the plaintiff or the person
under whom he claims discovered the fraud, or could with reasonable
diligence have discovered it. (eff. Sept. 1966, as amended)

    Section 213-a.   Actions to be commenced within four years; residential
                      rent overcharge
    An action on a residential rent overcharge shall be commenced within
    four years of such overcharge. (eff. April 1, 1984).

    Section 214. Actions To Be Commenced Within Three Years....
    The following actions must be commenced within three years: . . .
    2. an action to recover upon a liability, penalty or forfeiture created
or imposed by statute . . . .

    3. an action to recover a chattel or damages for the taking or detaining
of a chattel;

    4. an action to recover damages for an injury to property;

    5. an action to recover damages for a personal injury....

                            .... (eff. June 16, 1981, as amended)

    Section 214-a.   Action For Medical Malpractice To Be Commenced Within
                      Two Years And Six Months....

    Section 215.   Actions To Be Commenced Within One Year....

    The following actions shall be commenced within one year:

    1. an action against a sheriff, coroner or constable...
                            ....
    3. an action to recover damages for assault, battery, false imprison-
ment, malicious prosecution, libel, slander, false words causing special
damages, or a violation of the right of privacy...;

    4. an action to enforce a penalty or forfeiture created by statute
and given wholly or partly to any person who will prosecute...;

    5. an action upon an arbitration award;

    6. an action to recover any overcharge of interest or to enforce a
penalty for such overcharge;

    7. an action by a tenant pursuant to subdivision three of section two
hundred twenty-three-b of the real property law [prohibition of retaliation

against a tenant by landlord]. (as amended Sept. 1, 1979)

UNIFORM COMMERCIAL CODE: ARTICLE 2: SALE OF GOODS

Section 2-725. Statute Of Limitations In Contracts For Sale.

(1) An action for breach of any contract for sale must be commenced within four years after the cause of action has accrued. By the original agreement the parties may reduce the period of limitation to not less than one year but may not extend it.

(2) A cause of action accrues when the breach occurs, regardless of the aggrieved party's lack of knowledge of the breach....

....

1. Anderson, CPA, performed services for several years for Winfield doing
   business as Winfield's New Ventures. Since Winfield's business appeared
   to have excellent potential, Anderson did not press for collection of
   his fees. The balance owing by Winfield has grown substantially, and
   $1,000 of the balance cannot be enforced because it is barred by the
   Statute of Limitations. Winfield recently sent a check for $1,000
   marked "on account". Anderson applied the check to the balance barred
   by the statute. Anderson's application of the payment

   a. Should have been applied to the oldest balance not barred by the
      Statute of Limitations.
   b. Is proper.
   c. Can be reversed by Winfield as he has the option of determining how
      his payments are to be allocated.
   d. Is subject to review by the courts because the Statute of Limitations
      is involved.

2. The Statute of Limitations normally

   a. Does not apply to written contracts.
   b. Has no application to unilateral contracts.
   c. Requires that the lawsuit be concluded within a specific period
      of time.
   d. Commences (begins to run) from the date of the breach of contract.

3. When a lengthy delay has occurred between the breach of a contract and
   the commencement of the lawsuit, the statute of limitations defense
   may be raised. The statute

   a. Is three years irrespective of the type of legal action the
      plaintiff is bringing.
   b. Does not apply to an action brought in a court of equity.
   c. Is a defense to recovery if the requisite period of time has elapsed.
   d. Fixes a period of time in which the plaintiff must commence the
      action or be barred from recovery, regardless of the defendant's
      conduct during the period.

GLOSSARY OF SOME COMMON LEGAL TERMS AND PHRASES

The following legal terms and phrases are used in studying the law of contracts and in reading judicial proceedings. This list is not complete, but will aid students in understanding legal terms, court decisions, statutes and legal text material.

Abuse of discretion: Clearly erroneous legal judgment. The term is usually used to refer to a determination made by an administrative agency which the losing party claims has no foundation in fact or in law. The determination of an administrative agency may be set aside by a court upon the court finding an abuse of discretion.

Acceptance of offer: The offeree's assent to (or compliance with) the terms and conditions of an offer which results in the formation of a contract.

Accord: Agreement to a compromise settlement.

Accord and Satisfaction: An agreement between two disputing parties to settle an obligation, usually for less than the terms of the original contract. The accord is the agreement and the satisfaction occurs when the agreement is executed (payment is tendered). The legal effect of an accord and satisfaction is that the original debt is discharged.

Acknowledgment: A declaration made by a party to a notary public that his signature on a document was executed voluntarily by him.

Action: A lawsuit in court.

Action remanded: A decision of an appellate court to send back a judicial proceeding to the lower court for a new determination or a new trial.

Adjudge: To give judgment.

Adjudication: A decision of a court.

Administrative agency: A governmental agency created by legislative act which is given quasi-judicial powers to promulgate and to enforce particular laws dealing with specialized subject matter. (E.g., Federal Trade Commission, Internal Revenue Service, Worker's Compensation Board, or Motor Vehicle Bureau). Administrative agencies have power to make determinations which are binding upon the parties. The determination may be subject to judicial review by a court if a party wishes to appeal the determination on specific grounds (such as the agency exceeding its authority).

Administrator (Administratrix - f.): A person authorized by the Surrogate's Court (sometimes called Probate Court) to administer the disposition of the estate of a deceased person who dies without a will (duties are

312

similar to an executor of an estate).

Affidavit: a statement sworn to and signed before a notary public.

Affirmation: A statement of solemn declaration (usually has same or similar effect as an affidavit), but doesn't have to be sworn to before a notary public.

Affirmative defense: The setting forth by defendant of a legal reason why he cannot be held liable to the plaintiff. This is contained in the defendant's answer to the plaintiff's complaint, stating that defendant has a technical defense to plaintiff's action, such as Statute of Limitations, Statute of Frauds, Infancy, Bankruptcy, etc.

Agreement: Contract.

Allegation: A statement in the pleadings by either plaintiff or defendant as to what he intends to prove at trial.

Allege: To make a statement of fact; to plead.

Annul: To nullify or void a prior act.

Answer: Responsive pleading by defendant, setting forth the defenses to the plaintiff's complaint.

Answer dismissed (Answer stricken): A court decision, whereby the court has decided defendant's answer does not merit further consideration; in effect, judgment for the plaintiff.

Anticipatory breach: The assertion by one party to a contract repudiating the contract before the time for his or her performance of the contract; in effect the party gives notice that he will breach the contract and that he will not perform.

Appearance: The technical presence in court in person or by an attorney, either as plaintiff or defendant in an action.

Appellant: One who appeals a decision to a higher court.

Appellate court: A court where an appeal is heard, appealing a decision of a lower court.

Appellee: The person against whom the appeal is taken. (sometimes called "respondent").

Arbitrary and capricious: Without any rational basis in fact or law.

Arbitration: Submission of a dispute to an impartial third party (arbitrator), whereby the parties agree in advance to accept the decision of the arbitrator as a substitute for a court decision.

Assent: A declaration of willingness to do or accept something in compliance with a request.

Assignee: One to whom a right or interest is transferred.

Assignment: The transfer of one's right or interest to another.

Assignor: One who transfers his right.

Attachment: A legal procedure granted by a court at any time before, during or after an action has been commenced which authorizes a court officer, such as a marshall or sheriff, to take and hold property of the defendant until the end of the trial to secure satisfaction of any judgment that may ultimately be entered against the defendant in the action. An attachment will be granted by the court only on specific grounds such as defendant is about to leave the state or dissipate or hide his assets, or for various other statutory reasons.

Bankruptcy proceeding: A court proceeding instituted either by the debtor or the debtor's creditors in the proper Federal District Court according to the provisions of the Federal Bankruptcy Act which governs all bankruptcy proceedings in the United States. The bankruptcy proceeding is usually instituted because the debtor is unable to pay his debts as they become due and the debtor or the debtor's creditors seek to have the Bankruptcy Court adjudicate the debtor a bankrupt. In a bankruptcy proceeding the debtor turns over all of his assets (which are not exempt by statute) to the trustee in bankruptcy who administers the bankrupt estate. The trustee in bankruptcy collects and reduces to cash all assets, determines the validity of creditors' claims and distributes the bankrupt estate's assets to the creditors according to a priority list set forth in the Federal Bankruptcy Act. The legal effect of the debtor being discharged in bankruptcy is that the debtor has no further liability for the payment of those debts that are discharged in bankruptcy. In 1981, over 350,000 individuals who owed about six billion dollars to their creditors were discharged in bankruptcy while about 15,000 businesses that owed approximately four billion dollars were adjudicated bankrupt. Note: The inability of a party to pay his debts does not necessarily mean he is bankrupt. A party is not bankrupt until the Federal District Court adjudges him to be bankrupt.

Beneficiary: A party entitled to receive money, property, or other benefit. (see Trust).

Bequeath: Transfer of personal property pursuant to the terms of a will.

Bilateral contract: A contract formed by the offeror and offeree exchanging promises. (E.g., seller promises to sell to buyer in exchange for buyer's promise to buy from seller.)

Bill of Particulars: A written statement (which in certain cases must be sworn to or affirmed) filed in court by a party in a lawsuit specifying in

314

detail the claims of that party. The Bill of Particulars is furnished in response to the other party's request for specific information and may become part of the pleadings in the action.

Bona fide: In good faith.

Breach of contract: Failure by a party to fulfill the terms and conditions of the contract.

Cause of action: The legal basis of the plaintiff's action in court which is set forth in plaintiff's complaint against the defendant.

Certiorari: The legal procedure of bringing the record of a lower court before a higher court to determine whether the lower court acted within the limits of its authority.

Cestui que trust: The beneficiary under a trust.

Codify: To set forth rules of law in a statute or code.

Common law: The system of law that originated and developed in England based on court decisions rather than on codified written laws.

Compensatory damages: Monetary award made by the court or jury to a party in an action to compensate for loss or injury suffered, caused by a wrong of the other party.

Complaint: The pleading in which plaintiff alleges his cause(s) of action against defendant and sets forth a claim for relief. The complaint must be filed in court at some prescribed time.

Complaint dismissed: A decision of the court that dismisses the plaintiff's complaint because the court determines the complaint has no legal merit. (E.g., The complaint fails to state a legal cause of action against defendant.)

Composition agreement: An agreement between a debtor and two or more of his creditors whereby such creditors agree to accept a lesser amount as payment in full.

Condition precedent: An event which must happen before a certain right or duty is created under a contract.

Condition subsequent: An event which operates to discharge a party from his duty to perform under a contract.

Confession of Judgment: The debtor's written authorization that a judgment be entered against him without notice in the event he subsequently defaults in payment. The legal effect of a confession of judgment is that the debtor waives the right to assert any defenses to the action brought against him and consents in advance to the court entering a judgment against him without having the plaintiff's summons and complaint served.

Contempt: Conduct by a party which violates an order of a legislative or judicial body which interferes with the due administration of law and which is punishable by fine or prison or both.

Contract: An agreement between two or more parties which is enforceable by law.

Contribution: Right of one party who is liable to have another party(ies) share in the loss.

Conveyance: Transfer of legal title to property.

Counterclaim: A claim made by the defendant against the plaintiff in the same lawsuit in which the defendant claims to have a cause of action against the plaintiff. The counterclaim does not have to arise out of the same facts and circumstances as plaintiff's complaint.

Counteroffer: A different offer made by the offeree to the offeror in response to the offeror's offer. The counteroffer is a rejection of the offeror's offer.

Covenant: A clause contained in a written agreement or instrument (deed) which recites that a party promises to do a specified act or to refrain from doing a specified act. Covenants are usually included in deeds, agreements for the sale of a business, and employment contracts.

Creditor: A party to whom a debt is owed.

Crime: An act committed or omitted in violation of a law forbidding or commanding it which imposes punishment upon conviction. The government prosecutes offenders.

Cross-claim: In a court proceeding, a claim by one defendant against one or more of the other co-defendants in the action.

Damages: Monetary award which a party may recover in a proceeding as compensation for loss or injury.

Debtor: The party who owes something, usually money, to a creditor.

Decedent: Person who died.

Deceit: A tort involving intentional misrepresentation of a fact.

Decision: The judgment, order, or decree of the court.

Decree: Judgment or order of a court.

Deed: A written instrument signed by the grantor (seller or donor) which transfers title to real property.

Default: The act of failing to proceed in a court proceeding within the required time limits (e.g., defendant does not answer the plaintiff's summons and complaint within the time allowed by law or the failure to pay an obligation or otherwise perform within the required time.

Defendant: The party against whom a lawsuit is commenced by the plaintiff.

Defense: The answer opposing and contesting a charge or claim in an action commenced by the plaintiff. (See also affirmative defense as to one type of defense)

Demurrer: A motion to dismiss the other party's lawsuit on the ground that the other party's allegations are legally insufficient to state a claim, even if true.

Deponent: A person making an oral or written statement under oath (e.g., the person signing an affidavit or the person testifying under oath in a legal proceeding).

Deposition: Testimony of a witness under oath taken before the trial. The witness is questioned, the questions and answers are transcribed, and the witness signs the stenographic transcript under oath. The deposition may be used in subsequent court proceedings.

Devise: Transfer of real property pursuant to the terms of a will.

Dictum: An opinion or observation by the judge on a matter not before the court that has only incidental bearing on the case.

Disaffirm: To repudiate or rescind a contract.

Discharge in bankruptcy: An order or decree rendered by the Bankruptcy Court which discharges a bankrupt party from all debts which are provable except those debts specifically excepted by statute which survive bankruptcy (e.g., alimony, child support). (See bankruptcy proceedings.)

Disclosure Proceedings: Encompasses various legal proceedings to enable opposing parties in a lawsuit to obtain further information from each other about the allegations to be proved at trial. Disclosure includes Bill of Particulars, depositions, interrogatories, and discovery.

Discovery Proceedings: A legal procedure by which opposing parties in a lawsuit may obtain information from each other in order to assist each party in preparation for trial.

Dissenting opinion: The decision of one or more judges in an appellate court who disagree with the majority decision of the court. The dissenting

317

opinion is not the decision of the court. The majority decision is binding on the parties.

Divisible contract: A contract in which performance may be apportioned - usually to the price (as opposed to an entire contract).

Donee: A party to whom a gift is made.

Donor: The party who makes a gift.

Due process of law: A party's right to a fair hearing before the party may be deprived of life, liberty, or property. The essential elements of due process of law are notice and an opportunity to be heard and to defend in an orderly proceeding adopted to the nature of the case: the guaranty of due process requires that every party have protection of a day in court and benefits of general law.

Duress: The use of force or coercion to make a person act against his will.

Emancipated infant: An infant (under 18 years in New York) who is legally released from the control or custody of his parents or guardians.

Eminent domain: The right of a government (federal, state, or local) to take private property for public use upon paying just compensation to the owner.

Enforceable contract: A contract which imposes duties upon each of the parties to the contract and which affords legal remedies if there is a breach of contract.

Enjoin: To forbid the doing of a specific act by court order. The court order may be called either an injunction or restraining order.

Entire contract: A contract in which full and complete performance by one party is required to be given in exchange for full and complete performance by the other party. When there is an entire contract, performance cannot be apportioned (as opposed to a divisible contract).

Equity: A system of jurisprudence developed in England and adopted in the United States that is separate from the common law courts and supplements the common law. A Court of Equity has jurisdiction over the person and is empowered to administer justice according to fairness when there is no adequate remedy at law available. (E.g., a Court of Equity has the power to (1) decree specific performance of a real estate contract by a seller if requested to do so by the buyer, (2) issue an injunction, and (3) reform a contract which contains a mutual mistake.)

Escrow agreement: An agreement by which one party to a contract deposits documents and/or money with an agreed upon third party, called the escrowee. The escrowee holds the property until certain agreed conditions are met at which time the escrowee delivers the property held in escrow to the other party to the contract. The usual escrowee may be an accountant, attorney, or bank. The escrowee is also called an escrow agent.

Estate: All of the assets and liabilities owned and owed by a party on a particular date. (E.g., estate of a decedent; bankrupt estate).

Estoppel: A legal bar which prevents a party from saying something contrary to his prior words or conduct because the other party relied on his prior words or conduct. The doctrine of estoppel is applied to prevent injury to an innocent party who has relied to his detriment on the words or conduct of the other party.

Examination before trial: A discovery procedure where either party to a lawsuit may question under oath the opposing parties or witnesses as part of the judicial proceeding (sometimes called deposition).

Exculpatory clause: A clause in a contract that excuses a party from liability to another for his own negligence.

Executed contract: A contract which has been fully performed by both parties. Sometimes the term is used to refer to a contract that has been signed by all parties.

Execution of a contract: The signing of a contract by the parties.

Execution of judgment: A remedy given by the court, which directs a court officer, such as a marshall or sheriff, to enforce collection of the judgment, usually by seizing and selling the debtor's property and delivering the net proceeds to the judgment creditor (or as much as is necessary) to satisfy the judgment.

Executor (Executrix -f.): Party named in a will to administer the estate of a deceased person. The executor cannot begin to serve until authorized to do so by the Surrogate's Court (In some states called the Probate Court).

Executory contract: Contract which has not yet been fully performed by both parties.

Exemplary damages: See punitive damages.

Exempt property: Specific property designated by statute that a debtor may lawfully keep free from attachment or execution.

Ex parte application: An application made by a party in a lawsuit to the court seeking a court order which will bind the other party without giving notice to the other party that an application has been made. (E.g., temporary restraining order which legally restrains the party from transferring certain assets during the lawsuit.)

319

Express contract: A contract where the terms are agreed upon (as opposed to an implied contract).

Felony: A serious crime which imposes a minimum prison term of one year.

Fiduciary: A party who holds a position of trust and confidence and who is legally held to a high standard of conduct. A fiduciary has the duty to act with undivided loyalty and the duty to act in good faith at all times. (E.g., attorney, executor, administrator, trustee, guardian, agent, officer, director.)

Firm offer: A signed written offer made by the offeror which by its terms will be held open by the offeror for a certain period of time. A firm offer (made by a merchant) is irrevocable during the stated period (but not more than three months) even though no consideration is given for the firm offer. (See UCC 2-205 for special interpretation).

Forebearance: Refraining from doing an act that one has a legal right to do.

Foreclosure: A legal proceeding which enables the mortgagee to sell real property which has been mortgaged if the mortgagor defaults under the terms of the mortgage. The real property is sold in a foreclosure sale to satisfy the mortgage debt. The mortgagor is liable for any unpaid deficiency and is entitled to any surplus realized from the foreclosure sale.

Fraud: A false representation of a material fact, made with knowledge of its falsity, with intent to induce the other party to contract, which is relied on, and which causes injury.

Garnishment: A legal proceeding whereby money or property of a debtor in the possession of another party (the garnishee) is applied to payment of the judgment against the debtor. The garnishment proceeding is enforced by a court officer such as a marshall or sheriff. Garnishment of an employee's wages, known as an Income Execution, is a legal proceeding whereby the employer is directed to deduct 10% of the employee's salary and to deliver said sum to the Court officer for the judgment creditor of the employee until the judgment debt (principal and interest) is paid.

Good faith purchaser for value: One who purchases for value without know-ledge or notice of any defect in title or any other legal infirmity of the seller or the property.

Goods: Personal property which is movable.

Grantee: Party to whom a grant of real property is made. The instrument used to convey title to real property is called a deed.

Grantor: Party who conveys title to real property to grantee by deed.

Guarantor: Party who guarantees; a party who promises to answer for the debt, default or miscarriage of another.

Guaranty: Agreement made by a guarantor to the creditor that the guarantor will pay the debt of another or guarantee the due performance of a contract by another party.

Guardian: A person appointed by the court to have legal custody and control of another person or his property or both. Usually, a legal guardian is judicially appointed to act for another who is under a legal disability (such as an infant or an incompetent).

Holder in due course: The holder of commercial paper (checks, promissory notes, drafts, and certificates of deposit) who takes it for value, in good faith, without notice that it is overdue or has been dishonored, and without knowledge or notice that there is any defense or claim against it on the part of any person.

Illegal: Any act declared by statute to be a crime or unlawful.

Implied contract: Contract which is formed on the basis of the conduct of the parties rather than their express agreement (as opposed to an express contract).

Indemnify: To protect a party against any loss or damage or injury.

Indemnity: A duty of one party to reimburse another party or hold him harmless for any loss, damage or injury incurred.

Infant: A person under 18 years of age. (Statutory definition in New York State and almost all other states.)

Injunction: A court order that directs a party to do or not to do some specified act. A party who disobeys a court injunction is subject to fine or prison or both.

Injury: A wrong that results when one party violates another's rights.

Irrevocable offer: An offer in which the offeror agrees not to revoke the offer during a specified time. Any attempted revocation of an enforceable **irrevocable offer has no legal effect.**

Insolvency in the bankruptcy sense: A party is insolvent in the bankruptcy sense when his total liabilities exceeds his total assets at fair market value.

Insolvency in the equity sense: A party is insolvent in the equity sense when he is unable to pay his debts as they become due in the regular course of business. (Note: Do not confuse bankruptcy with insolvency.)

Intestate: A person who dies without a will.

Joint and several liability: When two or more parties are jointly and sever-
    ally liable, the creditor or claimant at his option may sue one or more
    of the parties separately or all of them together.

Joint liability: Liability which may be imposed only if all defendants who
    are liable are sued together in one lawsuit.

Judgment: The final order or decision of the court in an action.

Judgment affirmed: On appeal, the decision of the lower court is upheld by
    the appellate court.

Judgment by confession: See Confession of Judgment.

Judgment creditor: A creditor in whose favor a money judgment has been
    entered by a court of law and who has not yet been paid by the judgment
    debtor.

Judgment debtor: A party against whom a money judgment has been entered by a
    court of law.

Judgment for defendant: The court enters a decision in favor of the
    defendant (i.e. the plaintiff loses).

Judgment for plaintiff: The court enters a decision in favor of the plaintiff.

Judgment on the pleadings: A judgment whereby the court determines a party
    is entitled to a judgment after all pleadings are filed, on the ground
    there is no question of fact remaining to be decided.

Judgment remanded: On appeal, the appellate court sends the action or
    proceeding back to the lower court for a new trial or hearing.

Judgment reversed: On appeal, the appellate court overrules the decision of
    the lower court (i.e. gives opposite decision or modifies decision or
    sends back to lower court for new trial). (See also Judgment remanded)

Judicial proceeding: A court proceeding.

Judicial sale: A sale of property made pursuant to an order of the court.

Jurisdiction: The power of the court to hear and determine the subject matter
    in controversy between the parties.

Jury: A specified number of impartial persons who decide questions of fact
    at a trial under the guidance of a judge.By statute, the size of the
    jury depends on the type of judicial proceeding, such as, civil,
    criminal or grand jury proceeding.

Laches: An unreasonable delay by one party in initiating legal proceedings or asserting legal rights which bars the party from doing so.

Legacy: Personal property that is given to a party named in a will.

Letters of Administration: The appointment given by a Surrogate's Court (in some states called Probate Court) to a party called the administrator of the estate to administer the estate of a deceased who died without leaving a will. The administrator cannot begin to serve until he receives the letters of administration from the court.

Letters Testamentary: The appointment given by a Surrogate's Court (in some states called Probate Court) to the party named as executor of the estate in the deceased person's will, to administer the estate of a deceased. The executor cannot begin to serve until he receives letters testamentary from the court.

Levy: Seizure of property by a court officer (usually a marshall or sheriff) in execution of a judgment or other order of the court.

Libel: Any false written statement that damages a person by defaming (attacking, maligning) his character or exposing him to ridicule.

Lien: A legal claim that a party has on the property of another for payment of a debt. If the debt is not paid, the lienholder may institute a legal proceeding to sell the property to apply the net proceeds to pay the debt owed to him.

Liquidated claim: A definite and fixed sum of money that is owed, and about which there is no honest dispute between the debtor and creditor.

Liquidated damages: A specific sum of money which the parties to a contract agree will be paid by one party to the other as damages in the event of a breach of contract. A liquidated damage clause will be enforced by a court only if the amount of damages is difficult to determine and the amount of liquidated damages agreed to is reasonable in relation to anticipated loss. If these two tests are not met, the court will declare the liquidated damage clause to be a penalty that is void and unenforceable.

Mechanic's lien: A claim against another's real property created pursuant to statute to secure priority of payment for the value of work performed and materials furnished to another party. If the mechanic's lien is not paid within a specified time, the holder of the mechanic's lien may foreclose against the property and sell it and apply the net proceeds to satisfy the mechanic's lien.

Merchant: A person who regularly deals in a specific kind of goods. (See U.C.C. 2 - 104 (1) for formal definition).

Misdemeanor: A crime less serious than a felony which imposes a prison term of less than one year.

Misrepresentation: A false statement of material fact made without knowledge that it is a false statement.

Mitigation of damages: The duty of an injured party to take reasonable action to prevent damages from increasing as a result of a breach of contract.

Modification of agreement: New agreement which changes one or more of the terms of the prior agreement.

Mortgage: A legal interest in real property created by a written instrument which the owner (mortgagor) gives to his creditor (mortgagee) as security for a debt or other obligation that the owner owes to his creditor. If the debt or other obligation is not paid, the creditor (mortgagee) may foreclose against the property and sell it and apply the net proceeds to satisfy the debt or obligation.

Mortgagee: The party to whom a mortgage is given, usually the creditor.

Mortgagor: The party who gives the mortgage, usually the debtor.

Motion: An application to the court by one of the parties in the action or proceeding, requesting the court to make an order or give some form of relief.

Motion for summary judgment: Motion made by a party to the action that seeks judgment in his favor, by claiming there are no issues of fact to be determined and that the decision can be granted by the court on the pleadings, affidavits and other papers without the necessity of a formal trial.

Motion to dismiss: Motion made by a party to the action that seeks to have the other party's pleadings stricken, thereby obtaining a decision without a trial. (Sometimes, an application for a motion to dismiss the plaintiff's complaint is made by the defendant at the trial, alleging that plaintiff has failed to prove a prima facie case.)

Mutuality of obligation: Reciprocal obligation of the parties is required to make a contract binding on both parties. (Both parties must be bound to the contract or neither is bound.)

Negligence: Failure to exercise reasonable care. (An unintentional tort.)

Negative covenant: An agreement by one party not to do a specific act.

Novation: An agreement between the creditor and the debtor to substitute a new debt or a new debtor for an existing debt or debtor. When a novation occurs, the old debt or debtor is discharged from liability.

Offer: An oral or written communication made by one party to another party indicating an intent to enter into a contractual relationship.

Offeree: Party to whom the offer is made.

Offeror: Party who makes the offer.

Operation of law: A legal result happens automatically by operation of law when certain events occur (e.g., death of employee terminates employment contract by operation of law).

Option contract: An agreement to hold an offer open for a specified period of time.

Ordinance: A statute or regulation usually enacted by a local government or an agency of a local government (e.g., zoning board).

Parol evidence rule: A rule of evidence which prohibits a party from offering any evidence of a prior or contemporaneous oral agreement or a prior written agreement which contradicts the clear and unambiguous terms of a written contract that is the final expression of their agreement. (Note: there are certain exceptions to the parol evidence rule.)

Per curiam decision: The opinion of the entire court not attributed to any specific judge.

Personal property: All property other than real estate.

Petition: A petition is in the nature of a pleading seeking one or more specific remedies and is filed by the petitioner with the court in special judicial proceedings.

Petitioner: Party who signs and files a petition with the court.

Plaintiff: The party who initiates the lawsuit in court against one or more defendants by having a summons and complaint served against the defendant(s).

Pleadings: The formal allegations presented to the court by plaintiff and defendant which sets forth the causes of actions and defenses. Pleadings includes the complaint, the answer, the defenses, the counterclaims, and reply to counterclaim.

Pre-existing duty: A duty already existing under a contract.

Prima facie: Evidence which by itself establishes the claim or defense of the party. (Presumed to be true unless disproved by evidence to the contrary.

Privity of contract: The legal relationship of the two parties to a contract. The parties to a contract are in privity of contract with each other.

Probate: A judicial proceeding in the Surrogate's Court brought by the appropriate party (usually the named Executor) to prove that the will is the valid last will and testament of the testator.

Promissory estoppel: The doctrine of law that a promise will be enforced even though no consideration is given for the promise in order to prevent an injustice where the promissor should have expected the promissee to rely on his promise and the promissee substantially changed his position in reliance upon the promise.

Property rights: The rights and interests a party has in property that is owned by him or other parties.

Punitive damages: Damages awarded by a court or jury to a plaintiff against a defendant in excess of actual loss suffered by plaintiff. Punitive damages are imposed to punish the defendant for the wrong where there is evidence that defendant acted with malice when he committed the wrongful act. Punitive damages are also called exemplary damages.

Quantum Meruit: An action based on quantum meruit seeks to recover the fair and reasonable value of services rendered. Quantum meruit is sought when there is no contract between the parties and is based on equity that one should not be unjustly enriched at the expense of another, meaning payment as much as he reasonable deserves.

Quasi-contract: An obligation imposed by law whish arises from the voluntary act of one of the parties or some relation between the parties and not from any agreement between the parties. The doctrine of quasi-contract is based on the equitable principle that a party should not be unjustly enriched at the expense of another.

Ratify a contract: To adopt or affirm a previous voidable contract by words or conduct. (E.g., an adult may ratify a contract he made while he was a 17 year old infant.)

Real property: Land and anything permanently attached to land.

Receiver: A party appointed by the court during the litigation to take legal custody of property of a party involved in the litigation until the litigation is concluded.

Reformation: An equitable remedy that the court grants to revise or reform a written contract to conform to the real intention (agreement) of the parties. Reformation is usually granted where a mistake is made by both parties in the written contract.

Reimbursement: To pay back or refund.

Rejection of an offer: (rejecting an offer): The offeree's refusal to accept
     the offer made by the offeror. Rejection may be by oral or written
     communication or by conduct (e.g., not responding).

Release: To give up a legal right or claim which one party has or may have
     against another.

Remedy: A legal means of enforcing a right or redressing a wrong.

Reply: A pleading filed by the plaintiff in a court proceeding which re-
     sponds to the defendant's counterclaim.

Representative capacity: One who acts on behalf of another and not for him-
     self. (E.g., an executor acts on behalf of the estate of the decedent;
     an agent acts on behalf of a principal.)

Rescind: To disaffirm, annul, or cancel a contract.

Rescission: An equitable remedy granted by the court which results in the
     cancellation of a contract and the restoration of the parties to the
     same position they were in before the contract.

Res Judicata: A matter which has been finally adjudicated by a judicial
     decision. The rule of res judicata prohibits the same factual dispute
     between the same two parties to be tried again by a court after the
     final judgment has been entered and after all appeals have been
     exhausted.

Respondent: A party that answers a petition filed in a judicial proceeding.
     Respondent is also the party opposing an appellant on an appeal.

Restatement of Law: An exhaustive and scholarly statement and treatment of
     the common law rules of law for certain law subjects formulated and
     published by the American Law Institute (a group of legal scholars and
     judges organized in 1923). Restatements of the Law of Contracts,
     Agency, and Trusts are examples. The Restatements are not binding on
     courts but are consulted and considered by courts when deciding questions
     of law.

Restitution: An equitable remedy granted by a court directing a party
     involved in an action to return property to another party. Also an
     equitable remedy granted by a court directing a party to reimburse
     another party for the value of his services, even though there may not
     have been a contract between the parties.

Satisfaction of Judgment: A document that is filed in court by the judgment
     creditor stating that the judgment against the debtor has been paid and
     is therefore satisfied.

Scienter: A term used in pleadings signifying that the defendant had know-
     ledge that he committed a wrong or that he violated a duty (used in

criminal law and in intentional torts.)

Severable contract: A contract in which the items of performance may be
    apportioned to the consideration - as opposed to an entire contract.

Specific performance: An equitable remedy granted by a court which directs
    and orders a party to perform pursuant to the contract. A party who
    disobeys the court order is subject to fine or prison or both for con-
    tempt of court.

Stare decisis: The doctrine of law whereby courts follow and adhere to
    decisions by courts in prior cases.

Status quo: Leaving the parties in the same position.

Statute: A law enacted by the legislative branch of government.

Statute of Frauds: An English statute (1677) that specifies which types of
    contract must be evidenced by a signed writing in order to be enforce-
    able. Each state has enacted its own various Statutes of Frauds. There
    is no uniform Statute of Frauds in the United States.

Statute of Limitations: The legal time limit prescribed by state statute
    within which an action or proceeding may be commenced. If a plaintiff
    commences an action or proceeding after the statute of limitations has
    expired for that particular action or proceeding, the defendant may
    plead the statute of limitations as an affirmative defense and the court
    will dismiss plaintiff's action.

Subpoena: An order of the court directing a party to appear and testify in
    court on a given date; violation of a subpoena can subject a party to be
    held in contempt of court.

Subpoena dices tecum: A court order directing a party to appear in court and
    produce certain specified documents.

Subrogation: The substitution of one party in place of another with respect
    to rights and claims. (E.g., a guarantor who has paid a debt owed by a
    creditor is then subrogated to the rights of the creditor against the
    debtor). The legal effect of subrogation is the same as if one party
    assigned all his rights against a party to another party.

Summary judgment: A judgment entered by the court in favor of one party
    because the court concludes there are no triable issues of fact which
    require a trial. (See Motion for summary judgment).

Summons: A notice directed to and served on the defendant notifying him of
    the legal action being brought by plaintiff against him. The summons
    states that he is required to answer the complaint or file a notice of
    appearance within a specified time. If he fails to do so within the
    time limit specified by law, a judgment of default may be entered against

328

him.

Tender: An unconditional offer to perform the required act.

Testator (testatrix - f.): A person who makes a will.

Third party: A party who is not a party to the contract.

Third party beneficiary: A party for whose benefit a contract was made by the contracting parties. The third party beneficiary acquires rights under the contract even though he is not a party to the contract and gave no consideration to either party to the contract.

Tort: A civil wrong committed against a person or property that is not a breach of contract.

Tortfeasor: One who commits a tort.

Tort (intentional): A tort committed intentionally by one party against another (E.g., libel, false arrest, false imprisonment, assault, battery.)

Tort (unintentional): A tort unintentionally committed by one party against another due to negligence. (E.g., automobile accident caused by negligence.)

Trial: A judicial proceeding conducted by a judge alone or by a judge and jury to determine the issues raised by the parties in their lawsuit.

Trust: A legal relationship whereby one party transfers title to property to another party who holds it for the benefit of a third party. The three parties to a trust are the settlor (who establishes the trust), the trustee ,and the beneficiary.

Trustee: A party who has legal title to property which is held by him for the benefit of a third party called the beneficiary. A trustee may be an individual or a corporation.

Unconscionable contract: A contract that is so one-sided that a court of law may declare it void and unenforceable. Courts generally consider such factors as outrageous price, poor quality of merchandise, highly technical language used in contract, illiteracy of consumer-buyer and unequal bargaining power of one party.

Undue influence: Taking unfair advantage of another's weakness of mind.

Unenforceable contract: A valid contract which cannot be enforced for some legal reason such as an oral contract which violates the Statute of Frauds.

Uniform law: A model law drafted by the Commissioners on Uniform State Laws and proposed for adoption in all States. Some of the most common Uniform

329

Laws are the Uniform Commercial Code, Uniform Partnership Act and Uniform Limited Partnership Act. The Commissioners on Uniform State Laws **have** been in existence since 1890 and have drafted more than two hundred model laws.

Unilateral contract: A contract in which a promise is given in exchange for an act.

Unjust enrichment: Doctrine of law that a party may not profit or enrich himself at the expense of another. Under the doctrine of unjust enrichment a party will be required to pay the other party the reasonable value of what he received (goods or services) even though there may not be any contract between the parties.

Unliquidated claim: Uncertain amount (not exact amount, not fixed), or an amount honestly disputed by the parties. An unliquidated claim is the opposite of a liquidated claim.

Usury: A rate of interest on a loan which exceeds the maximum rate permitted by a state statute. The statutory definition of usury varies from one state statute to another.

Valid contract: A contract that is not void. A valid contract may not be enforceable under certain circumstances (E.g., violates Statute of Frauds).

Venue: The particular county in a state which has jurisdiction to hear and decide the lawsuit.

Void: No legal force or binding effect.

Voidable: A contract which may be voided or avoided by one of the contracting parties for some legal reason such as infancy, fraud, misrepresentation, duress, mutual mistake, or undue influence. The other party is bound by the contract until the party who has the right elects to avoid the contract (Note - voidable is different from void.)

Waiver: Giving up a legal right or claim.

Warranty: A statement concerning the subject matter of a contract (which may be expressed by the parties or implied by law). For example, every seller of goods impliedly warrants to the buyer that the goods are fit for the purpose intended.

Will: A written instrument executed with the formalities required by state statute declaring the person's wishes as to the disposition of his property after his death.